LAST DAYS OF THE SICILIANS

LAST DAYS OF THE SICILIANS

AT WAR WITH THE MAFIA

The FBI Assault
on the Pizza Connection

RALPH BLUMENTHAL

𝕿𝖎𝖒𝖊𝖘 BOOKS

Blumenthal, Ralph.
  Last days of the Sicilians.

  Bibliography: p.
  Includes index.
  1. Mafia—United States—Case Studies.   2. Organized
crime—United States—Case studies.   3. Organized crime
investigation—United States—Case studies.   4. Drug
traffic—United States—Case studies.   5. United
States. Federal Bureau of Investigation.   I. Title.
HV6446.B58 1988   364.1'06'073   87-49597
ISBN 0-8129-1594-1

Designed by Paul Chevannes

Manufactured in the United States of America

9 8 7 6 5 4 3 2

First Edition

To Annie

To Annie

ACKNOWLEDGMENTS

At daybreak on April 9, 1984, a heavily armed force of more than four hundred federal and local law enforcement agents burst into pizzerias, cafés, country homes, and apartments from the Midwest to Long Island. The raids were the culmination of the largest, most complex criminal investigation ever undertaken by the FBI and cut off the billion-dollar heroin pipeline that came to be known as the Pizza Connection. Equally significant, the case exposed a secret franchise of the Sicilian Mafia in America. The revelation caught even the nation's leading organized crime experts by surprise. Who *were* these obscure Sicilian pizza men and bakers and contractors operating here independently of their American mob counterparts while masterminding a flow of heroin into the United States and an outflow of literally tons of cash to Switzerland? An unintentionally macabre headline over a story I wrote for *The New York Times* evoked the confusion:

UNKNOWN ARM OF SICILIAN MAFIA
REPORTEDLY DISCOVERED IN THE U.S.

This is the true story of how that arm was uncovered and what it meant.

I could not have gathered and told this story without a great deal of help. When I began my research in 1985, I asked the FBI for access to the supervisors and agents most responsible for the case. William D. Baker, then the bureau's assistant director for congressional and public affairs, granted that access with no restrictions, although many of the interviews had to await the conclusion of the trial in March 1987. No one played a larger role in explaining the case and providing access to sources than Thomas L. Sheer, the bureau's criminal director, and later assistant director in charge, in New York. His insights and candor were invaluable aids, and he offered his help without any assurance that the outcome would be to his liking. He also opened the door to interviews with many other protagonists: Charlie Rooney and Carmine Russo, Bob Paquette, Frank Storey, Lew Schiliro, Tom Vinton, Jim Kallstrom, Bob Gilmore, Pat Luzio, Lou Caprino, Mike Slattery, Denis Collins, John Mauzey, Randy Prillaman, Jerry Cox, and dozens of others. Joe Valiquette helped make the arrangements. Joe Pistone, aka Donnie Brasco, the bureau's man inside the mob, provided guidance on his part in the story. The case was the product of hundreds of agents who exemplified the bureau's dictum of "We—not I." But short of publishing a telephone directory, there is no feasible way of acknowledging them all or weaving all their contributions into the narrative.

Needless to say, none of the agents or their superiors or any of the others I interviewed is responsible in any way for my conclusions. They may, understandably, have completely different perspectives.

Rudolph W. Giuliani, the United States attorney for the Southern District of New York, also granted me numerous interviews and access to his prosecutors after the case ended. His efficient deputy Dennison Young made many of the arrangements. Louis Freeh, the chief prosecutor, whom many consider the investigative mastermind of the case, generously shared his insights, as did his associates Richard A. Martin and Robert Bucknam. Special Deputy U.S. Marshal Domenico "Mimmo" Buda helped with court records, as did Carol Weiss and Janet LaForgia of the U.S. attorney's office. In Brooklyn Charles Rose, Mark Summers, and Reena Raggi graciously provided parts of the story, as did former U.S. Attorney Raymond Dearie, although Messrs. Dearie and Rose in particular were not at all in agreement with the way the case unfolded.

Thomas Cash, operations supervisor of the Drug Enforcement Agency in Washington, and Thomas Kelly, deputy DEA administrator, were extraordinarily helpful in describing the narcotics aspects of the investigation and making their experts available. Intelligence analyst Mona Ewell was a particularly invaluable source of information on the multitude of players and their interrelationships. She carries more information in her head than many other experts do in their libraries. Frank Panessa spoke movingly and often comically of the perils of undercover work inside the mob. The former DEA and CIA agent Thomas Tripodi was a rich source of information on the events leading up to the Pizza Connection case. DEA agents Anthony Petrucci and Mario Sessa patiently explained intricacies of the Sicilian Mafia and the role of Tommaso Buscetta.

Michael Fahy, operations supervisor of the Customs Service in New York, and Customs agent Thomas Loreto offered a behind-the-scenes look at key episodes in the case. In the New York Police Department, the encyclopedic Jack Clark was, well, encyclopedic, Joseph Polly highlighted the new cooperation between the NYPD and FBI, and James Mulally provided snapshots of the battles in the trenches.

Pino Arlacchi, a former member of Italy's Anti-Mafia Commission and probably that country's shrewdest analyst of the Mafia, taught me to see the criminal phenomenon in economic terms, so lucidly expressed in his classic treatise *Mafia Business.* He is a wise and brave man, and he has become a good friend. Sociologists Jane and Peter Schneider of Fordham University have also written some of the best accounts of the roots of the Sicilian Mafia. I am indebted to them and their work. Taking on the Mafia in Italy has been a deadly undertaking for many courageous officials and journalists. I salute them. Magistrates Giusto Sciacchitano and Paulo Borsellino in Palermo and police chief Alessandro Panza in Rome took time from their busy schedules to brief me on developments in Italy. Daniele Billitteri, an unbullyable reporter on the *Giornale di Sicilia*, guided me around the locations in Palermo that figured in the Pizza Connection story. I was also shown around Sicily by a gifted interpreter who let me see that this ancient island of temples and treasures is far more than the home of the Mafia. For reasons she will know, I shall not name her but convey here my deepest gratitude. I had the good fortune to have a similarly accomplished interpreter and translator in New York, but she, too, must remain anonymous. My interviews in Italy were expertly arranged by Cristina Fioravanti of the *Times'* Rome bureau.

Throughout the long course of the trial I also had discussions with lawyers representing many of the defendants. From them I gleaned much useful information and many important documents. I am sure I will make their lives much easier by not mentioning them by name, although I am nonetheless grateful for their help.

With all my information, this still would not have become a book without the encouragement and guidance of Jonathan Segal, vice-president and editorial director of Times Books, and Julian Bach, my agent. Their keen judgments and enthusiasm carried the long project over some rough spots. Ruth Fecych applied her most professional editing skills to the manuscript, Pearl Hanig was a scrupulous copy editor, and Beth Pearson diligently oversaw the editorial production. My good friend Stephen R. Conn read the manuscript and offered many valuable suggestions, as did my *Times* colleague Sam Roberts.

Editors at *The New York Times*, Arthur Gelb, Warren Hoge, and John Darnton among others, generously let me accumulate time off and rearrange my schedule to devote the necessary time to finishing this project.

To be written, a book needs a place to be written in. My friends Kelly and Joan Van Horn generously donated their vacant apartment for much of this endeavor. It made the task far easier.

Throughout this project my family and my in-laws, Marilyn and Herbert Danto, were unfailing sources of strength. Nothing was more sustaining than the love and good counsel of my wife, Deborah. She, alone, made it possible and she, alone, knows what she endured.

New York City
March 20, 1988

THE "PLAYERS"

Adamita, Emanuele: New York pizza man who unwittingly led DEA agents to Milan for major heroin seizure in 1980 at beginning of drug conspiracy. Rearrested in Brooklyn in 1988.

Aiello, Anthony "Commerciante": Owner of Caffè Aiello, Queens; drug customer of Salvatore Catalano/Giuseppe Ganci consortium.

Alfano, Pietro: Pizza maker in Oregon, Illinois; nephew of Gaetano Badalamenti; relative of Palazzolo; relative of Evola; narcotics middleman between Badalamenti and Catalano/Ganci groups.

Amato, Baldassare "Baldo": Partner of Cesare Bonventre.

Amendolito, Salvatore: Italian-Swiss money launderer for Sicilian Mafia drug consortium.

Badalamenti, Gaetano: Exiled head of Sicilian Mafia Commission; uncle of Pietro Alfano; drug supplier to Catalano/Ganci group.

Bonanno, Joseph: Boss of New York Mafia family in 1950's and 1960's.

Bono, Giuseppe: Sicilian Mafia boss and heroin kingpin; moved to New York in early 1980's.

Bonventre, Cesare: Captain of Sicilian crew of Bonanno family; suspect in Galante murder; cohort of Baldassare Amato; member of drug consortium.

Buscetta, Tommaso: Highest-ranking Mafia turncoat; former Sicilian Mafia leader, now in federal witness protection program in United States.

Cangialosi, Giovanni: Envoy of Sicilian Mafia, sent to United States to resolve drug supply problem.

Carol: Ganci's mistress, in Clifton, New Jersey.

Casamento, Filippo: Proprietor, with brother Frank, of Eagle Cheese Co., Brooklyn; convicted of narcotics violations in 1973; drug customer of Ganci.

Castronovo, Frank (Francesco): Partner in Roma restaurant in Menlo Park, New Jersey, with Gaetano Mazzara.

Catalano, Onofrio: Money launderer; brother of Saca Catalano, cousin of Salvatore Catalano; a fugitive.

Catalano, Salvatore "Saca": Drug trafficker; jeweler; brother of Onofrio; cousin of Salvatore "Toto" Catalano.

Catalano, Salvatore "Toto": Street boss of Bonanno family, Sicilian faction; Queens bakery owner; partner in pizzerias with Giuseppe Ganci and Bonventre; leader of Sicilian Mafia heroin consortium in New York–New Jersey.

Contorno, Salvatore: Major Sicilian Mafia turncoat, now in federal witness protection program in United States.

Della Torre, Franco: Italian-Swiss money launderer for Catalano/Ganci group.

Evola, Samuel: Contractor in Temperance, Michigan; husband of Badalamenti's niece and relative of Alfano in drug deals with Catalano/Ganci group.

Galante, Carmine "Lilo": Boss of Bonanno family and would-be heroin kingpin; slain in Brooklyn restaurant, July 12, 1979.

Ganci, Giuseppe "Pino," "Bufalone," "Buffalo": Partner with Sal "Toto" Catalano and Bonventre in pizzerias; Catalano's chief deputy in Sicilian drug consortium.

Greco, Leonardo: Brother of Salvatore Greco; leader of Bagheria Mafia family; power behind money-laundering operation.

Greco, Salvatore: New Jersey pizzeria owner; brother of Sicilian Mafia boss Leonardo Greco of Bagheria.

Lamberti, Giuseppe Joseph, "Mr. Joe": Long Island contractor and boutique owner; partner in Catalano/Ganci drug consortium; cousin of Salvatore Lamberti and brother-in-law of Salvatore Mazzurco.

Lamberti, Salvatore: Cousin of Giuseppe Lamberti; member of Borgetto family of Sicilian Mafia; accused in assault death of Italian policeman, 1982.

Ligammari, Giovanni: New Jersey contractor; member of Catalano/Ganci consortium; triggered crisis by pulling out of drug deal with Badalamenti-Alfano group.

Mazzara, Gaetano: Partner of Frank Castronovo in Roma restaurant; keeper of heroin for Catalano/Ganci consortium; murdered during trial.

Mazzurco, Salvatore: Long Island contractor, boutique and rink operator; brother-in-law of Giuseppe Lamberti; business agent of Catalano/Ganci heroin consortium.

Musullulu, Yasar: Turkish shipowner; supplier of morphine base to Sicilian Mafia; a fugitive.

Palazzolo, Emanuele: Pizza maker in Milton, Wisconsin; brother-in-law of Pietro Alfano; associate in Badalamenti drug deals with Catalano/Ganci group.

Palazzolo, Vito Roberto: (No relation to Emanuele Palazzolo.) Italian-Swiss money launderer; link between Catalano/Ganci group and Leonardo Greco.

Polizzi, Frank (Francesco) "Ciccio": New Jersey contractor and restaurant and motel owner; partner in conspirator consortium and member of New Jersey's DeCavalcante Mafia family.

Ronsisvalle, Luigi: Ex–hit man on Brooklyn's Knickerbocker Avenue; Mafia underling-turned-witness-turned-recanter-turned-witness, now in federal witness protection program.

Salamone, Filippo: New Jersey pizza maker; local money launderer for Catalano/Ganci group; brother of Salvatore Salamone.

Salamone, Salvatore: Gun buyer; Pennsylvania money launderer for Catalano/Ganci group; brother of Filippo Salamone.

Soresi, Giuseppe: Middleman between Sicilian Mafia traffickers and Catalano/Ganci group.

Tognoli, Oliviero: Italian businessman; associate of Bagheria Mafia boss Leonardo Greco and Salvatore Amendolito's link to Sicilian Mafia; a fugitive.

Waridel, Paul: Associate of Turkish shipowner and morphine-base supplier Yasar Musullulu.

Zito, Benny: Philadelphia pizza maker; drug customer of Ganci; missing, a fugitive or a murder victim.

PART ONE

A TRAIL OF BLOOD

That's how you die.

—Salvatore Contorno, Sicilian Mafia soldier

1

N A steamy July afternoon in 1979 a black Cadillac carrying two men thumped its way along the rutted asphalt of Knickerbocker Avenue in Brooklyn. All over New York that week a pillow of suffocating air smothered the city's face. In Bushwick, where the el still clattered past open tenement windows, throwing the street into a shifting lattice of inky shadows, the heat seared with a crueler intensity. Once a proud German enclave of brass-trimmed brownstones, the neighborhood received a tremendous influx of Italians between the world wars. Now they in turn were rapidly abandoning Bushwick to a growing population of poor Ecuadorans and Chileans and other Hispanics and blacks. Ravaged by arson and neglect, Knickerbocker Avenue had a boarded-up, derelict air. But not all the Italians had departed.

The Cadillac with the two men bounced past the *granita* peddlers pushing carts of shaved ice melting rapidly in the fierce heat. It passed espresso cafés and bargain stores with clothes piled helter-skelter in bins on the sidewalk. Above the shops women held babies at the open windows, trying to catch a breeze. Down on the street men in undershirts sat on vinyl dinette chairs, playing radios and swigging from bottles swathed in paper bags. The car, dodging potholes, skirted the green rectangle of Bushwick Park, where chicken siz-

3

zled on charcoal grills, wreathing the benches in clouds of barbecue smoke and lighter fluid.

The car stopped in front of a small Italian restaurant with dingy yellow curtains and a sign, WE GIVE SPECIAL ATTENTION TO OUTGOING ORDERS. The passenger, mob boss Carmine Galante, nodded good-bye to the jowly driver in aviator glasses, his nephew James Galante, and stepped into the Joe and Mary Italian-American restaurant, owned by his cousin Joe Turano and his wife, Mary. Carmine Galante, a small, cocky man with a terrifying reputation, felt safe there. He had recently taken steps to corner the heroin import trade, and not everyone was happy about it.

Galante passed the counter with the obligatory Frank Sinatra album propped up and a print of da Vinci's "The Last Supper" decorating the front wall. He strode through the dining room with its walls papered in brown velvet and tables covered in yellow oilcloth. Emerging onto the backyard patio, which was set in a garden of tomato vines, Galante seated himself just outside the door at a table under a yellow-and-turquoise-checked umbrella. Soon he and Turano were joined by another friend, Leonardo Coppolla, and Galante's sometime bodyguards, Cesare Bonventre and Baldassare "Baldo" Amato, who positioned themselves on either side of Galante. Despite the heat, the bodyguards wore bulky leather jackets—to conceal their guns.

The table was set with fish, salad, and red wine from a gallon jug. Bonventre didn't like fish; he ordered steak. Overhead, lines of laundry hung limply in the stultifying heat, suturing the sky between the narrow alleys. Galante lit a cigar.

Just before 2:45 P.M., James Galante called. Was his uncle still there? "I'll be right over," James said.

Turano's son, John, first saw the three men in ski masks as they bolted through the front door of the restaurant. One was wearing jeans and a T-shirt and carried a shotgun. Another, with a potbelly and a large nose, carried a pistol. A third, he would remember later, was tall and thin.

"Don't move," the man with the shotgun told John. "Keep your mouth shut."

Then the man called to his companion, "In the back, Sallie."

"Papa!" John shouted.

John's younger sister, Constanza, heard a shuffle of feet at the door and her brother's shout.

As two of the masked men headed toward the garden, John ran to a storeroom where he knew the family kept a pistol. The gunman with the potbelly followed him. John reached the storeroom and tried to slam the door shut. The gunman forced it open. John ran his hands along the shelf, feeling around frantically for the pistol. He couldn't find it; it was one shelf higher up. The gunman fired and shot him.

Constanza ran out of the kitchen and collided with her brother. John, bleeding from wounds, threw her to safety against the wall. She crawled away and hid behind the refrigerator.

Constanza heard her father say from the garden, "What are you doing?" The rest was drowned out by shots.

Outside on Knickerbocker Avenue a deliveryman was just passing by on his rounds. He saw a blue Mercury Montego double-parked in front of the restaurant. There was a man in a ski mask and a dark jacket leaning over the door. He had a rifle. He saw the deliveryman staring at him.

"Get the fuck out of here or I'll kill you," he growled.

Down the block the deliveryman ran into the supermarket and buttonholed a security guard. Together they flagged down a passing patrol car.

The gunfire lasted less than a minute. Constanza saw the gunmen running back from the garden and out of the restaurant. She made her way to the patio. On the floor, amid the overturned chairs and spilled food, she saw the blood-smeared bodies of her father, Coppolla and Galante, who lay twisted with a stogie clenched in his teeth. The top of Coppolla's head had been blown off. One pellet or bullet had taken out Galante's left eye. His cigar was still lit. The two bodyguards, Bonventre and Amato, had escaped unscathed.

2

OT since the murderous Vito Genovese, who dominated the five New York families in the 1950's, had there been a more fearsome Mafia boss than Carmine Galante of the Bonanno family. Like his wily chieftain, Joseph Bonanno, Galante traced his roots to the Sicilian seacoast town of Castellammare del Golfo, where colorful fishing boats bob at anchor under a ruined fortress. But if Bonanno fancied himself a statesman, Galante was a shark. A New York police lieutenant put it another way. "The rest of them are copper," he said. "He is pure steel."

Stubby, with an often disheveled air and an icy gaze, the five-foot-three-inch Galante, known widely by his diminutive of "Lilo," was frighteningly unpredictable. He could engage in philosophic discourse like a college professor, then fly into the psychopathic rage of an uncontrollable killer. Over a half century's criminal career he had been implicated in some eighty murders, including the shooting of a policeman during a robbery and the assassination of an anti-Fascist New York newspaper editor who had run afoul of Benito Mussolini. As Bonanno's underboss Galante surfaced in Montreal in late 1953 to seize and reorganize the city's rackets, including drug trafficking, on behalf of the American Mafia. But Galante had been too brazen, and the government was able to make a drug case against him in New York in 1962. The first prosecution ended in a mistrial after the jury foreman had been mysteriously pushed down a flight of stairs and injured. A second trial, during which one defendant hurled a chair at the prosecutor and another entered the jury box and shoved jurors around, ended with Galante's conviction.

While Galante was serving his twenty-year sentence in Atlanta, spooking many of his hardened fellow inmates, Joe Bonanno was ousted in New York, reputedly for plotting the murder of rival Carlo Gambino. In 1974, after serving little more than half his term, Galante had returned home on parole, eager to wrest back control of the Bonanno family, challenge Gambino's influence over the New York families, and rebuild his own disrupted drug network. Rival Bonanno boss Philip "Rusty" Rastelli was still in jail. Galante elbowed him aside and took over. Gambino solved another of Galante's problems by dying of old age. Galante stepped into the leadership vacuum and sought to restore large-scale Mafia trafficking in heroin, for which he was said to have received the endorsement of the other bosses.

Along with prostitution, drug trafficking had long been officially disdained and sometimes banned by mob bosses within their families—but it was nonetheless avidly pursued in the American Mafia. The drug racket carried an aura of unmanliness as well as high risk, but the assurance of huge rewards more than counterbalanced the hazards. A Mafia conclave at Apalachin, New York, in 1957 was to have affirmed a ban on drug dealing, Joe Bonanno said. But whatever compunctions many Mafia bosses felt about dealing in junk vanished in the face of the staggering fortunes to be made feeding the nation's growing demand for heroin, cocaine, marijuana, and pills. The Sicilian Mafia, on the other hand, merely segued from the tobacco smuggling of the fifties and sixties to the drug trade of the seventies and eighties. By the late 1970's all of Palermo's forty-five Mafia clans were in the heroin business, although the overseas delivery channels were controlled by just a handful of them. In 1979 their most promising customer in America was the sixty-nine-year-old Galante, who, with the help of a little-known arm of the Sicilian Mafia in the United States, was moving forcefully to dominate the multibillion-dollar heroin import market by charging importers a "license" fee of $5,000 a kilo. In return, Galante would oversee the distribution, matching up importers and drug wholesalers.

Hints of this had been picked up by the New York cops who regularly shadowed Galante on his daily rounds to the cleaners he owned in Little Italy and watched him harvest tributes from respectful underlings and favor seekers. The FBI and Customs Service had also stumbled across a perplexing influx of illegal Sicilians in recent years, along with unexplained and often violent shifts of mob power (such as the 1976 killing of Knickerbocker Avenue street boss Pietro Licata) that seemed to advance the fortunes of a shadowy cadre of Sicilians in the Bonanno family. But investigators had no idea how deadly the rivalries were about to become or who would lunge for Galante's prize. They also did not yet know what an undercover FBI agent planted deep within the Bonanno family had discovered shortly after the killing on July 12, 1979: that Galante had positioned himself at the spigot of the heroin pipeline. Galante alone was determined to turn it on and collect the gushing profits. There would be sharing only over his dead body.

The FBI didn't know any of this yet—but it was about to learn. After decades of denying the existence of organized crime, the bureau, armed with new technology, techniques, and legal weapons, was embarking on a momentous crusade against the Mafia and the scourge of drugs, although its cojurisdiction with the Drug Enforcement Administration was not formalized until 1982. By the late seventies the bureau's attitude toward other law enforcement agencies had also matured. Although it had always preached the virtues of cooperation among its agents, it had practiced the opposite in its relations with fellow agencies: The FBI had long been notoriously stingy, with some reason, about sharing its information with others, including the New York Police Department. But it was now, at long last, starting to pool information with counterparts at home and abroad, especially in Italy, where the authorities were gearing up for a serious assault on the "honored society," the "friends of the friends," La Cosa Nostra. It was all coming together: information compiled over twenty-five years by thousands of anonymous agents, a once-puny data base that had grown into a mountain of intelligence that the bureau now hoped to use, finally, to crush the Mafia once and for all.

FBI agent Carmine Russo was on temporary assignment in California on July 12, 1979, when he got a phone call from New York.

"Carmine?"

"Who's this?"

"Sweeney, NYPD."

"Yeah, Sweeney, what's up?"

"Lilo just got whacked."

Russo hung up the telephone and tried to channel his racing thoughts, which began with a realization, now that it had happened, of the inevitability of the hit. So the little bastard had finally bought it. Who had had the guts to turn on Lilo? Russo wondered. Why now? And had the hit been ordered or approved by the other bosses? Russo was not surprised, having followed Galante's gory career for five years, first as a special New York State anticorruption investigator and for the last year as a new agent in the FBI's Brooklyn-Queens office, where he was sometimes called in on organized crime cases. Nor was Russo overly sympathetic. As one of the few Sicilian-born agents he particularly resented the Mafia stigma that had come to taint all Sicilians, as the result, or so he liked to point out, of the criminality of a small minority. Bums Russo called them; they were the bums who gave Sicilians a bad name. "Sicilians are a law-abiding people," he would say, "an honest people. Some rotten apples, and everyone gets the blame." *But look at the system. Living conditions in Sicily stink. People can't get work. It's a forgotten society.* Russo kept his other thoughts buried. How far would a Sicilian go in the bureau? Only so far. Why? Because he was not a Mormon? Because he might drink wine with his meals? But he had pulled himself up, he thought proudly. He might have started out in the last row last seat, but he had ended up in the first row. Tautly built, with a finely shaped Italianate profile, closely cropped brown hair, and a thin mustache, Russo seemed from his fervor and volatility to have been packed under pressure. As an immigrant who had come to the United States from Sicily with his family as a boy, Russo also had a strong patriotic streak that could verge on the corny.

The call from Bill Sweeney in police intelligence had reached Russo while he was working on a case against Galante's longtime boss, the "retired" Joe Bonanno in Tucson, Arizona. Russo, in fact—and this was typical in the bureau—had barely settled into his first FBI posting on the bank robbery squad in the Brooklyn-Queens office in the summer of 1978 when, as one of the bureau's few agents fluent in the Sicilian dialect, he was rushed out west to Tucson to sit on wiretaps of Bonanno, who, in supposed mob retirement, was nevertheless dropping quarters in drugstore pay phones to call Mafia associates in Canada. The phones were duly tapped, and a year later, in July 1979, Russo was back in San Jose, California, poring over the transcripts he had translated for an obstruction of justice case the government had put together against Bonanno in California. Amazingly, it was the first successful felony prosecution ever of the longtime boss, whose only other brush with the law had been a $450 fine for a New York City rent law violation in 1945.

Three weeks later, as soon as his work on the case ended, Russo flew back to New York, where he had been assigned to the corruption squad investigating fraud and white-collar crime. As intrigued as he was by the Galante murder, Russo found that another squad was already working the case, along with NYPD homicide and organized crime units. White-collar crime and bank robbery were common first postings for new agents like Russo; it exposed them to the whole investigative process and allowed them to follow relatively uncomplicated cases from inception to conclusion. The way the FBI saw it, an agent would be in the bureau for up to thirty years. There was no sense forcing him or her into a specialty too soon. Better to provide a solid general grounding first. That was okay, Russo figured. He knew that when something came up involving the Sicilians, the bureau would call on him fast enough.

Russo and his two sisters had been born near Messina, Sicily. Their father, a bricklayer, moved the family to Brooklyn when Carmine was nine. Russo first learned about the Mafia in New York. He was seventeen, and it coincidentally was the day of President Kennedy's assassination. He and his father were passing a neighborhood hangout called the Dixie Tavern, close to their Park Slope apartment. "Don't you ever go in there! You hear me, never!" the elder Russo admonished his son with a vehemence that startled the youth. He explained about the Mafia.

"Whatever you say, Dad," Russo replied.

Dissuaded by his father from studying for the priesthood, Russo attended community college and then joined the Navy. Later he applied for work at the New York Police Department but narrowly failed the vision test; instead, he was hired as an investigator with the office of special state anticorruption investigator Maurice Nadjari; one of his cases was the sensational theft of the French Connection heroin from a NYPD safe. He and his partners felt sure they knew the cops who had done it, but they couldn't prove it. The case remained unsolved. In 1978 Russo applied for the FBI, doubting he would be accepted; he was Sicilian after all.

Among Russo's partners was an easygoing former part-time FBI clerk from Brooklyn, who had also served with Russo on the bank robbery squad and who liked to spend his spare time restoring steam locomotives. At twenty-eight, railroad buff Charles Rooney was five years younger than Russo. He was slightly flabby, with a helmet of thin brown hair that swept over his ears and curled over his collar. There was something childlike about his face that his light mustache only accentuated, like a kid trying to look more grown-up. His eyes were greenish brown, and they seemed to twinkle with good-natured, innocent wonder.

Rooney had been born in Flatbush, the only child of an Irish-American insurance broker. He had been studying history at Fordham University in 1970 when he took a part-time job as an FBI clerk in the New York office's old building on Third Avenue at Sixty-ninth Street, then often ringed by picketing demonstrators rallied by mob boss Joseph A. Colombo and his Italian-American Defense League. Rooney's job was filing and receiving coded messages through the teletype room on the premidnight shift. It was unglamorous duty, but Rooney impressed superiors as a dogged worker, an ambitious kid "with no off switch," as one later put it. After graduation, he continued as a full-time clerk, starting at the munificent salary of $4,621 a year, until 1976, when he was accepted at the bureau's academy in Quantico, Virginia.

Rooney and Russo sat in a large room in the bureau's Brooklyn-Queens office in a bronze-tinted monolith overlooking Alexander's department store on Queens Boulevard. They got along well, and when a desk opened up near Rooney's, Russo took it. They made an odd couple, the intense and brooding Russo and the casual and gentle-tempered Charlie Rooney, whose watchword was "Relaxio." They seemed an unlikely team of case agents for what became the biggest criminal investigation in FBI history.

Not too many years before, Russo and Rooney might have been passed over by J. Edgar Hoover's FBI. Hoover, his own gnomic life-style and bulldog physiognomy notwithstanding, clearly favored white, conformist, preferably Mormon or Protestant six-footers, who photographed well collaring the mad-dog killers and bank stickup artists whose mugs papered the bulletin boards of post offices across the nation. That was what passed for organized crime for most of the twentieth century in Hoover's view. The director had strong ideas about what constituted a menace—Reds topped the list—and the image his agents should project.

Following Hoover's death in 1972, the bureau was eagerly recruiting a broader spectrum of agents, still preferably lawyers or CPAs, whom the FBI always favored, but less stereotyped and therefore more suited to tracking and penetrating an ever more devious organized criminal underworld. Rooney and Russo may not have fitted the old mold. But they fitted the new.

Through the end of 1979, as an FBI "Galante squad" pursued the killing, Rooney and Russo worked their own cases. Rooney was probing possible payoffs behind the New York City Transit Authority's acquisition of federally subsidized R-46 subway cars. In November Russo was called in to help on another homicide and possible mob case. A young pizza cook dressed in his chef's whites had been found gunned down gangland-style outside his Queens home. He had some debts, the police learned, but nothing of a magnitude likely to cost him his life.

Several months after that killing, an anonymous letter in beautiful script arrived at the FBI's Queens office. Written by someone who appeared to have detailed knowledge of the killing (Russo speculated it was a woman by the cursive handwriting), it told the following story: The victim, Settimo Favia, had been gambling in the backroom of the Café del Viale on Knickerbocker Avenue and had lost $3,000. He tried to win it back and lost more. Then, the letter said, Cesare Bonventre and an associate, Filippo Ragusa, sat him down and made him a proposition. Favia could discharge his gambling debt by making a trip for them to Italy. All he would have to do was bring back a package containing some powder. But, the letter went on, he angrily refused, vowing he would pay back his debt but would have nothing to do with heroin. The letter was signed only "SOS." Russo had it checked against the bureau's anonymous letter file, comparing its script, ink, paper, and writing style to similar examples, but as expected, nothing matched. With no way of tracking down the writer, Russo tried a last desperate ploy, inserting an ad in the Italian-language New York newspaper *Il Progresso:* "Dear SOS, please contact us."

No one ever did. It seemed to be just another of many dead ends, and in fact, the Favia killing was never solved. But it played a part in the evolution of Russo's thinking as he pondered the role of Bonventre, whom Russo, along with practically everyone else who read the newspapers, knew as one of the mysterious survivors of the Galante restaurant slaughter. Russo began thinking about the Café del Viale, which he also knew was a mob hangout and reputed gambling den on Knickerbocker Avenue, three blocks from the Joe and Mary restaurant.

On the night of January 19, 1980, Russo and Rooney joined a team of agents on a gambling raid of the café. They rattled the locked door, then pounded on the wood. There was no response. The "stickman," or lookout, had peered through a peephole, seen the agents, and run to hide. Wielding sledgehammers and shotguns, the agents smashed their way in. The startled stickman barely had time to yell, "Everybody quick! Escape over the roof!" before diving headfirst out of a window, only to be yanked back by his feet by one of the agents. As the raiders burst in, one of the agents, taken for a holdup man, was nearly blown away by one of the pistol-toting guards at the baccarat game. Russo, who had drawn the small Smith & Wesson .38 he kept strapped around his left ankle, grabbed one of the patrons, who insisted, "I don't know what's going on. I'm here for a meeting of pizza makers from Castellammare." The raid yielded the standard gambling paraphernalia and a gun. But although Bonventre's yellow Peugeot had been spotted in front, neither he nor the others Russo had hoped to nab were found; they must have escaped out a back way. Again Russo seemed to have turned into a dead end. But the raid convinced him that the writer of the Favia letter had had it right. Bonventre and the Bonanno family, drugs and death were intersecting here on Knickerbocker Avenue.

On February 10, 1980, Russo found a file waiting in his mail slot in the Queens office. That was the way agents were customarily assigned a case. The name on the one Russo picked up was Cesare Bonventre.

Rooney also had a file waiting. His bore the name Salvatore Catalano, which meant nothing to Rooney. The thin file, which represented the entire compendium of FBI information on Catalano, identified him as a Queens baker and pizzeria operator sometimes called Toto, a member of the Bonanno family on Knickerbocker Avenue. Rooney checked Catalano's yellow sheet and found he had been arrested once, in 1975, riding with two companions in a car discovered to contain an unlicensed pistol. Catalano had got five years' probation and was discharged after three. The mug shot showed a stocky, stony-faced man in his thirties. Not a lot to go on. If anyone knew anything more, Rooney figured, it would be the NYPD's organized crime intelligence expert, Jack Clark, the NYPD's resident Mafia wiz. Clark, who could pass for a Hell's Kitchen street tough, had been tracking mobsters for nearly two decades, most of the time anonymously. "Unless you know me, I'm like the phantom," he would say. But FBI agents treasured his intelligence and, even before the NYPD and bureau were official collaborators, would cite him as a "CI," or confidential informant, to back up their reports. Clark and his associates in the NYPD intelligence section had been watching Catalano, without clearly understanding who he was and what he represented. Rooney called Clark and was rewarded with the names of some of the bad guys the cops had spotted around Catalano. Rooney had never heard of them either.

Elsewhere in the bureau's New York offices a number of important investigative strands had begun to twist together. The squad working the Galante killing had grown increasingly convinced from the circumstances of the hit that Bonventre and Amato weren't hapless bystanders but had actually participated in the executions. Bonventre was emerging as a brazen comer in the Bonanno family, a key figure in narcotics and other rackets. And Catalano was somehow hooked up with Bonventre.

By late 1979, under Special Agent in Charge Thomas Emery of the organized crime division, the bureau had come to the belated realization that La Cosa Nostra was impervious to prosecutions of scattered members or bosses. A new strategy was needed: an attack on the family as an entity. And not just one family but all five New York families. A decision was made to spearhead the effort with a thrust at the Bonanno family. A key informant had come forward, a disarmingly charming mob hit man who was able to provide the authorities for the first time with a road map to the Bonanno underworld of Knickerbocker Avenue. Perhaps the best reason of all was still a highly sensitive secret, shared by only a tight circle of bureau officials: The Bonanno family had something no other family had— an FBI undercover agent planted inside. The two relative neophytes who had been tapped to pursue what was now the new Bonanno investigation from different angles, Charlie Rooney and Carmine Russo, had not yet been apprised of that historic breakthrough.

They began by poring over witness accounts of the getaway after the Galante shooting. One report told that a neighbor who lived in a third-floor apartment on Knickerbocker Avenue had been looking out of her window at Joe and Mary's restaurant on the afternoon of the killings. She saw the blue Mercury double-parked and the masked man outside with the rifle. She also saw two men coming out of the restaurant without masks. One, she remembered later, was carrying a pistol. He had dirty blond hair and fitted the description of one of the two men who had come to dinner: Bonventre.

Forensic experts had collected the bullet fragments and shell casings and studied the pattern of shots. Curiously, some shells had ejected over a wire fence, behind which Bonventre had been sitting to Galante's right. It looked suspiciously as if Bonventre had fired a gun. Galante, who had been facing the door, had been hit by four shotgun blasts, some eighty pellets, fired at such close range that paper wadding from the shell had been embedded in his body. Turano, the host, also had been killed by a shotgun blast fired at point-blank range. Coppolla, facing Galante and seated on the other side of Bonventre, had been hit by both shotgun pellets and six bullets, several of which were fired into the back of his head, execution-style. From the different ammunition recovered, investigators were certain that the killers had used five guns—two shotguns and three pistols.

But there had been only three ski-masked intruders. Did three killers fire five guns? Or had there been five killers, counting Bonventre and Amato? Otherwise, how had they escaped? It had rained bullets and they stayed dry. How? Moreover, both had suspiciously disappeared right after the shooting.

Police reports also focused on another suspect. Half an hour after the shootings, an NYPD surveillance team concealed in a curtained apartment in Manhattan's Little Italy was peering across Mulberry Street at the Ravenite Social Club, a stronghold of the Gambino family. Detectives watched as a tan Lincoln pulled up outside. Looking down through the windshield, they saw the driver draw a pistol from under the dashboard and stick it in his waistband before stepping out of the car. They recognized the thin, dark, balding figure as Bonanno family soldier Anthony "Bruno" Indelicato. Later some of his fingerprints were found in the recovered getaway car of Galante's killers. On the sidewalk Indelicato seemed to be accepting congratulations, but he looked distracted, detectives thought. He also had a bruise over one eye and appeared to be limping.

Other men arrived, including Indelicato's father, "Sonny Red," and brother, "J.B.," but their entrance into the club of Gambino underboss Aniello Dellacroce was blocked by Bonanno *consigliere* Stefano "Stevie Beef" Cannone. Respect required that he present the news to Dellacroce first.

A parabolic microphone aimed through an opening in the lookout window sucked up Indelicato's words: "This has got out of hand, and this has got to stop."

He had to be talking about the murders. But why was a Bonanno delegation visiting the Gambino family right after the Galante murder? Both families had to be in on it, investigators reasoned. They were even more convinced after they pulled the records of visitors to imprisoned Bonanno boss Philip Rastelli at the Metropolitan Correctional Center in Manhattan. Right before the Galante hit, he suddenly seemed to be deluged with mob visitors who, it now seemed clear, had been seeking his blessings for the rubout. "The Sicilians wouldn't take out an American without the okay of Philly, or there'd be war," reasoned Jack Clark of police intelligence.

Nineteen days after the shootings Bonventre and Amato suddenly reappeared, surrendering with their lawyers to face questions about the murders from the Brooklyn district attorney. After three hours of confidential testimony, during which they claimed to have fallen backward during the fusillade and seen nothing, they emerged into the courthouse corridor: Bonventre, tall and blond and dapper in tinted glasses, a bold blue-and-white-striped shirt, and blue pants; Amato in a tan shirt and slacks, looking like a fierce Alain Delon, darkly handsome, a wave of thick black hair, deep-set sparkling eyes, full, sensuous lips.

They ignored the throng of jostling newsmen. "How did you escape?" one yelled.

"It was a miracle." said one of the lawyers.

"Carmine, look at these!"

Russo tilted back in his chair to see Rooney sitting behind him in the Queens squad room, waving a sheaf of black-and-white photos. It was June 1980, nearly a year after the Galante slaying and four months after Rooney and Russo had found the Catalano and Bonventre files in their mail slots. Rooney showed him the surveillance pictures taken by the police outside the DA's office the day Bonventre and Amato showed up. The two had gotten out of a car, and standing with them was a stocky man with a rounded head and a forceful deadpan gaze: Sal Catalano. Rooney recognized him from his mug shot. Next to Catalano was another man, squat, with a double chin and large, fat face framed by crinkly silvering hair brushed straight back. There was another stranger in the car at the wheel. And several other unknown men were standing nearby. What was Catalano doing there? He had nothing to do with it. Or did he? Was he the "Sallie" one of the shooters had called to?

Rooney showed the pictures to the NYPD's Clark and came up with some other IDs. The police had seen the fat man with Catalano before. He was Giuseppe Ganci, a partner of Catalano's in the pizza business and, it seemed,

Catalano's frequent shadow. Rooney later learned that one of the unidentified men in the photo was me—covering the story for *The New York Times*.

Why Catalano and Ganci had chosen to step into the glare of publicity with Bonventre and Amato was something Rooney couldn't figure out. Later it hit him: They wanted to send a powerful message. There was a new alignment: *Catalano and Ganci, Bonventre and Amato—we are now together.*

Something else occurred to Rooney: If Bonventre and Amato had been in on the hit, as he now believed, they must have had great faith that they would not be mowed down in the mayhem. They had trusted the shooters with their lives.

A miracle? Rooney didn't believe in miracles, especially not after he had heard about a seemingly unimportant bust that had taken place the previous June, five weeks before the Galante murder.

On that mild evening two Nassau County plainclothes cops had been patrolling the Green Acres shopping center, one of Long Island's largest, which was plagued by a crime wave of shoplifting, robbery, rape, and even an occasional murder. As the stores were shutting down for the night, the two cops, cruising in their green Plymouth Valiant with oversize tires, noticed a blue Cadillac with a tall blond driver and a hard-faced, dark-haired passenger. They appeared to be loitering around the California Pizzeria, which had previously been identified as a suspected drug location. Another team of plainclothesmen had spotted the same pair several hours earlier and, their suspicions aroused, ordered an ownership check on the Cadillac's New Jersey license tag. It had come up Cesare Bonventre of Brooklyn, a name that meant nothing to the cops at the time.

As the partners in the Valiant watched, they saw Bonventre's Cadillac and another Cadillac signal each other with flashing headlights and cruise to a rendezvous in the parking lot. They saw Bonventre step out, carrying a white plastic bag tightly concealed against his body. He delivered it to the other Cadillac and emerged clutching a leather jacket draped around something stiff, about three feet high, the shape of a shotgun, the officers surmised. He carried it over to the driver's side of the other Cadillac and handed it to the man at the wheel.

Suddenly the two cars shot off in separate directions. The officers gave chase and caught up with Bonventre's Cadillac a short distance away. Bonventre identified himself as a twenty-eight-year-old pizza man from Brooklyn, born in Castellammare del Golfo. The pizza business must be good, the officers thought; he was carrying $1,800 in $50 bills. His passenger, Amato, said he was a twenty-seven-year-old deli owner, also of Brooklyn and Castellammare.

One of the officers shone his flashlight into the Cadillac. On the back seat he saw a paper bag lying on its side. From the opening protruded the frame and hammer of a Smith & Wesson .38 five-shot, the same model he himself carried. The serial number had been obliterated. The gun was loaded.

The officers continued to search the Cadillac. In a rear pouch attached to the back of the driver's seat they found a Colt .38, also loaded. They found two black wool knit ski masks—unlikely gear for a soft June night. In a box on the floor by the front seat they found a switchblade knife and bullets. And in the trunk were three other knives, two pairs of rubber gloves, and a rubber Halloween mask. Not exactly, the officers thought, your run-of-the-mill shoppers at the mall.

The more Rooney and Russo learned, the less Bonventre and Amato looked as if they had been beneficiaries of a miracle when the killers had blasted Galante and his two companions at Joe and Mary's. It looked, thought Rooney, as if they had helped do the old man in.

Galante. Joe and Mary's. Bonventre and Amato. Catalano and Ganci. The Café del Viale. It occurred to the agents that there was a common denominator. It was Knickerbocker Avenue, for half a century the turf of the Bonanno family and a stewpot of bubbling underworld activity, according to FBI files. Aside from the Café del Viale's after-hours back room casino complete with ready loan sharks, there were other mob-owned espresso bars and taverns. At Joe and Mary's restaurant, Galante's cousin, the ill-fated Joe Turano, did a thriving side business in hijacked meat, according to an FBI informant. Knickerbocker Avenue also boasted Colosseo Imports, a small newsstand–gift shop run by Salvatore Catalano. It was a modest starting point for a man who would eventually mastermind a colossal heroin empire.

The maze of names and businesses and events that led like a boomerang back to Knickerbocker Avenue was described to the FBI beginning in 1979 by one of its most important informants, a hapless and diabolically funny mob hit man from Sicily named Luigi Ronsisvalle. If the slit-eyed Ronsisvalle, who admitted to killing thirteen people—five in Sicily, eight in the United States—had had a calling card, it might have advertised a boast he later made to the authorities: "Homicide is my business."

Ronsisvalle had come to Knickerbocker Avenue from Catania in eastern Sicily in 1966 at the age of twenty-six, carrying an introduction to one of the dozen triggermen Joe Bonanno had imported from Sicily to beef up his forces in the New York Mafia wars of the 1960's. Ronsisvalle quickly picked up some advice about rising in the organization: "Listen careful, follow orders, don't open your mouth, and do your job very good, the best you know how."

It echoed advice Ronsisvalle had received from his father years before in Sicily: "Luigi, when you see something, shut your mouth. If you see something you don't like, turn around. If you hear things that don't belong to you, don't hear them. Mind your business. That's most of the rules."

But Ronsisvalle broke the rules. After thirteen years in the United States as a contract killer, Bonanno family gofer, and drug runner, Ronsisvalle defected.

To avenge an insult, he became a secret government witness, one of the most valued mob turncoats since Joe Valachi nearly two decades before. Starting in early 1979, five months before the Galante shooting, he began providing the FBI with an intimate look at Mafia life on Knickerbocker Avenue. And a year later, when Rooney and Russo began leafing through the files, they came across Ronsisvalle's astonishing reports.

One of the first things Ronsisvalle did once he turned, according to the reports, was threaten to kill the FBI agents debriefing him if anything happened to his family before they could be placed in the federal witness protection program. The family was supposed to be under twenty-four-hour FBI guard, but Ronsisvalle's wife complained that after a few days she didn't see the agents anymore. Ronsisvalle was further shaken by a visit from two strangers to the Westchester motel room where he was being held, supposedly in secret. The men looked Ronsisvalle up and down, said they were detectives, and left. Ronsisvalle was convinced they had been sent by his former mob associates to verify his location. Shaken, he moved that night to another motel far away, then got down to work.

Shown an album of FBI surveillance photos of Bonanno family figures, Ronsisvalle had stopped at a picture of Salvatore Catalano, whom he said he knew as Toto. He said Toto was a captain in the Bonanno family and was "in charge" of Knickerbocker Avenue, where he worked in his brother Dominick's magazine and record store, Colosseo Imports. Ronsisvalle said that Catalano was made a captain about six months after a predecessor, Peter Licata, had been shot to death outside his home in 1976. Ronsisvalle had been an enforcer for Licata, accompanying him on rounds to collect loan-shark debts. Licata would point out those who owed money, and Ronsisvalle would terrify them into paying up. But Licata, like Galante after him, had become an obstacle, for different reasons. He didn't approve of drug trafficking. Moreover, Licata, who controlled the floating baccarat game on Knickerbocker Avenue, objected to removing the game from the Café del Viale to a new location. Traditionally the game rotated annually among several cafés and restaurants, which drew business from the game. The proprietor-host received up to $75,000 a year in royalties, while Licata made up to $200,000 a year from the house. Several loan sharks always stood by, offering money at 2 percent interest, which rose to 5 percent if the money was not repaid by the end of the next day. No wonder Licata was reluctant to let go. But others made up his mind for him. In November 1976 he was shotgunned to death outside his home.

About six months later the new boss of Knickerbocker Avenue was Sal Catalano. Ronsisvalle also saw two others rise to new prominence: Bonventre, who according to whispers was Licata's killer, and Bonventre's cousin and side-kick Amato. Subsequently, Ronsisvalle said, Catalano could often be found at the Café del Viale's postmidnight baccarat game, where he took a percentage of the proceeds. One of the shylocks at the game, Ronsisvalle said, was a pizzeria operator named Anthony Aiello, known as Commerciante, or businessman, and Ronsisvalle added, according to the FBI report: "Cesare Bonventre is in charge of the game. Baldassare Amato works with him. Salvatore Catalano is in charge of Knickerbocker Avenue for the Bonanno family."

"Mr. Catalano is an American who speak very little, almost nothing," Ronsisvalle said he was told by one of his underworld mentors. "He don't talk with nobody." And he said if FBI agents were looking at Salvatore Catalano for the Galante hit, "they were on the right track."

The picture of life on Knickerbocker Avenue that Ronsisvalle painted for the FBI was replete with violence and improbable mob characters. There was Paolo LaPorta, who dealt in hot cars and gave Ronsisvalle a .45 and arranged for them to stick up a Brooklyn drugstore. Actually LaPorta waited outside and fled after the pharmacist had pulled out a gun and pegged six shots, all wide, at the astonished Ronsisvalle. LaPorta also took Ronsisvalle periodically to Canada to deliver falsified American passports, at $500 apiece, to Sicilians waiting to cross the border.

There was Vincenzo "Enzo" Napoli of the Gambino family, an enterprising fence, who in 1977 was trying to unload $25 million in stolen securities, blank cashier's and airline checks, guns, Cartier watches, stolen credit cards, brand-name toiletries, shellfish, a fifteenth-century Italian sculpture, Picasso sketches, and Stradivarius violins. In the spring of 1977 Ronsisvalle, Napoli, and three associates staged a million-dollar robbery of a diamond dealer on West Forty-seventh Street in Manhattan. After the stickup Ronsisvalle got cheated out of most of his share; Napoli, he complained, then tried to fix him up with a woman in a hotel room and gun him down. Furious, Ronsisvalle resolved to kill Napoli first. But word of the feud leaked out, and Ronsisvalle was summoned by Catalano, who ordered him to cease his vendetta. The disputed spoils of the jewel heist were divided at a high-level interfamily sit-down. Paul Castellano, the powerful boss of the Gambino family, was presented with a $10,000 diamond—not the first evidence of close ties between the Bonanno and Gambino families. And a lawyer who had represented mob figures was rewarded with a three-carat diamond for the bargain-basement price of $7,000. Most of the proceeds that remained were invested in an abortive scheme to smuggle in heroin from Thailand.

Ronsisvalle also met another "peacemaker"—Pasquale Conte, Sr.—who, Ronsisvalle told the agents, had ties to the Gambino family and the Key Food supermarket chain. After a traffic accident involving Ronsisvalle, Conte got the hot-headed hit man to drop his vendetta against the other driver.

These episodes increased Ronsisvalle's disenchantment with the Americans, who he claimed dishonored the ideals of the Mafia. "They are a gang," he testified later. "I don't call them Mafia. A man of honor no go around stealing and killing for money. A man of honor, he kill for some reason, to help people."

One day in 1977 Ronsisvalle received a commission. A compulsive gambler could not cover his last bet in a poker game. In desperation he put up his wife. The man lost the hand and brought the other two cardplayers home to have intercourse with his wife. The next morning the wife complained to her brother, a policeman, who took up a collection for a murder contract on the husband that was placed with Ronsisvalle for $2,000. Ronsisvalle waited for the husband one morning until he left the house early to go fishing. Then he shot him to death. Asked later to identify the victim, Ronsisvalle was indignant. "I don't know his name," he said.

On an earlier occasion, in 1976, a man complained to the Mafia that his sister's fourteen-year-old daughter had been raped by a man he identified as a cook in a Brooklyn restaurant. Ronsisvalle tracked the accused culprit to his kitchen one early morning and felled him with five shots. Ronsisvalle later pleaded guilty to this homicide and did six years of his five- to fifteen-year sentence before he got out to become a star government witness.

In late 1978 Ronsisvalle was offered his biggest contract of all. Michele Sindona, the Italian criminal financier, was under investigation for bank fraud in the United States and Italy. Through an intermediary he offered to pay $100,000 for the murder of the assistant United States attorney on his case, John Kenney. As part of the plot cocaine or heroin was to be planted on Kenney's body to make the murder appear drug-related. Ronsisvalle had already served Sindona by trying to intimidate a Wall Street witness who was to testify against him, but this, even Ronsisvalle realized, was asking a lot.

"Whoa, you are talking about something heavy!" he told Sindona. Sindona, he said, also offered to pay $100,000 for the murder of a government-appointed liquidator of his bank in Milan, who, in fact, was later assassinated. But Ronsisvalle had backed out. Sindona himself later dropped the Kenney contract after one of the intermediaries had carelessly mentioned Sindona's name on the telephone. When Ronsisvalle was arrested shortly afterward for snatching the purse of a woman coming out of a bank, a cowardly crime he described later as deeply humiliating, he went to Sindona for the bail money, in effect a payment to guarantee Ronsisvalle's silence. Sindona refused to be blackmailed, believing

Ronsisvalle was bluffing. He wasn't. He turned himself in to the police in early 1979, saying he had a story for the FBI.

As he later acknowledged, he was willing to confess to thirteen murders just to get back at Sindona (who died in 1986 after drinking poisoned coffee in his prison cell in Italy). "I'm tired of this life," Ronsisvalle explained in his throaty and thickly accented English. "I'm tired of doing things against the law. I want to put myself straight."

Killing people, Ronsisvalle said, was just a job. "It was nothing personal, sir," he told a prosecutor. It was just a matter of money.

But, he was asked, couldn't he have shot innocent bystanders by mistake? "I don't think so," Ronsisvalle said. "I'm very careful in those things."

What really came to upset him, he insisted, was dealing in drugs. "In a sense, the way I believe it," he said, "you give to me thirty thousand dollars, and I am sent to kill a person. You kill him, not me. But to move pounds of heroin, you destroy hundreds of thousands of young American generations. That makes me shake." Eventually, Ronsisvalle said, he was drinking a liter of vodka a day to control his shattered nerves.

Ronsisvalle told how, as an associate not yet inducted into the Bonanno family, he became apprenticed to Carmine Galante's godson, a café owner named Felice Puma, who broke Ronsisvalle in on a couple of arson jobs and drug runs.

Puma taught Ronsisvalle how to hide cocaine or heroin in pockets sewn inside a loose-fitting suit and to evade airline checks by rushing for the plane at the last minute with an armful of bundles. Six years later, in a second round of FBI debriefings, Ronsisvalle came up with details he had never told the bureau in 1979. He related that he had flown to Los Angeles a dozen times in 1977, each time carrying a kilo of heroin for the same customer. He also carried nearly forty kilos of heroin on each of some fifteen trips to Chicago via Amtrak, representing, if Ronsisvalle was telling the truth, some $100 million worth of heroin at the Mafia's wholesale prices and over $1 billion if it was all cut and sold on the street. Sometimes, for $5,000 a trip, Ronsisvalle would fly to Florida to meet Puma, who had loaded up his red Porsche with heroin or cocaine, and they would drive back to New York together. Ronsisvalle would ride shotgun—literally. He sat with a sawed-off double-barreled shotgun between his knees and a .38 in his waistband. "Well," he later explained indignantly, "I don't move some heroin with a lollipop in my pocket."

Once in 1977, Ronsisvalle said, he flew to Miami and met Puma by prearrangement on Collins Avenue in Miami Beach. They immediately drove back to Knickerbocker Avenue with a hundred-kilo monster load of heroin stashed behind the rear seat. When they got back, as Ronsisvalle later described it, Catalano was standing outside the Café del Viale. Puma exchanged a few words with him. Then Catalano walked to the café and emerged with an associate who took custody of the heroin-laden Porsche. Ronsisvalle concluded it was Catalano's heroin. But Ronsisvalle never told the FBI this in 1979, and consequently Russo and Rooney did not learn of it until 1985, when he was debriefed by prosecutor Louis Freeh, long after the Pizza Connection case was cracked. Apparently Ronsisvalle had initially withheld it as leverage to get himself out of prison and into the federal witness protection program six years later. Either that, or he had remembered it only later. Or he had made it up.

Ronsisvalle's memory on another matter failed him—or remained unprobed— until 1985, when he remembered he had seen Puma in the summer of 1977 meeting with Catalano and a fat, silver-haired man he learned was Catalano's Sicilian associate, Giuseppe Ganci. At the time there had been a heroin drought —supplies had dried up. Later that same day Puma took Ronsisvalle aside.

"Luigi," he said, "do you know the pipe that brings the oil in the U.S. from Canada?"

Sure, Ronsisvalle had heard of the Trans-Alaska Pipeline.

"We have the same thing with heroin coming into the U.S."

The drought, he told Ronsisvalle, was over.

3

OST mornings in early 1980 Rooney and Russo would meet before eight in the large squad area of the Queens FBI office, which was jammed with littered desks and containers of leftover coffee. Dressed like other agents in the undercover uniform of the street—jeans, plaid shirt, and ski jacket—they compared notes and laid their plans for the day. If they had a strategy at this point, it was just to collect as much intelligence as they could about their two targets, piece it together, and see where it led them.

Searching for information about Bonventre, Russo had leafed through Gay Talese's best seller *Honor Thy Father* and had seen in the family tree printed on the flyleaf that Joe Bonanno's mother was a Bonventre. He knew that the Bonventres, like the Bonannos and Galantes, came from Castellammare. There was something about Bonventre that obsessed Russo, although it made him, as a law enforcement professional, uncomfortable to confront it. Detached as Russo tried to be, he had to admit that Bonventre, with his bravado and swagger, the way he draped his jacket European-style over his shoulders, got to him. He wasn't the only one. Bonventre was rumored to be alienating some of his own people as well. If this was the new face of the Mafia, Russo reflected, it was a hell of a lot more brazen and flamboyant than the old.

One morning Russo drove into downtown Manhattan to the offices of the Parking Violations Bureau. He had an idea. If he had Bonventre pegged, the brash young mafioso had probably accumulated a hefty file of parking tickets. Finding out where they had been issued might give Russo some clue to where he was hanging out and perhaps with whom. Then Russo could start running down license tags.

Rooney was also searching for an investigative opening. As the street boss of Knickerbocker Avenue and Bonventre's and Amato's apparent protector, Catalano was pivotal to the group, Rooney decided. But the chunky Sicilian seemed to enjoy some special status Rooney could not put his finger on. Although evidently influential in the American Bonanno family, he seemed closest to fellow Sicilians like Ganci and Bonventre. While most of the American mobsters spoke English, these four spoke the Sicilian dialect. Rooney had no way yet of knowing at that point that they had stumbled across a crucial underworld anomaly—a secret arm of the Sicilian Mafia in America.

Rooney's unwitting discovery was also anomalous in terms of the FBI's long-held perception of the Mafia's organization. Once it acknowledged the Mafia's existence, the FBI had sought to categorize its members into families, although the "genealogy" stopped abruptly at the Atlantic coast. There was little curiosity about the American mobsters' Sicilian roots and the transatlantic ties that bound the brethren. But the government's experts were naïve, just as their image of a monolithic Mafia was distorted. Beneath the often loose-knit families, the Mafia was composed of what the more experienced Italians called *cosche*, or cliques, geographical and kinship groups that formed shifting alliances and often murderous rivalries with other cliques, sometimes in the same family. In addition, the Atlantic was not the Mafia boundary it was long depicted to be: Here in America, a Sicilian clique was flourishing in Brooklyn, under the aegis of the Bonanno family. And at its head was Salvatore Catalano.

It was not surprising that the development caught the FBI unaware; it had enlisted late in the war on the Mafia and other organized crime groups. It was only within the last two decades that the bureau and other federal law enforcement agencies had really mobilized against traditional organized crime, which the bureau referred to by the euphemism used by many of its members, La Cosa Nostra, "the thing of ours." Joe Valachi, the first major Mafia turncoat in the United States, had sprung the term and the sinister reality of the Mafia on a surprised nation during the Senate investigating subcommittee hearings led by John McClellan in 1963.

It was an embarrassment for Hoover not to have prepared the public for the revelation. The director had long been on record denying that organized crime existed. Considering the mass of secret information he had been privy to for so many decades, no one inside or outside the bureau could adequately explain how Hoover could have for so long denied the existence of what was known to every street-corner punk and big-city cop. It was said that the director had resisted throwing his agents into a war against organized crime for fear they might show up badly or fall prey to corruption, but it is inconceivable that Hoover did not know of the Mafia. It is equally implausible, as detractors have suggested, that Hoover and the Mafia abided by some unspoken agreement to leave each other alone. Rather, Hoover probably felt that any acknowledgment of a nationwide or international organized criminal conspiracy would bring calls for an inter-agency national law enforcement response. And that, he sensed, could destroy the legendary independence and primacy of the agency he had built, virtually single-handedly, since taking control of the sixteen-year-old Bureau of Investiga-tion in 1924.

It was also no coincidence that the bureau's undercover program was launched only after Hoover's death in 1972. Hoover knew that agents sent into deep undercover roles would no longer be under the close control of the bureau. This undoubtedly explained much of Hoover's curious reluctance to use the bureau's prodigious resources against organized crime and the overriding criminal spectre of his last years: drug trafficking. The fact that the FBI was not given cojurisdic-tion with the DEA over drug laws until 1982 may have been a factor, but Hoover had never been shy about bending the rules when it suited him.

As it happened, Hoover accurately foresaw the coming interagency efforts in the organized crime war up to a point. In the years ahead the government's attack on the Mafia and an expanding universe of other organized crime groups did indeed force an unprecedented cooperation between the FBI and other federal and local investigative and law enforcement agencies. But the FBI was not weakened; it thrived.

In 1950, three decades before Rooney and Russo went to work, Senator Estes Kefauver's investigating committee had first torn the veil from the gambling and racketeering operations of "a sinister criminal organization known as the Mafia." Seven years later Senator McClellan's committee exposed Mafia labor racketeer-ing. Also in 1957, the New York State Police uncovered and raided a Mafia summit meeting of more than fifty mob bosses and associates at the Apalachin, New York, estate of Joe Barbera, a Castellammarese who had made a fortune in the soda bottling and distribution business. But Hoover still refused to throw the resources of the FBI into a war against the Mafia. When the Justice Department began its own investigation, Hoover dismissed it as "a fishing expedition," insist-ing that the bureau had "neither the manpower nor the time to waste on such speculative ventures." The Justice Department moved to establish a Special Group on Organized Crime. Hoover instead backed his own FBI "Top Hoodlum Program," which, characteristically, targeted individual crime kingpins rather than the shadowy enterprise they nurtured and served. It was a myopic view the bureau fortunately, if tardily, repudiated in years to come. Despite his public stance, Hoover quietly ordered background investigations into the men arrested at Apalachin, and the results stimulated FBI bugs and wiretaps that for the first time exposed inner workings of the Mafia, including the operation of a ruling national commission. Yet a full two years later, by 1959, there were still only a scant 4 agents in New York working on organized crime, while 400 were investigating Communists. Within three years the number of agents working on organized crime cases had grown to 150. By 1962, the year before Valachi's testimony electrified the country, many offices already had their own organized crime squads. But official skepticism and cynicism abounded. As a young assistant United States attorney in New York in the early 1970's, Rudolph W. Giuliani learned with dismay that his boss, Attorney General John Mitchell, had ordered the word "Mafia" stricken from the Justice Department's lexicon. The government's posture had a lot to do with its sensitivity to Italian-American voters and a lobby, including Joe Colombo's group, that picketed FBI offices to protest the Mafia stigma. The campaign of the Colombo family boss was decisively cut short in 1971 by a hit man's bullets.

The 1970's brought a turnaround. In 1968 the Omnibus Crime and Safe Streets Act had armed the government for the first time with wiretap authority in nonnational security investigations. The government's strongest investigative tool came two years later with passage of the pioneering legislation called the Racketeer-Influenced and Corrupt Organizations Act (RICO). The RICO statute, part of the Organized Crime Control Act of 1970, made it illegal to acquire or operate a business with funds derived from "a pattern of racketeering," a pattern being two or more proved racketeering charges within ten years. It also made it illegal to acquire or maintain an interest in an enterprise through a pattern of racketeering, conduct the affairs of an enterprise through a pattern of racketeering, or conspire to commit any of these offenses.

"RICO permits the scope of a corrupt organization as well as its methods of operation and enforcement to be presented in its entirety to a jury," noted one of the act's key authors, Notre Dame law professor G. Robert Blakey. In his words: "RICO is to an individual offense what a sphere is to a circle."

It took a long time for the authorities to understand how to wield RICO, particularly the surprisingly potent civil RICO offshoot that allowed the government for the first time to sue the Mafia under laxer, noncriminal standards of proof to halt long-entrenched racketeering schemes. But it finally impelled them to broaden their targets from individual criminal acts to criminal enterprises. By early 1987 RICO had been used to convict more than a thousand bosses, soldiers, and associates of the Mafia—and twice as many leaders of other ethnic crime groups and gangs. Ironically, however, while the FBI had 1,100 agents assigned to organized crime in 1981, by 1987 the number was down to 617, many agents having been shifted to FBI antidrug units.

When they began the Catalano-Bonventre part of the bureau's larger Bonanno investigation in early 1980, Rooney and Russo were still a long way from figuring out Catalano's role or piecing together his history. They knew from immigration records that he had been born in 1941 in Ciminna, south of Palermo, and had come to the United States in 1966. That in itself was something of a revelation.

Hey, Rooney asked Russo, only half-kiddingly, Catalano was Italian, wasn't he? Didn't Italians come from Rome?

Russo's response was to find a large map of Sicily and lay it out on Rooney's desk. "This is Sicily, Charlie," Russo explained. They would be dealing with Sicily in this investigation. He pointed to a dot on a wiggly line of a road thirty miles south of Palermo. That, he said, was Ciminna. Originally Punic, the rustic hilltop town of four thousand had been developed by the Romans, whose coins and artifacts were still being turned up there two millennia later. Like many of western Sicily's towns, Ciminna had a strong Mafia tradition going back to the nineteenth-century peasant gangs that guarded the interests of the absentee landlords.

Catalano's saga emerged slowly. Catalano was one of six children, the oldest of three boys. His mother died when he was a child; his father was a conductor who sold tickets on the Palermo-Agrigento bus line. In 1966, with his two brothers and one of his sisters, the twenty-five-year-old Catalano came to the United States, settling in a $180-a-month apartment on Hemlock Street in Queens, near the Cypress Hills Cemetery. According to information later provided by his lawyers, Catalano's first job was as a machinist in a scientific corporation, a claim that Rooney viewed with skepticism. "What was he building? F-14's?" he asked. Later Catalano ran his brother's gift shop on Knickerbocker Avenue. In 1977 he bought a Queens pizzeria that he operated with two associates: Ganci, who had also come to America in 1966 from another traditional Mafia stronghold, San Giuseppe Iato, south of Palermo, and Bonventre of Castellammare.

For Catalano, 1979 was a busy year. Shortly after the Galante murder he went to Sicily. There he married a distant relative in a civil ceremony but came back to New York alone. He arranged to return later for a large formal wedding—and some other business. He had already opened a bakery on Metropolitan Avenue in Middle Village, Queens, with his brothers Dominick and Vito and sister Vita. Catalano had made a tightly knit world for himself. His Italian bakery was around the corner from Ganci's orange brick garden apartment building. Ganci's wife, too, was a Catalano, though not a close relative of the baker. Catalano lived in a modest garden apartment a short distance away in Glendale.

Rooney and Russo were getting to know this little world. Often, separately or together, they drove past the Catalano and Ganci houses, the bakery, and the pizzeria and then swung down the pitted length of Knickerbocker Avenue, taking down license numbers. Russo particularly liked to cruise Brooklyn seeing if he could spot Bonventre and Amato at the Café del Viale or another one of their hangouts. Russo liked working the street. He saw himself as a man of action, and he got antsy if he was stuck too long in the office. But neither of them saw much. Either their targets were lying low or were managing to carry on their business surreptitiously. The investigation had not reached a point where the two men were put under regular surveillance. The FBI, in fact, had no reason yet to think they merited constant watching, just periodic monitoring while Rooney and Russo and the rest of the Bonanno squad tried to figure out the players and what they were up to.

In early February 1980 Catalano and Ganci were four thousand miles away, stepping off a plane at Palermo's Punta Raisi Airport under the surveilling eyes of the Italian Treasury Police. The airport, built on a point of land between the blue Tyrrhenian Sea and the rocky spine of mountains that cradles Palermo, drew its name from the ancient *rais*, or leader, of the Arab fishing crews that once hunted tuna in these waters, as the Sicilians were to do through modern times. The giant fish were encircled in a tightening ring of boats and nets and then hauled to the surface to be clubbed to death in a grisly slaughter. It was not an altogether unfitting association for an airport that since the 1960's had served as a notorious transshipment point in the smuggling of vast amounts of heroin to the United States.

A few days after Catalano and Ganci arrived in Palermo, the Italian police had listened in on a telephone call placed to Bagheria. The small city on the coast some ten miles east of Palermo was renowned for its perfumed orange groves, which spread from the sea in labyrinthine profusion, making fine hiding places for Mafia fugitives, another local product for which Bagheria was also renowned. One of the local Mafia rackets, in fact, was to cheat the European Economic

Community by pretending to destroy subsidized excess oranges and lemons but keeping the fruit for resale.

The monitored telephone call was to longtime suspected heroin trafficker Giorgio Muratore who had recently returned from a visit to New York.

"Is something wrong?" asked the caller.

"No," Muratore replied. "But the . . . tangerines."

"Will they arrive?"

"I don't know. Maybe," he said. "I planted three of them, I believe. Today I am going to water them. I was hoping, after, to have a few lemons, things."

To the eavesdropping Treasury agents, tangerine trees that yielded lemons and a flurry of similarly enigmatic calls were signs of a major drug deal in the works. The first weeks of the new year had seen a heavy influx of suspicious Americans into Palermo and the Treasury officers, tipped off that Palermo Mafia traffickers were hatching a series of drug deals, had been busy shadowing the visitors and trying to divine their mission by tapping the telephones of their Sicilian contacts.

The day of the call, February 7, 1980, some of the figures under surveillance made their way to Ciminna, where 250 wedding guests filled the Piazza Bellini outside the red sixteenth-century mother church, Santa Maria Magdalena. Some of the guests had come from as far away as America to celebrate the union of Caterina Maria Catalano and Salvatore Catalano.

High over the central nave, a fourteenth-century Gothic rose window spilled shimmering ruby light onto the tiled floor. Light shafts streaming through the clerestory windows illuminated particles of ancient dust floating in the incense-scented air. Under the limestone columns—Sicily had no marble of its own—bride and groom exchanged vows at the baroque altar before a choir of burnished carved walnut. From above, a peeling portrait of the Virgin surveyed the celebrants. Afterward the wedding guests sped to a catered party at La Nave restaurant in Palermo, where they plied the newlyweds with the traditional envelopes of cash. Receptions at catering halls and restaurants had become fashionable in recent years, especially among the new moneyed bourgeoisie, but more traditional Sicilians looked askance at such displays of ostentation. After the party the couple spent a three-day honeymoon at Caterina's mother's house while planning a longer escape to a Palermo hotel at the end of March.

A week after the wedding, Italian Treasury officer Calogero Scarvaci parked his unmarked police car on the Piazza Ruggiero Settimo (widely known as the Piazza Politeama) in the heart of Palermo, hefted his camera, and kept his eye on four men meeting in the corner Extrabar at the Sicilian capital's central square. At one end of the large piazza loomed the antique dome and columns of the Politeama, the theater of "all things," built as a circus and music hall in

1874, when this part of Palermo was still out in the country. On this mild February afternoon the square was aswarm with buzzing motorbikes and three-wheel scooters darting like mosquitoes through the flow of produce vans and construction trucks. A cacophony of horns and the blaring music carts of tape cassette peddlers, the updated version of the nineteenth-century barrel organ grinders, periodically drowned out the squeal of children chasing pigeons under the high palms and the chatter of couples lining up for *gelato* at the sidewalk stands.

Palermo fairly bowed under the weight of history. By the pinnacled, filigreed gate of Porta Nuova commemorating Spanish victories in Africa three hundred years before, high windows in the royal palace marked the World War II Sicilian headquarters of General George S. Patton. Resplendent with gold mosaics, the Palatine Chapel exalted the enlightened conqueror Roger II, who bequeathed Palermo a legacy of Arab-Latin harmony in an age when the city yielded its Norman rulers more riches than all England. A section of Palermo by the antique and flea market still bore the name Papireto, from the days of the Phoenicians, when papyrus had grown abundantly there. Dust storms frequently coated the city with sand blown from the deserts of North Africa. Under the Saracens, Palermo was a city of five hundred mosques, a cultural center rivaling Cairo and Córdoba; some of the domes still rise above the relatively modern, merely seven-teenth-century buildings of today's skyline.

There were grimmer monuments as well, testimony to another army of occu-pation, as entrenched as the Bourbons or Angevins had ever been: the orange-roofed Mediterranean stucco villa on the Via Messina Marina by the sea where a clandestine laboratory had refined fifty kilos of heroin a week and the decrepit storehouse near Brancaccio, the South Bronx of Palermo, where one of the more vicious Mafia chieftains had tortured victims in his "room of death" before himself falling prey to assassins. Other modern landmarks, seemingly benign, masked the same insidious force: All along the Viale Strasbourg, phalanxes of bright new apartment blocks marched west into the fast-growing suburbs of Palermo, where, it was well known, no significant construction took place without the approval and participation of the local Mafia boss. The building surge coin-cided with the booming Mafia drug traffic. Much of the new western part of the city stretching toward Punta Raisi Airport, it was said, was built on heroin money. How else, skeptics asked, could Palermo rank seventieth among Italian cities in per capita income yet come out an astonishing seventh in per capita consump-tion? Similarly, the Conca d'Oro, the golden shell of mountains spilling down to Palermo and the sea, was becoming a vast construction site as villas sprouted like poppies on the steep hillsides. Later, when the Mafia investigations rocked Sicily,

hundreds of the buildings would be left unfinished, testimony to panic and suddenly evaporating fortunes.

Through the Extrabar's glass doors, Officer Scarvaci could see customers sipping espresso at the counter and ordering up desserts in the rear. A line had formed at the cashier, where people were buying tickets for their pastries and drinks.

When the four men came out, the officer followed them with his camera. Two were later identified as Muratore of the "lemons" conversation, and Filippo Ragusa, a bakery owner from Queens, New York, mentioned in the anonymous letter to the FBI about the murdered pizza chief in November of 1979. Caught on the film, approaching a double-parked black Mercedes, was Catalano, in a three-piece suit. An Italian police report concluded that the Extrabar meeting at the Piazza Politeama "constituted the fundamental 'moment' when the criminal plan that had been developing was concretized." The plan was to send a large heroin shipment to America.

Several weeks after the meeting at the Piazza Politeama, a gruff Sicilian butcher named Salvatore Contorno ran into a friend who was looking for a lift to Bagheria, the citrus center and Mafia stronghold east of the capital. Contorno didn't mind driving him. Like his friend, who was on the run from Italian justice, the thirty-three-year-old Contorno was a member of the Mafia family of Santa Maria di Gesù, an outlying neighborhood of Palermo. He came, as a police report put it, from "Mafia family extraction," his father and older brother having embraced the brotherhood before him. The tall, long-haired Contorno had a busy career in crime, with theft, smuggling, swindling, drug trafficking, carrying weapons, and receiving stolen property being among his many charged offenses. He had been sentenced to exile in Venice from 1976 to 1979 and was wanted again for ransom and kidnapping.

For a mere soldier, Contorno was unusually well placed, reporting directly to his boss, Stefano Bontade, a particularly influential member of the ruling Sicilian Mafia Commission known as the Cupola, the dome or big heads. Contorno and Bontade had been young hunting companions in the sixties, and Bontade, after rising to head the Santa Maria di Gesù family, had kept his eye on Contorno. One night in 1975 Contorno was tested by one of Bontade's men, who took him to witness a killing. As the victim expired before Contorno's eyes, his escort explained simply, "That's how you die." Contorno didn't flinch. Shortly afterward Contorno was picked up without warning and driven to Bontade's house, where a number of family members had gathered. They placed a picture of a saint in his hand. They pricked Contorno's finger and let the blood run over the image of the saint. Then they set fire to the picture in his hand, warning him that if he ever betrayed them, he would burn like the flaming paper. "You can't just show up and say, 'I'd like to join the Mafia,'" Contorno explained years later. You had to be invited. Strikingly, Contorno's account of his initiation into the Mafia in Sicily—and a similar account given by Mafia turncoat Tommaso Buscetta—matched one given by Joe Valachi two decades earlier in America.

Contorno's story—like Valachi's and Ronsisvalle's and Buscetta's—came out because like the others, Contorno agreed in 1985, after three years in custody, to follow Buscetta's lead and testify against the Mafia and, eventually, to enter the federal witness protection program in the United States. Guiding him to his perilous decision was the killing in 1981 of Bontade and many of his key lieutenants by the rival Corleonesi and an ambush attack shortly afterward on Contorno himself, one he narrowly escaped.

Contorno's account was to highlight one of the key episodes of the case. At the end of the Bagheria autostrada Contorno and his companion turned off the highway and drove past the citrus groves to an iron factory belonging to Leonardo Greco, the boss of the Bagheria family, who directed them to a nearby country farmhouse. On the awning-shaded terrace Contorno saw Catalano and Ganci from America, recognizing them from a previous encounter at Mafia boss Michele Greco's country estate, a well-known port of call for mafiosi, politicians, and even policemen. (Leonardo and Michele Greco were not believed to be related.) Ganci reminded Contorno of a bull; in fact, he learned, Buffalo was one of his nicknames. He also met Salvatore Greco, Mafia boss Leonardo Greco's brother and operator of a pizzeria in New Jersey. Contorno said he was introduced to Sal Greco with the comment "La stessa cosa" ("the same thing")—a mafioso's term for another "man of honor." There was not a lot of chatter. As Contorno later explained, "In circles like ours, where the less said the better, half a sentence is sufficient."

Later, when he was being debriefed in Palermo and Rome starting in 1984, Contorno first maintained that he did not recognize the Americans at the farmhouse. He didn't even tell Russo he could identify Catalano. But subsequently Contorno whispered to an American DEA agent, Anthony Petrucci, that he could indeed identify Americans at the farmhouse, although he would not do so in the presence of the Italian authorities. To Petrucci, Contorno identified photographs of Frank Castronovo—known as "Ciccio L'Americano"—and Gaetano Mazzara, partners in a New Jersey restaurant.

It was Contorno's first encounter with Castronovo, whose cousin and brother-in-law, Carlo, Castronovo said, had been in the cigarette-smuggling business until the contraband of choice switched to heroin in the mid-seventies. The profits in drugs dwarfed those in cigarettes, Carlo Castronovo told Contorno; if Contorno

had 40 million lire (then about $47,000) to invest in a heroin shipment, he could quickly double his money. Carlo belonged to Leonardo Greco's Bagheria family and confided that Frank ran a pizza restaurant in America as a front. "It means," Contorno understood, "that you make pizza but actually deal in drugs."

The guests took out two plastic garbage bags and extracted packages of white powder in clear plastic envelopes, each bearing different tiny scissor cuts or pen or pencil marks to identify the individual owner. They poured samples of the powder into a bottle heating on a hot plate. Soon an acid stench filled the room. Contorno, overcome by nausea, ran downstairs to the open air and picked a lemon to suck on to ease the dizziness. His more experienced friend had taken the precaution of bringing a handkerchief to hold over his face. Within an hour he came downstairs and assured Contorno that the batch was good. But the heroin would never reach America.

A few weeks later another Sicilian-born New York pizza man, Emanuele Adamita, flew into Milan's airport accompanied by a companion in a yellow windbreaker, who, unbeknown to Adamita, was a DEA informant. Frank Rolli had been an Alitalia cargo employee who helped heroin smugglers in the Gambino family, including Adamita, slip their loads through Customs checks at Kennedy Airport. The previous year DEA and Customs agents at the airport had intercepted two unclaimed parcels being sent to a fictitious Brooklyn address. One of the packages had contained canisters that were labeled "talcum powder" but turned out to be heroin. Ordinarily the authorities trumpeted such seizures. This time they kept it quiet. As they hoped, the disappearance of the load without the usual announcement of the seizure had spread paranoia among Adamita and his partners. Suspicion quickly had fallen on Rolli and his fellow cargo handlers, who were ordered to come up with the drugs or $900,000. In an effort to extract a confession, one of the employees had been strung upside down from a rafter with a gun stuck in his mouth. Only then had the terrified employees been able to find documentation that the packages had indeed been seized by the authorities. Meanwhile, agents had traced the package waybill to one of the employees, who agreed to cooperate and finger others. Rolli, too, then had agreed to work secretly for the government although he knew the risks. He drew the line, though, at wearing a wire; several times, after being carefully fitted with a microphone hidden under his clothes, he waited until he was away from the agents and then ripped it off. He was brave, but he wasn't crazy.

Now, with the unsuspecting Adamita, Rolli was leading a trail of DEA agents back to Milan, to the source of what Rolli believed would be a six-kilo shipment. To his amazement, it turned out to be forty kilos—$8 million worth at Mafia importer's prices and at least $80 million worth at street prices—after Ganci and

Catalano and others in the Bagheria farmhouse unexpectedly added their loads to the shipment.

Adamita and Rolli hailed a taxi and drove off toward Milan, followed by the police. Within a few miles the cab broke down, and the two visitors had to scramble for other transport to their destination, which surveilling officers established was the small suburban villa of Adamita's brother.

Several days later a light truck from Sicily arrived at the house. The driver unloaded half a dozen crates of lemons, oranges, and fennel, the heroin carefully concealed underneath. That afternoon Rolli and Adamita's brother drove to a hydraulic equipment supplier and purchased three zinc canisters with covers and welding tin. At a music store they bought seventy long-playing records and thirty tapes of Italian music.

That evening, as surveilling officers watched from a distance, a red Ford van pulled up to the rear of the house and was loaded with three very large cartons and a smaller one. The van continued on to the Jumbo freight forwarding agency in a nearby town, where the cartons, weighing eighty-two kilos, were consigned for shipment as free record samples for a customer in New York.

As soon as the men who had brought the cartons left, the Italian police entered and opened them. On top of the cartons were records. They dug deeper, through a layer of polystyrene and red cloth, to a zinc container with a soldered lid. Inside were nine cellophane bags wrapped in tinfoil and beige adhesive tape, and in them was white powder. Altogether the cellophane bags held 40.610 kilograms of 85 percent pure heroin.

Many of the bags were later found to bear the small scissor cuts and other identifying marks, the codes that Contorno had noticed during the chemical test in Leonardo Greco's farmhouse. Also recovered was Adamita's phone book, listing, among others, Catalano and Ganci and two names still unfamiliar to investigators, Giuseppe Lamberti and Salvatore Mazzurco.

What the Italian police had unknowingly uncovered was the new heroin pipeline Ronsisvalle had been told about in 1977, a pipeline from Sicily to New York, with Catalano and Ganci and a cadre of their Sicilian cohorts at the receiving end—where Carmine Galante had hoped to be. But it was to take four more years of investigations on both sides of the Atlantic to piece it all together.

After the news of the big bust in Milan had been splashed all over the Italian press, Contorno ran into his friend again. "Remember the batch they were testing in Bagheria?" he asked Contorno. "That's the one that was seized," he added, confiding that the heroin was to have been hidden in the mats around a shipment of tiles.

Now, he said, they would have to try other channels.

4

 N the FBI's Brooklyn-Queens office, the case was stalled in a morass of detail. The trace on Bonventre's parking tickets had, as expected, yielded a sheaf of them, sending Russo on a tortuous search of state corporate records to find who owned the businesses around the places where Bonventre's car had been ticketed. Those names then had to be run through FBI files listing mob-owned companies and organized crime members and associates. They in turn led to other names and they all had to be checked out. So far nothing striking had turned up. The tedium and pressure took a particular toll on Russo, who, as his wife, Carmela, had noticed, had turned sullen and uncommunicative at home.

Frequently alone at night, she lay awake in the dark Brooklyn apartment listening to the sleep murmurs from the boys' bedrooms. Often when the apartment door clicked open it was after midnight. It sickened her to see Carmine come home so late. He always looked so drained and angry.

Now, Carmela heard a key in the lock.

Carmine had been in the Navy when they had met fifteen years before. The loneliness of shipboard duty in Guantanamo Bay, Cuba, and Greece had become unbearable, as he complained in letters home. His father knew someone he could write to, a Sicilian girl from a good family near Milazzo. He had already taken the liberty of contacting her parents, his father told Carmine: It would be permissible for Carmine to write to her. He sent a letter and a picture, which puzzled Carmela at first. "What happened to his hair?" she asked her cousin. "Nothing," said the cousin. "He's in the Navy." Carmela sent a picture in return. Carmine stared at her features—a soft Sicilian face framed in dark tresses—and fell in love.

In the apartment, Carmela waited for the sound of Carmine's footsteps. She sat upright in bed and pushed her dark hair out of her eyes. She tried to peer through the hall shadows. Somewhere there seemed to be a light burning. Had she left it on? She didn't think so.

Carmela had never come to terms with Carmine's strange hours. She could never sleep until he was safely home. She had tried to stop asking him what he was working on; not that he would tell her anyway, but she couldn't help herself. He was always nervous on a case but she had never seen him like this. He never smiled, he didn't eat. He was a phantom.

"Carmine? Is that you?" Why didn't he answer?

She swung her feet out of bed and into her plastic slippers, wrapped herself in her robe, and made her way down the hall.

There was a light burning in the living room! She thought of the boys asleep and her heart twisted with panic. She didn't know whom to worry about most —Carmine or herself and the boys.

There was someone moving around in the apartment!

Carmine.

"I thought you'd be asleep," he said in Sicilian.

"You didn't hear me calling?"

"No." His eyes were rimmed in purple.

She touched his arm. "What took so long tonight?"

"Nothing."

"You want to eat something?"

"I don't want to eat."

"Carmine," she persisted, "what happened?"

He shrugged.

"Carmine, you don't tell me anything anymore. My friends say, they say, 'What happened to Carmine? He looks sick. He never laughs anymore.' "

He knew. But what could he do? How could he tell Carmela what was going on when he didn't know himself?

In the midst of all the tensions, Rooney had a bit of blind luck. A book on another agent's desk caught his eye one day, and he began leafing through it. To his amazement, the thick volume entitled *The Canadian Connection* turned out to be an exhaustive account of international Mafia drug trafficking since the 1930's, as uncovered by the Quebec Police Commission Inquiry into Organized Crime. Published in 1976, the book by Canadian criminologist and later parliamentarian Jean-Pierre Charbonneau was crammed with names and intelligence derived from virtual daily surveillances of hundreds of mob figures, including many Americans. In the index Rooney found the name Salvatore Catalano, identified in the text as "an important international trafficker." Intrigued, he read on: "Catalano, a Brooklyn resident, had been exposed in 1963 by Italian authorities as a dangerous member of the Mafia." It said that Catalano was listed by the American Bureau of Narcotics and Dangerous Drugs as an associate of Tommaso Buscetta "and several other U.S. and Italian crime chiefs." In 1970, the account went on, Catalano had been picked up on a Canadian wiretap trying to set up a Mexican company to import sardines, tomatoes, and pasta, anything—"That doesn't matter," Catalano said on the phone. The man in Mexico would understand. It was to be a cover for drug smuggling.

How could he have missed this? Rooney wondered. This could not be his Salvatore Catalano. But that meant there had to be two of them.

A few days later in the Queens office Rooney looked up from a book to see Russo at his desk moving a pencil down a line of what looked like phone numbers.

"Carmine, you got something?"

He walked to Russo's desk. Below the tinted windows midday traffic was beginning to thicken on Queens Boulevard. Lunch hour. Reflexively Rooney conjured up the culinary delights of the Hwa Yuan Szechuan Inn on East Broadway, one of his favorite Chinatown restaurants, although deep down he believed that there was no such thing as a bad Chinese restaurant. He could do with an egg roll and some chicken and peanuts right now. Instead, he'd probably send down to Perdue in the lobby for the usual chicken takeout and seltzer.

Scattered over Russo's desk were calling cards, scribbled notes, driver's license and auto registration papers, and lined sheets with hand-printed names and phone numbers. Rooney picked up one of the phone lists.

"From Bonventre and Amato," Russo explained. "When they were grabbed in the Nassau parking lot."

"Whose is whose?"

"They don't know," Russo said, making a face. "Cops got them mixed up."

Rooney picked up one of the scraps, listing half a dozen names and numbers, including entries for Sal and Lilo and the figures 700 and 100.

"What's this mean?" he asked.

Russo shrugged. "Your guess." They could be references to business dealings with Galante and Catalano—one of the Catalanos anyway. Then again they could not. And the numbers: Debts? Investments? There was no way to tell. Another sheet bore the name and Sing Sing Prison address of a jailed Bonanno soldier, Anthony Mirra. There were business cards from a travel bureau, an insurance adjuster, an auto sales agency, a bakery, a surgeon, several lawyers, and a restaurant, Talk of the Town, in Belleville, New Jersey.

The restaurant card was an interesting clue, but the investigation would not follow it for another three years. Rooney and Russo, missing its significance— a lead pointing to a Sicilian cohort in New Jersey—skipped over it. Russo handed him the sheet of names and phone numbers he had been scrutinizing. Bonventre was on the list. Rooney also recognized entries for Catalano and Ganci under their nicknames of Toto and Pino. There was a listing for "Commerciante," whoever that was. They didn't immediately remember that Luigi Ronsisvalle had cited Anthony Aiello, nicknamed Commerciante, as one of the loan sharks at the baccarat game behind the Café del Viale. On most other names, too, they drew blanks. All would have to be run down.

The New York cops had been periodically tailing Catalano as part of their own intelligence-gathering operations. One day in early October 1980 they watched him and Ganci enter a Cadillac that called for them at Catalano's bakery and drove them to Martini's Sea Food restaurant, in Bay Ridge, Brooklyn. Half an hour later the agents recorded the arrival of—Paul Castellano and his top aide, Tom Bilotti.

"Paulie? Big Paul?" Rooney was bowled over when the cops told him. The Gambino family boss didn't meet with just anyone. These players had to be really plugged in. Just the way they met suggested that the Sicilians were on equal terms with the top boss of the New York Mafia. Later, in fact, FBI intelligence indicated that Catalano was serving as boss of the entire Bonanno family. But by March 1981, it was said, the Sicilian was compelled to step aside because of a language problem—he found it difficult to communicate with other family members and outsiders.

The cops had run the tag of the Cadillac that had picked up Catalano and Ganci; it was registered to 4205 Supermarket Inc. The number rang a bell with Rooney. He used to shop at a supermarket in his old neighborhood at 4205 Avenue D in Flatbush. The address had always stuck in his mind. It was a Key Food market. But what was a Key Food car doing carrying Catalano and Ganci to a meeting with Paul Castellano? Rooney wondered. He checked the bureau files on Key Food and found one clue: Pasquale Conte, Sr., the man Luigi Ronsisvalle said he had heard had ties to the Gambino family.

Immigration records, meanwhile, had yielded more information on the other Salvatore Catalano who had mystified Rooney in the pages of *The Canadian*

Connection. He was a jeweler in the diamond district on Forty-seventh Street and, it turned out, a cousin of the Queens baker and pizzeria operator. To avoid confusion, Rooney decided to call his original Catalano just Catalano or the baker or Toto, the traditional diminutive for Salvatore. He tagged Catalano the jeweler with the name of his jewelry business, Saca.

Ganci's presence at the meeting with Paul Castellano targeted him for closer observation. In November surveillance agents saw Ganci carry a suitcase into the Alrae Hotel (now the Plaza Athénée) on East Sixty-fourth Street in Manhattan. They also watched him escorting around an as yet unidentified bespectacled, round-faced man whom NYPD intelligence officers photographed eating a slice of pizza at Ganci's Little Italy Pizza Parlor near Columbus Circle.

The pizza eater was Giuseppe Bono, one of Sicily's most powerful Mafia bosses and longtime master of the heroin trade. In the fall of 1980 he came to New York for his wedding at St. Patrick's Cathedral. Bono, a short, balding man whose fleshy face and rimless eyeglasses gave him a misleadingly bland countenance, had a huge dossier in Italy, where magistrates were compiling a major case against him and other masterminds of the Mafia drug trade. But he was completely unknown in the United States. Despite their common law enforcement interests, Italy and the United States had long hesitated to share their Mafia files, to their own detriment and the benefit of the underworld. Less conspicuous outside Italy, Bono had found it advisable in the 1970's to shift some of his operations to Venezuela and America. He bought a $250,000 mansion in the southern Westchester community of Pelham and became engaged to an Italian-American woman whose family ran a pizzeria in Queens.

On November 16, 1980, in a tableau that might have walked off the pages of *The Godfather,* up to three hundred Sicilians, including dozens of Mafia figures, converged on St. Patrick's to celebrate Bono's wedding, with the bulbous Ganci at Bono's side as his best man. Afterward the celebrants reconvened for a lavish reception at the Pierre Hotel on Fifth Avenue. "There were so many flowers it was difficult to see," Caterina Catalano recalled. The hotel's bill came to $64,000 and was settled in money orders. The FBI did not learn of the affair until the following year, through an informant's tip to the DEA.

In contrast, when Catalano that same November staged a New York celebration to mark his wedding in Ciminna the previous February, the cops caught wind of it, tailing some of their Bonanno mob targets to the party at the Marina del Rey in the Throgs Neck section of the Bronx. Rooney, as it happened, was out bowling with an FBI league in Brooklyn when the cops reached him by patching a call through the FBI switchboard. Rooney rushed to a Bonanno social club, hoping to catch some of the boys leaving for the party. He was too late;

they had already left. Rooney made his own way to the restaurant and cruised the parking lot, copying down license numbers.

Clearly Catalano was a man of growing respect. But information on his position in the Bonanno family was hard to come by. The Mafia yielded few reliable informants; the bureau had to rely on scraps of intelligence and on surveillance, for court-sanctioned wiretaps were not yet in place. But near the end of 1980 Rooney and Russo first learned that the FBI was in the midst of one of its most startling investigative operations in its war on the Mafia. For five years FBI agent Joseph D. Pistone had been working inside the Bonanno family, accepted as a promising Mafia acolyte while exposing the mob's secrets to the government.

Pistone's success was the culmination of the bureau's new emphasis on bolder investigative approaches, including storefront sting operations masquerading as stolen property outlets to snare mob fences. The FBI, the DEA, and Customs all graduated to more elaborate operations, using mob informants to vouch for undercover agents, to help insinuate the agents into the fringes of the mob, where, with skill and luck, they might be swept into the power centers. "With the right stool," avowed DEA operations chief Thomas Cash, "Jesus would sell you dope." By the end of the seventies the FBI had mastered so-called proactive and undercover operations to such a degree that for the first time an agent was close to being "made," formally inducted into the Mafia. Pistone's unprecedented penetration of the mob was to open up vast new areas of organized crime intelligence and expose the Mafia to a wave of successful prosecutions.

Undercover agent Pistone was six feet tall with olive skin and receding salt-and-pepper hair. For a while he had a mustache, until his mob bosses let him know that the Mafia favored a clean-shaven look. His most striking feature was his eyes, a luminescent walnut that signaled his Sicilian and Calabrian lineage. Pistone communicated a potent sense of self-confidence and an indomitable will. "I had a job to do," he said later, "and I did it."

According to the minimum of biographical information Pistone later parceled out, he was born in Pennsylvania and grew up there and in New Jersey. His father worked in a steel mill and ran some bars. Pistone won a basketball scholarship to college but dropped out after two years at the age of twenty to marry a nurse. After a year Pistone went back to college and graduated. He taught social studies for a while and in 1968 joined the Office of Naval Intelligence as a civilian investigator. He had always wanted to be an FBI agent, and this was his way of fulfilling the law enforcement prerequisite. After joining the bureau, he started off in the New York office's criminal division, working investigations into gambling, bank robbery, prostitution, truck hijacking, and fugitives. In 1975 he went down to Florida as trucker "Donald Brasco" for a half-year undercover operation that penetrated hijacking rings. He was back in New York when a supervisor suggested another undercover role aimed at identifying the fences who bought and sold stolen property for the mob.

Pistone set himself up as a purported burglar and jewel thief from California and Florida. In early 1977 he began hanging out on Madison Street on the Lower East Side of Manhattan, where he sold jewelry that he said he had stolen but that he actually got from the FBI. He also used FBI money to buy stolen goods to establish his criminal bona fides. Pistone's first contact inside the Bonnano organization was a psychotically vicious soldier and hit man, Anthony Mirra, who had once hurled a chair at a prosecutor in court, narrowly missing him and the jury. (Russo found Mirra's address at Sing Sing among Bonventre's and Amato's papers that were taken when they were stopped in the Green Acres shopping mall in 1979.) Through Mirra, Pistone met another family member, Benjamin "Lefty" Ruggiero, who operated out of a clubhouse near the Manhattan federal courthouse. Ruggiero was a high-strung bookie who fancied himself a sport but would borrow the ten-dollar bills he liked to slip headwaiters and hatcheck girls.

Mirra, a rugged Zorba-like character with a violent streak and a magnetic appeal to women, introduced Pistone to the Toyland Social Club, Nicky "Glasses" Marangello's innocent-sounding Bonanno clubhouse on Hester Street tucked among the Chinese noodle shops and Jewish talis makers. One day Mirra greeted a quiet heavyset young man. "That's Sal Catalano," Mirra told Pistone afterward. A lean, blond-haired man with Catalano, Mirra said, was Cesare Bonventre.

"They're Zips," he explained. "The Zips are into drugs. Drugs is their business." Zips, Pistone learned, was the American mobsters' pejorative word for their Sicilian Mafia brethren. The origin of the term remained obscure, but one expert, Lieutenant Remo Franceschini of the Queens DA's squad, thought it derived from a derogatory reference to the Sicilians' liking for ziti. Others thought it came from the silent, homemade zip gun.

One summer night Pistone was called on to guard a Little Italy restaurant where Galante was holding a meeting. "We're standing out here to make sure nothing happens to the old man while he's inside," explained Ruggiero.

Pistone suggested stepping inside to join them.

"Look, Donnie," Ruggiero replied, "you don't understand. With this guy, he doesn't sit down with soldiers or anybody like you. The only people he sits down with are captains or above. He's a mean SOB, and he's got certain people that he sits with and that he's close to."

"Well, who are these people?" Pistone asked.

"These people that he has and that he controls are the Zips," Ruggiero said. "Galante and Carlo Gambino were the first ones to bring the Zips over from Sicily to this country. And what they did is when they brought them over, they set them up in various businesses like pizza parlors."

"Why pizza parlors?" asked Pistone.

"Well," Ruggiero said, "it was a good place for them to wash their money. He leaves them there, he leaves the Zips in the businesses until he needs them to do some work, to make hits or something. And the reason that he does this is that they don't have any police records here in this country."

Ruggiero told Pistone that "the Zips control the drug trafficking in the family" and that Galante "controlled the Zips."

Ruggiero confided that he had recently been inducted into the Mafia. "It was a long time coming on account of my gambling," he said. "When you get made, you go up to a meeting, which is also attended by the bosses, and each new member gets voted on. One no vote and you don't get made. If everybody votes yes, you get made."

In 1978 Pistone traveled to Milwaukee to vouch for another undercover agent who was penetrating the powerful Midwest family of Frank Balistrieri. The agent, a burly Scotsman with the unlikely name of Gail Tyrus "Ty" Cobb (no relation to the baseball player), was masquerading as Tony Conte, an Italian vending machine operator. Like Pistone in New York, Cobb had insinuated himself into the fringes of the Chicago Mafia as a fence and used his credibility there to infiltrate Milwaukee. Pistone helped Cobb cement an alliance between the Bonanno and Balistrieri clans, a successful operation that sent Balistrieri to prison. "What would I look for in a good undercover?" Cobb reflected later in an interview. "I'd look for a guy who was happily married to the same woman for twelve years. And who she had no idea was cheating on her all twelve years."

Back in New York, Pistone stayed close to Ruggiero, who promised to school him so Pistone, too, could be made someday. He explained some of the rules. Soldiers had to share with the bosses, he said. A captain could pull in as much as $30,000 a week. There was a dress code, Ruggiero said: "A wise guy doesn't have a bushy mustache and long hair." And nobody, Ruggiero said, worked on Mother's Day.

Ruggiero called Pistone one day in the summer of 1979. "Buy the paper," he told Pistone excitedly.

"Why, what happened?"

"Buy the paper and you'll be in for a big surprise." Galante had gotten whacked.

The next time they met, Ruggiero explained that "Galante got hit because he wouldn't share his drug business with anybody else in the family. Now that Galante's killed, Rusty Rastelli is going to be the next big boss." Rastelli was trying, once and for all, to oust ex-boss Bonanno from the last vestiges of his power, Ruggiero confided. For more than a decade Bonanno had been exiled to Arizona after other bosses had learned he was scheming to kill Carlo Gambino.

"There's a new captain," Ruggiero added.

"Who?" asked Pistone.

"Cesare Bonventre."

There was another new power as well, Ruggiero said. "Sal Catalano is the new street boss of the Zips. The Zips are part of the Bonanno family, but they're the Sicilian faction. They're separate from the Americans."

"Who's your new captain?"

"Sonny Black," said Ruggiero.

Pistone was delighted. He got along with Dominick Napolitano, known as Sonny Black because of his dyed jet black hair. Napolitano had his headquarters in Brooklyn, where he kept an apartment with a pigeon coop on the roof. Pistone had been helping set up Florida operations for the Bonannos, and Sonny Black was impressed.

"I heard you were a good guy," he told Pistone. "You keep your mouth shut. You're an earner. You got any drug arrests?"

"No," said Pistone truthfully.

"That's good," said Napolitano. "The cops won't look so hard at you."

Later Napolitano asked him again, "You sure, no drug arrests?"

"I'm sure," Pistone said.

One of these days, he assured Pistone, the books would be opened in the family and Napolitano could propose five new members. Pistone might be one of them. In fact, Napolitano said, he was personally taking over sponsorship of Pistone from Ruggiero. Napolitano boasted of cementing a new alliance with the Sicilians. He had done some big favor for Paul Castellano, the Gambino family boss. Perhaps it had something to do with arranging Galante's murder, which Bonanno hit man Bruno Indelicato's presence at the Gambinos' Ravenite Club after the Galante murder seemed to suggest. As a result, Napolitano had gotten a piece of the drug action Galante had been monopolizing. Napolitano, too, was dealing with a Sicilian faction that existed as a distinct group within the Gambino family just as the Catalano faction existed within the Bonanno family, but Napolitano was wary of the Sicilians. With Galante's successor, Rastelli, in jail, the new Bonanno acting boss, Salvatore Ferrugia, wanted to promote more Sicilians to captains. Napolitano called that crazy. "Then they'll have more power than us, and they'll be looking to take over," he objected.

Pistone could see that new strife was destabilizing the families. Angelo Bruno, the mob boss of Philadelphia, had just been murdered. Pistone asked Ruggiero what had happened. Santo Trafficante, the Mafia boss in Florida, had traded Bruno a part of Florida for a part of Atlantic City, Ruggiero related. But Bruno wanted to keep all of Atlantic City to himself, he explained. "He didn't want to share."

In 1981 three Bonanno captains seen as threats—Dominick "Big Trin" Trinchera, Philip Giaccone, and Alphonse "Sonny Red" Indelicato—were called together and ambushed on Napolitano's orders. Giaccone seemed to know it was coming: He had told his family a decision had been made about him and he sold his trucking company. "You should have seen when they shot Big Trin," one of the executioners told Pistone afterward. "Fifty pounds of his stomach went flying." His corpse was later cut up with a chain saw. Another hit man on the mission, Santo Giordano, caught some of the shotgun fire and was paralyzed, Pistone heard later. Only Sonny Red's body was ever found, after a rainstorm had washed away the topsoil of his shallow grave near Kennedy Airport.

A fourth member of the now-eliminated faction, Sonny Red's son Bruno— one of Galante's killers, to judge from fingerprints later found in the getaway car —had been spared, but soon Napolitano wanted him dead, too. He suspected that Bruno was plotting against him. Also, he was said to be a heavy cocaine user, $3,000 worth a day. "He's a dangerous little kid," said Napolitano. "We've gotten the other three. Now we have to clear this one up as well." The hit man was to be Pistone.

Ruggiero was thrilled to hear that Pistone had been given the contract on Bruno. "It will look very good in the eyes of the bosses," he said. Pistone pretended to agree. But somehow he could never catch up with Bruno.

Pistone was pulled out by the FBI in July 1981, amid growing fears by his superior, Jules Bonavolonta, and others that he could be unmasked as an agent or whacked for being on the wrong side of a family feud. (Ten days after Pistone turned up on the witness stand in Manhattan federal court the following year, the remains of a body with the hands cut off washed up in a Staten Island creek. It took three months to identify the corpse as that of Dominick "Sonny Black" Napolitano. Of Pistone's other associates, Tony Mirra had been found shot to death in a Manhattan parking lot earlier in 1982, and Ruggiero was tried, convicted, and sentenced to twenty years.)

Later that summer Pistone met with Rooney and Russo. His invaluable information helped the two agents place Catalano, Bonventre, and the other "Zips" distrusted by Napolitano in the framework of the Bonanno family.

5

A s Rooney and Russo were struggling to fathom the activities of Catalano and his associates, a notorious fugitive from Italian justice, Tommaso Buscetta, was walking away from a halfway house in Turin, Italy. Rooney had come across Buscetta's name in *The Canadian Connection,* but he and Russo had made little of it, for the Sicilian was of no concern to the FBI in 1980. Yet four years later, after the courtly, soft-faced mafioso was apprehended once and for all, he became the government's star witness, a dark oracle of the underworld spilling secrets from the innermost sanctums of the Palermo Mafia and for the first time putting into an authoritative framework the disparate information investigators had been collecting over many years on both sides of the Atlantic. It was a saga of how American Mafia boss Joe Bonanno spurred the reorganization of the war-ravaged Sicilian Mafia, how the shattered French Connection was restored by Sicilian heroin traffickers, and how the Sicilian Mafia was undermined, perhaps fatally, by the corrupting influence of easy drug billions and the murderous vendettas of rival cliques headed by the poisonous Corleonesi.

Buscetta, aristocratic and vain, was a most precious criminal turncoat, the Mafia's ultimate Deep Throat, and one of the most complex and contradictory figures ever to emerge from that underworld. He commanded without giving orders and bossed without ever being a boss. "I was never rich," he said later. "But I was important." Why did he turn? "The time had come for me to do so," he said. Two of his sons had been murdered, along with many other relatives, and the Mafia, he said, had been corrupted to a gang of baby killers. The bosses sporting their Rolexes had also been co-opted; as soon as they had enough lire, Buscetta scoffed, they bought a silk shirt. That he professed ever to believe in the Mafia's nobility, having seen firsthand how it functioned, was a mark of either stunning naïveté or cynicism. And nobody thought Buscetta was naïve.

Later in court he was asked: "Was it a big moment in your life when you became a member of the Mafia?"

"Filthy!" he insisted, drawing hisses from Sicilian defendants in the dock. But although Buscetta became renowned for exposing Mafia secrets at landmark trials on both sides of the Atlantic, there were darker secrets he vowed to carry to his grave.

The youngest of seventeen children of a middle-class Palermo glassmaker, Buscetta was born in 1928 and grew up dreaming of medieval knights, Napoleonic battles, and airplanes. He attended school for seven years until World War II, during which, he claimed, he served as a partisan, shooting German soldiers. After the Allied victory the Buscetta family's glass factories prospered in the postwar reconstruction of the bomb-shattered Sicilian capital. Buscetta displayed his legendary independence early on, unionizing the workers at his family's own plants and leading a protest for better wages. When one of his brothers was courting a local girl, Buscetta seduced her sister. Tommaso, then sixteen, was made to marry the nineteen-year-old Melchiorra Cavallaro, the first of the many romantic escapades that later blackened him in the eyes of his censorious Mafia bosses.

An eager apprentice in the resurgent postwar Mafia, Buscetta was summoned one day in 1946 to the home of a member of the small Porta Nuova family. In Sicily, Mafia cliques took their names from the neighborhood or town they controlled. Porta Nuova was the section of central Palermo named for the splendid ceremonial gateway at the royal palace. For some time, Buscetta learned, he had been scouted by family leaders as a promising new recruit. "I didn't make out any application," he explained later in an account echoed by Contorno. "I was called."

The ritual was calculatedly melodramatic. One of his fingers was pricked, and he rubbed the blood onto a picture of a saint. Then the paper was placed in his hands and set afire. As he passed the flaming paper quickly from hand to hand, he repeated the oath: "Should I betray the organization, may my flesh burn like this image." La Cosa Nostra, he was told, comes before everything, before one's own blood, family, kin, or country. "Always be discreet," his boss counseled him. "Behave with dignity and silence. Don't look at other men's wives. And when you are called, rush."

There were other rules and conventions as well, Buscetta learned. Nothing was written down; everything was passed on orally. The family was composed of the capo, or boss; underboss; *consigliere,* or counselor; *capodecina,* or boss of ten; and soldiers. A member questioned by another member could decline to answer, but if he spoke, it had to be the truth. A member of one family could contact a member of another family only through his own boss. For protection, a member could be introduced to another member only by a third member known to both. The greeting then was commonly *"La stessa cosa."* A member introducing a second member to a third said, "This is a friend of ours." But if the stranger was not a man of honor, the member said, "This is a friend of mine." Like Tolstoy's happy families, all Cosa Nostra families were more or less alike and subscribed to the same rules. But in practice, the rules were often applied against each other.

There was one further requirement of every new man of honor: He had to have killed in the service of the family.

For the record Buscetta contended that his wartime shootings of Germans fulfilled the murder obligation. But he was accused of a double murder—the charges were later dropped—and suspected in the mass poisoning of dinner party guests. "How could I bring seventeen people together and poison them?" Buscetta protested later.

Buscetta's revelations, while sometimes less than the full truth and seemingly shaded when it came to his own part in the drug traffic, exposed hitherto unknown chapters in the evolution of the American and Sicilian Mafias and how the gap between them came to be bridged.

Romantic accounts have portrayed the Sicilian Mafia as a response to three millennia of repression under foreign occupiers and in particular to the rebellion that broke out against the Angevin occupiers in 1282—the so-called Sicilian Vespers, reputedly triggered by a French soldier taking liberties with a Sicilian woman he was searching for weapons outside the walls of Palermo on Easter Monday evening. The word "Mafia" itself is of obscure origin, possibly related to Arabic words for "refuge" or "stone." By the late 1800's "mafia," used as an adjective, had come to denote admirable qualities of beauty, strength, and self-reliance. But with the upheaval following the mid-century unification of Italy and Sicily, the word came to be applied by northern Italian administrators and diplomats to bands of Sicilian brigands and strong men. The first official reference to Mafia cliques came in 1838 in the dispatch of a Bourbon official noting efforts by local groups in Trapani to influence judicial proceedings. In 1863 the popular success of a play, *I Mafiusi della Vicaria*, set in the main Palermo prison, gave the word a popular criminal coloration; in the play a group of prisoners treated deferentially by the other inmates termed each other *mafiusi*, for "men of respect."

The criminal phenomenon known as the Mafia actually took root in the second part of the nineteenth century in western Sicily, where absentee landowners rented their estates to local leaseholders, who formed peasant gangs to enforce order against outside bandits. These leaders drew on a Sicilian tradition that exalted cunning, ferocity, friendship, and, perhaps most of all, "honor"—Sicily's "national anthem," in a sociologist's felicitous phrase. Honor was a person's worth as judged by others. It embodied an immediate and personal response to offense. Recourse to police and courts, in turn, was an unmanly confession of weakness. Justice was a private matter, and the Mafia code of silence that became known as *omertà* was really an ethic of tight-lipped, self-reliant manliness. There was cynicism here, too. "He who has money and friends has justice by the ass," went one Sicilian proverb. The traditional mafioso shunned the limelight, preferring to let his deeds and fearsome reputation speak for themselves. The mafioso mediated local disputes, offered protection, and enforced his brand of social order as a surrogate of a remote and impotent central government. Idealized, the mafioso was "a knight at the service of the weak," available to any suitor to settle a grievance or enforce order, for a favor, or a price.

As the grain-exporting economy of Sicily slipped into obsolescence, mafiosi reacted forcefully to fend off change that threatened their power. They formed cliques and entrenched their control over their own territories in western Sicily. But dislocations of the changing economy, the two world wars, and repression under Mussolini conspired to sweep Sicilians in great waves of migration to all corners of the world. This diaspora served the purposes of the secretive criminal cartel. Along the way some of these Mafia cliques acquired formidable economic power. The frightening thing, warned sociologist Pino Arlacchi, a consultant to the Italian government's Anti-Mafia Commission, was not that the Italian Mafia had become a parasitic drain on the financial systems but, to the contrary, that it had become such a diabolically innovative force. Powerful Mafia families had accumulated industrial fortunes in the hundreds of millions of dollars, rendering them economic as well as criminal powers.

Yet in a sense the skeptics and cynics were right: The Mafia as popularly presented was a fiction. A centralized organization of members bound to each other by secret sworn ties never did exist, Arlacchi wrote in a landmark study of Mafia capitalism. Instead, he argued, what popular writers had for years been depicting as a monolithic Mafia was in reality webs of no less fearsome criminal cliques founded on blood kinship, geographic ties, and shifting alliances.

In the late 1880's these cliques crossed the ocean with the waves of immigrants streaming to the New World. Among the first cities to encounter them was New Orleans. After a series of brutal murders on the docks Police Chief David Hennessy exposed a Mafia war for control of the Latin American shipping trade. Hennessy ended up a victim, shotgunned to death as he walked home one night. Nineteen Sicilians were later accused of murder conspiracy, but when the jury was unable to agree on convictions, a mob attacked the jail, lynching and shooting eleven of the prisoners. Hennessy's fate awaited another early anti-Mafia investigator, New York Police Lieutenant Joseph Petrosino. In 1909, on the trail of the so-called Black Hand, Petrosino, supported by private funds after the city fathers had refused to underwrite the mission, traveled to Palermo to confer with his Italian counterparts. On his way to police headquarters, unaware that his mission had already been fatally compromised by a leak, he was slain by four shots in the head, fired by Don Vito Cascio Ferro, an early Sicilian Mafia boss, who later boasted of the deed. Petrosino's squad was the forerunner of Jack Clark's NYPD organized crime intelligence unit.

As in Sicily, the families in America were constituted for racketeering and defense; they curried particular favor among immigrant Sicilians here as a bulwark against rampant discrimination. New York, where the bulk of all immigrants settled, supported five families. Each was originally named for its geographic roots; later it took the name of its leader. Thus the Palermitano family of Albert Anastasia, Carlo Gambino, and others became known as Gambino. And when mafiosi of Castellammare del Golfo traded their Sicilian seacoast town for New York, they eventually took the name of their boss, Joe Bonanno.

On a late spring day in 1931, with the country sliding deeper into the trough of the Great Depression, three hundred overlords and soldiers of crime from around the United States made their way to a small resort hotel near the woodsy Hudson Valley village of Wappingers Falls, New York. It was not the first conclave for the nation's crime bosses; they had met in Cleveland in 1928 and the following year in Atlantic City (it was en route home from the 1929 meeting that Al Capone was caught with a gun by sharp-eyed detectives in Philadelphia, an offense that earned him a year in state prison, eroding the myth of invincibility that Eliot Ness and his Untouchables shattered for good two years later). At the Wappingers Falls summit the "fathers" of America's emerging Mafia families sat together at a long table. At its head sat the charismatic Castellammarese Mafia warrior Salvatore Maranzano. In the audience was a young *picciotto* from Castellammare named Joe Bonanno.

The vicious Castellammarese war that had left the streets of New York littered with bullet-ridden corpses had culminated in 1931 in the killing of Joe "the Boss" Massaria, head of the city's most powerful Mafia clan. He had been dining in Scarpato's Italian restaurant in Coney Island with Salvatore Lucania, better known as Charles "Lucky" Luciano. Luciano, of course, had seen nothing. As he later told the police, he had excused himself to go to the bathroom. He heard shots. When he came back, Massaria's body was slumped over the table. Massaria had been seen as a stumbling block to the bolder racketeering schemes of Luciano and cohorts Albert Anastasia and Joe Adonis. At the Wappingers Falls conclave Maranzano sought to bind the wounds of war and prepare for a more important summit: the first Mafia national convention in Chicago later that month. Capone, the Neapolitan boss of Chicago, who was a family unto himself, was picked as the host. Maranzano and Capone had made a deal: Capone would be left alone to run Chicago, and Maranzano would be recognized as the national boss of bosses. The lavish Chicago convention at the Hotel Congress, obligingly ignored by the police, thanks to Capone's influence, memorialized the accords and laid out the new leadership lineup. But the fragile peace was scarcely affirmed when Maranzano, too, was shot and stabbed to death at his Park Avenue office by men posing as IRS agents. The new boss, soon to give his name to a potent new dynasty and leave an indelible imprint on the American Mafia, was twenty-six-year-old Joe Bonanno.

In the early decades of the century ties between the American mafiosi and their more entrenched Sicilian brethren were strong and close. Sicilian mafiosi could travel to the United States and start families of their own, provided they had the permission of their boss at home. These new families were independent of their Sicilian progenitors. The iconoclastic and ruthlessly innovative Luciano, for example, went so far as to forge alliances with Jewish gangsters like Bugsy Siegel, Louis Lepke, and financial wizard Meyer Lansky. But this laissez-faire approach was short-lived, crumbling after about 1932. After 1950, communication between Sicilian and American Mafia families was further curtailed, perhaps as a consequence of the spotlight thrown on the American Mafia by the hearings of the Kefauver Committee. Subsequently the Sicilian Mafia generally operated exclusively in Sicily and the American Mafia operated here. But the ties extended across the Atlantic.

Tommaso Buscetta met Luciano in Palermo in 1957, eleven years after Luciano had won early release from federal prison and been deported from the United States in consideration of his services to the Navy in World War II. Buscetta was twenty-nine and already a fast-rising star in the Porta Nuova family. Palermo in 1957 was a city still sunk in wartime decrepitude. Allied bombing had flattened many neighborhoods, and the drug-fueled building boom was still nearly two decades away. But beneath its impoverished facade the city seethed with a thousand schemes and rackets. One day Luciano passed on the intelligence that that year the leaders of the American Mafia, probably at the raided Mafia summit meeting in Apalachin, had forbidden its members from participating in drug trafficking. Up to that point, Buscetta was told, only the family of Vito Genovese had been dealing in drugs. Buscetta became convinced that the commission was serious. Years later, he said, he learned that fellow mafioso Angelo La Barbera had sought to smuggle five kilos of French heroin into the United States from Mexico but that Carlo Gambino had supposedly warned La Barbera that if the drugs crossed the border, La Barbera would die. So far as Buscetta knew, the heroin stayed out.

Years later, Gambino's successor and brother-in-law, Paul Castellano, was said to have issued a similar edict banning drug trafficking by family members, on pain of death. The threat backfired when some drug traffickers, fearing Castellano more than the authorities, agreed to turn informant and accept official protection rather than face Mafia justice. Despite the ban, dealing in drugs remained endemic in the families—the profits were too tempting to pass up.

Bonanno's account of the Mafia's drug platform was slightly different. A summit meeting had been held at Joe Barbera's estate in 1956. At that conclave participants aired the drug issue and concluded that their tradition "outlaws narcotics." The judgment was to have been reaffirmed at the Apalachin summit the following year, but the meeting was aborted by the momentous raid by the New York State Police. Buscetta's and Bonanno's self-serving accounts, however, had to be viewed with skepticism if only because Mafia figures never admitted to trafficking in drugs.

October 1957 saw a major conclave of Sicilian and American Mafia leaders at Palermo's Grande Albergo e delle Palme. Amid the marble columns, tapestries, and Venetian glass chandeliers, Buscetta recalled, the bosses decided that the savage and ambitious Albert Anastasia would have to be expunged. A contract was fulfilled almost immediately afterward as Anastasia reclined in a barber chair at New York's Park Sheraton Hotel.

The same month, Buscetta recalled, he, Luciano, and Bonanno met for dinner in Palermo. Also present were Carmine Galante and other trusted Bonanno aides, and several other Sicilian "men of honor," among them a severe and taciturn man of thirty-four with deep-set eyes and a steely glare. His name was Gaetano Badalamenti.

Badalamenti was five years older than Buscetta. He was born in 1923 in Cinisi, a rural town near the coast fourteen kilometers west of Palermo. With its white-washed stucco city hall on the pretty town square, Cinisi was built on a hill along a road that opened into the orchards spreading between the mountains and the Tyrrhenian Sea. Cinisi was small, but it was no village. There were virtually no villages in all of Sicily, colonial exploitation and Mafia violence having long since grouped the population into larger concentrations for protection.

Gaetano was the baby, last of the family's five boys and four girls. His father had a string of seven parcels of land on the outskirts of Cinisi, where the family raised cows and goats and sheep and produced the creamy, warm, and faintly musky ricotta cheese that is one of Sicily's great culinary delicacies. In the ancient tradition the boys worked the farm with their father; the girls stayed home and helped their mother tend the house.

To young Gaetano, Cinisi was idyllic. Cattle roamed over the fertile plain, and the land blossomed with lemon trees. It was financially rewarding, too. As war fever engulfed Italy and the Fascist regime turned to rationing, farming not only guaranteed a family a steady source of good food but also provided ample opportunity for lucrative black-market dealings. Six-year-old Gaetano was permitted to attend school, but by his tenth year he had been called back to the farm. He had had more schooling than anyone else in his family.

World War II was already largely lost for the Italians when Badalamenti was called up, an eighteen-year-old draftee with little interest in dying for the fatherland. He was assigned to an infantry division and posted to Calatafimi. During the American bombing onslaught, Badalamenti claimed, he deserted his unit and rejoined the conflict as a partisan in the summer of 1943, as American troops liberated Sicily and began their sweep up the boot of Italy. Later, Badalamenti continued to insist in the face of skeptical questioning that he had been consulted by American OSS officers about the invasion of Sicily and had served with the invading American Army and participated in attacks on retreating German soldiers in June 1943. Unfortunately for his account, the Americans did not land in Sicily until July 7. And Badalamenti admitted he had never heard of General Patton, and could never come up with the name of a single partisan. Moreover, historians say there was no partisan activity in Sicily.

As Italy's supreme *capo di tutti capi* Mussolini had brooked no rivals, certainly not the violent Mafia clans that infringed on the Fascists' monopoly on terror. Mussolini had been particularly outraged by the cavalier and insulting treatment accorded him by one especially revolting Mafia boss in Piana dei Greci during the duce's visit to Sicily in 1924. The ensuing crackdown on the Mafia was masterminded by a career policeman, Cesare Mori, employing repression and torture on a scale unseen in Italy since the Inquisition more than four hundred years before.

During Italian fascism's quarter century the Mafia was beaten and hounded underground, to the point where the shattered brotherhood and the occupying

American forces saw themselves as natural allies in the years before and after the Italian surrender. In 1942 U.S. naval intelligence had called on the imprisoned Lucky Luciano to use his still-considerable influence to curtail sabotage in the port of New York, controlled then, as later, by the heavily Italian longshoremen's union. Luciano's cooperation won him the reward of an early release from federal prison and deportation to Italy in 1946.

After the American invasion of Italy, mafiosi were only too happy to serve their liberators, and feckless American officials encouraged the alliance, installing Mafia mayors in city halls across Sicily. The vaunted Office of Strategic Services, predecessor of the CIA, even conspired with the Mafia to blunt the political gains of the fast-growing Italian Communist party. In one comic opera scenario, there briefly flourished a secession movement to make Sicily an American state.

With the end of the war the Sicilian Mafia came surging back, and with it, Badalamenti, who had already made a name for himself as a young mafioso from Cinisi. In March 1946 he was named in an arrest warrant on charges of conspiracy and kidnapping. His oldest brother, Emanuele, was in Monroe, Michigan, operating a supermarket and gas station. America beckoned like a refuge. As Badalamenti later told U.S. immigration authorities, he boarded the SS *Saturnia* in Naples on the pretext of buying cigarettes from a sailor and, with the help of a 10,000 lire bribe, stowed away until the ship docked in Port Newark or Baltimore; at that point his story got a little fuzzy. Prosecutors later suspected that Badalamenti had really slipped into the country from Canada. In Monroe Badalamenti claimed that he worked in Emanuele's store and gas station, sorting stock and cleaning windshields. He also became a favorite playmate of Emanuele's little daughter, Cristina.

In 1950 the immigration authorities caught up with Badalamenti and deported him to Italy. Within several years he had married and had two sons, had begun exporting lemons, and had founded a successful construction business that supplied the crushed rock for Palermo's Punta Raisi Airport, which, along with its booming transatlantic drug traffic, fell within the Cinisi Mafia family's sphere of influence. An indignant Badalamenti later denied that he had had anything to do with selecting the site of the airport, which was abutted by mountains.

As for meeting with Buscetta, Bonanno, and Luciano in Palermo in 1957, Badalamenti insisted, it never happened.

Was he a member of the Mafia?

"I have never said it, and if I were, I would not say it," he answered, staring down his accusers. "I have never betrayed, and I will never betray my secrets.

"If I am depository of a secret, there is no one who can get it out of me. So many have tried all different ways, torture included."

For whatever reasons, Buscetta, whose memory about the bosses' dinner in

Palermo in 1957 was obviously clearer than Badalamenti's, recalled that Bonanno drew Buscetta aside. "You should set up a commission like we have," Bonanno urged the Sicilian. "In the United States no man of honor can be killed without the approval of the commission. This system works very well."

Whether the irony of Americans counseling Sicilians on the value of a Mafia organization struck any of the participants at the time was not recorded. But Bonanno's suggestion stirred avid interest. The idea particularly excited Luciano, who saw in it the possibility of reconstructing links between the American and Sicilian Mafias that might ease his return to power in the States. It proved an idle dream; he died in Italy, possibly poisoned, in 1962.

Buscetta acted enthusiastically on Bonanno's recommendation. Within a year he and an associate had crisscrossed the triangular island, setting up commissions in the main western cities of Palermo, Trapani, and Agrigento. At Bonanno's suggestion, the Sicilian commissions were to be composed not of family bosses but rather of soldiers designated by their bosses to represent their families. In truth, however, the bosses insisted on sitting on the commission. So they concealed their exalted positions or pretended to step down. For five years the commissions functioned smoothly, arbitrating interfamily disputes so successfully that Buscetta could not remember a single killing. But the harmony could not last. Beneath the placid surface, fierce rivalries were pitting established bosses against upstarts like Buscetta. Ahead lay a period of ferocious strife.

It began insignificantly enough, as a Mafia *Romeo and Juliet.* A soldier in Buscetta's Porta Nuova family had sought permission to marry the daughter of a Noce family member. The Noce boss opposed the union, arguing that relatives should always be members of the same Mafia family. But Buscetta blessed the marriage. The commission backed up Buscetta, shaming the Noce boss. As the bitterness spread, the Noce boss was murdered, and suspicion fell on Buscetta. Buscetta insisted on his innocence and, in turn, pointed the finger at Angelo La Barbera, a longtime ally who had been the drug trafficker forbidden by Carlo Gambino from smuggling a heroin shipment into America. La Barbera fled, and his brother Salvatore disappeared. The Palermo police suspected that Buscetta had switched sides and had had Salvatore killed and incinerated in the furnace of his glass factory—another accusation Buscetta denied. The violence escalated, embroiling the Grecos, who were aligned with the fearsome Corleonesi.

On June 30, 1963, a bomb planted in a Fiat Giulietta in front of a garage in Villabate, Sicily, killed two passersby. The same day a telephone call had alerted the carabinieri to a suspicious Fiat Giulietta parked in Palermo's rural Ciaculli district, near the home of one of the Grecos. The police found and disarmed a primitive bomb in the back seat. Then another bomb—the real bomb—exploded in the trunk, killing seven of the policemen and three bystanders and transforming the otherwise innocuous cars into symbols of terror across Italy (which cut deeply into the model's sales). What became known as the Ciaculli massacre produced an immediate outcry and led, within days, to formation of an anti-Mafia investigating commission. The government ordered a wave of arrests all over Sicily, sending many mafiosi fleeing abroad to the United States, South America, and elsewhere. Had the Italian government pressed its initiative and continued to make arrests, it might have struck the Mafia a crippling blow. But its zeal evaporated. There were too many powerful government officials secretly indebted to the Mafia. The opportunity passed. It would not present itself again for nearly two decades.

PART TWO

MONEY BY THE TON

What's inside the bags—gold?
    —A New York City cabdriver to a Mafia money launderer

6

"**G**uess who I saw this morning," said Rooney.

It was October 31, 1980. He and Russo were at their desks in the Queens office. Russo, who was scowling over pages of scrawled surveillance logs, tilted his chair back to look at Rooney. They often played this guessing game.

"Cesare?" Russo ventured.

"Cesare," said Rooney. He knew how the tall blond Bonanno captain, so aptly named, galled Russo. It had to do with the way Bonventre swaggered around, so secure with his Cadillac, gold chains, and tinted glasses, and his coat slung over his shoulders. If the mob ever turned on cops and agents and judges here the way it was doing in Italy, Russo was convinced, Bonventre would be right up there leading the charge.

As the FBI stepped up surveillance of Catalano, Ganci, and their cohorts, there were signs of Bonventre's growing independence and stature. He and Amato were spending less time on Knickerbocker Avenue and more time around Brooklyn's Thirteenth Avenue, at a place called Caffè Roma. It could be Cesare's new hangout, probably his own place, Russo figured.

Bonventre was spotted leaving Catalano's bakery on Metropolitan Avenue near Ganci's house in Middle Village, Queens, Rooney said. Moments later

Ganci entered. What, if anything, that signified, neither agent had any idea. They had been monitoring a lot of seemingly uneventful comings and goings. Four weeks earlier they had seen Catalano being driven home in a silver Audi they traced to Frank Castronovo, a New Jersey restaurateur and native of Bagheria, Sicily. The next day, October 3, agents had watched Catalano step out of his bakery to make two calls from a pay phone on the street. Three days later, the same day that Catalano and Ganci had been followed to their meeting with Gambino boss Paul Castellano, the pair had been seen leaving the bakery with a cardboard box that Ganci placed in the trunk of his Cadillac. He and Catalano were then tailed to a Catalano relative's house in Queens, where Ganci delivered the box. Then both drove to a Key Food supermarket in Queens. Key Food was a co-op, Rooney had learned, and on its board sat Gambino capo Pasquale Conte, Sr., and it was a Cadillac traceable to Key Food that had recently carried Catalano and Ganci to meet Gambino boss Paul Castellano. But what did it all mean? With undercover agent Joe Pistone still secretly in place in the Bonanno family, he had little time to sit down with superiors, let alone Russo and Rooney, to explain the family's inner workings.

Lefty Ruggiero's accounts of the "Zips" who were running pizzerias as drug covers were not to be imparted to Rooney and Russo for at least a year. Meanwhile, the two agents slogged through surveillance reports and ran down car licenses and phone numbers. It was slow going. Rooney had time in between to talk to IRS agents about the corruption he was uncovering in the Transit Authority's purchase of R-46 subway cars.

While Rooney and Russo were pondering the movements of the Sicilians, another FBI agent they had never met was embarking on an investigation of his own, one that would provide some of the answers Rooney and Russo were searching for. It started with a phone call to Special Agent Robert L. Paquette in late October 1980.

Paquette's specialty was white-collar crime. From his small regional office, which the FBI called a metropolitan resident agency, in the Sheraton Hotel in the Westchester suburb of New Rochelle, he was usually busy tracking money launderers and stock manipulators through the concrete canyons of Wall Street. Paquette, part French Canadian, part native American Indian, part Irish, Greek, and Czech, stood six feet two and weighed well over two hundred pounds, despite periodic diets drawn up by his wife, a cancer nurse. A balding pate and a mustache gave the soft-spoken agent a homespun, avuncular air. He was then thirty-three and had been in the FBI for six years.

When the call came in, Paquette was on the bureau's semiannual antiterrorist SWAT exercise in rural Pennsylvania, dangling from a rope hanging out of a helicopter. The chopper floated down, its beating blades whipping the dry country soil into whirlpools of stinging dust, as Paquette slid to the ground and was called over to the phone. It was one of his sources, a businessman with an extensive professional financial background who called Paquette periodically with tips. The informant quickly got to the point. "I know a guy who's looking to move a large sum of money out to Switzerland," he told Paquette.

"How large?" Paquette asked.

"Sixty."

Paquette wasn't sure he got it right. "Sixty what?" he asked.

"Million."

It took a moment for the amount to register. Sixty million dollars! He had never run across anything that big. The financial crimes he had been exposed to often involved sums that ran into the millions but not $60 million at a clip. That kind of money usually signaled one thing—drugs.

The caller provided names and an address, which Paquette quickly copied down. He was unwittingly about to cross Rooney and Russo's investigative trail by doing the obvious, following the money.

The address was on Third Avenue at Forty-second Street, one of Manhattan's busiest intersections, a nexus of banks, hotels, and office towers in the shadows of the Mobil Building, the *Daily News* headquarters, and the Chrysler Building. The southeast corner boasted a particular New York landmark, the last Horn & Hardart Automat in the city. On November 3, 1980, the intersection was clogged with its usual crush of traffic. Near Horn & Hardart a beat-up, plain blue van was parked at the curb. There was nothing distinctive about it, but hidden in the darkened interior crouched an FBI surveillance agent, dispatched at Paquette's request by the New York office's chief of special operations.

James Kallstrom, a large, shy Bostonian and former Marine with hands like baseball mitts, commanded the unit that fielded a fleet of camouflage vans, tracking cars, and electronic gadgetry aimed at secretly monitoring the underworld of criminals, terrorists, and spies. "The miracle worker" was how Tom Cash of the DEA described him. Kallstrom's boss Thomas Sheer agreed: "Jimmy can bring an agent within spitting distance of anyone within twenty minutes." Paquette liked to say, "Give him a nickel, and he'll buy you a dime cup of coffee."

From the van parked outside 655 Third Avenue, where Paquette's informant said the money was being delivered, the surveillance agent saw a silver Audi pull up, driven by a husky, gray-haired man fingered by the informant. A rugged-faced passenger got out with a heavy black bag, which he carried into the building's glass and marble entrance. One of Paquette's sources was later able to verify that the bag contained money—about $200,000. The car was traced to Frank Castronovo, the same New Jersey man who had driven Catalano home three weeks before in one of Rooney's surveillances. For now nobody made the connection.

Three weeks later Kallstrom's agents, staked out around the same Third Avenue building, spotted a young man in a light suit carrying a Gordon's vodka carton inside. The box must have been heavy, for the man struggled to carry it. With the agent snapping photographs through the van's darkened window, the man, who appeared to be in his twenties, disappeared into the building, emerging empty-handed a few minutes later. The agents followed him as he drove uptown and parked outside an ornate office building on Madison Avenue at Fifty-sixth Street. Positioned with studied casualness in and around the building at 575 Madison Avenue, the agents watched the man make a call from the lobby. A few minutes later a man in a black leather jacket came out of the elevator and joined him. The second man looked about forty and wore glasses. Together they went out to the car and hauled two cartons out of the trunk, while one of the surveillance agents shot pictures from a nearby van. As luck would have it, the men had their backs turned so the agent had to be satisfied with rear views. The two then carried the cartons into 575 Madison Avenue. Quickly one of the agents followed the pair into the elevator and rode up with them. The agent feigned boredom, but his eyes probed the box for clues to its contents. There were none. It was taped tightly shut. The elevator stopped on 10, and the two men got out. The agent resisted the urge to follow them; it would have been too obvious. The agents later followed the young, husky driver in the light suit to his home on Staten Island and, by running his license tag, identified him as twenty-five-year-old Filippo Matassa of Cefalù, Sicily. Paquette's instincts told him he had stumbled onto something big. Who were these guys with their boxes of money?

From his New Rochelle office he called New York headquarters in the federal skyscraper near City Hall, to see if Matassa's name or plate number had come up before in FBI files. Never. He then drove down to check the files himself. In 1980 the bureau had just inaugurated its computerized Organized Crime Information System, OCIS (pronounced Oh-sis.) The system, a specialized adjunct to the bureau's broader National Crime Information Center set up in 1967, was devised to store vast intelligence on organized crime, including subjects and their car licenses and every piece of property believed owned or controlled by the mob. The information, fed in from FBI offices around the country, was to be the bureau's most sensitive data base. But for now Paquette's best shot was still to thumb through the card index cross-referencing investigative subjects and their vehicles. Agents were trained to begin any new case with a check through such records.

Paquette saw that Castronovo, who had driven up with the first cash delivery to 655 Third Avenue, had been tailed recently driving someone named Salvatore Catalano. An investigation was being conducted by Charlie Rooney in Queens.

It was early evening, and the Queens squad room was emptying out when the phone rang on Rooney's desk. "Bobby Paquette from New Rochelle," said the voice. Did Rooney know that one of his targets was smuggling cash out of the country?

"Negative," said Rooney, his phlegmatic exterior masking his excitement. "We got to get together."

First thing the next morning he and Russo drove up to New Rochelle, where Paquette laid out the story of the surveillances on Third and Madison avenues.

Rooney turned to Russo. "What do you think?" he asked.

"Pick one of three," said Russo with a thin smile. "Life savings? Nah. Loan sharking? Probably not. Narcotics? Has to be."

They and Paquette, it was clear, had gotten hold of different ends of the same case. Suddenly it was looking like a much more important case.

Paquette thought it would not be too hard to identify the tenth-floor company Matassa had visited, but he thought wrong. To his dismay, he found by checking the lobby directory that the floor housed the labyrinthine offices of World-Wide Business Centres. World-Wide subleased one-room offices to what looked like a hundred or more small businesses, many of them largely paper entities that needed little more than a desk, a telephone, and a telex and that shared the same receptionists. His guy could be anywhere in there. Paquette hardly knew where to start.

Meanwhile, four thousand miles across the Atlantic, unbeknown to the FBI, police in Milan were probing a company called Citam that Mafia boss Giuseppe Bono (who had just gotten married at St. Patrick's Cathedral), operated with his brother Alfredo from a purported powdered milk factory on the Via Larga. Starting in the fall of 1979, the Italians had put Citam under surveillance and the following year began tapping its phones. Among those who visited the milk factory was a squat New York pizza man named Giuseppe Ganci. The phone calls were mysterious. For one thing, there was a lot of talk about exchanging money.

"Listen," a worker was recorded saying, "there's my friend . . . who must make an exchange of about five thousand lire of the green type."

In the background a voice was picked up interjecting, "American."

"Eh, green," said the caller.

"And when does he need them?" the worker answered. "Eh, even tomorrow. I'll bring you."

". . . For five thousand?" the caller asked.

"You bring the equivalent," he said.

A few minutes later the same caller rang back. "Could I have them this afternoon?" he asked.

The enigmatic calls were followed by others involving problems withdrawing certain funds from a bank. "You still don't understand . . . what it is to deal with the Swiss . . ." the first caller complained. "You have no idea what shits they are."

Money changing appeared to be unusually integral to the milk factory's operations, the Italian police found. In fact, they determined, the Bonos had arranged for couriers to transport suitcases of dollars from the United States and for the dollars to be exchanged through Citam for Swiss francs at a Lugano bank called, of all things, Cop Finance.

But neither the Italians nor the FBI knew what had preceded these deliveries, although it would come out later. Earlier in 1980 two money movers, or *spalloni* —from *spalle*, or "shoulders" in Italian—told a Swissair operations clerk at Kennedy Airport that certain "Swiss businessmen" had large amounts of money to be transferred to Switzerland. What, they wanted to know, was the customs procedure for leaving the United States? There was none, the clerk, Claudio Esposito, assured them. The *spalloni* then packed the money into square duffel bags on wheels and checked them through on Swissair flights out of JFK. Esposito was appalled. The bags were flimsy, and the wheels often got snagged in cracks in the airport concourse. The bags frequently arrived torn, with the money clearly visible inside. One of the "Swiss businessmen," it turned out, was Ganci, whom Esposito came to know by another of his nicknames, Bufalone. Esposito arranged for Ganci himself to deliver the bags to him at the airport's International Hotel. From his car Ganci hauled two burgundy two-suiters with straps. Esposito asked him to open one. Inside were neatly stacked dollar bills. Esposito sent the suitcases to Switzerland with his wife and one of the *spalloni*, who traveled as a couple to allay suspicion. Still, when they landed in Zurich, Swiss Customs asked to see the contents. It took the inspectors more than two hours just to count the money in one suitcase. It came to $500,000. The weary Swiss Customs agents then estimated that the second suitcase probably contained a comparable sum and put the total down at $1 million. Then, without further ado, they passed the bags and the couple through.

In New York Esposito admitted to some qualms about the arrangements he had made. "This Bufalone," he said to one of the money movers one day, "he doesn't seem like a Swiss businessman."

Once Esposito received two suitcases of money, but the courier who was supposed to pick up the bags never appeared.

"Just put them aboard the flight anyway," Esposito was instructed.

"Are you crazy?" he said.

"Well, take them home then and hold on to them," Esposito was told.

After several days at home with his curious children asking more and more questions about the strange bags, Esposito sent them with his wife to Geneva. Next, according to later trial testimony, Esposito was instructed to go to Pennsylvania to pick up suitcases from a stranger named Filippo Salamone. This was too much. He refused. Okay, he was told, Salamone will bring the suitcases to you.

None of this yet had come to the attention of Paquette, who was still struggling to decipher the money scheme and identify the players, including the man Matassa had met on Madison Avenue. Presumably, he worked somewhere on the tenth floor, where he and Matassa had been followed delivering the cartons. But with the hundred or more paper companies operating out of World-Wide Business Centres, there would be no easy way to track him down. Paquette would have to ask a lot of questions. Perhaps the staff was in league with him. Wouldn't it tip him off? Paquette decided to take the safer course. He would try to run down each and every one of the companies on the tenth floor. Maybe he'd get lucky.

Paquette would hunt for the man in the leather jacket for two and a half more years. His name was Salvatore Amendolito. A former financial analyst from Milan, Amendolito had had several collisions with Italian justice, including convictions for passing bad checks and fraudulently turning back the odometer of a rental car. He had come to New York in 1977, when he was forty-three, and began exporting fresh fish by plane to Italy, France, and Greece. In 1979 three Sicilians visited him with a proposition. One was Giorgio Muratore, who would be overheard the following year talking about lemon-yielding tangerine trees and who would be photographed at the Piazza Politeama with Catalano and Ganci in February 1980.

"We'd like to buy your fish," Muratore said.

Amendolito was delighted. Business had been off lately. He could use a good order.

"Where would you like me to ship it?" he asked.

"We'll ship it ourselves," Muratore said. He was very insistent on this; they would do their own loading and shipping. Also, Amendolito would not get paid until the fish reached Sicily. The offer struck Amendolito as odd. Since timely shipping of the fish was so crucial, why would these Sicilians with no expertise insist on handling the transport themselves? They had to be interested in shipping something besides fish. It couldn't be drugs; heroin moved the other way, from Sicily into the United States. Still, it sounded peculiar. And for what? To get paid only after whatever it was had reached its destination? Amendolito turned down the deal.

By 1980 his fish business had gone bust. Angry creditors wrecked his office, throwing papers into the street. Amendolito's northern Italian business representative, Salvatore Miniati, knew the gravity of Amendolito's financial plight. As Amendolito later recounted, they had been partners in a financial consulting business in Milan, where Miniati had specialized in the export of lire to Switzerland to skirt Italy's currency control laws. Now Miniati called Amendolito with a proposition that could wipe away Amendolito's $100,000 debt.

"There are pizzerias in New York and New Jersey that have to send money to Europe," Amendolito remembered Miniati's telling him. "The money belongs to them, but it's going to a large construction company in Sicily that wants to use the money to build a hotel or a resort. After the construction is finished, the money will be given back, with no interest."

It sounded peculiar. "Who are the owners of the funds?" asked Amendolito. Miniati skipped over the question.

"Where is the money going?" Amendolito asked.

"Switzerland," said Miniati. "Your job would be to get it from New York to Switzerland."

"How does it get from Switzerland to Sicily?" Amendolito wanted to know.

"That's not your problem," Miniati said. "The construction company has its own channels."

Amendolito voiced his skepticism.

Miniati was getting impatient. "Look," he said, "I told you. These people don't want to give all their money to the IRS. They're not that sophisticated about business, so they can't do the transfers themselves. Are you interested or not?"

"Okay," said Amendolito.

"Now remember," Miniati said, "be very careful not to give the names of the owners of the money to the U.S. government. In America, if you take over five thousand dollars out of the country or you deposit over ten thousand dollars in the bank, you have to file a report, and they don't want to do this."

"What's my fee to move the money?" Amendolito asked.

"Try one percent to start," Miniati said. "Afterwards we'll see."

Amendolito had one more question. "How much money is it anyway?"

"Nine million dollars," said Miniati.

Amendolito's contact, Miniati said, would be Oliviero Tognoli, a prominent Milan area businessman. Miniati didn't mention that Tognoli was closely associated with Leonardo Greco, one of the most powerful bosses of the Sicilian underworld and a kingpin of the heroin trade. Greco owned the iron factory near the Bagheria farmhouse where Contorno had seen Catalano, Ganci, Giuseppe Bono, and others testing the forty-kilo heroin shipment that informant Frank Rolli later helped the authorities seize in Milan.

"The guy with the money for you, his name is Ciccio," Miniati said, a common nickname for Francesco, or Frank. He gave Amendolito a New Jersey phone number.

Amendolito called the number and reached the Roma restaurant in Menlo Park. Ciccio had been expecting him. He asked him to come by, and Amendolito drove out the next day.

The bright, paneled restaurant sat in a corner of the vast enclosed shopping mall near a Radio Shack and a Pearl Vision Center. There was a counter and register at the door, a front room of tables with plastic checkered cloths, and several banquet rooms in the rear. Ciccio turned out to be a husky, round-faced man with a thinning thatch of graying hair, Frank Castronovo. Castronovo cautioned Amendolito to keep his identity confidential. "Once the IRS hits on you," he said, "they can be very tough."

Amendolito explained how he proposed to do the transfers.

"How you do it is your business," Castronovo said. "If you've been recommended by Tognoli, you know what you're doing."

The next day they met at a hotel near the restaurant. Castronovo brought a bag containing $100,000. They counted the bundled money, and Amendolito transferred it to his briefcase.

Over the next few days Amendolito visited a dozen banks, making deposits just under $10,000, the amount that had to be reported to the government. At each he then bought bank checks and had the funds wired to Swiss accounts.

Over the next few weeks the process was repeated seven times, with Castronovo and sometimes his nattily dressed and carefully coiffed partner, Gaetano Mazzara, handing over sums ranging from $50,000 to $550,000. Usually the cash was packed in cardboard liquor boxes. It settled into a routine. Amendolito would drive into a covered loading dock behind the restaurant. After he had waited there a few minutes, Castronovo would come out with the boxes, and they would load them into the car. As Amendolito recalled, he would drive to the various banks, while an employee transferred the money from the carton to a soft bag, counting it as he went. Amendolito was not concerned that someone was counting and repacking hundreds of thousands of dollars in his car as they sped along the New Jersey Turnpike. "On highways people are too busy driving to look in your car," he said later.

But buying bank checks in denominations under $10,000 had become cumbersome. By mid-July 1980 Amendolito tried a variation. Carrying $28,000 in bank checks, he chartered a plane and flew directly to Nassau in the Bahamas to deposit the funds in the Banca Svizzera Italiana.

A week later Castronovo gave Amendolito $550,000. Miniati had new instructions. "There's a company in New York called Finagest," he told Amendolito. "Take the money over there." Finagest was a Swiss firm with headquarters in Lugano and a New York office in the Seagram Building on Park Avenue. Its nominal business was real estate development, but it was heavily involved in currency transfers.

Amendolito ultimately testified that he called Finagest and made an appointment with the public relations manager, who, it turned out, had little to do but keep track of company offices around the world by sticking pins and little Swiss flags into a large wall map. Amendolito told him he wanted to make a cash transfer to Switzerland of half a million dollars. The manager called Lugano for instructions and spoke to Franco Della Torre. Amendolito was instructed to bring the money to a commodity trading company in the World Trade Center. Several days later Amendolito, in his red Fairmont wagon, picked up the Finagest manager outside the Seagram Building. Amendolito had four yellow leather bags.

They were so garish that the man from Finagest was compelled to ask, "What's in the bags?"

"The money," said Amendolito matter-of-factly.

At the trading company the two were escorted downstairs to the Chase Manhattan Bank. But there was a problem. "This branch is too small to handle this amount of cash," they were told. They were directed to Chase's main office.

Amendolito and his escorts then hoisted the yellow bags with the $550,000 onto their shoulders and trudged through the sticky July heat to Chase's lower Manhattan headquarters, where they entered a huge vault lined with money-counting machines. Amendolito started hauling the cash out of his bags and piling it on a table. But the money-counting machines were busy on another job, and the deposit had to be left for the next day. Amendolito picked out a few bundles of cash and put them in his attaché case for himself. The deposit would be $2,500 short.

On the last day of July, and again a week later, Amendolito received $500,000 from Castronovo. Both times he chartered a small plane to the Bahamas, where the branch manager of the Banca Svizzera Italiana in Nassau was waiting for him with a limo.

A few days before, Amendolito had heard from Miniati in Italy. "Tognoli has another source of funds," he said.

"Who is it?" Amendolito asked.

Miniati paused. "I don't know his name."

"Where can I reach him?"

"You can't," Miniati said. "He'll call you."

Shortly afterward, by Amendolito's account, he got a call in an office he was using in Queens. "Is this Salvatore?" said a man's voice in Sicilian.

"Who is speaking?"

There was no answer. "Are you ready to meet for the transfer?" the caller asked. He mentioned a corner near Amendolito's office.

"A corner?" questioned Amendolito.

"There is no problem," the other man said. "It is a deserted place."

The next day Amendolito arrived in his red Fairmont. A few minutes later a blue car drove up, and two men got out. One, Amendolito later learned, was named Sal. He was stocky, although Amendolito would somehow remember him as skinny. His companion was named Vito. He was shorter but bore a distinct resemblance to Sal; they could have been brothers. They were. Amendolito later learned their names—Salvatore and Vito Catalano.

"Shall we go to a restaurant?" suggested Amendolito.

"There is no need to go anywhere," Sal said. "There is this doorway here, very big, and nobody is here. Let's get in and let's talk."

Amendolito waited to be given the money.

"It will be a million or more to be transferred," Catalano said. "But it is not ready yet. It will be ready in a few days."

"But how can I reach you?" Amendolito asked.

Vito took out a small notebook with a phone number and the names Sal and Vito on one page. "You can reach me at my friend's business," Sal said, giving Amendolito the paper.

A few days later Miniati called back. "Sal is ready now," he said.

Amendolito fished out the paper Catalano had handed him. He had carried it around in his pocket for a few days before sticking it in his Rolodex. He called the number and asked for Vito. He was out. So was Sal. Amendolito left a message.

Catalano called back the next day. "I am ready to meet you with one point five," he said.

"Where?"

"Same corner," said Catalano.

Amendolito showed up first again. Then Catalano drove up in his blue car.

"Where can we go to count it?" whispered Amendolito.

"No need," said Catalano. "Just come with your trunk close to the trunk of my car, and I deliver you the box. About the counting don't worry."

Amendolito maneuvered his car so the two trunks were practically touching. Catalano hoisted out two suitcases and handed them to Amendolito. They were very heavy. Amendolito shoved them into the back of his station wagon. He looked around to make sure no one was watching. The street was deserted. He got into the car and drove back to the city, heading for the Barbizon Plaza on Central Park South, where he had reserved a room.

To his dismay, the lobby was crowded with guests checking in and out. Amendolito kept his hands on the suitcases. Suddenly he felt a tug on the handles. The bags were being pulled from his grasp!

He whirled around.

"Checking in, sir?"

It was only the bellhop.

In the room he first opened the suitcases. The money was wrapped neatly in bundles. He counted it carefully. It came to $1.54 million. He removed $53,900 for himself. One percent was a miserable commission, he had decided. Three and a half percent was better.

There was a knock at the door. Amendolito slammed the suitcases shut and pushed them under the bed.

"Who is it?" he asked.

"You know who it is."

Then he remembered. He opened the door to the banker from the Bahamas.

Amendolito retrieved the suitcases and handed them to the banker. "Where are you taking them?" he asked curiously.

"To our correspondent bank," came the answer.

Amendolito waited for the name, but the banker didn't volunteer it. Later Amendolito learned it was the Bank of Boston.

Business was booming. In August Amendolito installed his money-laundering enterprise, Overseas Business Services, at 575 Madison Avenue. Actually it was just a cubicle in World-Wide Business Centres' vast warren of rental offices. But clients wouldn't know that. The address sounded impressive.

In September 1980 Amendolito flew to Lugano to meet Miniati. This time Miniati had some encouraging news. "I found someone else who can move the money," he said. He took Amendolito to the offices of Finagest, where a dapper Italian was waiting for them. "This is Franco Della Torre," said Miniati.

Della Torre said he had recently left Finagest and opened his own office. "I'll be doing what you were doing," he told Amendolito. "There's no more need to fly down to the Caribbean. *Spalloni* will come into the U.S. and take the money out with them. I'll be handling everything," Della Torre assured him. "I'll be in New York often myself."

Before sending Amendolito back to New York, Miniati had a surprise in store. "We are going to Sicily," he said. They flew to Catania, where a car and driver were waiting. To the north they could see the vast gentle cone of Etna exhaling wisps of vapor. With the volcano at their back they drove south to Pozzallo below Ragusa to meet Tognoli, who was managing one of Sicily's three large iron factories. After all their telephone conversations it was the first time Amendolito had met Tognoli. He cut an impressive figure, Amendolito thought. Carefully groomed and expensively dressed, he seemed the quintessential wealthy Italian executive. They drove across the island to Bagheria. "We will be meeting a special friend of mine," said Tognoli. The car stopped in front of another iron factory. It was the same one Contorno had visited earlier that year. Outside the gate Amendolito was introduced to a man of medium height, with rough-hewn features and dark scimitars for eyes.

"So you are the famous Amendolito," Leonardo Greco said. "I understand you are very interested in fishing."

Amendolito was taken aback. He and Miniati had discussed getting back into the fishing business, perhaps organizing some commerce between the Bahamas and Sicily. Miniati was going to set up a meeting with an interested party in Sicily. But Amendolito had no idea that Leonardo Greco was involved. Miniati or Tognoli must have been keeping him posted. For nearly an hour they discussed the possibilities of the fishing business without reaching any conclusions. Before leaving Sicily, Amendolito met Greco once more, over dinner, during which Greco asked him, "Can you help me get a visa to America?" Amendolito didn't know why Greco was asking him, and he wasn't sure what he could do. Actually, according to immigration records later found by the FBI, Greco had been in America several months earlier.

Amendolito was getting nervous about the money. He could hardly have doubted that he was laundering drug proceeds, although he accepted Miniati's assurances that the funds were nothing worse than "black" money—legitimate business proceeds being shielded from the tax collector.

He raised his doubts again with Miniati, who said he had been assured by Tognoli's father that the money was clean: "He swore on his grandchildren, his grandchildren, Salvatore." Amendolito shrugged.

Later in New York, when Tognoli and Castronovo visited him, Amendolito said he wanted the money brought to him from now on; he would not go to various locations to collect it. Tognoli said he had just the person to make the deliveries—Filippo Matassa, whose cousin was married to Tognoli. Soon Matassa began picking up the cartons from Castronovo and taking them to Amendolito. Della Torre was providing a separate channel.

One day Matassa was instructed to meet two men in a Korvette's parking lot in Brooklyn. A Cadillac with two men inside pulled up alongside Matassa. They told Matassa to follow them. The Cadillac led him to Bay Parkway near Bath Avenue. Matassa and the two other men got out. One was Onofrio Catalano, Sal the baker's cousin; the other, he later learned, was Ganci. They took a carton and a soft bag out of their trunk and placed it in Matassa's trunk.

Matassa ventured a question. "Isn't it a little unusual or risky to be doing this here in the open?"

"It is a matter of convenience," said Ganci. "In the future it will be done differently."

Uncomfortable as he might have been, Matassa followed the instructions and took one of the boxes to a company called Idea Development in the Horn & Hardart building on Third Avenue at Forty-second Street. Other times Matassa delivered the money-stuffed boxes to Amendolito on Madison Avenue. They had no idea they had been photographed by one of Kallstrom's surveillance agents, but Matassa had picked up one of the tails. After visiting Casamento's *salumeria* in Brooklyn, where Ganci had handed him a carton and a vinyl bag, Matassa was heading back through Manhattan to drop off the box on Third Avenue when he noticed a car following him. Abruptly he made an illegal U-turn on the West Side Highway, losing his pursuer.

He told Ganci he had been followed, but Ganci just grunted. This wasn't for him, Matassa decided. He wasn't getting paid a penny. This was all a favor for his cousin's husband. The hell with it. He broke the news to Tognoli and then called Ganci. From now on, Matassa said, Ganci should deliver the money himself.

"Me?" Ganci's voice rose two octaves.

Matassa started to give him the address where the money had to go.

"Wait!" Ganci cut him off. "Don't say it on the phone. Tomorrow morning at eight, come to the Café Sicilia on Eighteenth Avenue in Bensonhurst. Someone will meet you there."

A stranger showed up the next morning in a maroon Datsun. If it wasn't Sal Catalano's maroon Datsun, it was its twin. Matassa gave the man a slip of paper listing the places to drop off the money. He was out of it.

In October Miniati and Amendolito spoke again. "Tognoli is trying a different channel," Miniati said. "Part of the money will still go through your banking contacts. The rest will be delivered to other people in New York."

"Who?" Amendolito asked.

"Furriers."

"Furriers?"

"Furriers," said Miniati. "Furriers from Naples." The furriers had lire in Italy and needed dollars in the United States, he explained. Instead of bothering to transport the dollars overseas, Amendolito would give the dollars to the furriers here, and the furriers would credit them for the lire in Italy. What could be simpler?

A few days later Amendolito again made a pickup from Castronovo at the Roma restaurant. There was a carton Castronovo said had $299,000 and a plastic bag with $320,000. Amendolito transferred the two batches to a Samsonite suitcase, each in a separate compartment. Then he drove to the Southgate Hotel near Penn Station in Manhattan to meet the furriers.

Four of the furriers were in the hotel room. Amendolito dumped the $299,000 on a table. He removed $9,000 for himself and locked it in his briefcase while he went to use the toilet. When he came back, he started counting the $320,000 left in the suitcase and found $100,000 missing. He looked at the furriers. They were at the table, busily counting the money he had spilled out for them.

"Excuse me." The furriers looked up expectantly.

"Has anyone by chance seen some other bundles, about a hundred thousand dollars?"

The furriers all shook their heads adamantly. "You should check with the person who gave you this money," one said.

Amendolito panicked. He must have left it in the car. He raced downstairs and searched the boxes from Castronovo. Empty. He rushed to a pay phone and called Castronovo. "The three hundred and twenty thousand dollars you gave me?" he said. "I can only find two hundred and twenty thousand."

Castronovo explained that the extra $100,000 had been packed with the other money, with the $299,000. Actually it was $399,000.

Amendolito gasped. He had inadvertently dumped the extra $100,000 onto the table for the furriers. He rushed back to the hotel room. But the furriers were out, gone to dinner. Amendolito settled himself in the lobby and waited. They returned at two A.M.

"Let's go back and count the money again," he pleaded. "I think there was some mistake."

"We counted it already," said one. They refused to let Amendolito back into the room. There was nothing for him to do but call Miniati and report the loss.

In December Amendolito made three more journeys to the Roma restaurant to pick up another $3 million from Castronovo. He had flown some of the money to a new account in Bermuda, smoothing the way with a large "loan" to a local official. Altogether he picked up about sixty cartons of cash—about a metric ton of money.

Once he narrowly escaped leaving Kennedy Airport with close to $300,000 in cash in a traveling bag. A security guard asked to look into his bag. Reluctantly Amendolito opened it.

As soon as the guard saw all the money, she called the police. Several officers came running. "What is all this money?" one asked.

"I am in the fish business, and I am going to Bermuda," Amendolito lied. "I need this cash to purchase equipment."

"Did you fill out a currency transfer report?"

Amendolito played dumb. "A what?" he said.

The police summoned a Customs agent who explained the need to file a form for all cash exports over $5,000.

"Okay," Amendolito said, "I do it."

How much money was he carrying? the Customs agent wanted to know. Amendolito told him $210,000, although it was substantially more. He filled out the form with the agent. But he had already missed his plane. Amendolito said he would not fly out after all. In that case, the Customs agent decided, there was no need to count the money. Amendolito went home.

A few days later he returned to the airport with the money. He did not fill out a reporting form. This time he was not stopped and flew to Bermuda unhindered.

The greatest peril was yet to come. Amendolito had, all along, been skimming funds from Leonardo Greco. Instead of immediately putting through the money he had received to the specified Swiss accounts, Amendolito was depositing it in his own accounts in the name of a Miami-based trading company he had started. Tognoli had caught him at it and was furious. In Sicilian that Amendolito barely understood, Tognoli demanded that he make immediate restitution. Amendolito flew to Milan to talk to Tognoli personally.

"You are using the funds for your personal advantage," Tognoli told him icily. "That is totally unacceptable."

Amendolito argued that he was only depositing money in his own accounts in order to facilitate the transfers. The accounts, in any event, he insisted, were noninterest-bearing, so, he said, he was getting no economic benefit. His deceitful protestations won Tognoli over. But Tognoli urged Amendolito to shorten the time the funds were in his accounts.

Amendolito then dangled his own bait before Tognoli. "Perhaps my company can be of assistance to your family's business?" Tognoli's brother ran a family factory producing bicycles. It had been seeking to break into the Caribbean market. "With an investment by you, a lucrative deal could certainly be concluded," he told Tognoli. Tognoli said he had some friends who might be interested.

In January 1981 an angry Tognoli again summoned Amendolito, this time to a meeting in Montreal. Castronovo, who had been supplying the funds, was separately summoned. To their embarrassment, the two found themselves on the same flight, although Castronovo was in coach and Amendolito in first class. At first they tried to pretend they didn't see each other. In Montreal Tognoli castigated Amendolito. "You must restore—immediately—all the funds you have skimmed," he said. "Our dealings are halted until the situation is cleared up."

Amendolito was undaunted. "Have you thought any more about an investment in my company?" he asked. "All we are talking about is a mere five hundred thousand dollars."

Tognoli said he would consider it only after Amendolito had made full restitution. When he returned to New York, he sent Tognoli two checks totaling $488,550. Both bounced.

Tognoli was beyond patience. In March 1981 he ordered Amendolito to Sicily. Amendolito would make his explanations personally to the owners of the funds. It had by then dawned on Amendolito who that was. The Sicilian Mafia.

Amendolito was picked up at Palermo's Punta Raisi Airport by a driver he had seen before but could not quite place. They stopped in the suburbs at a small hotel to meet a nervous Tognoli. "I am losing my credibility with these people," he said. "You must explain to them yourself what you have been doing. First of all," he added, "you have to make good on the checks you bounced." Tognoli told him to stay at the hotel overnight. "Tomorrow," he said, "you will be called for."

The next day Amendolito was picked up by car and driven across Palermo to a small coffee shop. There a second man in an old jalopy drove him back through the city to a street corner Amendolito did not recognize. A third man met him there. He drove Amendolito out of the city to a villa in the suburbs. The house, built of stone, was well fortified. It sat on the top of a hill at the end of a dead-end road. There was a gate and a few steps up to the house. Amendolito was dropped off and left alone. He didn't scare easily, but this place gave him the creeps.

In a few minutes Tognoli arrived. He unlocked the house with a key and let Amendolito in. The house was airless and dusty. The windows were sealed, as if no one had been there for a long time.

"I am very worried," Tognoli whispered. "I must tell you I am more worried than I was yesterday. I am afraid nothing you say will be of help."

A few minutes later they heard someone enter the house. Amendolito recognized a grim-faced Leonardo Greco, the ironworks owner he had met in Sicily the previous September. Soon they were joined by another man Amendolito did not know. He was in his fifties or sixties, medium height, with a mustache. He wore an elegant blue jacket with gleaming gold buttons.

Amendolito took a deep breath and plunged in. "May I explain my company? Italia Presenta. It is based in Miami. In the free-trade zone. I think it could be of great assistance to you." He rattled on with his presentation for nearly two hours. He was afraid to stop. He concluded with an appeal: "All I need is your investment of five hundred thousand dollars; that is all the project requires."

Greco and the other man murmured back and forth. To Amendolito it appeared that the other man was the senior of the two, that Greco was consulting him for approval.

"Okay, we are interested," said Greco. "But first let us talk about our other business. Why do you owe so much?" Amendolito's eye fell on a slip of paper on a table by the two men. With a stab of fear, he recognized it as one of his bounced checks.

Amendolito explained his transfer procedures and the story of the Neapolitan furriers, how they had stuck him for $100,000. He acknowledged the bad check but said he had been expecting money to flow into the account. He promised to make good.

"Okay," said the other man. "But before we go into any new business, you must clear the balance you owe." They told Amendolito they were striking the furriers' $100,000 from his debt. They warned him to repay the rest fast.

The meeting broke up jovially, and Amendolito returned home to New York. He never repaid the money.

Paquette, who still did not know that the prize he was searching for was named Salvatore Amendolito, spent much of 1981 trying to find out where in the World-Wide Business Centres labyrinth Matassa had delivered his boxes. Paquette had started running background checks on the dozens of tenants that the directory listed for the tenth floor, but finally he had to admit defeat. Many were little more than mail drops with no recorded officers. A year had passed since he had gotten his information about the money. He had to take the kind of risk that could either break the investigation open or tip off the target. He had to visit World-Wide. On a crisp fall morning he drove from his office in New Rochelle to the building on Madison and Fifty-sixth Street. In his pocket was the blurry photo of the back view of the man who had come down to meet Matassa the day Kallstrom's surveillance squad had shot the pictures from the van on November 3, 1980. He took the elevator to the tenth floor, pausing for a moment after the door opened. The man he had been tracking for a year could be somewhere in that warren of offices. He could be right there at the receptionist's desk. If so, Paquette would have to make up a story fast. He walked down the short corridor and pushed open the glass-paneled door.

"Can I help you?"

Paquette turned right to face a receptionist with glasses and curly hair. "Uh, can I see the manager please?" he said. He hoped she wouldn't ask why, and she didn't. The fewer the number of people who knew about this, the better. When the manager arrived, Paquette showed his badge and said he had a confidential matter to discuss. The manager ushered him into his private office. Paquette fished out the picture. "We're interested in this man, and I'm wondering if he looks familiar," Paquette said. "I'd appreciate it if you don't mention I asked about him."

The manager stared at the photo. He smiled. "I couldn't do that," he said.

"You can't keep it confidential?" Paquette was annoyed.

"Nah, I'm glad to help. But I couldn't tell him anyhow," the manager said. "That's Sal Amendolito. Overseas Business Services. I recognize the leather jacket. He's been out of here some time."

"Where can I find him?" Paquette asked.

"If you find him, tell me," said the manager. "He skipped owing us a bundle. I'd like to find him, too."

"Did he leave any forwarding address?"

"Nope." The manager shook his head.

Paquette tried to hide his disappointment.

"Strange guy, Amendolito," the manager added. "He put a huge safe in his office."

"He did?"

"It was big as two refrigerators. He had to specially reinforce the floor. I was afraid for the elevator cables."

"Really."

"And a burglar alarm."

"You don't say."

"He also put in a money-counting machine."

Paquette's spirits rose. "Did he leave anything behind?"

"Nope."

Paquette's hopes sank.

"But the way we bill here," the manager continued, "I have all his phone and telex records. Everything goes through us."

Paquette left elated, promising to return shortly with a subpoena for the material. Later he and the manager located it after a hunt through a storeroom of various company records. The papers he took contained Amendolito's telephone and telex charges as well as copies of the telex messages themselves. There was also a list Amendolito had provided World-Wide, naming employees of Overseas Business Services who had authorized access to his office.

With the help of two IRS agents, Paquette tracked one of them down in the city. Before risking an approach, however, Paquette ran a background check on him, too, just in case he might still be with Amendolito. He seemed clean. Paquette took the chance and visited him in Brooklyn.

"Yeah, I worked for Sal," he told Paquette. "We didn't really get along."

Paquette was glad to hear it. "Do you have any of his records left?"

"Only his phone book," said the man. "Sal once gave me a copy to make calls for him when he was out of the country."

With Amendolito's phone book and charge records spread out over his desk in New Rochelle, Paquette called a colleague at the Customs Service. Mike Fahy was a senior special agent Paquette had worked with on earlier money cases. Fahy, a tall, bluff Irishman of forty-one, had been a part-time Customs trainee in college when he searched a Ford Galaxie aboard the SS *Raffaelo* in 1971 and uncovered eighty-two kilos of heroin that investigators later heard had been sent by Gaetano Badalamenti. Paquette specialized in money laundering and financial crime, but Customs agents like Fahy had one big advantage over FBI agents, Paquette knew: Customs was empowered to follow any suspect item to its destination anywhere in the world and to search it without a warrant as long as it always remained in sight. Customs had also accumulated an impressive computerized data base through the Financial Law Enforcement Center (FLEC). It listed every recorded bank currency transaction of $10,000 or more and every movement of $5,000 or more into or out of the country, provided the required paperwork had been filed with the government.

Paquette leafed through Amendolito's phone book, reading off the unfamiliar names for Fahy to run through FLEC. One of the names he gave Fahy was Franco Della Torre. "And while you're at it, Mike," Paquette said, "put Salvatore Amendolito on the watch list." If and when Amendolito showed up at an American airport or border crossing, Paquette wanted to know.

Paquette suddenly had a lot of new information to check out: all the names in Amendolito's phone book and the subscribers to the phone and telex numbers Amendolito called. He had verified that the boxes contained money. But where was it coming from? Amounts like that could come only from drugs, Rooney and Russo agreed, but where were the drugs?

"I'll find the money," Paquette promised Rooney. "You find the drugs."

7

T HE Sicilian Connection—for that was what Rooney and Russo and Paquette had unwittingly stumbled across—was the successor to the French Connection, the postwar heroin pipeline from Marseilles that at its peak in 1971 was pouring an estimated ten tons of heroin a year into the United States. One character who bridged both worlds, according to many accounts, was Buscetta. Another was a Sicilian-speaking former CIA agent named Thomas C. Tripodi. Tripodi, an oak of a man at six feet three and 240 pounds, tried out for the Giants football team, but when he found himself warming the bench, he quit to join the Treasury's Bureau of Narcotics in 1960. Two years later he transferred to the CIA, handling counterintelligence and internal security out of New York and Miami. He transferred back to the Bureau of Narcotics in 1968, when the agency was being merged with the Food and Drug Administration's Bureau of Drug Abuse Control to form a new agency, the Bureau of Narcotics and Dangerous Drugs under the Justice Department. He was still with the BNDD when it merged with elements of the Customs Service to create the DEA in 1973.

Tripodi traced a sinister continuum in the reemergence of drug trafficking after World War II. The war's curtailment of commercial shipping and stepped-up border security measures had virtually wiped out the smuggling of heroin along with other contraband into the United States. Consequently, the number of American heroin addicts was estimated to have plummeted from the 200,000 of prewar 1940 to only 20,000 five years later, a fraction of today's half-million or more heroin addicts and nearly 6 million cocaine users. For the first time in this century the addict population had been reduced to manageable proportions. After the war the Corsicans in France and the Mafia in Sicily resumed their supply lines. Although the American authorities were instrumental in the revival of the Sicilian Mafia, they persuaded the Italian government to mount a successful crackdown on the heroin smugglers. This left the Corsicans, who had also been buttressed by the CIA as an anti-Communist force, as the major providers of illegal heroin to the United States. The Corsicans had two powerful advantages: their connections to the Southeast Asian heroin market through the French colonial presence in Indochina and their influence in the French secret services through the Corsicans' involvement in official anti-Communist agitation. Often, it emerged, they used their intelligence connections as covers for heroin trafficking. Moreover, as French popular support for the war in Indochina dwindled, French forces turned to heroin trafficking as a means of discretionary funding. This expediency culminated in the French military's Operation X, which, Tripodi's research showed, involved collecting opium from Indochinese mountain tribes, transporting it to Saigon, and transmitting it to the Corsican underworld. Clandestine laboratories in Saigon processed the base into morphine, and the Corsicans arranged for its shipment to Marseilles for further refinement into heroin.

Two other developments fostered the emerging French Connection, Tripodi wrote in reports submitted to the CIA. One, he said, was penetration of French intelligence by the Soviets, who encouraged the trafficking as another means of undermining the West. The other, Tripodi said, was the defeat of the French forces at Dien Bien Phu in 1954. French President Charles de Gaulle was so angered by the refusal of the Eisenhower administration to come to France's aid, Tripodi contended, that he encouraged the French intelligence service's efforts in the heroin trade as it adversely affected the United States. Tripodi reached that conclusion after interviewing operatives in the French security establishment. "De Gaulle had to know about it," Tripodi said years later. "And he obviously permitted it because he could have stopped it if he wanted to."

After 1972 growing American law enforcement pressure took a toll on French Connection traffickers. French sources of heroin base and laboratories dried up, although the French authorities uncovered a heroin laboratory and forty kilos of morphine base near Marseilles as late as February 1978. Sicilian traffickers who had been relying on French suppliers were forced to look elsewhere. Drawing on years of experience as tobacco smugglers, they sought buyers for Asian and Mexican heroin. To maximize their profits, they began to create their own labs in Sicily. Initially the Sicilian labs were dismissed as amateurish compared with their more accomplished French models, but they were quickly upgraded.

By the late 1970's the growing role of the Sicilian Mafia in drug trafficking was evident from accelerating seizures in New York and other North American gateways. One confidential DEA report cited five busts that pointed to mounting deliveries of large quantities of Middle Eastern heroin to New York City, Detroit, Chicago, and Toronto by Sicilian groups that acquired opium, morphine base, and raw heroin from sources in Turkey and Lebanon as well as Iran, Afghanistan, and Pakistan. The base was transformed into heroin in laboratories in Palermo, Campania, and Reggio di Calabria. There were also reports of heroin labs operating aboard ships off the Italian coasts.

One Customs check at Kennedy Airport uncovered six kilos of heroin in plastic bags hidden in a large can of olive oil. The can had been deviously modified to contain a smaller can, soldered off center, in which the heroin had been concealed, frustrating the usual probe to test the can's contents.

As a result of intelligence gained from such seizures, the DEA developed a profile for screening cargo, particularly personal effects, sent from Palermo. In 1979 it focused on two such shipments consigned to a fictitious addressee in Brooklyn. Investigators studied the shipments and found that certain items had been removed by collaborating Alitalia employees to avoid detection. The inquiry implicated a ring of airline cargo workers who were helping smuggle the shipments in. One employee, Frank Rolli, caught by the government, on the one hand, and fearing retaliation from his Mafia superiors, on the other, ended up working secretly for the government, leading the DEA and the Italians to the forty kilos seized in Milan in 1980.

The proliferating drug busts pointed to a growing smuggling plague. Something more was needed. The U.S. government's answer was Operation Caesar. Started with the Italian authorities in late 1978, the operation targeted Gaetano Badalamenti among other suspected Sicilian traffickers and built a crucial intelligence base that paved the way for more than a thousand convictions on both sides of the Atlantic. Just as Operation Caesar was getting under way in September 1978, a key underworld meeting was taking place in Palermo. According to an Italian investigation, it drew together members of the Badalamenti trafficking organization and a number of Turkish, Greek, and Dutch nationals. The meeting broke up before the Italian authorities learned of it, so there was no surveillance. But they established that among the attendees had been a notorious underworld chemist, Ismet Kostu who, they found, had been in Palermo for about a week.

For three of those days he had disappeared. Investigators later discovered that he had taken a taxi thirty kilometers outside Palermo, where he was picked up by a Mercedes. Three days later the cab returned to the drop-off point to take him back to Palermo. The police subsequently heard that the Badalamenti group had been operating a clandestine lab and had nearly ruined a batch of heroin. It had rushed in Kostu with six kilos of pure heroin to doctor the defective batch and render it marketable.

The bulwark of Operation Caesar was the DEA's Tom Tripodi. In Palermo Tripodi worked closely with Deputy Police Chief Boris Giuliano and went undercover to gather information firsthand. But it had not taken the Mafia long to identify Tripodi. Giuliano concluded that Palermo was too dangerous for Tripodi despite his being guarded by carloads of heavily armed security officers, and he persuaded Tripodi to leave. Even back in Washington Tripodi continued to get threats. "Hey, baby," said one caller, "your time has come." Tripodi survived. Giuliano didn't. In July 1979 he was gunned down at a café where he had gone to meet an informant. Four men were later arrested and tried for the killing but were acquitted. In an eerie postscript, Tripodi heard that nine male relatives of the accused were later killed by either rival Mafia factions angry over the provocative assassination or vengeful police.

Witnessing the cataclysmic events from his special vantage point was Buscetta. With other powerful mafiosi, he had fled Sicily in the wake of the Ciaculli bomb blast in 1963. His odyssey, which was just beginning, was to take him through the rise and fall of the French Connection and to end two decades later with his astonishing exposure of the Sicilian Mafia.

Buscetta had drawn the wrath of his boss, Giuseppe "Pippo" Calò, who retired him from the Porta Nuova family for leaving his wife for another woman. At the same time he was getting increasingly disenchanted with the mounting strife in the Sicilian families. He moved to Milan, where he set up a company to market dairy products in partnership with a distant relative of Guglielmo Marconi, the inventor of the wireless radio. But remaining anywhere in Italy had become risky for him. Buscetta slipped into Switzerland and under a false name flew to Mexico City, where Saca Catalano brought him $500 from Carlo Gambino, then head of the American Mafia Commission. The proud Buscetta sent it back. He soon fell in with a group of Italian expatriates who recognized his photo from newspaper accounts of the Mafia uproar in Sicily. One of the Italians was a young clothing salesman, Giuseppe Catania, nicknamed Pino. Buscetta, who by this time was separated from his wife and living with a vivacious Italian television star named Vera Girotti, moved in with Catania and his wife. In early 1964 the two couples relocated to Toronto. On one occasion Catania accompanied Buscetta to two clinics in Mexico City for plastic surgery "to have the line of my nose changed," Buscetta later said, vanity being among his acknowledged vices. The results were unremarkable; even Buscetta's son Benedetto didn't notice any change.

For years the Canadian underworld had been boiling with activity, monitored closely by investigators from the Royal Canadian Mounted Police and the old U.S. Bureau of Narcotics. One catalytic event had been Carmine Galante's visit to Montreal in 1953. He had crossed the border at the behest of his boss, Joe Bonanno, to reorganize gambling and other rackets for the American Mafia. Among the most lucrative markets was America's emerging appetite for illicit drugs. The quantities of smuggled drugs had not yet reached the flood stage of the 1970's and 1980's, but the tide had begun. In late 1955 a tipster led police to search the SS *Saint-Malo* when the freighter from Bordeaux docked in Montreal. In a hollowed-out area in a crew member's cabin, searchers uncovered fourteen kilos of pure heroin, then valued at more than $14 million on the street. At that time it was the largest such seizure ever in North America.

From Canada, Buscetta and Vera Girotti slipped across the border illegally into the United States and made their way to New York. Later he also sent for his wife and their three sons and a daughter, whom he installed in a separate apartment. One of the first fellow countrymen Buscetta looked up in New York was Saca Catalano, then a more notorious mafioso than his cousin Salvatore "Toto" Catalano. Buscetta had known Saca as a "man of honor" in Palermo, and Saca had brought him the $500 from Carlo Gambino. Like his cousin, he came from Ciminna and had also fled Sicily's Mafia strife after 1963. Saca put up Buscetta in his home and got him a construction job. Buscetta was also introduced to a Brooklyn deli owner, Filippo Casamento, a pinched, distracted-looking man with a tangle of graying locks who ran a successful Brooklyn deli or *salumeria* called Eagle Cheese. Casamento helped Buscetta land a job as a pizza maker, where he might keep a low profile while perhaps pursuing other options. Carlo Gambino sent for Buscetta and presented him with $10,000, warning Buscetta that he had made a "mistake" by rejecting Gambino's money the first time. He also cautioned Buscetta that Sicilians were not to conduct their own criminal business in America.

In 1966 the Immigration Service caught up with Buscetta. The slippery mafioso presented a Mexican passport in the name of Manuel López-Cadena and managed to convince the investigating agent, Anthony J. DeVito, that he was a Mexican national who had come for the New York World's Fair and to study the prospects for opening his own glass business here. DeVito, who happened to be a cousin of *Godfather* novelist Mario Puzo, was particularly concerned that "López-Cadena" might be a Cuban or a Communist. The United States began deportation proceedings, but Buscetta slipped away, to resurface later under various aliases.

Buscetta's new employer lent him $5,000 to buy one of his other pizzerias on Brooklyn's Pitkin Avenue. By his own later account, Buscetta was a hardworking and solicitous businessman who at closing time gave customers the leftover pizza free. Within two years Buscetta had sold that pizzeria and bought two others with silent Mafia-connected partners. More lucrative deals soon beckoned.

By 1969, according to Catania, he and Buscetta were partners in the drug business along with another Sicilian, Carlo Zippo, who ran a Brazilian-Italian electronics and gift boutique near Times Square. Several years later, when American authorities were questioning him in Italy about his possible extradition to the United States, Zippo was asked whether he had ever dealt in narcotics. "By narcotics, what do you mean?" Zippo replied.

In early 1970 Buscetta made a trip to Madrid and Mexico City, emerging with big news for Catania: Buscetta confided he had obtained up to eighty-nine kilos of heroin in Europe, Catania recalled later. It was coming via Panama and would arrive in Mexico shortly. Did Catania know of a buyer?

Catania had good contacts in the Bonanno-affiliated Cotroni Mafia family in Montreal and with some of the French Connection's most notorious traffickers: ex–Gestapo agent Auguste Joseph Ricord, Michel Nicoli, Lucien Sarti, Claude Pastou, Christian David, Guido Orsini, and Jean Paul Angeletti. With a gang of rightist French expatriates, they frequented the Club Ex-Combattants in Buenos Aires and specialized in body couriering into the United States the heroin cooked by the renowned French chemists from morphine base smuggled in from the Orient. Yes, Catania said he assured Buscetta, he and his contacts could find a buyer for the eighty-nine kilos. Buscetta, he said, then arranged for a suitcase of heroin to be placed in Catania's car in Mexico City.

Buscetta later insisted that he had nothing to do with these drug deals, that while Zippo and Nicoli and Catania and the others were hatching their trafficking schemes, he was merely seeking to acquire another set of false identification papers through them. But sworn statements by Catania, Nicoli, Pastou, and others were remarkably consistent regarding Buscetta's central involvement. Even his son Benedetto told the FBI in 1972 that he knew his father had been a big man in the narcotics traffic.

In June 1970, investigators later suspected, Buscetta turned up under an alias with three companions in a car stopped by the police in Milan. One was a fellow mafioso named Gaetano Badalamenti.

Near the end of August 1970 Buscetta and his son Benedetto drove from their home in Queens to Zippo's midtown hotel, where they were promptly arrested by surveilling New York State troopers. Buscetta tried to claim once again that he was someone else and showed a driver's license in another name, but fingerprint checks quickly established his identity. As far as the police and government knew, however, Buscetta was just an illegal immigrant, albeit one wanted by the Italians on several charges of murder. At the time, however, American and Italian law enforcement authorities regarded each other with suspicion, and the intelligence on Buscetta was not properly pooled. He was held in the federal detention center in Manhattan until his release on $40,000 bail. When Italy sought his extradition, Buscetta fled, driving first to Mexico City to link up with Catania, then continuing on to Guatemala, Paraguay, and Brazil. On Rio's Copacabana beach, Buscetta met the love of his life.

She was Cristina Guimarães, a blond psychology student some twenty years his junior and the daughter of a politically connected, wealthy Brazilian labor lawyer. Buscetta's flings had become legendary, but this was the real thing. Sexual electricity crackled between them. "When they're together," said one DEA analyst who later interviewed them, "you just want to get out of the room." Once Buscetta was accused of using a prison infirmary to make love to the visiting Cristina, but he disdainfully dismissed the charge. "This runs totally counter to my dignity," he said.

Cristina knew all about Buscetta's lurid past and shrugged off his trespasses. "I thank those women because they prepared him for me," she told Buscetta's biographer.

Buscetta, in contrast, found it difficult to shed his natural macho possessiveness and jealousy. But he was ready to die for Cristina. When it appeared some years later that he might once again be jailed and permanently separated from his family, he penned Cristina a haunting last letter—"please cancel my shadow," he pleaded—and swallowed strychnine. As usual, he survived.

Buscetta's first order of business in Rio de Janeiro was to arrange for a new set of phony identification papers supplied by a fugitive Italian trafficker, masquerading as a Brazilian police officer, who had once devised a scheme to smuggle heroin in hollow statuettes of Christ of the Andes. Guglielmo Casalini was so impressed with Buscetta, in fact, that when he obtained a book on the Sicilian Mafia, he went through it, underlining mentions of his idol—a fateful mistake, as it turned out. Buscetta soon fell in again with Casalini's associates, Michel Nicoli, Carlo Zippo, Catania, and other French Connection traffickers.

Nicoli said later that he met Buscetta and Carlo Zippo in May 1971 and arranged, in Buscetta's presence, for Lucien Sarti to deliver 50 kilos of heroin to a representative of Zippo's in New York. Two months later Buscetta and Zippo asked for another 50 kilos to be delivered to a customer of Buscetta's in Mexico City. And in November Sarti delivered another 120 kilos, for $840,000, Nicoli said. Claude Pastou, another prominent French Connection courier for Auguste Joseph Ricord, told of delivering a 50-kilo shipment to Buscetta's friend Filippo Casamento at his Eagle Cheese shop in Brooklyn for $500,000.

By 1971 the Italian police crackdown on the Mafia had eased. Buscetta had supposedly slipped home to Italy the previous year to meet with Mafia leaders on reconstituting a Sicilian Mafia Commission, although he denied it. By 1971 the commission was re-created around a triumvirate of top bosses Salvatore Riina of Corleone, Stefano Bontade of Santa Maria di Gesù, and Gaetano Badalamenti of Cinisi. Buscetta, back in Brazil, was confident they had set the stage for a new period of interfamily collegiality and peace. In reality they ushered in an era of unprecedented bloodletting.

In February 1972 Lucien Sarti and his girl friend were arrested in Rio; it cost associates $60,000 in bribes to gain their release. A few days later Sarti, carrying $200,000, was arrested again, this time with his wife in Bolivia. They were released after four days, but the Bolivian authorities kept the $200,000. In April Sarti and his wife and daughter were stopped by the Mexican police. According to the official police account, he drew a pistol, but the police shot him dead first.

Meanwhile, Nicoli said, he and Buscetta's son Benedetto traveled from Rio to São Paulo, where Buscetta had agreed to purchase a 60-kilo heroin shipment coming in from France. When a hitch developed in securing the heroin, Nicoli arranged for 400 kilos of opium base from Turkey, processible into 180 kilos of heroin for sale in the United States through Buscetta. When he reached Rio, Nicoli was warned that the police were around. He fled to São Paulo while his wife found a new refuge in Rio, but when he returned, the police were there, too. Nicoli rushed to Buscetta's house, where he found, to his mounting panic, that everyone had left in a hurry the day before. He returned to São Paulo to hear that Cristina's parents had been arrested and that Buscetta was in hiding. Nicoli rushed to another friend's apartment, followed by the police—who arrested everyone. By November 1972 they had also tracked down Buscetta. The key traffickers were sentenced to twenty years in prison without parole. Christian David chose twenty years in an American prison rather than face the guillotine in France, where he was wanted for the killing of a policeman investigating the 1965 assassination of Moroccan opposition leader Mehdi ben Barka. Buscetta was expelled to Italy, where he began serving a three-year sentence for Mafia association, based on a 1969 conviction in absentia. The Justice Department sought his extradition to the United States to face a drug-trafficking indictment in Brooklyn. The Italians refused but used the American charges to increase his sentence to ten years, later reduced to eight by an appellate court. With Sarti dead and Ricord, Nicoli, David, Pastou, Catania, and Buscetta in jail, the French Connection was severed.

The Sicilian Mafia soon filled the vacuum. In the mid-seventies one of the Mafia's most lucrative rackets was the smuggling of untaxed cigarettes into Italy. Initially, loads of five hundred cases of cigarettes were considered substantial; at its height the racket dealt in shiploads of up to forty thousand cases, providing a livelihood for thousands of otherwise unemployable Sicilian poor. Mafiosi and their allies in the Neapolitan Camorra masterminded the traffic, but the armies of dockworkers and street sellers were not "men of honor." Thus, traditional Mafia discipline was eroded, and notice of the schemes circulated widely among the populace.

By the end of the 1970's growing pressure by the Italian Treasury Police and internal squabbling had robbed cigarette smuggling of much of its profitable allure. However, a new, far more lucrative racket was at hand, one tailor-made for the oceanic and overland smuggling routes developed by the tobacco traffickers. One of the old-time cigarette smugglers was Nunzio La Mattina of Buscetta's Porta Nuova family, who quickly saw ways of turning his expertise to drug trafficking. In conjunction with an associate, Antonio "Carlo" Rotolo, he secured sources of opium from Turkey and the Orient and devised means of refining the product into heroin in clandestine Sicilian laboratories.

Unusually sinister and powerful forces were at work. The drug trade and its easy billions came to the Sicilian Mafia during a period of growing interfamilial strife. The Corleonesi and Greco clans had upset a traditional balance of power and were jockeying to subjugate the other families on the ruling commission. The timing was explosive.

The reconstituted Mafia Commission was dominated by the ruthless boss of the Corleonesi, Luciano Liggio, who at nineteen was reputed to have been the youngest Mafia chief in Sicilian history and exemplified the new Mafia—vicious and flamboyant. During one of Liggio's frequent stays in jail the commission leadership fell not to either of his Corleonesi successors, Salvatore Riina or Bernardo Provenzano, but to the leader of the Cinisi family, Gaetano Badalamenti. The Corleonesi, however, took every opportunity to goad and undermine Badalamenti, once incriminatingly collecting a kidnapping ransom in his territory and even ridiculing him publicly at commission meetings for his unlettered peasant diction. On the grounds of some undisclosed offense, Badalamenti was finally ousted from the commission in 1978 and replaced by his cousin and hated rival, Antonio Badalamenti. Michele Greco of the powerful Greco clan took over as head of the commission but remained a figurehead, according to Italian investigators. Behind him, it was said, lurked the real powers, Liggio and the Corleonesi. After Liggio was jailed for life in 1982, power continued to be wielded by Provenzano and the legendarily elusive Riina, a short, roly-poly man of whom the Italian police had not even been able to secure a photograph in thirty years.

Badalamenti's ouster by the Corleonesi had far-reaching implications for the drug trade, according to Italian investigators. Badalamenti had been supplying the Gambino family in New York. Now that he was deposed, the Gambinos would have to secure other sources of heroin. The victorious Corleonesi, meanwhile, were favoring a new group of customers in New York. They were Sicilians allied with the Bonanno family and under the control of Salvatore "Toto" Catalano.

The strife turned bloodier. The Corleonesi embarked on a terror campaign of assassinations of rival members and police officials. Many of the killings, Buscetta later said, were deviously engineered to throw suspicion on other families, and a wave of counterterror and slaughter ensued. One member of the commission, Buscetta's idolized Stefano Bontade, plotted to shoot Salvatore Riina at a commission meeting but was instead ambushed on his birthday in 1981. Another boss, Salvatore Inzerillo, who believed that owing Riina money for a heroin deal amounted to life insurance, miscalculated. Inzerillo was gunned down while visiting his mistress. A killer whom Buscetta identified as the Sicilian Mafia's most fearsome murderer, Pino Greco, also slaughtered Inzerillo's teenage son after hacking off his arm as a gruesome warning to would-be avengers.

Salvatore Contorno, the later turncoat, was targeted for assassination, too, by Pino Greco. Driving in an old section of Palermo in June 1981, he was ambushed by Greco firing a Soviet-made Kalashnikov automatic rifle from the back of a motorcycle. Contorno managed to escape the blaze of bullets, draw his own pistol, and fire back, hitting Greco, or so it seemed. He later learned that Greco was wearing a bulletproof vest and escaped. From the bullets fired at Contorno, the police later established that Greco's rifle had also been used to kill Inzerillo and Bontade. In 1982 Contorno was arrested and convicted in Rome of conspiracy and drug and gun possession. After three years in jail he, like Buscetta, agreed to testify against the Mafia. Some twenty-five of Contorno's relatives were massacred in retaliation.

The Mafia killings targeted the authorities as well. Between 1979 and 1982 the victims included Boris Giuliano, deputy chief of the state police in Palermo, and his two successors, Cesare Terranova, a judge and member of the parliamentary Anti-Mafia Commission, and police captain Emanuele Basile; in one day, Palermo's chief prosecutor Gaetano Costa and anti-Mafia politician Piersanti Mattarella; the secretary of the Sicilian Communist party Pio La Torre; investigating magistrate Rocco Chinnici; and General Carlo Alberto Dalla Chiesa, who had been sent to Palermo to curb the Mafia but who suffered from a critical and, many thought, calculated lack of support from Rome, where influential politicians were secretly indebted to the Mafia.

The killings were meant to be seen as signs of strength, but they betrayed the Mafia's growing vulnerabilities. Schemes once plotted quietly with the help of strategically placed political allies now came undone in a paroxysm of slaughter. The attacks on the judiciary and police also fed an unusual public outcry from a population and officialdom not used to denouncing the Mafia. Buscetta saw it all coming apart.

"Drug trafficking will lead to the collapse of Cosa Nostra," Buscetta quoted Bontade as prophesying shortly before his assassination. Bontade, Buscetta said, was the only one who could have stood up to the rampaging Corleonesi. "Once he died," Buscetta said later, "the Mafia, in the traditional sense, no longer existed."

8

HILE Paquette was blindly working his way through the roster of World-Wide Business Centres in search of the elusive money launderer he later learned was Amendolito, Rooney and Russo were looking for the drug connection. For the kind of money they had been seeing, there had to be a steady flow of multikilo loads. If Catalano wasn't moving the money and drugs himself, he had to have people working for him who were. Those were the people they had to find. Then they could follow the ladder up. But there was no immediate way of differentiating Catalano's criminal associates from casual acquaintances or even passersby. To be safe, the agents shot pictures of everybody near Catalano: bakery delivery-men; people waiting for the bus; and, one day in late February 1981, a bushy-haired man in a turtleneck and plaid jacket to whom Catalano seemed to be explaining something.

Three weeks before, Russo had learned from the encyclopedic Jack Clark of police intelligence that Bonventre, Amato, and Catalano, along with doomed Bonanno captains Phil Giaccone and Dominick "Big Trin" Trinchera—soon to be killed—had been among a group of Bonanno members surveilled by the Suffolk County police at a rendezvous at a caterer's on Brooklyn's Avenue U. What made the gathering of unusual interest, Clark told Russo, was that it

91

included representatives of the Gambino and Colombo families. Gambino consigliere Joseph N. Gallo reportedly presided. Something that needed the approval of several families, Russo guessed, possibly something to do with drugs, was being decided. Operating on a hunch, he immediately set off in his own car to see if he could find Bonventre and Amato. He finally spotted the duo in Bonventre's blue Cadillac near the Caffè Cesare, Bonventre's new power base on Thirteenth Avenue. Russo tailed them to the Café del Viale on Knickerbocker Avenue. It was impossible to follow them in, but as Russo drove past, he could see them through the open door sitting around a large table with a bunch of other men. He kept circling the block, trying to peek in each time he passed. His impotence angered him. It was well past midnight when he returned home.

On a mild May morning in 1981 new tenants quietly moved into a wood-frame house on Metropolitan Avenue in Middle Village, Queens. They didn't need a lot of furniture, clothes, or dishes. The FBI traveled light. Charlie Rooney had first spotted the place. He thought it would make a perfect lookout, but he called in special operations to make an expert assessment. They liked it, too. It was part of the neighborhood yet a little separate. It had a private entrance. Most important, its upper floor offered a good view of Catalano's bakery.

A few nights later, while Middle Village slept, a cherry picker stopped nearby, across from a low orange-brick garden apartment building on Seventy-eighth Street. The truck driver scaled an electrical pole and tinkered with an installation. If any neighbors saw him, they did not give it much thought. Utility repairmen were a common sight in the neighborhood, and with the firehouse down the block, there was always quite a bit of traffic. When the man finished his work on the pole and clambered down, a small video camera was trained on Giuseppe Ganci's house. The camera beamed a microwave signal to a television monitor on the top floor of the wood-frame house that overlooked Catalano's bakery and that the FBI had just rented under a subterfuge. Although it was common for the bureau to set up such lookouts or "plants" as a base for extended surveillances, it was apparently the first time a closed-circuit video system had been permanently trained on the house of a criminal suspect. Jim Kallstrom had struck again.

The surveillances were carried a step further. On the basis of the investigation into the emerging web of Mafia and cash interconnections, a federal magistrate had granted the government's application to install pen registers on the phones of Ganci and Castronovo and the growing circle of those they were found to be calling and meeting. These devices, similar to a wiretap, and named for a twenty-year-old prototype that used a stylus pen to record outgoing numbers as a series of dots and dashes, preserved the numbers dialed and the times they were made —but not the conversations themselves—on paper. The devices had since been computerized. Rooney soon had a printout of hundreds of phone numbers, each of which then had to be checked with the phone company for the name of the subscriber. It would have been easy enough for Kallstrom's FBI technicians to plug in a little clip to allow an agent to hear the conversations themselves, but the standard of proof required for what was known as a Title III intercept—a wiretap—was much higher than that for a pen register, as befitted the constitutional distinction between just knowing to whom a citizen was talking and actually listening to what he or she was saying.

On the morning of May 6, 1981, Rooney was in the Queens office when all the pen register teletypes seemed to go off at once. Suddenly everybody was calling everybody. It wasn't until a few days later that Rooney learned the reason from Joe Pistone, who was winding up his undercover assignment inside the Bonanno family: May 5 was the night the three Bonanno captains were killed on orders of Sonny Black Napolitano. The pen registers had obviously picked up the telephone activity as the news of the killings went from house to house the next morning—a tip-off, Rooney thought, of the probable involvement of the Sicilians.

Rooney soon heard of other intriguing developments. Also on the busy morning of May 6 a police surveillance team spotted two Bonanno mobsters driving in Queens in a car registered to one of Catalano's brothers. The cops tailed the pair to a diner, where they watched them switch cars and then drive across the Whitestone Bridge to the Capri Motel in the Bronx. Shortly after noon, with the cops surreptitiously photographing the scene, the two emerged from the motel with two other men, who got into a pickup truck and drove off, but not before the cops took down the plate number. It came back to a New Jersey contractor, Giovanni Ligammari. And when Rooney saw the pictures the cops had taken, he recognized Ligammari as the bushy-haired man in the plaid jacket who had been photographed walking with Catalano in February. Rooney wondered whether the Capri Motel rendezvous had something to do with the murders of the three captains the night before. Perhaps one of the triggermen was being spirited out of town. Who was Ligammari, and what was his connection to Catalano? Was Catalano involved in the hits?

Russo, meanwhile, was pondering another small piece of the puzzle. The night of the captains' murders a surveillance agent had been staking out the Queens house of one of Ganci's associates, Santo Giordano. Giordano, the agents had since learned, was the fifth man with Catalano and Ganci when they accompanied Bonventre and Amato to the Brooklyn DA's office after the Galante killing. His fingerprints had been found with Bruno Indelicato's in the getaway car, and investigators now believed Giordano had been the masked man with the rifle waiting outside Joe and Mary's.

As the agent watched Giordano's house the night of May 5, he saw his car come tearing out of the driveway and peel off down the street, too fast for the agent to follow. A few days later Russo found Giordano in a Queens hospital's intensive care unit. His chest was swathed in bandages, and he was partially paralyzed from a bullet wound. Russo suspected he had been wounded while doing in the captains—an account Pistone later confirmed.

"I heard you had some trouble," Russo said.

"Me?" Giordano said. "Oh, this? Nah, this is nothing."

"The doctors say you were shot."

"An accident," Giordano said.

"How'd it happen, Santo?" Russo asked.

"Argument over a parking spot."

"Where?"

"I don't remember," Giordano said.

Russo smiled a thin, tight-lipped smile, shook his head, and left Giordano propped up on the hospital's crisp white sheets.

Well, Russo reflected, he didn't really expect Giordano to admit he got shot killing some guys.

Through a 300-mm lens on a tripod in the lookout, Rooney and other agents photographed Pistone's mob mentor Lefty Ruggiero paying two visits to Catalano's bakery at the end of May 1981. They also shot pictures of a short, drawn-faced man with rimless spectacles who was walking with Ganci in and out of Catalano's bakery. He was the same unknown subject the NYPD had photographed in November 1980 eating a slice of pizza outside Ganci's pizzeria off Columbus Circle. Now they started following him around, tailing him once to a mansion in suburban Pelham, New York, that they found Saca Catalano also visited. They got a name for the occupant of the fourteen-room Colonial house on exclusive Esplanade Avenue and tried it on the Italian authorities in Rome. Had they ever heard of a Giuseppe Bono? The Italians were stunned. Bono was a Sicilian Mafia drug kingpin then under growing investigation in Italy. They knew Bono had dropped out of sight, but they presumed he was in Venezuela, where he was known to have extensive business interests. What was he doing walking around Queens? The FBI opened a new file and put a squad just on Bono.

An informant who walked into the DEA one day shortly afterward added astonishing new information. Bono, he said, had gotten married at St. Patrick's Cathedral in New York the previous November, celebrating the wedding with a gala reception at the Pierre Hotel. His wife, Antonia, was from a family that ran a pizzeria near St. John's University in Queens. Dumbfounded DEA agents verified the story with the hotel and soon tracked down the wedding pictures. Suddenly Rooney had a portrait gallery of the three hundred people whom a top Sicilian Mafia boss had invited to his New York wedding. Rooney recognized Ganci posing alone with Bono; he must have been Bono's best man. Catalano and his wife were there. So were Bonventre and Amato. It was an extraordinary bonanza, Rooney realized, an illustrated Mafia who's who. Ganci and his friends were tied to a Sicilian drug baron. Now, Rooney thought, if he could only get someone to identify all the people in those pictures. From the lookout he and other agents had been snapping hundreds of additional photographs of unidentified people outside Catalano's bakery. Many were innocent passersby or bakery customers. Others, Rooney felt, were undoubtedly bad guys. Sometimes the agents just photographed cars parked nearby on the street, hoping to tie them to people around Catalano. One day in September they snapped a picture of Catalano stepping out of a white Cadillac outside the bakery. The driver couldn't be seen, but the license plate could. When the agents ran the tag, it turned up Francesco Polizzi of Belleville, New Jersey. Who was Polizzi?

In addition to the pen register printouts, Russo and Paquette had been going over phone tolls, the long-distance telephone records subpoenaed from the telephone company. They were still dealing with Ma Bell; the court-ordered breakup of the nationwide communications monopoly had not yet taken effect. Kallstrom dreaded the day the bureau might have to deal with a half dozen competing phone companies whenever it needed to subpoena toll records or install wiretaps.

Paquette found that Frank Castronovo, the New Jersey restaurateur surveilled during some of the cash deliveries to Third Avenue, had made calls to an iron factory and relatives in Bagheria, Sicily, in 1980. There were calls from his Roma restaurant to a New Jersey pizzeria operated by a Salvatore Greco and calls from Castronovo's restaurant partner, Gaetano Mazzara, to pizzerias in Philadelphia. There were calls from Roma to Ganci and to Amendolito's Overseas Business Services. And to an Onofrio Catalano, another cousin of Sal and brother of Saca Catalano's, who turned out to be the rugged-faced man with the black bag whom Castronovo had driven to the Horn & Hardart building in November 1980 when Paquette first learned of the money deliveries. Three Catalanos, two of them Sal! Russo marveled.

With the additional phone tolls on the people who were coming up in the pen registers and surveillances, Rooney and Russo soon accumulated boxes of file cards listing all the telephone numbers they had found. Other agents in the Queens office were starting to shake their heads. Who knew what those two were doing anymore? Did they know themselves? Maybe, some of the others were beginning to whisper, they were just spinning their wheels. But you couldn't argue with Russo; he took things personally—especially anything involving Sicilians, an area in which he regarded himself, with some justification, as an expert. Carmela, too, suffered through her husband's bouts of moodiness, which Carmine tried to work off kicking around a soccer ball with their four sons. She was seeing less and less of him at home.

Rooney seemed unflappable. At least he rarely permitted his frustrations to show. He, too, was married. His sandy-haired wife, Jane, a policeman's daughter, had been a typist at the FBI office when she met Charlie, then a part-time FBI clerk going to school at Fordham. They dated for two years while he finished school, then married and moved into a $160-a-month apartment in Flatlands, Brooklyn, suited to a new agent's $18,000-a-year salary. Now, at the end of 1981, they had moved into a small, black-shuttered Colonial house on Long Island and had a boy and a girl, five and three. Weekends, if he didn't drive in to the office, Rooney looked for distractions. He was putting an addition on the house, supervising and sometimes helping the contractors. After all the mental strain of trying to piece together the growing piles of names and numbers, it was a relief to do something with his hands. He especially liked to drive out to the rail museum in Riverhead and tinker with the steam locomotive he and other rail fans were trying to restore. For buffs like Rooney, the great trains had never lost their allure. But Jane was unhappy competing with a locomotive. Sharing a husband with the FBI was bad enough. When the case left him free time, Jane felt Charlie should spend it at home. "Get to know your kids!" she would say.

The issue was becoming moot. There was less and less free time to spend anywhere. Jane threatened to hang up a photograph of Charlie with a sign for the children: "This is your father."

Now that Pistone had time to sit down with them and brief them on doings inside the Bonanno family, Rooney and Russo had gone back to old surveillance files and had made a surprising find—photos taken by FBI teams from an apartment across from the Bonannos' Toyland Social Club on Hester Street over nearly a year, starting in March 1977. There were shots of Pistone in his undercover role of Donnie Brasco—whom the surveillance agents at the time took for just another ambitious Bonanno hood—and of Pistone's first mob mentor and later his nemesis, the psychotically violent Anthony Mirra. Photos showed Mirra joking outside the club with Catalano and Bonventre and giving a handshake and kiss to Catalano. Ganci was also in some of the pictures. At the time the photos were taken, the FBI had only the vaguest idea who these subjects were. Since then Pistone had provided Russo and Rooney a rundown of his encounters with the "Zips," but Catalano remained a shadowy figure. Pistone had heard his name as "Tato" and other variations of "Toto," leaving Rooney to wonder if they were talking about the same guy. But the Catalano they had been following was clearly the heavyset, laughing man in the plaid open-necked shirt and gold chain and medallion photographed outside Toyland in 1977 with Bonventre and Mirra. The case was coming together. The bureau had given the Bonanno family investigations the code name of Genus, the Latin word for "family." The Catalano case now got a subtitle. Officially it was now called Genus: Cattails— the Bonanno family and the tales of Catalano.

In April 1981 Bonventre and Amato each began serving a year's sentence in the Nassau County jail for carrying the illegal guns found in their car when they were stopped nearly two years earlier in the Green Acres shopping center, shortly before the Galante killing. By Thanksgiving, after serving eight months, the two had been released. Russo and Rooney made a point of waiting for them outside the jail with subpoenas for their appearance before a grand jury investigating the killing of the three Bonanno captains that May. Russo didn't expect them to say much, but he wanted them to know he was watching them.

"Have a good time on Thirteenth Avenue," he said.

"Thanks," said Bonventre, impassive. He stepped into the car his wife had brought and sped her to a motel in Sheepshead Bay as the surveillance agents followed. Russo shook his head. A piece of work, that Cesare.

As Bonventre and Amato were freed to rejoin their comrades and varied business interests, a crucial transfer was under way in the ranks of the FBI. Francis J. Storey was moved from the Philadelphia office to New York. A former part-time FBI clerk like Rooney, the Spartan Storey had studied accounting and made his way up the bureau ladder to organized crime supervisor in Philadelphia when he was named in November 1981 assistant special agent in charge of the three organized crime squads at New York district headquarters and the regional offices in New Rochelle and Queens, where Rooney and Russo worked. The three OC squads were a throwback to the earlier semiautonomy of the regional offices, and Storey, whose mind was as tidy as the button-down shirts and dark suits he favored, wondered how much sense it made to splinter the bureau's OC work that way, but what did he know? He was a newcomer. As such, though, he had one advantage in approaching the Cattails investigation he learned was going on in Queens under Rooney and Russo: He knew absolutely nothing about it. He could start fresh.

Rooney tried to explain the investigation to him with some charts in Paquette's office in New Rochelle one day. It looked amazingly complicated, but Storey thought it seemed to boil down to some kind of Mafia heroin ring. What else could generate such mountains of money?

"Are you working on Title Threes?" Storey asked.

Rooney knew about wiretaps but wasn't sure if they had enough probable cause to convince a judge to permit telephone eavesdropping.

Storey rolled his eyes. "You guys just don't have enough experience with Title Threes," he said, perhaps a little too sharply. Rooney and Paquette might have resented that, he realized. Well, it was the truth, wasn't it? "If you're not working on getting Title Threes, you're spinning your wheels," he said. "You could follow these guys around forever and not know what the hell they were doing. You have an informant?"

Aside from Pistone, who had little to do with Catalano and the other Sicilians, they had no one feeding them information from inside, Rooney admitted.

That was tough, Storey thought. An informant's account that can be corroborated, at least in part by surveillance, could often establish enough probable cause for a Title III interception, especially under the doctrine of "dynamic probable cause" that judges were increasingly accepting. In this approach, the government, lacking clear-cut evidence of hard-to-prove conspiracies, strung together bits and pieces of informant accounts, surveillances, and other intelligence to document an otherwise elusive conspiracy. Often it was sufficient to make a case for a wiretap. These agents, Storey thought, weren't close to that. They had come in in the middle. It would have been a lot easier if an informant had come forward in the first place with a tip that Ganci was coming to the United States to set up a heroin transfer. Then they could have tailed him from the beginning. But Ganci was already here, and this thing, whatever it was, was in full swing. It had to be traced backward.

"This case ain't gonna work this way," Storey told them. "You're going off in ten different directions at once. Time out, guys." They had to start gathering probable cause for a Title III, he said.

Next, Storey checked in with the DEA. Maybe it knew something about these Sicilians. To his surprise, it had nothing. Like Russo, Rooney, and Paquette, and everyone else before him, Storey found himself wondering, Who are these guys, and why don't we have anything on them?

This Storey comes on pretty strong, thought Paquette. He might be right about the Title III's, but for now, Paquette thought, he had a money trail to follow. He had still not tracked down Amendolito, but he didn't need him to figure out that the money was undoubtedly destined for Swiss bank accounts.

As slow as it had been to acknowledge the Mafia itself, the federal government was equally lax in catching on to the mob's money laundering, the science of disguising the origins of dirty money that Lucky Luciano's demonically brilliant disciple Meyer Lansky had pioneered in the 1930's. The tax evasion conviction of Al Capone by Eliot Ness and his Untouchables in 1931 had impressed the Mafia with the need for a more secure refuge for their billions. Lansky devised a network of money couriers and secret bank accounts that was serving the mob more than half a century later. He perfected the use of the loan-back to launder criminal funds. The money was secretly deposited in Swiss accounts or offshore banking centers and then "loaned" to mob enterprises in the United States. Suddenly the orphan dollars had a pedigree.

It was not until the late 1960's that the federal government recognized the laundering problem, but enforcement was fragmented among a dizzying profusion of agencies, among them: the Comptroller of the Currency, the Federal Reserve System, the IRS, Customs, the Securities and Exchange Commission, and the Federal Home Loan Bank Board. Although the Treasury Department was responsible for coordinating the efforts, it was little wonder that the government lacked a comprehensive strategy of attack.

Meanwhile, the profits of the richest racket in history were adding to a growing pool of "hot money" that started ricocheting around the globe in the 1970's, destabilizing world financial markets and creating an intriguing monetary mystery: Each year the nations of the world were exporting some $100 billion more in capital than they received. Ideally, for each nation's capital export, there had to be an import by some other nation. But here was the global financial system running a balance of payments deficit with itself. The lost capital wasn't going to the moon. Obviously there was money being received and not officially recorded. Not all the volatile hot money stemmed from criminal enterprises. Some of it was legally earned and then hidden as "black" capital for purposes of tax evasion or speculation. Still, federal estimates in the early eighties put the total of illegal drug money earned in the United States each year at $50–$75 billion, of which $5–$15 billion was said to find its way into international financial channels. These were the channels for which Paquette was now hunting.

In June 1981 he had worked up a trip to Switzerland to run down a lead on the destination of the money delivered to 655 Third Avenue. Paquette's informant had named a Zurich financial counselor as the recipient of some of the funds in Switzerland. There were also several Swiss phone numbers Paquette wanted to trace. The Swiss were not known for their cooperation when it came to exposing their bank customers. The rigid Swiss bank secrecy statutes, in fact, had long been the bane of investigators like Paquette. But a subtle shift was taking place. The Swiss were growing increasingly disenchanted with their image as bankers for the Mafia, callous custodians of billion-dollar fortunes built on the deadly narcotics addictions of hundreds of thousands of American—and now, increasingly, European—young people. Besides, tainted Mafia money represented only a small portion of the capital flowing into Swiss accounts; it could be eliminated without a serious impact on the banking economy. For the first time American investigators found the Swiss receptive to their inquiries.

"Hey, Bobby, what European spa are you touring now?" Paquette took a ribbing for his trip to Switzerland. Some envious agents saw it as a boondoggle. Some boondoggle. Everything went wrong. The flight out of JFK was delayed just long enough so that he missed his connecting flight in Paris. There was a six-hour layover until the next flight to Zurich, where he scrambled for the train to the Swiss capital. All told, the trip to Bern took twenty-seven hours. He flew coach, of course, and the cost of his hotel room consumed his modest FBI per diem allowance of eighty dollars. He ended up dipping into his own pocket to eat and travel around. It was worth it. In Paquette's presence the Swiss police interviewed the Zurich financial counselor, who revealed he had been recruited by a Swiss money mover named Adriano Corti of Cop Finance in Lugano. The Swiss agreed to look for him while Paquette returned home to dig up more leads. When he returned to Switzerland several months later, it was with the names and numbers that had turned up in Amendolito's phone book and telexes. One of the numbers in Lugano came back to Franco Della Torre. Paquette was at last on the money trail at the end of which loomed Leonardo Greco, Giuseppe Bono, and other drug overlords of the Sicilian Mafia.

It was a fateful breakthrough, for the storybook land of cuckoo clocks, snow-capped peaks, and chocolate was a nexus of the Mafia's money-drug network. But as was the case with Amendolito, the participant who would allow the FBI and DEA to piece this story together was, in 1981, a long way from surfacing.

He was Paul Waridel, a Turkish-born used-ship dealer and shady businessman who trafficked in protected Turkish archaeological treasures and, until he was caught, heroin. Waridel was a huge man, built, as an American prosecutor later described him, like a Norge refrigerator. Waridel grew up in Istanbul, where his father was an exporter of Turkish products, and as a twenty-two-year-old business graduate, he moved to Switzerland in 1963. His younger brother later became director of the Swiss social security system in Zurich. Waridel sold used ships out of Spain and Mexico and owned two computer agencies in Switzerland. In view of his interest in circumventing Turkish laws against export of highly prized Ottoman antiquities, it was perhaps inevitable that he would meet a far more expert smuggler and plunderer.

Yasar Musullulu was a mysterious Turkish shipowner who procured morphine base for Sicilian heroin producers, who then sold their product to traffickers, who in turn sold to the Badalamentis, the Catalanos, and the Gancis. Swarthy and powerfully built, with a curved nose and mustache, Musullulu, who also went by the names of Avni Karadurmus and Atilla Oksuz, was estimated to have provided up to seven thousand kilos—nearly eight tons—of the sticky opium distillate that the Mafia's chemists cooked into heroin, a quantity that by itself would have fed almost the entire American heroin habit for a year. At wholesale prices of $13,000 a kilo to the Sicilian traffickers, the volume represented sales of $91 million, of which Musullulu was said to have kept at least $57 million. Had all of it been made into heroin and been delivered, cut, and sold to addicts on the streets of America, it would have generated up to a staggering $28 billion. Musullulu obtained the morphine base from a Pakistani who shipped the product overland from Pakistan, Afghanistan, and Iran to Turkey and then by freighter to the Tyrrhenian Sea, where it was put aboard a speedboat for transfer to another vessel controlled by the Sicilians. Once they received it, smuggling it into Sicily became their responsibility. Musullulu guaranteed delivery of the morphine base in five-hundred-kilo lots to an area seventy sea miles from Sicily, around the island of Marettimo between Sardinia and Sicily, where an underwater transmitter had been installed. When one of Musullulu's ships passed over the transmitter, it triggered a signal, alerting a plane that would make a series of low passes over the freighter to verify the shipment prior to unloading.

Musullulu also knew ways of smuggling antiquities out of Turkey, an expertise that attracted Waridel to him. They met in Turkey in 1972 and became friendly. Musullulu confided that he had access to drugs seized by Bulgarian Customs. Several years later, in Rome, when one of Waridel's associates was looking for drugs, Waridel remembered Musullulu, and a deal was struck. But when Musullulu sent several kilos of heroin through the mails, it was traced to Waridel, who was arrested and convicted and spent from 1977 to 1980 in Rome's Regina Coeli Prison, then crowded with notorious dope traffickers and mafiosi, including Nunzio La Mattina, who learned that Waridel was a friend of Musullulu's.

After he got out of jail, La Mattina became one of Musullulu's best customers. The glowering Sicilian ex–cigarette smuggler had applied his skills to drug smuggling, selling morphine base to the Sicilian Mafia. La Mattina sold Musullulu's raw material so fast, in fact, that he had run up an $11 million debt with the Turkish shipowner. Musullulu insisted that he pay up, but La Mattina protested that he was waiting for his customers to pay him. They were stalemated. Then La Mattina remembered his former prison mate Swiss businessman Paul Waridel. Perhaps Waridel could intervene with his old friend Musullulu.

When Waridel was released from prison in Rome in 1980, he was met by La

Mattina, who confided he needed Waridel's help to break the stalemate. Waridel tried, but Musullulu would not budge. Not long afterward La Mattina was murdered. He had reported that one of his couriers lost $1.3 million in a holdup, but his associates doubted his word; they suspected La Mattina of stealing the money and killed him.

Waridel and Musullulu kept in touch. One day in 1982, when both men were in Zurich, Musullulu summoned Waridel. "I have someone in my office," said the Turk. "I need a Turkish interpreter." When Waridel arrived, he met Antonio Rotolo, also called Carlo, a fearsome dark-skinned Sicilian with a pencil-thin mustache, who was taking over from La Mattina.

Rotolo needed four hundred kilos of morphine base from Musullulu. At $13,000 a kilo, it came to $5.2 million plus La Mattina's remaining $11 million debt to Musullulu. How the money would be paid and the shipment delivered were matters that took more than twenty days of negotiation to resolve.

Two weeks later, on Good Friday 1982, Waridel found himself in his large Pontiac driving to Switzerland with one of Musullulu's relatives. They drove to an office in Lugano, where Waridel recognized Rotolo, among other Italians. Also present were Vito Roberto Palazzolo, an ostensible dealer in precious stones who invested drug profits for the Mafia, and another Swiss banker, Enrico Rossini.

Waridel's attention was immediately riveted on the center of the room. A long table supported two-foot-high stacks of twenties and fifties, wrapped in piles of $10,000 each. He was dumbfounded by the gigantic pile of cash being counted with the help of a money-counting machine. It came to $5 million.

The money was loaded into six large suitcases and heaved into the trunk of Waridel's Pontiac, which Waridel drove to Musullulu's house in Zurich. Even Musullulu's relative was flabbergasted. He knew the money had come from accounts at the Pradeplatz Bank Verein in Munich. "Is this the Pradeplatz bank of the Mafia or what?" he asked Waridel.

Musullulu said nothing when the suitcases with the $5 million arrived. "Musullulu was a man who talked very little," Waridel recalled later, "the absolute necessary, and unless it was absolutely indispensable, he made no comment as to what he did."

Not long afterward Waridel accompanied Musullulu to Zurich to take delivery of another shipment of cash. They were waiting at a roadside when Rotolo and Palazzolo drove up with bags containing $3 million. Waridel helped Musullulu transport the money back to his office. Later the money was deposited and changed at the Pradeplatz Bank Verein in Zurich. Some days later there was a third delivery. Waridel and Musullulu were waiting in the parking lot of a hotel in Zurich when Rotolo drove up and handed Musullulu several bags containing

$2 million. There was one last delivery: Rotolo brought Musullulu fifteen Prade-platz Bank checks of $100,000 each.

Altogether, Waridel had helped collect $11 million owed to Musullulu by Rotolo. Some of the remainder, Musullulu later told Waridel, had been paid in the United States and then transferred into Switzerland through Bulgaria, where Musullulu had many contacts in banking and government.

Musullulu and the heroin traffickers of the Sicilian Mafia tried to move their hoards of millions as anonymously as possible, but out of necessity, as money launderer Amendolito knew well, there was no alternative to relying on the international banking community. When they did that, they inevitably left a trail —one that Paquette picked up in 1982.

On March 25, 1982, a few weeks before Paul Waridel's Good Friday trip to the bank in Lugano to watch the counting of Yasar Musullulu's $5 million, Louis E. Brown, regional director of security at Merrill Lynch headquarters in lower Manhattan, got a call from a supervisor in the commodity operations division.

"Lou," he said, "we have a customer who's coming in with a large deposit in small bills. We'd like you to provide security from his hotel into the office."

Brown had been an FBI agent for twenty-three years before retiring and going to work for the brokerage house. The request was highly unusual. Brown checked with another supervisor and was told it would be okay.

"Meet him at the Waldorf," Brown was told. "When you get there, call his room from the lobby. We'll call to tell him you're on your way."

"Who's the client?" Brown asked, curious.

"Franco Della Torre."

Brown picked up a colleague and headed uptown to the Waldorf. They called the room and were invited up to an expensive suite. The man who opened the door was in his forties, of medium height with dark hair. Oddly, Brown thought, he did not introduce himself. There was, in fact, no conversation whatsoever. Nor was there any sign of the deposit they were to escort. Then Della Torre pulled aside a thick curtain to reveal several hidden suitcases. They were extremely heavy, so Brown helped Della Torre lug them downstairs to a taxi. "Wow!" the cabby said, shaking his head, as the suitcases stowed in the trunk visibly lowered the rear end of the taxi. They drove in silence to Merrill Lynch's commodities office in the financial district, where they hauled the suitcases upstairs to the third-floor vault. The suitcases were opened, revealing stacks of fives, tens, and twenties. The amount totaled $1.31 million.

The next day Brown was again summoned to provide security for Della Torre and his suitcases. By this time Della Torre had moved out of the Waldorf and into the Parker Meridien. More suitcases were waiting. They decided that instead of carrying the bags to Merrill Lynch's offices, it would be safer to take the money directly to Bankers Trust, where Merrill Lynch maintained an account. Once again they dragged the heavy bags to a taxi, and once again the driver marveled at their weight.

"What's in the bags—gold?" he joked.

Della Torre said nothing.

"By the way," Brown asked in the taxi, "where's all this money coming from?"

"Real estate," said Della Torre.

Brown waited for the rest of the explanation. It didn't come. Della Torre was his usual reticent self, Brown thought. He didn't press it.

Merrill Lynch commodities representatives were waiting outside Bankers Trust when they arrived. Inside the bank, Brown noticed, Della Torre hung back when the bags were carried into the vault. Most clients insisted on accompanying their money into the vault to verify the count. Of course, Brown realized: the cameras. Della Torre did not want to be filmed.

This time there was $700,000.

Brown called the Parker Meridien to check on Della Torre. Yes, he was told, Della Torre was from Zurich. Brown took the further step of calling FBI friends to check the bona fides of Della Torre and the banking company he used, called Traex. As he later wrote in a memo to Merrill Lynch officials, "Reliable and confidential sources familiar with criminal and organized crime activity in the New York metropolitan area were contacted concerning Mr. Della Torre and Traex. Sources advised based on available background information they could furnish no information about either Mr. Della Torre or Traex."

Writing about himself and the other security officials who escorted Della Torre, Brown continued:

> For your information, it is the considered opinion of the investigators who participated in this activity that the transaction of business involving the transfer of extremely large sums of money in small denominations ($5, $10, $20) from an unidentified source is highly suspect. Although the investigators were nonchalantly informed by Mr. Della Torre that the funds were obtained through Traex real estate activities, the practice of conducting business in cash, particularly large amounts, is highly questionable.

Nevertheless, Merrill Lynch rode shotgun for two additional large deposits of small bills by Della Torre, on April 22, when he brought in $500,000, and on April 23, when he brought in $1.4 million.

At some point during the pickups, Brown became highly suspicious. He called the Merrill Lynch manager in Zurich, where Della Torre's bank, Traex, was based. According to Brown, the manager of the Lugano office assured him that "the principal of Traex, a personal friend of his, is an honest and reputable individual. He said the Traex Company is a firm that has holdings and is well-known throughout the world. He said those transactions are legitimate transactions of which he was well aware of."

In fact, according to Waridel, Rossini had just been present with Musullulu in Lugano when $5 million in drug profits was counted on a table and that Rossini, like many bankers in Lugano, had gotten used to receiving and depositing suitcases of cash from all over the world without asking embarrassing questions.

Even if Brown had been told that Della Torre's partner was an ostensible gem dealer named Vito Roberto Palazzolo, it would have meant little—unless Palazzolo could have been identified at that point as a leading money launderer for Leonardo Greco and the Sicilian Mafia. One of those bringing in money to Traex, in fact, was Greco's iron factory manager, Oliviero Tognoli, who earlier had had such frustrating dealings with Amendolito.

Brown was increasingly troubled by the way Della Torre had kept the suitcases stashed behind the curtains and by Della Torre's practice, when the deposit count was short, of extracting a large roll of bills from his pocket and casually making up the difference.

Merrill Lynch closed the Traex account in April. Traex asked the officials to reconsider. On July 8, 1982 Merrill Lynch attorney Donald Gershuny and credit manager Joseph Schmidt met in New York with Rossini and Merrill Lynch's Lugano manager "to discuss future business possibilities, particularly involving large cash shipments," as Gershuny's internal company cable put it.

According to the cable, Rossini identified Franco Della Torre as a customer of Traex, and not an employee of the company.

Merrill Lynch realized they had been transacting business against stated policy by taking deposits from clients of Traex rather than employees of Traex. Ordinarily they wouldn't even take deposits by check from Della Torre. *And he's bringing in suspect cash?* "Such pretty much forecloses our even meeting with Della Torre should he show up here next week as was mentioned," Gershuny cabled.

Rossini was not easily put off and asked if Merrill Lynch would reconsider if he would deposit $25 million in cash.

Schmidt advised Rossini that Merrill Lynch was simply not prepared to accept large cash payments.

Rossini asked if their answer would be different if he deposited $50 million.

Again, Merrill Lynch stated that they did not want cash.

Gershuny didn't rule out future dealing with Traex if the Lugano office was satisfied with Traex's operations and reputation and didn't use Merrill Lynch's name. If Lugano only dealt with Traex personnel and not its customers Traex might continue to remain an acceptable customer "subject of course to credit arrangements." But the relationship between the two firms was never reestablished.

Brown later heard that Rossini and Della Torre shifted their account to E. F. Hutton. There was an external frauds committee of industry security officials who exchange information about common problems. Brown called a counterpart at Hutton and told him of Merrill Lynch's experience with Della Torre. It was the last that Brown or Merrill Lynch had to do with Della Torre.

"Bobby, we got a hit!"

It was October 1982, and Mike Fahy of Customs was calling Paquette. In March he had passed on to Fahy the names found in Amendolito's address book provided by one of the money launderer's disgruntled ex-employees. Fahy had stored the names in the computers of the Financial Law Enforcement Center (FLEC) that recorded bank transactions of $10,000 or more or currency imports or exports of $5,000 and above—provided the individuals involved in the financial dealings had filed the requisite forms. Some money launderers and couriers did, to avoid the federal criminal penalties for nondisclosure. Now half a year later the computer paired one of Paquette's names with a transaction.

"Who turned up?" asked Paquette.

"Some guy named Franco Della Torre."

Della Torre's disclosure forms showed $17 million in transactions through Merrill Lynch and E. F. Hutton between March and late September 1982. On October 4 Paquette rushed down from New Rochelle to Merrill Lynch's headquarters near the World Trade Center. Ex-Agent Lou Brown said Merrill Lynch was prepared to cooperate, although Paquette said a subpoena for the account records would be duly served. Brown related the story of the four Della Torre cash deposits totaling nearly $4 million, and he was happy to advise the FBI that Merrill Lynch had terminated the relationship "due to the questionable nature of the cash transactions."

Later that day Paquette called Hutton's chief of security, Bill Condon, and explained the sensitive nature of the investigation. Paquette was shortly called back by one of Hutton's assistant counsels, Loren Schecter, who said he understood the situation and pledged Hutton's cooperation. He said that Della Torre's accounts were still open and that he expected additional deposits shortly.

Schecter said Della Torre was not in New York now but was expected shortly and that he would let Paquette know of Della Torre's next contact. Within the next few days, as he had promised, Paquette served subpoenas on Merrill Lynch and Hutton for their records.

When Paquette failed to hear from Hutton again, he went back to Schecter. The agent later described the meeting: "Has Della Torre surfaced yet?" he asked. The lawyer had trouble meeting Paquette's gaze. "The accounts have been closed," Schecter said.

"Closed?" Paquette was dumbfounded. "How? Why?"

"The clients were notified in Switzerland."

Paquette slumped back in his seat. He had been counting on finally catching up with Della Torre and tailing the elusive money launderer to his Mafia contacts in America.

According to Paquette, Schecter then referred further questions to Thomas Rae, an executive vice-president and general counsel of Hutton. Paquette recalled later that Rae confirmed that he had ordered the closing of Della Torre's accounts and had told Hutton's office in Lugano of the FBI inquiry. The manager in Lugano had then informed the account holder, Vito Roberto Palazzolo.

That was the worst news of all. Paquette was stunned.

"You told him?" Paquette repeated, struggling to master his rage. "Why?"

"It was a management decision," Rae said, according to Paquette. "Our employees could be endangered."

Paquette was furious, but he bit his tongue. "What if you went back to him to reinstitute the deliveries?" he ventured. "Maybe the relationship could be reconstructed." He was desperate to salvage this trail.

"No," said Rae, "I don't think so."

Paquette left the office spitting mad. But his fury paled beside that of the assistant U.S. attorney to whom he reported the episode. Louis Freeh was a former FBI agent who earlier in 1982 had prosecuted the government's case against Lefty Ruggiero and the other Bonanno members exposed by Joe Pistone. Freeh was one of the government's toughest investigators, a ramrod-straight and ferocious crusader against the mob who had been named to work with the FBI on the Catalano and money-laundering investigations. He was then thirty-two and already enjoyed a reputation as an investigative genius. A Jersey City–born son of a real estate broker from Brooklyn, Freeh had studied criminal law at New York University and had spent five years in the FBI, where he had helped run its large waterfront investigation, before becoming a prosecutor in the Southern District. Paquette's account sent Freeh into a tirade against Hutton.

What had happened became clear only after Della Torre's arrest in November

1984 and his questioning by American prosecutors and defense lawyers in Switzerland the following June. Della Torre told them that in the fall of 1982 Hutton had warned his partner, Vito Roberto Palazzolo, the money launderer for the Sicilian Mafia, that the FBI had shown an interest in their accounts at Hutton, whereupon, Della Torre said, he stopped going to the United States. To thank him for lending him his time, Della Torre testified that he presented another Hutton executive, Arnold Phelan, with an $8,000 gold Rolex watch from Cartier.

Paquette was exhausted. The trail had vanished with Hutton's tip-off to Della Torre. Who had expected Hutton to rat them out? Paquette had lost months, maybe a year of work hunting Della Torre, although Amendolito's phone tolls provided many other leads. In addition to calls from his office at 575 Madison Avenue, he had charged calls from Miami and Utah, providing new clues to his possible whereabouts. The calls went to Frank Castronovo of the Roma restaurant and to numbers in Italy, where the police traced them to Salvatore Miniati and Oliviero Tognoli, Amendolito's connections to Sicilian Mafia boss Greco, although this was the first Russo or Paquette had heard their names. There was a risk now that Hutton's tip-off could blow the entire case.

There was one bright spot. In the middle of his investigation of the cash deliveries by Catalano and his associates, Paquette had been named case agent in another hot inquiry. On April 12, 1982, three CBS technicians were shot to death when they happened onto the roof of a West Side garage during the abduction of a diamond company bookkeeper, who was also later found slain. The shocking murders were a bizarre mystery, but the police soon came up with a suspect who had been parking a van in the garage. Paquette had the plate number run through OCIS. To his astonishment, the van had been spotted the month before the murders during one of Rooney's surveillances of a Queens bakery owned by an associate of Catalano and Ganci. It turned out that the van's owner had nothing to do with Catalano—he was stalking the bookkeeper near her home prior to killing her to cover up fraud at the diamond company. The fortuitous FBI surveillance of the van was a crucial bit of evidence tying the suspected killer to his victim.

Gratifying as the solution to that case was to Paquette, it didn't help him find Della Torre. Now, at the end of 1982, more than two years after his first tip on the cash deliveries, Paquette was trying to pick up Della Torre's lost trail. For lack of a better idea, he went from hotel to hotel to see whether Della Torre had stayed at any of them as a guest. So far he was coming up dry. In desperation, Paquette subpoenaed American Express Company records to see whether Della Torre showed up as a cardholder. He did. Card receipts showed, in fact, that Della Torre had stayed at the Waldorf, the Sheraton Centre, the Vista, the

Barbizon Plaza, and the Parker Meridien in New York City, as well as hotels in Palm Beach. Paquette hadn't checked those yet. He was elated. He would hit them one by one.

Paquette gazed at the deep cranberry rug and pink Art Deco ceiling of the Waldorf's sumptuous lobby. Behind him the tall 1893 clock sounded the quarter hour with resonant Westminster chimes. In Peacock Alley off the lobby, men in dark suits and women in furs murmured over drinks against the floral murals. When the manager appeared, Paquette asked about Della Torre. In the office the manager found that Della Torre had been a frequent guest that year; a signature card for charges to his room was on file. Adriano Corti, the Swiss money mover whose trail Paquette had been following in Switzerland, had also turned up at the Waldorf in January 1981. Paquette retrieved copies of their room bills. Records of their phone calls were there, too, Paquette saw with mounting excitement. With the help of the Swiss police, he traced one of Della Torre's calls to a hotel guest in Lugano—Vito Roberto Palazzolo. There were other calls to New Jersey numbers the FBI traced to the New Jersey pizza man Salvatore Greco, whose name had come up before in calls from Francesco Castronovo. And there were still other calls to a Pennsylvania and New Jersey pizza man named Filippo Salamone.

Each hotel Paquette visited yielded a similar bonanza of Della Torre phone records. The calls meshed dramatically with phone numbers turned up by the pen registers. There were calls between the Roma restaurant and its partners, Frank Castronovo and Gaetano Mazzara, Sal Greco's pizzeria, Giuseppe Ganci's house and pizzeria, and Filippo Salamone's home and pizzeria. And when Salamone's phone records were pulled, they showed calls to Vito Roberto Palazzolo at a number in West Germany.

The money trail had heated up again.

9

A world away in the teeming megalopolis of São Paulo, Brazil, Tommaso Buscetta, who had watched the Mafia begin to devour itself in Sicily, was about to embark on the last leg of his fateful odyssey, which would intersect the lives of the men Paquette, Rooney, and Russo were tracking in New York. Buscetta had been arrested in São Paulo in November 1972, about a month after the roundup of the French Connection Corsicans. Guglielmo Casalini, whom Buscetta thought was a Brazilian police officer, turned out to be a wanted drug trafficker. Police who searched his house found a book mentioning Buscetta, with many of the references to him underlined. Buscetta was then quickly rounded up with his sons Antonio and Benedetto.

He insisted he had nothing to tell the Brazilian military police about drug trafficking. But they were convinced he was a dangerous Sicilian mafioso and were determined to extract his secrets. He was given electric shocks on his genitals, anus, teeth, and ears, and the nails of his big toes were pulled out. Other times he was hooded and tied to a stake in the blazing sun. He kept silent. In December 1972 he was expelled to Italy, where he was promptly jailed on his 1963 conviction for Mafia association. To his surprise, Buscetta arrived in Ucciardone Prison with a fearsome reputation and the aura of a big-time drug trafficker and ruthless

Mafia boss. He attributed the myth, as he called it, to his "strong and proud personality" and to a naturally reserved nature that his fellow inmates, who ran the prison as a preserve of the Mafia, took as sure signs of Mafia power. The more he sought to dispel the aura, Buscetta found, the more it grew. He protested his innocence, and his jail mates laughed knowingly.

Yet for all his prestige, Buscetta felt abandoned by his Mafia family and its boss, Pippo Calò, whose spreading power was masked by a mild, clerklike appearance. It was customary for a boss to provide for a jailed family member. Buscetta complained Calò took no interest in his case. A generous fellow inmate who was not even a mafioso volunteered to provide Buscetta's wife, Cristina, with a $1,000 monthly stipend. Buscetta heard that Calò had expelled him from the family for having left his first wife, Melchiorra, to live with Vera and then Cristina. Buscetta could hardly believe it. But when Badalamenti joined Buscetta in Ucciardone for a brief prison stay, the Cinisi boss confirmed it. Through intermediaries Buscetta sought an explanation from Calò, who denied that he had expelled Buscetta and sent back word that Badalamenti was "overly dramatizing." Later, when Buscetta confronted him personally, Calò said it was all a mistake and that Badalamenti was a "pessimist." But it rankled, the more so because Buscetta had originally nominated Calò as a Mafia member after Calò had distinguished himself by wounding his own father's murderer.

With less than a year to serve, Buscetta was transferred to a halfway house in Turin. As the time of his release approached, the police stepped up their surveillance, suspecting that Buscetta was preparing to resume his criminal career. For his part, Buscetta felt the authorities were looking for a pretext to pin new charges on him. Finally he appealed to the parole judge. "Your Honor," he said, "these men are always in plain clothes. I don't know what service they represent or what they are looking for. But please, Your Honor, stop them from harassing me."

The judge shrugged. "I cannot stop the police from carrying out their investigation," he said. "Besides," he added, "I ordered them to."

The climate in Turin had turned stifling. Buscetta decided it was time to leave. By mid-1980 he had spent nearly eight years in Italian prisons and was ready to claim his freedom, even if the state was not quite ready to hand it to him. One night he did not return to his halfway house. "Somewhat reluctantly," as he put it later, "I left the city before my time was up."

In early June 1980 the AWOL Buscetta headed first for Palermo and his son Antonio's apartment. He moved carefully, largely restricting his travels through the city to the afternoon hours between one-thirty and four, when, everyone knew, it was hardest to find a policeman in Palermo. Buscetta was astounded by the changes in the Sicilian capital. All his old associates seemed suddenly to have grown rich on tobacco smuggling and heroin trafficking. Calò, too, had grown wealthy and established a strong power base in Rome. Officially he ran a butcher shop, but he had amassed a fortune in the drug trade and invested the funds in legitimate enterprises. He was also rumored to have gotten involved in kidnappings. An emissary from Calò contacted him and arranged a meeting in Rome.

Calò could see Buscetta's displeasure. "I did not send you money, Tommaso, because I thought you were well provided for," he insisted. Besides, he said, the Palermo districts had been reorganized. There would be fat profits for everyone now. And, he said, "you will no longer have to deal through the *capodecina*. You will be reporting directly to me."

Buscetta was unconvinced. Deadly intrigues and confusion were taking their toll on La Cosa Nostra. It was not the world Buscetta had left. He felt betrayed. There were new grounds for estrangement. Calò warned Buscetta that his son Antonio was paying for groceries with bad checks. Buscetta summoned Antonio, who admitted that he was in such dire financial straits he had even begun to pawn his wife's jewelry. Whereupon Calò presented Antonio with a wad of lire totaling about $10,000, saying it was for his birthday. When Antonio used the money to redeem his pawned jewels, the bills turned out to be on a list of money paid for kidnapping ransom, and Antonio was arrested as an accomplice. An angry Buscetta confronted Calò, who contended that the tainted bills must have come from tobacco smuggling and promised to underwrite Antonio's legal expenses.

Calò urged Buscetta to settle in Rome, where the Sicilian boss spent much of his time. "I will put a house at your disposal. Your children can go to school here," he said. Buscetta wondered why Calò was courting him so assiduously. He decided it had to do with the growing strife against the Corleonesi and Calò's need of an ally. What the Mafia boss told him next confirmed it.

"Bontade is behaving very badly," he told Buscetta. "He has allied himself with Salvatore Inzerillo, who is a child. He had Gaetano Costa killed without orders from the commission." Buscetta resisted being drawn in. "Listen to me," he told Calò, "you must meet with Bontade and Inzerillo. You must resolve this before it consumes all of you."

Back in Palermo from his visit to Calò in Rome, Buscetta met first with Bontade, who confirmed that Inzerillo had killed the prosecutor Costa to demonstrate his autonomy from the commission and to protest, in a bizarre way, his rivals' killing of police captain Basile. Bontade, the boss of the Santa Maria di Gesù family, also readily admitted plotting to kill Salvatore Riina at a meeting of the commission.

"Believe me, Tommaso," Bontade said. "This is the only way I can avoid getting crushed myself." Antonio Salamone, boss of the San Giuseppe Iato family, had agreed to support him before the commission, after Riina of the Corleonesi was dead, Bontade said.

"What about Calò?" Buscetta asked. Where did his own Porta Nuova family boss stand in all this?

"He is completely dominated by the Corleonesi and Michele Greco," Bontade said. "When they give their views, Calò doesn't even say anything. He just nods his approval."

Suddenly Buscetta felt overwhelmed with disgust and exhaustion. "Ahhh," he told Bontade, "you are lost."

As a parting gesture Buscetta arranged a meeting in Rome between himself and Calò, Bontade, and Inzerillo. The four gathered at a highway snack bar, the Autogrill Pavesi, on the Naples-Rome autostrada just outside the capital. Truckers and travelers stopping for fuel or a *gelato* paid little heed to the Mafia quartet huddling in a corner. Prodded by Buscetta, the other three agreed to avoid an open break with the Corleonesi and to consult each other before taking matters to the commission.

In January Buscetta departed the Sicilian capital for Brazil traveling by car ferry to Calabria and driving on to Paris, where, using a false passport, he caught a flight to Rio, accompanied by his eldest son, Benedetto. Cristina, with their two small children, flew under her own name from Rome to Rio.

Buscetta remembered Brazil fondly. In 1951, when he had grown tired of Argentina, he had moved to Brazil, where he established a mirror factory called the Conca d'Oro in São Paulo. Twenty years later, when he was out on bail in New York and Italy requested his extradition, he fled to Brazil. Now, with his Brazilian wife, it beckoned him again. Buscetta's first task upon arriving was to drive across the border into Paraguay, where he purchased a new set of false documents identifying him as Tommaso Roberto Felice, the surname from his mother's first name. His own name was an acute embarrassment in Portuguese-speaking Brazil, where "Buscetta" was uncomfortably close to the slang word for vagina. Buscetta began managing a cattle farm owned by Cristina's father, Homero Guimarães.

After the savage conspiracies of Palermo, Brazil seemed idyllic. But bad news from home kept filtering through. Within a few months Buscetta learned of the ambush murder of Bontade on his birthday. Antonio Salamone of the San Guiseppe Iato family had also found refuge in Brazil, in San Pedro, a spa town an hour and a half south of São Paulo, and Buscetta sought him out for information.

Salamone told him that an associate of Bontade had learned Bontade would be spending the night at his country villa. The killers, alerted by walkie-talkies, were lying in wait nearby. They let his escort car pass and then shot him to death.

"I just telephoned Papa," Salamone said, referring to Michele Greco, the Corleonesi ally who was heading the Sicilian Mafia commission. "He told me he was very surprised about this murder and knew nothing about it.

"I also spoke with Inzerillo," Salamone went on. "He is convinced the crime was the work of the Corleonesi. He doesn't believe Greco's denials. He said it would be impossible for him not to know since a man from his family had tipped off the ambushers. Inzerillo also told me he was not afraid for himself because he still owed Riina payment for a fifty-kilo shipment of heroin."

It wasn't insurance enough. Two weeks later Inzerillo was murdered. Again Buscetta sought out Salamone, who said the newspapers ascribed the killings of Bontade and Inzerillo to a double cross of the Corleonesi over drugs. Buscetta scoffed. More likely, he told Salamone, the Corleonesi were spreading this story to sully their rivals. Then Salamone articulated a chilling thought. He reminded Buscetta of Bontade's plan to shoot Riina at a commission meeting. "You, I, and Inzerillo knew that Bontade intended to kill Riina," he said. Now Inzerillo and Bontade had been killed. He left the next sentence unspoken.

Buscetta dismissed the thought. "I knew nothing of the kind," he insisted. "And neither did you."

Salamone let it drop. "In any case," he said, "invited or not, I'm going to Palermo to find out what's what."

When he returned to Brazil after seeing Michele Greco, Salamone told Buscetta that the Corleonesi had arranged the killing of Bontade and Inzerillo even before learning of their plot to kill Riina. Afterward it became ex post facto justification for the murders. The plot had been revealed by a member of Bontade's family, who was rewarded by the Corleonesi in their own fashion. After taking his information, they abducted and killed him and his son.

There were disturbing signs that Buscetta, too, had drawn the ire of the Corleonesi. Buscetta called Calò, who urged Buscetta to return to Palermo, where Antonio Salamone happened to be visiting. Buscetta was disquieted by Calò's entreaties. Was it a trap? When Salamone returned to Brazil, he accused Buscetta of dangerously exposing him by telling Calò of their contacts in Brazil. Buscetta ridiculed Salamone's concerns, but he no longer trusted Calò. It was all becoming dangerously Byzantine.

Buscetta was happier than ever to be in Rio. The pleasure-driven life of a Carioca suited Buscetta and Cristina and their growing family. They had some friends, visited the beach where they had met, and let their sizzling love melt away their sorrows. Buscetta also spent long periods on the 62,000-acre Amazon ranch that was a land grant to his father-in-law, Homero Guimarães, from the

Brazilian government under a program to tame and cultivate the jungle. Gui-marães later transferred the land to him, Buscetta said. There may have been more to it, however. According to intelligence reports reaching the Brazilian police, Buscetta was still or again involved in the drug traffic, perhaps working with Salamone to smuggle Southeast Asian heroin into South America for trans-shipment to the United States. If so, the remote ranch on the Amazon would be a perfect cover, investigators felt. There were even reports that the elusive Buscetta had been spotted in Bangkok. The accounts, as always with Buscetta, remained unsubstantiated.

In August 1982 Buscetta's routine was jarringly interrupted by a phone call. The familiar Sicilian voice of Gaetano Badalamenti set Buscetta's stomach churn-ing.

Buscetta had never considered the Cinisi Mafia boss a particular friend, but as he later put it, "among evils, he was one of the best." His word could also be relied on, Buscetta reflected. When Badalamenti was expelled from the commis-sion for reasons Buscetta still did not understand, some told Buscetta he would be the gainer. "No," Buscetta replied, "I lost someone I could trust." Nonethe-less, he was not happy to hear Badalamenti's voice on the phone.

"I need to talk to you," Badalamenti said, as Buscetta later testified. "Can I come to Brazil?"

Buscetta paused. "Yes, of course," he said.

"I'll call you from the airport or the hotel," Badalamenti said. "Then you can pick me up."

Buscetta remembered Salamone's warning. The last time Buscetta saw the San Giuseppe Iato boss in San Pedro, Salamone said, "He will try to get in touch with you." Salamone had little use for Badalamenti, whom he knew from their days together on the commission. "Guaranteed," Salamone predicted, "he is only trouble, for all of us."

"But if he wants to come to Brazil," Buscetta reasoned, "how can I stop him?"

Several days later Badalamenti phoned that he had arrived in Belém, a jungle boom town in the Amazon delta where Buscetta had been ranching. Badalamenti seemed down on his luck, Buscetta thought with a twinge as he settled his visitor at the Regente, a comfortable, but less than super-deluxe, three-star hotel in the city.

Badalamenti quickly got to the point. "You must help us back home," he said. "Help—how?"

"You must come back to direct the revolt against the Corleonesi," Badala-menti went on, in Buscetta's recounting. "Only you with your influence can do it."

Buscetta saw through the flattery in Badalamenti's statements, but he knew the wily peasant was speaking the truth. He, Buscetta, had the influence. Who else could rally disaffected commission members against the Corleonesi? Certainly not Badalamenti. But getting involved with the murderous Corleonesi was the last thing on Buscetta's agenda.

The situation was irredeemably compromised, he knew. The Corleonesi were now indisputable masters of the Sicilian Mafia, having crushed opponents like Badalamenti. At least Badalamenti was alive. Perhaps he wouldn't be for long if the Corleonesi knew where he was. The thought suddenly alarmed Buscetta.

"Does anyone know you came here?" he asked Badalamenti.

"Are you mad?" Badalamenti replied. "Of course not."

Things were in a bad state at home, Badalamenti continued, trying to entice Buscetta into returning. Salamone had left a mess, he insisted, exposing many of their allies to the vendettas of the Corleonesi. After Bontade was killed, Badalamenti said, he had placed himself at Inzerillo's disposal to take revenge against their enemies, but Inzerillo had demurred. As for his murdered cousin Antonio Badalamenti, who had replaced him as regent of the Cinisi family, Badalamenti said he was convinced he had been killed on orders of the commission. There had been little love lost between the two cousins, but from Badalamenti's vantage point it had been better that Antonio rather than someone else had been named to head the Cinisi family after his ouster by the commission.

"I have another plan," Badalamenti said. "Can you kill Liggio?"

"Can I what?"

"Kill Liggio," repeated Baladamenti. "You made a lot of friends in the Ucciardone. Maybe someone from Catania or Milan would undertake this contract for the right price?"

Badalamenti was mad, Buscetta decided. He had not the slightest inclination to be drawn into a murder plot against the Corleonesi's most vicious boss. "Out of the question," he told Badalamenti.

Buscetta was nervous enough. During Badalamenti's visit Cristina's brother, Homero Guimarães, Jr., had disappeared. Things like that happened all the time in Sicily but not in Brazil.

Buscetta thought of his ranch. "You should stay here," he counseled Badalamenti. "Enough of this mayhem. Forget your hunger for revenge. Fighting is useless. Here you would be safe. You were born a peasant. This land suits you. Bring your relatives here and live in peace."

In the month that Badalamenti spent visiting Buscetta in Brazil, Buscetta showed him and his son Leonardo a ranch they could farm with the rest of their family, far from the terrors of the Corleonesi. Leonardo dismissed the idea with contempt. "I hate the climate," he said. "I could never live here."

On an evening in early September Buscetta, Badalamenti, and Leonardo were at the Hotel Regente watching television when the news carried the murder of General Dalla Chiesa in Palermo.

"You see," said Badalamenti. "This is the answer of the Corleonesi, their arrogance."

A few days later Buscetta called Palermo to speak to his son Antonio, who had recently been released from jail. Antonio's wife picked up the phone but she could hardly speak for crying.

"Antonio has disappeared," she wailed.

"When?"

"Two days ago—Saturday," she said. "I have heard nothing from him."

"Was he alone?" Buscetta asked.

"He was with Benedetto."

So, Buscetta thought, his heart pounding, two of his sons. "Go to the police," he said. "Maybe they have been arrested." When he called the next day, she told him the police knew nothing. Buscetta had been in the Mafia long enough to recognize a *lupara bianca* ("white shotgun")—a killing in which the victims' bodies are never found. Several days later Badalamenti, who was still in Brazil, visited with condolences.

"You see," he said, "how important it is for you to lead the revolt against the Corleonesi?"

Buscetta was sick. The suspicion gnawed at him: Was Badalamenti involved in this plot? "My sons are gone," he told Badalamenti. "My only hope is that now the Corleonesi will leave me in peace."

Badalamenti was loath to give up. "You can get back at Michele Greco," he suggested, "by arranging the disappearance of his son Giuseppe."

Buscetta was suddenly very weary. "What good would that do?" he said. "What does Giuseppe have to do with this? He is a harmless young man."

"Wrong," said Badalamenti. "He is *combinato*"—settled, inducted as a "man of honor."

"And?"

"And nothing," said Badalamenti.

Recent events were giving Buscetta the creeps. "Are you certain," he asked Badalamenti once more, "no one knew you were coming here?"

"Of course," Badalamenti said.

Buscetta soon had reason to think otherwise. After Badalamenti returned to Sicily in late 1982, having apparently given up hope of enlisting Buscetta in his war against the Corleonesi, Buscetta heard that the ousted Cinisi boss plotted his own assault on the Corleonesi. He laid an ambush for Pino Greco, the ferocious assassin and leader of the Corleonesi-aligned Ciaculli family, who had killed Bontade, Inzerillo, and Inzerillo's son and had tried to kill Contorno. But Greco escaped Badalamenti's revenge and unleashed a wave of counterterror. Before the end of 1982 Buscetta's son-in-law had been killed with two other relatives in the Palermo pizzeria that he had run with Buscetta's two missing sons. Within a few days Buscetta's brother Vincenzo and Vincenzo's son Benedetto were also killed.

Buscetta related the murders to the abortive plot against Greco, which Badalamenti had hinted of during his visit to Brazil. If Buscetta was telling the truth, he had taken no part in Badalamenti's vendetta, but the Corleonesi were making him pay for it anyway. It even crossed Buscetta's mind that Badalamenti may have engineered the attacks on his family as a devious way of turning Buscetta against the Corleonesi. It sickened Buscetta to think that someone who had once embraced his children might have plotted their murders. He had no way of confirming this, but he was more convinced than ever of the folly of getting drawn into Badalamenti's vendetta. The killing of his sons, he reflected later, "was nothing more than a sinister warning to me."

10

Tom Sheer sometimes thought he was in a jalopy, a '49 Hudson bomb with the brakes shot, flying downhill at seventy-five miles an hour. It was moving like a sonofabitch, it was going somewhere, but Sheer, a beefy ex-Marine who had just taken over the FBI's criminal division in New York, wasn't sure where the hell that was. It was August 1982, three years after Galante's retirement lunch at Joe and Mary's restaurant, and Sheer, a forty-six-year-old former college football guard with a flattened nose who bore a passing resemblance to the actor Albert Finney, had suddenly found himself catapulted into the leadership of half a dozen major organized crime cases, including one called Cattails that was rapidly becoming the most complex criminal investigation ever mounted by the FBI.

By now, Sheer learned, scores of agents in New York and New Jersey were tailing dozens of Sicilians, who were leading them to still more Sicilians turned up by the telephone pen registers. The next step would be to "go up on the wires," collect enough probable cause to turn the pen registers into full-fledged wiretaps so the FBI could start listening to the calls themselves. That would take dozens more agents, but aside from Rooney's partner, Carmine Russo, whom did Sheer know who spoke Sicilian? Maybe the DEA had some people. Trying to get a grip on this case, Sheer thought, was like trying to mold a cloud and stuff it into a bag. But whatever the hell it was, Sheer was now in charge of it. Not that he was complaining. He had asked for it. He had been inspecting the New York office as part of the bureau's rigorous internal affairs unit when he discovered that the directorship of the criminal division was available. He lobbied for it and got it.

For a onetime waif from the streets of Cleveland, it was a triumph to savor. His mother died when he was three, and his father, a mechanic, then left to join the Army, sending little Tommy to live with his mother's sister in Chagrin Falls, Ohio. He grew into a husky youth, a decent student with a flair for football that won him admission to the University of Florida, where he studied market research. In his senior year the football team, with Sheer playing guard, made it to the 1959 Gator Bowl but lost to Mississippi. That same year Sheer met his wife-to-be, Luisa, a petite, black-haired beauty. Sheer enlisted in the Marine Corps, and the couple settled down at Camp Pendleton, California, for what promised to be a quiet domestic tour. Instead, Sheer was almost immediately sent to a roving combat battalion off Okinawa. Back at Pendleton for his discharge from the Corps in 1962, Sheer ran into an FBI agent at the camp PX. An agent was what he really wanted to be, Sheer decided. Accepted in 1962 at Quantico, he was first sent to New Haven and then assigned to California for Spanish-language training in preparation for a longed-for posting to Lusia's native Puerto Rico. Instead, the bureau intercepted him en route in Denver, where Sheer stayed for a year before getting transferred to the bank robbery squad in New York, where he arrived in the midst of a chaotic New Year's transit strike and the upheavals of campus revolution, protest, and terrorism. Next, it was back to Washington for the auto theft and Indian affairs units. But three days after Sheer's assignment to what he bleakly assumed would be a dead-end job, a shoot-out between Indians and FBI agents on a lone western reservation at Wounded Knee thrust him into the center of the country's hottest investigation. Over the next seven years Sheer ricocheted through a half dozen more assignments in the FBI, including the inspection unit in Washington, transporting his dizzied wife and son, Sean, from city to city until mid-1982 when they landed once again in New York, where Rooney and other agents had been tracking a group of Sicilians driving around with cartons stuffed with money.

Sheer was astounded by the breadth of the investigation. Was this thing raging out of control? The criminal division in New York had 375 agents, 165 of them assigned to organized crime, and this was already beginning to consume a good percentage of the force.

He wondered about Rooney, who kept pushing this case. "Close your eyes and picture a 'rock 'em, sock 'em' FBI agent," Sheer joked. "Then you open your eyes, and there's Charlie Rooney. Not what you'd expected, is it?"

And Russo. Was he real? Sheer had never met anyone so straight. He couldn't even get Russo to stop calling him Mr. Sheer.

"Tom," he'd correct him.

"Yes, Mr. Sheer."

Often, over bottles of Heineken in a Greek restaurant across from the FBI Manhattan offices, Sheer and his OC assistant, Francis Storey—Frank to his colleagues—discussed the case.

"Tom," Storey said one day, leaning over the blond wood table, "this is the biggest thing I've ever seen."

"Where's it heading?" Sheer asked.

"I don't know," said Storey.

Sheer decided that something was cockeyed. Bureau operations were peculiarly duplicative. There was the headquarters office in the federal building at Foley Square, where he worked. There was the Brooklyn-Queens office on Queens Boulevard, where Rooney and Russo worked with other agents on the Cattails investigation. There was another satellite office in New Rochelle, where Paquette worked. Each of the three offices, it turned out, had its own organized crime unit, a legacy of the reorganization in the early 1970's, when the New York office moved downtown from East Sixty-ninth Street and the two regional offices were created to spread FBI coverage to the outer boroughs and suburbs. But did La Cosa Nostra also draw its lines at the East River and Bronx border? Ridiculous. *Hey, you Bonanno wise guys, you get back into Brooklyn where you belong!* Then why, thought Sheer, should the bureau?

The New York office lacked "program purity," Sheer decided. Lines of authority were muddled, as they were in the three OC squads. In his mind Sheer was always redrawing the office flow chart. Sheer loved charts. He could see a problem best when it was diagrammed on paper. "We've been case-oriented for too long," he told Storey, his eyes lighting up with a zeal his staff came to know as Sheer's trademark whenever he talked reorganization. By being case-oriented, Sheer decided, the bureau focused on one separate crime after another, missing the significant patterns that linked them. The office needed to become "problem-oriented" to address the criminal challenge properly. Sheer pondered a solution.

With the Swiss police helping Paquette trace some of his money launderers, American and Italian investigators, too, were closing ranks. The two nations had a history of sometimes prickly relations in law enforcement, stemming largely from their different legal systems, although the Americans also suspected, not without cause, that the Mafia had infiltrated the Italian government. Moreover, the Italian investigating magistrates combined the functions of judges and prosecutors and were akin, in their strictures of secrecy, to American grand juries. Thus American prosecutors often found themselves stymied in gaining access to the files of magistrates like Giovanni Falcone of Palermo, perhaps the Sicilian Mafia's most intractable foe. At the same time Italian magistrates had difficulty understanding American legal requirements of probable cause and considered it an insult to have to prove to American courts the need for evidence that the magistrates wanted obtained in America. But dedicated investigators on both sides of the Atlantic soon devised their own links to circumvent the bureaucracy. When the Italians were eager for the extradition of the mastermind underworld financier Michele Sindona, who was convicted of bank fraud in New York in 1980, they found an ally in a feisty and strikingly attractive Eastern District narcotics prosecutor and later federal judge, Reena Raggi. She, in turn, learned that if she wanted investigative material from Italy, she had to get it before it became an official part of the magistrate's record. She and a Milan magistrate regularly shared information in English and Italian. He would read her a document, and if she wanted it, he would put a copy aboard an Alitalia flight. She did the same for him via TWA.

Such collegiality became the norm in the 1980's as Italians and Americans embarked on a period of unprecedented law enforcement cooperation. Some of it was attributable to personal contacts between Attorney General William French Smith and Italian justice officials and to a new American-Italian extradition treaty fostering the exchange of arrested fugitives. But much of it had to do with stepped-up wars against the Mafia being waged on both sides of the Atlantic. The effort was particularly urgent in Italy, where police officials and judges were being targeted for assassination, an epidemic that had never spread to America. As nothing before, the killing of General Dalla Chiesa and his wife on a street off the Politeama sparked a popular outcry from citizens, Italian officials, and the Vatican against the sinister hand of the Mafia and the drug plague that was claiming an ever-higher toll all over Europe. "It may look like an operetta," said Judge Raggi, "but when people you know start ending up dead . . ."

In June 1982, two months before Sheer arrived in New York, Russo was dispatched to Italy to confer with his Italian counterparts. The idea of returning to his ancestral homeland representing the Justice Department of the United States of America filled Russo with unalloyed pride and patriotism. As the plane banked over the Ostia seacoast and approached Rome's Fiumicino airport, he couldn't stop thinking: *Here I am, a Sicilian bricklayer's son, coming back to represent my country. My country!* Russo's eyes filmed over with tears.

If Sheer could have seen him then, he undoubtedly would have brought Russo down to earth with a growl of mock disgust: "Chrissake, Russo! You're on the job! You can fuckin' well weep later on your own time!" But Sheer came to admire the sometimes corny Russo—as much admiration, anyway, as Sheer could summon up for a non-Marine. "That's not put on, that's real," Sheer would say of Russo, shaking his head in exaggerated disbelief.

Russo was in for a letdown in Rome. Although he brought the Italian police a two-inch-thick packet of information on the burgeoning American investigation, the Italians, he complained later, had mostly out-of-date material to give him in return. There was one revelation they did share, however: They confided to Russo that they had been tapping the phones of Giuseppe Bono's powdered milk company, Citam, in Milan and had uncovered a connection to drug trafficking and money laundering. The evidence linked Ganci, who had entertained Bono in Queens the year before and who had been the best man at his wedding in 1980, to one of Italy's most notorious Mafia drug kingpins.

Disappointed as Russo was with the results of his visit, the contacts between the Italians and Americans proliferated. In October 1982 law enforcement officials of both nations assembled at FBI headquarters at Quantico for a historic conference aimed at pooling some of their fast-growing intelligence on organized crime. Among those present was Judge Falcone, who, freed for once from his usual iron girdle of security guards, chased butterflies over the vast forested campus the FBI shared with the U.S. Marines. Another visitor was the Palermo magistrate Rocco Chinnici, who spoke so emotionally about the struggle to bring the Mafia to justice in his homeland that his eyes glistened with tears. Shortly after returning home, he was killed by a bomb.

Before the audience of Italian and American officials Russo and Paquette traced the case from the murder of Galante in 1979. Russo described the "miraculous" escape of Bonventre and Amato and their association with Catalano and Ganci, whom Pistone had identified as part of a hitherto unknown Sicilian affiliate of the Bonanno family. Paquette told how Castronovo and Catalano's cousin Onofrio had been spotted carrying cash to a money launderer and how the trail had led to Amendolito, Della Torre, Merrill Lynch, and E. F. Hutton. Paquette was still hunting for Della Torre.

Next, a short, fresh-faced blonde with a cheerleader's élan strode to the stage. She had chosen to wear a navy blue suit and tie to communicate authority and purpose, but inside, Mona Ewell was queasy with anxiety. No DEA analyst had ever addressed a gathering like this before.

The previous spring the DEA's Tom Tripodi had returned from Venezuela, bringing her a precious load of wiretaps implicating Canadian Mafia figures in drug-trafficking deals with Giuseppe Bono. Tripodi's information showed that in addition to Milan, Bono had established a presence in Venezuela, which was fast becoming a center of Mafia money laundering. A Philadelphia DEA investigation of a pizza chain had also traced some calls to Venezuela. Some of this material had been studied at a DEA and FBI conference in August. Ewell reviewed this material and added some especially fresh intelligence: The night before the Quantico conference she had learned that Antonio Salamone, the San Giuseppe Iato Mafia boss, was probably en route to the United States, to Texas or Las Vegas. He had been in touch with a woman called Maria Liguori in Los Angeles. The DEA had also overheard calls from Bono about a shipment of French lamps from Canada to the United States. An Italian who had packed the lamps in Italy was panicking because he had inadvertently dropped his ID badge into the container. Don't worry, he was assured, the people doing the unpacking in Port Newark would find it and remove it. The DEA and the Customs Service were convinced the conversation was about a shipment of drugs concealed in the lamps.

As she spoke, Ewell, to her crushing embarrassment, saw the Italians turning their backs and leaving the room. *I knew it,* she thought with shame, *I bored them.* Suddenly she realized that they were not walking out; they were running out—to the telephones to call Italy with the news. Maria Liguori was the wife of Michele Zaza, the head of the Camorra, Naples' own criminal brotherhood. Zaza was a former tobacco smuggler who, like the other bosses, had turned to drug trafficking when the market in contraband shifted. He was Antonio Salamone's godson and had been tied to a recently seized shipment of thirty kilos of heroin secreted in coffee machines.

The Quantico conference cemented relations with the Italians. Several weeks later, in the improved climate of cooperation, Russo was dispatched back to Rome and Palermo for follow-up discussions with Judge Falcone and a police supervisor, Gianni de Gennaro. This time Russo was blunter. "We need timely information, not stuff six months out of date," he insisted. When he returned home this time, it was with Italian wiretaps of Bono and Ganci and, for the first time, the surveillance pictures showing Ganci and Catalano in the Piazza Politeama in 1980. It was the meeting the Italians believed confirmed the plans for the forty-kilo heroin shipment that was seized shortly afterward in Milan.

Within three months the emotional roller coaster Russo was riding was to plummet once more, and he was to feel betrayed anew. The Italians suddenly issued 153 warrants for a wave of arrests of mafiosi across Italy. Russo felt sure that the action was based on the confidential information he had brought and that it would tip the hand of the FBI investigation in New York. A second St. Valentine's Day massacre, he raged, throwing down a cable reporting the raids and cursing in Sicilian. Rooney buried his head in his own work and pretended not to hear. "What are you going to do, Carmine?" Rooney finally soothed. "Relaxio."

But it was virtually impossible for Russo to "relaxio"—even off duty. One day in late 1982 the Russos, then expecting their fifth child, walked into their obstetrician's office in Brooklyn. There, sitting in the waiting room, was another expectant couple, Baldo Amato and his wife. They exchanged wan smiles.

"Hi, Mr. Russo, how're you?" asked Amato. He remembered how Russo had welcomed him upon his release from jail the year before.

"How's the deli doing?" asked Russo in return. The Amato family operated a deli on Second Avenue at Eighty-fourth Street in Manhattan. So far as the agents had been able to determine, it seemed to be a legitimate business.

"Oh, you know about that?" Amato sounded surprised. Was he flattered or nervous? Russo wondered.

Later, outside, Carmela asked, "Who was that couple you knew?"

Russo blanched. "A guy I know from work." He tried to sound casual. Carmela was nervous enough these days. She didn't have to know that they and one of the suspected killers of Galante shared the same obstetrician.

Back in the office, Russo wrote out a detailed report on the encounter. It was a good bet that Amato was under surveillance. How would it look for Russo to be photographed meeting him in some doctor's office?

One morning toward the end of 1982 Storey sat in Sheer's twenty-eighth-floor office with its panoramic view over the white-collar crime capital of the world. Sheer had his feet on the desk, his black brogues resting on strewn cables and reports.

Storey had a proposal. "Who's the best supervisor we have?" he asked Sheer rhetorically. "Schiliro," Storey continued. Lew Schiliro, a thirty-two-year-old native Brooklynite with a sinister-looking droopy mustache, was a lawyer and a shrewd and instinctive organized crime supervisor with a predilection for action that inspired his agents in Queens. "He's got a great squad, all three-hundred hitters," Storey went on. "Let's take Rooney and Russo and bleed them into Schiliro's squad." Storey was rolling now. "And Paquette, too, from New Rochelle. And Tommy Vinton from New Rochelle." Vinton was a fierce-eyed narcotics supervisor in New Rochelle who had worked with Schiliro in the past. Storey knew Sheer admired Vinton's organizational skills. Vinton was also an ex-Marine.

"We'll make Schiliro the squad supervisor," Storey went on. "It's a drug case,

so Schiliro will report to Vinton. Vinton," Storey concluded, "will report to me."
He saved the most important thing for last. "And we'll bring them all into
Manhattan to work right here."

Storey was exhilarated with his plan, which Sheer endorsed. But Storey was
not prepared for the backlash. "Storey is nuts," Schiliro decided. He doubted the
case was as big as Storey was making out. Maybe Storey's ego was affecting his
judgment.

The others were also disgusted. Their postings were generally rewards for their
seniority—the more time in the bureau, the more they could pick and choose
their assignments. Besides, Paquette was fond of his leisurely drive into New
Rochelle each morning from his home in Danbury, Connecticut. Now he had
to get up at four A.M. for the seventy-mile crawl through the nightmarish suburban commuter traffic into downtown Manhattan. Vinton was losing an even
closer commute into the New Rochelle office. Rooney, who lived thirty miles out
on Long Island, and Russo, who had since moved his growing family from
Bensonhurst to Staten Island, were similarly inconvenienced. They moped
around the new squad area in Manhattan. Some squad members who were pulled
in from Queens to Manhattan blamed Rooney and Russo for their fate. "They
want us to work their case," one complained. "They got nothing, they're blowing
smoke."

Sheer was understanding. "Let's give them some more time to adjust," he
urged Storey.

But Storey was getting fed up. "You're too indulgent," he told Sheer. Finally
Storey called the squad together in Queens. If they wanted to see him as the bad
guy, as an asshole, that was okay with him. He wasn't there to win a popularity
contest.

"Are you the agents I thought you were?" he began. "Then cut the bullshit!
You guys got to take that hill. Some of you think you already proved yourselves,
you already took one hill. Well, behind each hill is another hill. Some of you are
asking, 'How can I get out of this?' You can't. There's no way out. The only way
out is to solve this case. That's the way out. Now stop the bitching."

Paquette tried to strike a bargain. "After this," he asked, "can I put in for an
OP in New Haven?" OP was office of preference.

Storey said it would be favorably considered. His tough talk was bracing. The
revolt simmered down.

Since his arrival in New York more than a year before, Storey had been urging
Rooney, Russo, and Paquette to collect their evidence for a wiretap application.
Now, at the end of 1982, Russo, Rooney, Paquette, and Louis Freeh, who was
supposed to begin shaping their findings into a prosecutable case, closeted them-

selves in Paquette's former office in the New Rochelle Sheraton and sat down to pull an affidavit together. As the days stretched into weeks, and amid periodic impatient goadings from narcotics supervisor Vinton, they assembled their findings to date. What emerged after several weeks was an application under Title III of the 1968 Crime Control Act to intercept telephone communications. In the conventionally dry and legalistic language of such documents, it set forth the early history of the Bonanno family, going back to Joe Bonanno's birth in Castellammare del Golfo in 1905. But it soon got down to the particulars of what the FBI had found in the three years of investigation that began in 1980. The affidavit outlined the case as it appeared to investigators at the end of 1982, from Catalano and his mysterious band of Sicilians operating under the Bonanno family, as described by Pistone, to the $1.7 million cash known to have been delivered by Matassa, Castronovo, Catalano's cousin Onofrio, and others to the office on Third Avenue at Forty-second Street, to the $3.9 million cash known to have been delivered by Della Torre to Merrill Lynch, to the unknown millions that had passed through Amendolito and E. F. Hutton—perhaps the balance of the $60 million cited by Paquette's initial tipster. It was drug money—everyone agreed on that—but no one had yet seen any drugs. Rarely, if ever, had so much detailed information collected from so many visual, photographic, and electronic surveillances in so many countries been focused on a single FBI investigation. But as the wiretaps would show, it was barely the beginning.

PART THREE

BOREDOM AND TERROR

One who speaks little makes mistakes. Imagine the one who speaks a lot.

—Sicilian saying

11

Carmine Russo snapped the cassette into his tape recorder, adjusted the headset over his "golden ears," as he liked to call them, and punched the green play button. Disembodied voices, spoken fragments vacuumed up by the technology of the FBI, came spilling through the wires into his brain.

"*Porca miseria.*" The caller used the mild Sicilian oath "pig misery" as a greeting. "What are you doing?"

"I'm planting four onions," said the man who answered, also in Sicilian.

"Really, at this time?" The caller laughed.

"What am I going to do? They are all sprouted." He said he had just come from the other man's *paesano.* "He had about four bags of onions, all sprouted. Give me four, and I'll plant them."

Planting four onions? All sprouted? Russo pushed the stop button and spun the tape back for a replay in another effort to identify the voices and decipher the enigmatic conversation. It was March 16, 1983, and Russo was back in his old office on Queens Boulevard. It was typical: Two months after Sheer and Storey had pulled the squads from Queens and New Rochelle into Manhattan headquarters, turning Russo's life upside down, he was spending more and more time in Queens, listening to phone calls. He and Rooney had appealed for a

131

rehearing. The case was centered a mile from the Queens office, around Ganci's house and Catalano's bakery. Why couldn't they move back to Queens? But Sheer had made up his mind.

After three years of extensive surveillances, cited in the wiretap application Rooney, Russo, and Paquette had drawn up with prosecutor Freeh, a United States district court judge had agreed there was sufficient evidence of crimes being committed to justify violation of an American's most fundamental constitutional right, the right to be left in peace and privacy by the government. "Few threats to liberty exist which are greater than that posed by the use of eavesdropping devices," Notre Dame law professor G. Robert Blakey once observed, citing a federal judge's ruling. But in enacting the wiretap provisions of Title III, Blakey added, Congress found organized crime to constitute one of those threats.

Starting on March 7, 1983, and lasting for more than thirteen months, Russo and other agents became a secret party to an estimated hundred thousand phone conversations, representing about a year of uninterrupted around-the-clock talk in the largest single wiretapping operation ever mounted by the FBI. For the agents who had already spent three years puzzling over the activities of Catalano and Ganci and their associates, it was as if they had been standing in a dark room and suddenly been given a flashlight.

Although surveillance abuses and scandals had periodically tarnished the FBI, it had come to take wiretapping very seriously and approached this sensitive area with great scrupulousness. The director or designated director personally had to approve each application.

Armed with their court order, bureau supervisors then went to the phone companies to locate the lines of the designated phones, although some, like Ganci's, had already been isolated when the pen registers were installed. Once the lines had been found, the phone signal was shunted to an unobtrusive apartment or office usually within a few blocks of the tapped phone. As long as the plant, or listening post, had phone lines to begin with, technicians did not have to string additional wires from the tapped phone; the regular phone lines carried in the intercepted signal.

The calls had to be monitored throughout, in order for the listening agents to minimize, or tune out of, conversations that were personal and not pertinent to the case. Although a considerable number of agents spoke Italian and some of those spoke Sicilian, few aside from Russo could identify the voices, translate the dialogue, and quickly decide whether the discussion really was about a sick aunt, tomatoes, and rain or something more devious.

Beyond telephone taps the electronic surveillance arsenal comprised such wizardry as tracking aircraft, night-vision scopes, concealed video cameras, body recorders, parabolic microphones to pick up distant conversations, beacon transmitters to track moving vehicles, secure radio bands for agent communication, and powerful bureau computers to organize all the information pouring in.

Physical surveillance had also become a specialized bureau art, if not quite a science. For many years the job of watching and tailing subjects was something agents did for themselves on their own cases. But with growing FBI recognition of the value of pursuing quality cases over quantity, surveillance had been increasingly turned over to special operations squads trained to tail subjects invisibly and to snap photographs from inside strategically parked vans. It was a marriage, as Kallstrom said, of "people and widgets." The people were the more important part, men and women quickly able to size up fast-changing situations, instantly adopt subterfuges and disguises, and uncomplainingly endure, as one said, "hours of boredom and moments of terror." They led rootless lives. They might start out in Long Island, travel through three or four or all five New York City boroughs, and wind up fifteen hours later in a high-speed chase in New Jersey. But it suited the agents who chose this life. One of them, a mild, soft-spoken agent named Robert Gilmore, treasured an ad for Timberland boots that, he thought, nicely captured the romance: "Some men go to the office," it said. "Other men go to work." If you needed a desk with pictures of the wife and kids, Gilmore said, this was not the job for you. Besides, he never had to worry what to wear each day. Jeans and a work shirt and baseball cap were fine. So was a two-day stubble. It was a far cry from agent school, where, he remembered ruefully, wearing bell-bottom slacks or wire-rim eyeglasses was ground for disciplinary action.

The Title III's had been a watershed. Everyone now agreed that this was a big case and getting bigger. In January 1983 the FBI and U.S. attorneys from Newark to Los Angeles had met to map strategies and compare notes with the DEA amid the security of Governors Island in New York Harbor. There were still lingering wounds over the upheaval of the agent transfers to Manhattan. Schiliro spent weeks shell-shocked and guilt-ridden over what he viewed as a failure to protect his men from Storey's reorganization. Storey was afraid Schiliro might resign, a step that would be a grave setback for the investigation. Storey hoped he wouldn't; Schiliro was still the best organized crime supervisor he knew. Sheer still wasn't sure where the investigation was leading—nobody was—but Rooney's organizational skills in particular had won Sheer's confidence. And Rooney never quit. As Sheer said, he had no off switch.

As if reading his boss's thoughts at the Governors Island conference, Rooney twitted Sheer: "Do you know what you got yourself into?"

For once Sheer was thrown on the defensive. "What the hell is the matter with you?" he said. "Would you please go home and spend some time with your wife? She's pregnant, in case you forgot."

Sheer was right; Jane was due in three months with their third child, and Rooney had hardly seen her lately. Often he worked late into the night until Sheer or Schiliro or another supervisor who happened to stop by ordered him to leave. It was almost as if Rooney needed someone to tell him to go home. It was hard to tear himself away. At night they had to review the day's "T-3's"—wiretaps—to plan their surveillance strategy for the next day. And Rooney spent hours on the phone keeping other offices abreast of the investigation.

As the two case agents in charge of coordinating the day-to-day investigation, Rooney and Russo had found a natural division of labor. Russo handled the wiretaps, often listening to the calls as they were in progress and being simultaneously recorded by the bureau's reel-to-reel Revox machines. One original tape had to be maintained "virgin," as a sealed copy for the court, so conversations were dubbed onto cassettes for more detailed study afterward. Meanwhile, Rooney took care of a lot of the paperwork, and that suited Russo just fine.

The call Russo overheard about the onions had come into the home telephone of Filippo Salamone, a pizza maker in Jackson Township, New Jersey, and a figure at the end of a long trail painstakingly cleared by Paquette that had begun with the surveillances at the Horn & Hardart building. The movements of Matassa and Amendolito and the mysterious deliveries in New Jersey and Queens had led Paquette to Della Torre, whose name had shown up in Amendolito's address book. And Paquette, after running into some dead ends, had followed through on Della Torre's American Express records to uncover hotel phone logs of calls made from Della Torre's New York hotel rooms to the New Jersey number of Filippo Salamone. Now, two and a half years after Paquette's search had begun, Salamone's phone was being tapped. Who, or what, was Salamone, besides a pizza man who looked like the thin half of Laurel and Hardy? And why would a money launderer like Della Torre have been calling him?

To Paquette's questions, Russo now added his own: What did Salamone mean when he said he was planting four onions? He had to be talking about something else. And who was the caller?

Identifying the voices was always the hardest part. Nobody, least of all these guys, started off a call by giving his name. One side of the conversation—the tapped end—was relatively easy to figure out. But who called that number or whom that number called out to, those critical facts were something else again.

Russo did not know then, although he would figure it out within a few weeks, that Salamone was calling Gaetano Mazzara of the Roma restaurant in Menlo Park, New Jersey, and the *paesano* Salamone was referring to was Mazzara's restaurant partner, Frank Castronovo, the one who had been supplying all those cartons to Amendolito and Matassa. Once Russo figured that out, he could also guess that the sprouted onions were cash, ready for planting, possibly in Switzerland.

Five pairs of eyes and a video lens on the telephone pole watched Ganci one morning as he left his orange-brick garden apartment building on Seventy-eighth Street, a pleasant one-way street in Middle Village, Queens. Years before, when the surveillances had begun, agents would see Ganci in a T-shirt and work clothes, attire that earned him the radio code name Ralph Kramden. Since then, however, they noticed, he had traded in his *Honeymooners* look for a more prosperous image: Now his 17½-inch neck and thick shoulders were draped in shirts custom-made by Chris-Arto, the tailor who supplied Sulka, the elegant men's store on Park Avenue. He shopped at Ted Lapidus near Bloomingdale's and drove a midnight blue Mercedes 500 SEL. Now they called him simply the whale.

With Ganci that morning was a short-haired child of about six or seven. At that point the agents could not tell whether it was a boy or a girl; they later learned it was Ganci's daughter, Mary Jo. As Ganci's blue Mercedes pulled out, the engines of five cars scattered through the neighborhood revved to life, seemingly coincidentally. Inside the cars the radios crackled with transmissions.

"Okay, we got movement!"

"The whale's pulling out."

"Eleven's got him."

"Ah, he's getting red-balled on Metropolitan."

"Gotcha!"

The light turned green.

"Rolling again, turning left."

"You see him?"

"Ah, he's got a white-over-red Caprice behind, blue van in front."

In one of the pursuit cars Bob Gilmore gave silent thanks again for the innovation of secure radio bands that assured the privacy of communications between the cars and headquarters. Before the bureau got them, surveillance agents, like the targets they tailed, had to resort to their own elaborate codes. Names were simplified to letters and letters were rendered as numbers: Metropolitan Avenue might be simply M Street and M might be eight, so an agent on Metropolitan Avenue might say on the radio he was on Eighth Street. But the codes were often difficult to remember, and agents had to keep decoder sheets clipped to the sun visors. In a fast-moving chase it was cumbersome to have to consult the code sheets all the time. Now it became unnecessary; they could say where they were.

That left the agents free to worry about the driving, which was replete with its own hazards. "You never realize how many assholes drive in New York until you try to follow someone," Gilmore often remarked. "You're tempted to get out and move their cars out of the way yourself." That was why the bureau had its own advanced driving course for agents. Gilmore liked to have only New Yorkers in his surveillance squad. You really had to know the city to follow someone. You had to know instinctively which streets and avenues went which way and you had to know that the light on Steinway Street and Thirtieth Avenue in Astoria was red for an interminable two and a half minutes, so getting stuck there meant saying good-bye to the guys you were chasing.

Gilmore now watched Ganci's rearview and side-view mirrors to catch any quick glances by Ganci, signs that he might be alert to the surveillances. He seemed not to be. The unsuspecting pizza man led the parade only a few blocks before stopping at a Roman Catholic school. The child jumped out, and Ganci drove home and parked the Mercedes.

Gilmore exhaled in disgust. He had hoped for a little more action. He and the other agents scattered their unmarked cars around the streets leading to the Ganci house. Some parked facing away from it to allay suspicion, adjusting their side-view mirrors so they could slump down in the driver's seat and keep the house in view through the reflection. It attracted less attention. Still, with all the paranoia about crime, neighbors seeing a man alone in a car parked on a quiet side street sometimes called the police to report a pervert. Sometimes Gilmore told nosy neighbors he was an Immigration Service agent looking for illegal aliens. If a radio car then passed by to check, he would just flash the badge he kept over the sun visor and say he was "on the job." The police knew when not to interfere. It was worse when he left his car, shotgun in the padlocked trunk, for a foot surveillance. The car might or might not be there when he got back. If the "brownies," the traffic agents, didn't tow the car away, these crazy bastards in New York would steal it right out from under you. "Burning" a surveillance and getting "made" by their targets was usually not the biggest danger surveillance agents faced in New York in 1983; it was losing their vehicles to car thieves.

Minutes later they saw Ganci come out again, this time on foot. He walked up the block past a weed-grown lot, crossed the street to a candy store, bought a newspaper, and walked home. He was shortly followed by Catalano. After a few minutes they could be seen leaving Ganci's house and walking together around the corner to enter Catalano's bakery, with its glass showcases stacked with loaves of fresh bread, cannoli, "lobster tails," and other pastries.

That evening Ganci called home from a New Jersey restaurant and spoke to his wife, Margherita. If anyone called, Ganci said, he was at Frank's. Margherita was obviously annoyed. Russo could hear that. Ganci had been spending a lot of time away from home lately, especially in New Jersey. Clearly Margherita suspected the reason.

"And who is going to call you?" she asked her husband sharply. Almost immediately, it appeared, she felt guilty. "One guy named Vito called," she said.

"And what did he say?"

"Nothing, he'll call you later." Before hanging up, Margherita could not resist another dig. "Okay, enjoy yourself," she said.

Earlier Russo had listened to a woman who called Ganci uncle talk to him about setting up an incoming call to him the next day at a pay phone in New Jersey. Ganci couldn't keep the appointment, so they agreed on either a later hour or the day after. Russo wondered what was worth all the trouble.

In anticipation, Kallstrom quickly arranged for a hidden video camera to be hooked up outside the telephone booth in Belleville, New Jersey, where Ganci was to get the call. Within hours the camera caught Ganci driving up in a silver gray Audi. He made a call from the booth, then the agents saw him hang up and take an incoming call.

Russo was eager to listen to the tape of the call. It had obviously been sensitive enough to require special arrangements. To his disgust he learned it had not been recorded. "I don't believe it! I just do not believe this bullshit!" Russo fumed. "The guy gets an overseas call at a pay phone, we know the place, we know the time, and it's not covered! Of all the dumb, idiotic—"

"If we missed it, we missed it," Rooney said. "It'll happen, Carmine."

"Well, it better not happen too often or how're we going to be in business?" Rooney shrugged. "It's over," he said. "Relaxio."

After the call Ganci was tailed to the Belleville Motor Lodge, a large motel with an Italian restaurant, Casa Polizzi, near the center of Belleville. Agents ran a quick check on the ownership and came up with the name Francesco Polizzi, whom surveillance revealed to be a rugged, prosperous-looking man who dressed expensively and wore his hair in a wavy pompadour. A year and a half before, Rooney in the lookout had seen Catalano dropped off in front of his bakery by a Cadillac with a license plate traced back to Polizzi, but this was the first time they had gotten a look at him. He also had a construction company, Polizzi Builders, whose office, agents found, was near the phone booth where Ganci had received the call. And hadn't Ganci told his wife he was at Frank's?

Rooney and Russo would have been intrigued to know that Casa Polizzi used to be called Talk of the Town. A card from Talk of the Town had been found with the papers of Bonventre and Amato at the time of their arrest at the Long Island shopping mall shortly before the Galante hit. Rooney and Russo had seen the card when they looked through the Sicilian pair's papers in 1980, but at the time it had meant nothing to them; there were too many other leads to run down. Now, nearly three years later, they saw a connection among Polizzi, Ganci, and Bonventre that they might have made long ago. But without all the intervening investigation, it would have been impossible to make sense of it.

Ganci, who had disappeared into Casa Polizzi with its owner, later drove home to Queens. He was not back long before Catalano called. "What does it take to find you?" Catalano asked, annoyed. Ganci was never home when he called, Catalano complained.

"But you call when I'm not home," Ganci countered, with impeccable logic.

"Listen to what you should do," Catalano said. "Call that guy there, that guy down there, and tell him he should come here tomorrow, that I have to give him a thing. . . ."

The next evening agents, hoping to see whomever Catalano had been talking about get whatever it was he referred to, were staked out around Catalano's house near a cemetery a few blocks from Ganci's in Middle Village. It was a red-brick garden unit in a complex set diagonally off the street, creating a sawtooth effect. It had two small balconies with metal roofs and a chocolate brown garage door, the same color as Ganci's.

They watched as a dark car double-parked in front. The passenger could be seen directing the driver to carry a brown paper shopping bag into Catalano's house. The passenger, wearing a leather jacket draped over his shoulders, followed him in. It was Catalano's cousin Saca, whom Rooney had read about in *The Canadian Connection* and whom surveillance agents had come across before. He was a jeweler in the diamond district who lived in Howard Beach and had a house south of Poughkeepsie adjacent to an airstrip. As far back as 1963 the Italian police had identified Saca Catalano, then thirty, as a member of the Mafia, and in 1970 the Italians had once overheard him on the phone instructing Tommaso Buscetta's old friend Pino Catania to set up a front company in Mexico for heroin shipments.

After appearing on Toto Catalano's balcony for a smoke, Saca Catalano left, trailing a line of surveillance agents to his next stop, Caffè Aiello in nearby Ridgewood, Queens. The agents had no way of knowing yet that owner Tony Aiello was Commerciante, the businessman listed in the phone numbers taken from Bonventre and Amato nearly four years before and that his principal business, like Catalano's and Ganci's, was heroin. Shortly afterward Catalano and Ganci, who had been in the house when Saca arrived, also left, in separate cars. The pair converged at Ganci's house, where Catalano could be seen lugging at least two cardboard cartons out of Ganci's garage and putting them into the trunk of his Oldsmobile. Catalano then drove the boxes home. Interesting, thought Rooney. But what did it mean?

12

few days after the "sprouted onions" conversation between Filippo Salamone and Gaetano Mazzara, Rooney drove over to the Queens lookout, the
gabled wooden house with a direct view of Catalano's bakery and the video
hookup trained on Ganci's house. As always, he took a moment to gaze at the
television cue cards from the Jack Paar *Tonight Show* that some previous occupant of the house had used to insulate the exposed top-floor ceiling. Bored agents
doing surveillance duty could look up and read the corny jokes, provided the cards
with the punch lines weren't out of order, as they often were. "If George
Washington, who had no children, was the father of our country," one joke went,
"what does that make of the rest of us?" Rooney greeted black-bearded Pat Luzio,
a gentle, soft-voiced midwesterner who had become the regular agent on duty
in the lookout. Luzio was spending a lot of time in Middle Village and could not
afford to be recognized. The beard, neatly trimmed, made him look more Italian
than ever, helping him blend into the neighborhood. Besides, the beard was
becoming to him, and he continued to wear it long after it had served its purpose.

The video monitor showed one of Ganci's cars, a rust-colored Cadillac Seville,
in the driveway. They watched for a while. Nothing was happening. Rooney left
and drove over to the pizzeria Ganci and Catalano owned on Queens Boulevard.

140

Al Dente, with its faded red awning and a window sign promising "ROMPT" delivery, sat on a busy block in Forest Hills between a travel agency and a glatt kosher food supplier. Rooney could see a brown van parked nearby at the curb. Inside, he knew, was John Mauzey, his six-foot-two-inch frame pretzeled into the back, peering through a telephoto lens afixed to his Canon F-1 and undoubtedly dreaming about mountain climbing. With the van's interior upholstered in dark fabric, it was impossible for anyone outside to see in. Across the twelve lanes of Queens Boulevard, Rooney also spotted Bobby Gilmore, slouched at the wheel of his old Pontiac watching Al Dente. He hoped the gypsies who read palms alongside a white Cadillac parked nearby had not been drawing too much attention to Gilmore; they had been driving him crazy lately.

Peering inside Al Dente as he walked past, Rooney could see the squat Ganci at the counter, talking on a red telephone. These guys were tireless, Rooney marveled. When it came to making a buck, he knew, wise guys never slept.

In the ensuing days the agents learned something else about Ganci, something his wife Margherita tried to shut her eyes to. Ganci had a *commare*. Often, after dropping his daughter at St. Margaret's Catholic School and his wife at St. Margaret's Church for daily mass, Ganci led his tail of surveillance agents across the Hudson River to Clifton, New Jersey, where he met a woman who usually arrived in a black Mercedes sports car. She was in her thirties, pretty and petite, with delicately drawn features, sculptured short dark hair, and legs that seemed made for a miniskirt. Her name, the agents discovered, was Carol.

In addition to Carol, the surveillances and wiretaps were introducing the agents to a growing cast of characters. One day Ganci called a Long Island number and asked for "Mr. Joe." Russo had the number traced to a subscriber in Baldwin, Giuseppe Lamberti. Lamberti quickly acquired an FBI tail. He turned out to be a six-footer with a large, round face. He had a construction business and a men's clothing boutique upstate. He was followed to a meeting in New Jersey with Ganci and Frank Polizzi, the Belleville builder, motel operator and restaurateur who turned out to be a relative of Ganci's from San Giuseppe Iato. The recordings also led to Filippo Casamento of the Eagle Cheese shop in Brooklyn, who ten years before had been convicted of heroin trafficking and sentenced to fifteen years, although he was released after five. What Russo didn't know was that Casamento had been one of Tommaso Buscetta's first contacts in New York. But, then, Russo had hardly heard of Buscetta.

"I am doing the prosciutto," Casamento told Ganci one day. "Did you want a piece of prosciutto?"

"Those things are always liked."

"When you feel like it," invited Casamento, "come pick it up."

Several hours later agents followed Ganci to Casamento's shop on Avenue U, where Ganci picked up a small white bag from a wiry man with a tangle of graying curls. Ganci put the bag under his front seat. It was possible, Rooney reflected, that someone in Queens would drive to Brooklyn for a piece of prosciutto. But you would not hide prosciutto under the front seat.

A few days later Russo listened to another intercepted call to the home of New Jersey pizza maker Filippo Salamone, who had talked earlier about the sprouted onions. Salamone's wife told the caller she was urgently waiting for him to return from the pizzeria. A team of New Jersey surveillance agents—FBI offices in Newark and elsewhere in New Jersey had joined the investigation—stuck with Salamone as he headed home, stopping en route to change cars at the house of a business partner, a thin, white-haired man. Telephone toll records had shown that the partner, Salvatore Greco, had received calls from Frank Castronovo three years before, when Castronovo was delivering cash to Manhattan. What the agents did not yet know was that Greco was the brother of Bagheria Mafia boss Leonardo Greco, the heroin kingpin behind Amendolito's money laundering. Nor did the agents know anything of Salvatore Greco's 1980 voyage to the Bagheria farmhouse to test the heroin shipment.

The surveilling agents tailed the Salamones and their two children, whom the couple had picked up from school, as they drove west across the Verrazano Narrows Bridge and sped through Brooklyn to JFK Airport.

Salamone, dressed in a black leather jacket and gray slacks, parked in a lot near one of the international terminals and entered the arrivals area, where he greeted a man in a blue sports coat and white shirt. Then they walked to Salamone's car. Salamone opened his trunk and handed the man a brown gym bag. They walked back toward the terminal and stopped at the line of yellow cabs waiting for fares. Salamone's young son came out of the terminal, struggling with the visitor's large suitcase. The man took his own suitcase together with the gym bag Salamone had given him, stepped into a cab, and sped off. In the confusion none of the agents tailed the taxi, but they had gotten the cabby's plate. They tracked him down and noted that his trip sheet listed the passenger's destination as an apartment building on East Seventy-second Street in Manhattan. The information was added to the fast-growing file.

Given what they had already seen of cash deliveries and been hearing on the phone, Russo and Rooney along with Paquette strongly suspected that the bag handed over by Salamone contained money—four sprouted onions, as he had said on the phone. The agents learned later that it was stuffed with $400,000 of heroin proceeds that the visitor, a money courier, had flown in from Switzerland specifically to pick up and take back the next day.

Russo indulged the fleeting fantasy that there would be time to drive home to Staten Island for dinner with Carmela and the boys. But there were still tapes to listen to. So far only three phones had been tapped—Ganci's, Filippo Salamone's, and the one at the Roma restaurant owned by Castronovo and Mazzara —although others would soon be added. (Catalano's phone was never tapped. The government needed probable cause to get a judge's order for a wiretap, and phone records showed that the Catalano household was making only a few calls a day from home.) Just three tapped phones were generating dozens of calls a day. Nobody said Russo had to listen to them all himself, but he found that if he didn't review the translations personally, things would slip by: meetings that had to be surveilled; new phones they had to apply for authorization to tap. This was no reflection on the other Sicilian-speaking agents; it was just that they didn't know all the little things he knew from following the case for three years. How long had it been since he had sat down to dinner with the family? Two weeks? A month? He couldn't remember. It must have been before the wires anyway. Russo wrapped himself in a sweater and snapped in another cassette.

On March 24, 1983, surveillance agents followed Ganci in his Cadillac to Frank Polizzi's Belleville motel, where Polizzi and three other men got into Ganci's car. One was "Mr. Joe"—Giuseppe Lamberti—the big, round-faced Long Island contractor Ganci had called and met with a few days before. The agents hadn't seen the other two before. One had thinning hair and a stern, cold face; the other was small and rounded, almost elfin. Ganci drove them to the Menlo Park Mall in New Jersey, where they got out near the Roma restaurant and were greeted by one of the partners, Gaetano Mazzara. Mazzara had shown up in Rooney's album of Bono wedding pictures, along with his partner, Frank Castronovo, and deli owner Filippo Casamento. The agents recognized Mazzara by his hair, which was full and swept back in a blow-dried look. Rooney was excited to hear of the gathering. It put Ganci in contact with some new people whom the bureau could start checking out, and it linked them to the Roma restaurant, the starting point for the boxes of cash. A few hours later, when Rooney got a look at the surveillance pictures, he realized he had seen the small, rounded man in a photo taken the year before, though he still had no idea who he was.

Later that afternoon Ganci was followed to Clifton and to a brown garden apartment complex called Patricia Village, built by Polizzi and named for the niece who had set up the incoming overseas pay phone calls for Ganci not long before, although Russo had not yet identified her. Screened by the trees of the

IT&T corporate campus across the way, surveillance agent Gilmore watched Ganci raise the fourth garage door in from the street and enter the attached garden unit. A few minutes later Gilmore recorded the arrival of a black Mercedes two-seater convertible. That would be Carol, Gilmore guessed correctly. He watched them talk, silhouetted in the kitchen window. A few minutes later the pair emerged and entered Ganci's car, Carol swathed in a white fur coat. With Gilmore and other agents in pursuit, Ganci drove to Manhattan, to the renowned Four Seasons restaurant in the Seagram Building on Park Avenue. *Well,* thought Gilmore, *it sure beats pizza.* That reminded him of his own growling stomach. Ganci and his paramour wouldn't be moving for a while. He had time to duck into a coffee shop for a sandwich.

The next day, typically, Ganci left home early with his wife and Mary Jo. He dropped his daughter at the nearby Catholic school and his wife next door at the church. Then he drove over to Catalano's garage, where he put a large white wastebasket into his trunk. Next he drove to his tailor at 141 Fifth Avenue; he soon exited with a new suit. A flurry of other errands behind him, Ganci made his way to Clifton and to Carol's apartment.

Later he drove to the Caffè Aiello in the staunchly Italian neighborhood of Ridgewood, Queens. When he was a youngster, Rooney remembered, the neighborhood was largely German. Now it was overwhelmingly Italian. The café, with its omnipresent knot of hard-eyed regulars standing around outside—where they knew their words could not be overheard by any bug planted inside—had long been of interest to Rooney and Russo, who had found FBI and police intelligence files listing the proprietor, Anthony Aiello, as a suspected narcotics trafficker. Ganci left Caffè Aiello with a package that he put in the trunk of his Mercedes.

Ganci had another stop to make, one that Gilmore and the rest of his surveillance team were soon to dread. He threaded his way into an industrial quarter of Greenpoint, Brooklyn, where he entered a red-brick warehouse building on Provost Street. It bordered a sewage treatment plant whose stench commingled with the pungent exhaust of industrial pollution and chemical waste. Gagging on the vile vapors, the agents walked over to the unmarked building, hemmed in by behemoth refuse trucks and construction machines marked PRONTO DEMOLITION COMPANY. The name was not familiar. They did not yet know that one of Pronto's founding partners was Giuseppe Bono, the powerful Sicilian Mafia boss whose surprising presence in New York had been picked up two years before; that Ganci and Giuseppe Lamberti and Giovanni Ligammari—the Catalano associate who turned up at the Capri Motel the day after the Bonanno captains were murdered two years before—were among the other partners; and that the company was a front for drug smuggling.

Another link between the Sicilians and the murders soon emerged. Two weeks later, in early April 1983, Ganci was tailed to the Queens home of Santo Giordano, whom Russo had questioned in May 1981, while he recovered from bullet wounds in the hospital a few days after the three captains were killed. Giordano had also been identified through fingerprints as the driver of the Galante killers' getaway car, and he had been with Catalano and Ganci when they accompanied Bonventre and Amato to the Brooklyn DA's office. Ganci was definitely in with the killers of Galante and the captains, Rooney decided.

The next days brought a flurry of movements that kept surveillance agents streaming between New York and New Jersey, photographing exchanges of mysterious paper bags. Ganci traveled to Brooklyn to pick up a bag at Casamento's Eagle Cheese. Castronovo crossed the Hudson to pick up a white plastic bag at a Brooklyn pizzeria and a brown grocery bag at a tile store. Ganci picked up packages at Catalano's bakery and Polizzi's motel.

The agents also followed Filippo Salamone and his wife and children from New Jersey to Kennedy Airport. They were wondering whether he would hand over another gym bag when they saw Salamone check in at a Swissair counter for a flight to Zurich. When his wife phoned him several days later, the wiretap traced the call to a subscriber in West Germany, Vito Roberto Palazzolo. Paquette had come across Palazzolo's name in the hotel records of calls made by Franco Della Torre. He knew Palazzolo had something to do with the laundering of the millions smuggled out by Castronovo and Amendolito, but he had no way yet of knowing of Palazzolo's central role as a money launderer for the Sicilian Mafia.

Meanwhile, Ganci in his rust-toned Seville was followed to a jeweler on the Lower East Side. He left with a small, white, tightly wrapped package that the agents somehow doubted was for Mrs. Ganci. Later he met Carol, and they drove off together to Clifton. Still later Ganci called home to tell his wife he would be home by six. Margherita sounded pleased, Russo thought. He guessed that she was not fooled by her husband's infidelity but chose to overlook it. She said she would make the pasta that was left over from yesterday "and I'll put a little sauce . . . a little cheese and I'll place it in the oven."

In the background Mary Jo could be heard bubbling over with eagerness to see her father, which reminded Ganci to ask, "How did you do on the test? How did the test end today?"

"Good."

"How much did you get?" Ganci pressed.

"I don't know."

"How much you think you going to get?"

"Something in the nineties," Mary Jo said. ". . . Yeah, because there was one question that was hard. Maybe a ninety-five."

"Well, in the nineties!" Ganci sounded proud.

The next day the surveillance net scooped up Baldo Amato, in a gray sports jacket, white shirt, and black tie, stepping out of a gray Audi at Casamento's *salumeria* in Brooklyn. As Amato drove up to the deli, Filippo's brother Frank Casamento appeared. They entered the shop together. Amato exited with a very full large white shopping bag that he put in the trunk of his car. Then he drove Frank to several locations in Brooklyn and Manhattan. Sometime later Ganci arranged to meet Filippo in Bensonhurst Park, where surveilling agents photographed Ganci perched on the back of a bench, huddling with the deli owner.

The calls Russo was listening to, meanwhile, were getting more and more elliptical. Giuseppe Lamberti, the big, round-faced contractor, told Ganci: "The architect . . . who had to come over here . . . he wants a raise in salary . . . for those plants that I had told you about."

Salamone's wife told her husband, Filippo, in Italy: "The grass is all grown."

Gaetano Mazzara of the Roma restaurant told Ganci: "We reached an accord concerning those stores." The bigger one, Mazzara said, "was to be mine."

"I understand," Ganci said.

To Russo, the "architect" probably signified a drug supplier who wanted more money for his goods—the "plants." The "grass" was also drugs, as were the "stores." Russo figured he was on the right track immediately after listening to a conversation about Filippo Salamone's brother, Salvatore. Sal was supposed to be paying 10 percent for something but had welched, according to a caller: "Sal agreed ten percent while he was changing all that money into hundred-dollar bills, and then, when it came down to it, he gave him gas money." The phrase echoed in Russo's ears: "changing all that money into hundred-dollar bills."

He was still pondering it when a call came into the Roma. The caller was looking for either of the partners, Castronovo or Mazzara. "I'm Benny," the caller said. Both were out. Benny said he'd try them at home.

Benny who? Russo wondered, but he didn't worry about it for long. There were too many other calls. He had no way of knowing just how important Benny would become.

The next day Ganci was followed to a medical office in Queens. Agents checked the name plates of the physicians. Internal medicine. Ganci looked strong as an ox, though he smoked incessantly, Rooney noted. Or was this another of his business deals? Ganci was well enough the following day to make another trip to his Lower East Side jeweler and to drive out to Patricia Village to see Carol. He and Catalano were also photographed in late April coming out of the

Villa Maria restaurant in Ridgewood, Queens, with Sal Ferrugia, the stout, acting-boss of the Bonanno family, whom Catalano referred to as the horseman, apparently for a relative in the racing or breeding business. It was another sign, Rooney thought, of how well Catalano and Ganci were plugged in.

Between Russo's eavesdropping on the calls and Rooney's examination of the photos that the surveillance agents were snapping by the hundreds, they had succeeded in identifying two other members of Ganci's circle who had so far eluded them. One was the little man who had turned up with Ganci, Polizzi, and Giuseppe Lamberti in the Menlo Park shopping mall on March 24. He turned out to be Salvatore Mazzurco, a brother-in-law and contracting associate of Lamberti's and a partner in Pronto Demolition. The other man, who had thinning hair and a stern, sometimes icy face, was Lamberti's cousin Salvatore. What the agents didn't yet know was that Salvatore Lamberti was an important member of the Borgetto family of the Sicilian Mafia and had arrived the year before from Sicily, where he was wanted to face charges in the murder of a policeman.

Russo was especially intrigued with a call the pint-size Mazzurco made to Ganci on April 30. ". . . Tomorrow I'm supposed to meet those people," Mazzurco said.

Ganci grunted assent.

". . . But I'm supposed to bring them ninety-five cents," Mazzurco said.

"Here, I've got about forty," Ganci said. ". . . About forty I can . . . accumulate."

They were hardly pooling pennies, Russo reflected. What were they counting?

By May 1983 the wiretaps had been in place for nearly two months. Rooney would always remember the date because Brian, his youngest, was born in the second month of the wires. He had begun measuring his life against the slow unrolling of the case. Paquette had found his money; at least, with Amendolito's records, he seemed to be on the trail of it. Where was the powder that was Rooney's part of the bargain? It was probably in some of those bags. Where was the mother lode? How was it getting into the country?

It was evening in the FBI offices at 26 Federal Plaza, and Russo and Rooney, along with other members of the Cattails squad, were still at their desks, sorting through files, trying to find a pattern: Who was giving what to whom?

They didn't see Tom Sheer approach. "What're you guys waiting for? The case to solve itself? How's it coming?" They turned at the sound of Sheer's sardonic midwestern twang.

Rooney was caught off guard. "It sucks, pal," he blurted.

(Later supervisor Lew Schiliro pulled Rooney aside. "You can't talk to the SAC like that," he said. "Well," said Rooney, "he asked me.")

Usually, Sheer left him tongue-tied. To many of his men, Rooney included, Sheer was an intimidating figure. Agents said he looked like an FBI boss and an ex-Marine.

"Hey, just shittin' around," said Sheer. "You guys are doing a bang-up job." He apologized again for hauling them into Manhattan. "But I don't have to tell you," he said, dropping his voice, "this has become a gigantic fucking skunk-works," Sheer's way of saying the case had become of special interest to headquarters. He had been fielding increasing inquiries from Washington and other FBI offices about the growing manpower the investigation was consuming. Sheer readily agreed it was worth it. But he was clearly under pressure himself. "The wives holding up?" he asked them.

"Well, Mr. Sheer . . ." Russo said.

"Tom."

Russo admitted he hadn't been home much. Sheer sympathized. He had dragged Luisa all around the country for twenty years, most recently disrupting a travel agency she was trying to start. But it was the clients, not the travel agents, who were supposed to be constantly on the move. Sheer, too, was rarely home. Agents said he did more work in his car than the hookers on Thirty-fourth Street.

Sheer put his arm around Pat Luzio. "How's the house? Sold yet?"

Luzio shook his head. "Not even a bite." Luzio, the main agent in the lookout, had been sent up from West Virginia, where his $30,000 a year had gone considerably further than in New York. He not only had to cope with New York housing prices but couldn't find a buyer for his house in Wheeling.

"Don't forget, guys," Sheer added, "stop to smell the roses." That at least brought a laugh. Sheer knew what they were going through. You didn't uproot a bunch of agents and their families without stirring some discord. Maybe, Sheer thought, it was time for some quality circles, bring the agents together, let them forage for new ideas. It was better when they did it themselves than when he told them what to do.

"Hey, Russo," Sheer asked as a parting shot, "are you losing weight deliberately?" It was Sheer's idea of a joke. Russo smiled weakly.

"Now," Sheer said, "all of you guys, get the fuck home."

Rooney had his moments of doubt about their ability to keep up with the ever-expanding number of players and leads. He mostly kept them to himself, although he did confess his concerns to supervisor Lew Schiliro. Schiliro, who had begun by doubting the importance of the case, was now a believer. "Go for it," he told Rooney. "There's nobody in this world who can't be gotten."

Increasingly Rooney had to remind himself to "relaxio." It had seemed so straightforward in agent school in Quantico. The organized crime families were neatly laid out. Nobody talked about Sicilian factions and coded Sicilian conversations. There the challenges included the SWAT swim: Fully dressed and each holding an M-16 overhead, the trainees had to jump off the high board into the pool and swim the length three times. Some days they had to run the academy's three-mile perimeter carrying a shotgun, scale a wall, climb a rope, race for ammunition, load, fire at a moving target, and then sit down and write a report on the exercise. Sometimes Rooney would go back to find slower members of the class, see if they needed help. That was the spirit of the academy they drummed into them: not "I" but "we." Through the hum of a class lecture one day Rooney heard an instructor intone: "Someday you will get a file in the mail, or someone will hand you a folder. It will look like just another case. But it will be a big case. It will be the biggest case of your career."

The Salamone brothers, Filippo and Sal, continued to provide Russo fragments of conversation pointing to the laundering operation. In one call Sal confided his disgust with an employee. "Before I went to Switzerland," he said, "I gave Gary a lot of money to cash. Now he's spilling his guts all over the world, like he's doing with everything else."

Russo also listened to Sal calling a New Jersey food distributor named Pino to complain about a bill of $9,000. As Salamone pointed out, a former company salesman, Damiano, had cheated him of $3,500.

But it was Salamone's own fault, Pino insisted, ". . . because it was an illegal operation."

Russo's ears perked up.

"Sal, you know better than me," Pino continued, "that an operation of this kind with a bank is illegal."

Salamone claimed not to understand. He had asked the salesman, who was going from pizzeria to pizzeria anyway, to change some money, "and then he didn't bring me the money back." Was that right?

"What you have to admit," Pino said, "is that Damiano screwed you out of this money."

"Look," Salamone said, "I have nothing to worry about. We could go in front of the bank, we can go before the federals, we can go before everyone, okay?" People were perfectly free to change small bills into large ones anytime, he said.

Sure, agreed Pino. "But people will ask: 'What was he doing with this money? Why was he changing them into hundreds? Where was he bringing it? Where this and where that?'

"This three thousand is nothing," Pino warned pointedly. "Tomorrow could be worse. . . ."

So Salamone was changing small bills into hundreds, Russo reflected. It made the money easier to transport and less suspicious-looking. Funny, he thought, how these tough guys were always such patsies for a con man. And how they spent half their time arguing over who owed whom what. But what did anyone expect? They couldn't exactly go running to a lawyer or the police. Filippo Salamone's name had first come up in Franco Della Torre's phone records. Now the agents had evidence that his brother Sal's employees had been sent around to nearby banks with cash to purchase cashier's checks for just under the $10,000 bank reporting limit.

Filippo had other deals going, Russo soon discovered. He had called a specialty automobile shop outside the city to find out how much it would cost to adapt an imported Mercedes to American safety and emission standards. The price was $7,500. Salamone later relayed the information to Vito Roberto Palazzolo in Europe. The two agreed it was worth it for a car that sold for $50,000 in the United States.

Russo's suspicions were aroused. Why would a pizza man go into the car-importing business? Cars, he knew from dealing with the Customs Service, had long been a favorite way of smuggling drugs into the country.

On April 30, 1983, Ganci's girlfriend, Carol, began to keep a diary. Pitifully vacuous as it often was, it recorded events in her life and the lives of the men she touched over the next year. Her first entry recorded a lunch at Tavern on the Green with Ganci and her friend Paula. Afterward they sat in Central Park. Carol was pleased with herself. "Look nice," she wrote approvingly.

Several days later she met Ganci again, and they drove to her apartment in Clifton. Her diary memorialized the encounter. "Sex," she wrote.

She marked it down again several days later, also noting that she went to the drugstore and cleaner's and paid the oil bill for the house.

Ganci's wife, Margherita, was not as blind as Ganci and Carol might have thought. When Frank Polizzi, the Belleville contractor and motel owner and a Ganci relative, called to chat one day, Margherita let out a deep sigh. "Oh, Frank, don't tell me anything. I can't take it anymore," she said. ". . . Still, he says that it's not so. Am I crazy? I am not crazy! He created the craziness when he went with that whore. It wasn't necessary because we had always gotten along and we always cared about each other. It wasn't necessary to seek love from a pig."

Russo eavesdropped on other dramas. Catalano complained in one conversation that nobody told him anything; plans for a meeting had been changed, and he hadn't been told.

"Pass by here and we'll go," said Ganci.

"You pass by here," Catalano corrected him. "I'm just getting in now."

Ganci caught Catalano's tone and twitted his associate. "Hey, God, owner of three or four cars, Mercedes this and that."

"Who, you?" Catalano demanded.

"You."

"Bullshit! Bullshit!" bellowed Catalano. "You're too much bullshit."

Ganci couldn't resist a parting shot: "The people know about it. There is no need for me to tell them."

Ganci had hit a nerve. Catalano prized his low profile. He took pains to drive his smaller cars, not the Mercedes, which was leased anyway. Once he started to attract attention, he was in trouble.

May 5 brought Ganci, Polizzi, Bonventre, and Amato together at Casa Polizzi in Belleville. Agents concealed outside shot a wonderfully clear series of photographs showing the foursome in earnest discussion. Cesare stood out as usual, resplendent in a boldly striped collarless shirt open to the sternum, revealing a thick gold chain. The date made Russo ponder. It was the second anniversary of the killing of the three captains. Were these four celebrating?

Ganci drove to Clifton to see Carol. "Sex," she wrote.

For all his visits to Carol, Ganci was still a devoted father. Mary Jo was wild about him. When Ganci called home one day from New Jersey, Russo heard her shouting in the background, "I want to speak with my father!" She got on the phone. "When you get home, can we take a ride?" she begged.

"Sure," Ganci said.

"Dad, listen, I got a ninety on my religion test."

"Ninety?"

"Yeah."

"My God!"

Ganci wanted both—Carol and his family. At the end of May the Catalanos and the Gancis flew down to Florida for a long weekend. In a maneuver fraught with peril, Ganci also brought Carol without, of course, telling Margherita. As it developed, the tryst quickly turned to farce when Carol's luggage was mistakenly delivered to Catalano's room and Catalano opened Carol's suitcase by mistake, exposing Ganci's duplicity. Margherita had tried to look the other way for a long time, even when she once came across Carol's utility bill in her husband's pocket. But this was too much.

Back home after four days Ganci and Carol continued to meet, although there were often tiffs. "Had small argument, made up, sex," Carol confided to her diary.

In the following days Carol waxed her eyebrows and did "lots of thinking," as she wrote: "Please Carol for your own good try to organize your life." She got caught in traffic jams and recorded that in her diary. She washed the black Mercedes Ganci had bought her. She got a facial. She took a judo class. She met someone named Frank. She had breakfast or lunch with Ganci—and sex with Frank in the evenings.

Early June brought a mysterious visitor to Ganci's house, a full-faced, broad-shouldered, black-haired man who drove up with Giuseppe and Sal Lamberti. Catalano arrived separately. None of the agents had ever seen the stranger before, and not even the omniscient Jack Clark of police intelligence recognized him in the surveillance photo. Not until much later was he identified as Giuseppe Soresi of Borgetto, Sicily, an envoy of the Sicilian heroin suppliers. John Mauzey, hidden in his van, caught a telltale moment. As the visitor drove off, Ganci and Catalano remained standing on the sidewalk. Ganci then gave a noticeable nod and wink that seemed to say: "We've done it!"

Russo meanwhile was pondering a disquieting development. The investigation, it seemed, had been exposed. It began with a panicky postmidnight call on June 2 from Filippo Salamone's brother, Sal, in Scranton, to his sleeping wife at home in Bloomsburg, Pennsylvania.

"I can't talk on the phone!" he blurted.

"Prick!" she said. Had he woken her up to tell her he couldn't talk to her?

Something very important had happened, Sal said. He told her to call Filippo and he would call back.

"At this hour? What, are you crazy?"

"Yes, at this hour."

He gave her a number where Filippo could reach him.

"Why?" she asked. "Is there a problem again?"

"Yeah, enormous problems. You. Your father. Me. Everybody . . . I can't talk on the phone. They put a bug on this phone."

Shit! The bureau had been investigating the money changing by Salamone's pizza employees, but how did Sal know about the phones? Was it only a guess?

Filippo Salamone soon called back.

"There's a problem," Sal's wife told him.

"What kind of problem?"

She was reluctant to go into detail. Sal would explain it himself, from a safe phone.

Filippo was insistent. What was it about?

"Ah . . . about the mess," she said. ". . . You know what we did the last . . . that time."

"Huh?" Filippo didn't get it.

"The thing that you know . . . the thing . . . you remember, that we want."

"But what?" Filippo asked. "Did somebody come around?"

"Yeah . . . ah, well, not yet. But ah . . . you know . . . they're getting in touch with everybody." Filippo finally understood. The FBI knew about the money changing.

Later Sal's wife relayed his warning to her parents: ". . . be careful just in case they come over by you . . . because they have everybody's name, I guess. All of the ones that exchanged money and everything."

She went on: "So see if you can, you know, make up an excuse, in case they come, you know, that you needed the money . . . to buy another store . . . they took the photographs from the banks, you know, that they went to exchange it. . . . Perhaps you could tell them that you were making change or getting change, exchanging . . . making a deposit, something you know. . . . Even if they have the photos, there's no way they could know what you went there for . . . anyway, warn the guy from the bank who knows, since you are friends with him."

So the banker was in on it, Russo thought. Maybe he was the leak. Agents in Scranton had been checking the bank and the DEA's Tom Tripodi and other agents had searched a car and conducted some interviews. Maybe Sal had just pieced the evidence together from the interviews. Now that the investigation was exposed, Russo realized, they would face some hard decisions.

He called Rooney. "We may have to grab the Salamones," he said. He explained the calls.

"But wouldn't that tip off the others?" Rooney asked.

Russo agreed it probably would.

"So let's wait," Rooney said.

"But if he skips?"

Over the next few days the agents repeatedly hashed over the dilemma with Schiliro, Vinton, Storey, Sheer, and other FBI supervisors in New Jersey and Pennsylvania. In the end they decided to hold off. There was too much at stake to move precipitously.

Several days later Russo heard Filippo's wife tell her sister-in-law, "This month I leave."

"The end, the end of this month?"

Yes, she confirmed.

So, Russo realized, they were going to skip. But the decision had been made to let them go.

Sal and Filippo then conferred in low tones. "Did the tomato arrive?" Filippo asked.

"Yeah," said Sal. "And a . . . when it comes . . . when it arrives, when the tomato arrives, don't bring it to the house . . . call me, and I'll tell you where you have to bring it."

In fact, Sal added, "That one arrived . . . this morning it arrived."

In that case, Filippo said, he would come and get it "because here I'm running out."

Later that night Filippo called his wife from the road. He asked if someone had called.

"He came already. He planted the trees," she said. "He planted cherries, and peaches, plum fruit . . . three types."

By mid-June the Salamones were getting ready to sell the house and leave the country. Filippo's wife relayed these facts to Vito Roberto Palazzolo in Europe as Russo listened. She was just waiting for the kids to be finished with school, she said.

It was the FBI's last chance. Grab Filippo and show its hand? Or let him flee and keep the already compromised investigation as quiet as possible? The decision was set. The Salamones could go.

Several days later a call came in to Filippo Salamone's house. An unfamiliar voice answered. Russo realized he had heard it before. It was Salvatore Greco, Filippo's partner in the pizzeria. A few days before, Greco had been photographed in deep discussion with Gaetano Mazzara outside the Roma restaurant in the Menlo Park Mall.

"No Salamone, no here anymore," Greco told the caller.

Then who was that? wondered the caller, surprised.

"This the . . . the owner of the house," said Greco.

Where had the Salamones gone?

"I don't have an idea," Greco said.

June 18, 1983, was a Saturday. At one minute past five P.M. the telephone rang in the orange-brick Ganci house in Middle Village. Margherita answered.

"Hello, good evening, madam," said a voice Russo did not recognize. He had heard it for the first time the month before. "I am Benny."

The heroin Rooney and Russo had been anticipating so impatiently was about to appear.

13

O N a tranquil Saturday afternoon in the spring of 1983 Rudolph Giuliani
put a Bach cantata on the stereo, settled into a comfortable armchair in the living
room of his Washington home, and began to leaf through the book *A Man of
Honor* once again. He could not get over it. Here was Joe Bonanno laying out
in cold print, in his autobiography of all things, what Giuliani and other prosecutors had long taken for granted but had never convinced a judge to allow them
to say in the courtroom: that there was not only a very real Mafia but a ruling
commission that made policy, resolved disputes, and ordered or approved murders. The realization electrified Giuliani; Bonanno was laying out the illegal
enterprise—one that judges had always found too prejudicial or speculative to
introduce in court. Here it was from the horse's mouth, all set forth, with
surprisingly few euphemisms, complete with photos of the tall and rugged crime
boss meeting and partying and hunting and sightseeing with other "men of
tradition." Why was Bonanno admitting all this? Giuliani wondered. Was it his
overweening pride? His arrogance? His self-image as a virtual head of state? Or
his way of outdoing his son Bill, who had nakedly exposed the family in Gay
Talese's Mafia chronicle *Honor Thy Father*. Whatever the reason, it was an
extraordinary confession. If Bonanno could admit all this, Giuliani thought,

imagine what he was hiding. He pictured Bonanno before a grand jury. He would be gravely ill, of course, too frail to testify. The Sicilian flu. Too bad he couldn't haul the whole Mafia Commission into court, indict the whole— *Wait a minute! Wait a minute!*

Giuliani was preparing to return to New York from Washington as the United States attorney for the Southern District of New York, the nation's showcase prosecutorial post, just as Tom Sheer's office across the street was the FBI's flagship district. At thirty-nine, the mournful-eyed Giuliani was well on his way to becoming the nation's most exuberant racket buster since Thomas E. Dewey. With his pale, angular face, flat, woolly crown, and faint lisp, Rudy—as he was familiarly called—was soon to become a trademark presence on the nightly news and Sunday talk shows as he publicly drew a bead on the mob, white-collar crime, and political corruption. New Yorkers might have been pardoned a yawn. They had heard all this before. But within four years Giuliani not only masterminded the successful prosecution of the longest federal criminal trial in memory and jailed in the process one of Sicily's most notorious Mafia bosses but picked off as well a good chunk of the American Mafia's ruling commission, an idea which Giuliani made sure to credit to author Joe Bonanno. He also exposed and tried more crooked New York City officials than anyone in at least half a century and simultaneously prosecuted some of the biggest insider traders and market manipulators on Wall Street. Although he had his detractors, rival prosecutors who found him grabby, and targets whom Giuliani paraded before the media in his press conferences, there was no doubt that Giuliani was set on compiling an extraordinary record as chief prosecutor of the Southern District, one striking enough, or so it seemed, to propel him into a political career.

After Sheer's transfer to New York the summer before, followed by the former FBI agent Louis Freeh's assignment to the prosecution team, Giuliani's arrival proved the management catalyst that transformed the case into an epic.

Giuliani was born in Brooklyn in 1944. His maternal grandmother, one of twenty-two children, had come to the United States from Avellino, east of Naples, as a baby in 1884. Giuliani's father ran a tavern and pizza restaurant in Flatbush, and young Rudy sometimes helped out, waiting on tables. For years afterward young Rudy could not stand pizza. Harold Giuliani felt that the unschooled immigrant Italians had missed a stage in their social development, and he pressed his son to continue his education. The family moved to Garden City, Long Island, where Giuliani attended Catholic grammar school and high school. Until college, he said, he did not know what it was like to start classes without a prayer. Giuliani had considered the priesthood and a missionary life before acknowledging that he was probably not cut out for celibacy, although he was shy with women and far from a rake. He went to Manhattan College and New York University Law School and clerked for two years for a federal judge. In 1970 he joined the Southern District as a young prosecutor, handling, among other cases, the testimony of rogue cop-turned-witness Bob Leuci, whose story was later told in the hit book and movie *Prince of the City.*

After a two-year stint in Washington as associate deputy attorney general, Giuliani returned to New York to go into civil practice. In 1981 the new Reagan administration named him associate attorney general, the Justice Department's third highest official. Two years later Giuliani was back in Manhattan, making a prosecutorial splash. In one much-publicized performance he donned dark glasses, a T-shirt, and a leather vest for undercover buys of crack from the legions of drug dealers infesting Manhattan's Upper West Side. Even Giuliani's seventy-four-year-old mother could get into it. Sensing the reluctance of her son to discuss a controversial case on the phone, she once asked, "Rudy, you want to call me back from a pay phone?"

While in Washington as associate attorney general, Giuliani had kept close track of the widening Cattails investigation in one of the ninety-four regional prosecutor's offices he supervised. The FBI briefed him monthly on its major cases, and this was as major a case as it had running anywhere in the country. From what Tom Sheer and Louis Freeh told him, it was clear that the bureau had tapped into an extraordinarily large and powerful drug organization, one able to inundate the nation's largest brokerage houses with truckloads of cash. It was the Mafia but not the Mafia that Giuliani or anyone else recognized. These were Sicilians operating here through the Bonanno and Gambino families. Frighteningly, they were virtually unknown, these men who spoke in code in the Sicilian dialect, often on pay phones. Some had slipped into the country illegally from Canada with no immigration history or had entered long ago to live quietly, running pizzerias and other small businesses until they might be called upon by relatives or associates to assist in dope-trafficking schemes or other criminal plots, including murder. It was a secret, far-flung empire, reaching from one end of the country to the other and across the Atlantic to Italy, Switzerland, and Bulgaria and undoubtedly to the heroin centers of the Middle East and Asia. Under the circumstances, Giuliani realized, the bureau had amassed a vast amount of intelligence, a perfect foundation for a successful RICO case. It was not individuals he was after—there would always be more of them—it was the enterprise, the organization that nurtured them and that they in turn had fashioned into an all but impervious shield for their outlaw schemes. Giuliani targeted the Mafia itself. If Bonanno could write about it, Giuliani decided, he could haul it into court.

The time was propitious. It was at his office's behest in the Justice Department, Giuliani reminded Sheer, that the FBI in 1982 had been given cojurisdiction with the DEA over drug enforcement. And it was just this kind of long-range case that the FBI was most suited to pursue. The DEA had its own special expertise, Giuliani said, but it did best on the street, penetrating drug rings and busting up lower-level networks. This case was made for the FBI. In Sheer, Giuliani found a kindred spirit. Like Giuliani, the FBI's New York criminal chief had enough self-confidence to direct his efforts at solving the task at hand, rather than worry about how to protect his butt from Washington bureaucrats. Sheer felt likewise about Giuliani. He didn't have to waste time explaining to the prosecutor why the case was important. "You dragged it under his nose," Sheer said admiringly, "and he smelled it."

June 1983 brought another major law enforcement development. FBI agents were staked out around the Caffè Aiello, Tony "Commerciante" Aiello's suspected heroin dispensary in Ridgewood, where Ganci and Catalano made frequent visits, when the agents noticed some other men in cars outside. They ran the plates and saw they had competition—the NYPD was also watching the location. The Brooklyn cops had been running their own narcotics investigation, code-named Brooknor for Brooklyn North. Previously, such an overlapping might have triggered a turf squabble over who was there first. In fact when the bureau set up a meeting with the NYPD to coordinate their surveillances, one of the police supervisors was quick to see an FBI plot. "They're here to steal our case," Lieutenant Joe Polly warned his fellow cops. "We have a good case going. Why do we need them?" But to the surprise of Polly, a beefy, animated six-footer, the bureau agreed to share its information, an unheard-of largess to many of the hard-bitten cops who knew the FBI as an agency that always took information but never gave any back. Clearly things were changing. "They made me a believer," gushed Polly later. At a subsequent meeting, Polly's men showed the agents a picture they had snapped of an unknown subject. Rooney was ecstatic. This was Filippo Ragusa, the Queens baker from Bagheria who had been photographed in the Piazza Politeama with Ganci, Muratore, and others in February 1980. So he was around here now. Out of the new spirit of cooperation grew a series of joint police, FBI, and DEA task forces formed to combat drug trafficking, organized crime, and terrorism, among other threats. Police Commissioner Benjamin Ward, in his headquarters at 1 Police Plaza, soon began referring to the FBI across Foley Square as "2 Police Plaza."

When Benny phoned Ganci again on June 18, 1983, Russo didn't think that the portly pizza maker immediately recognized his caller. Benny gave only his first name, and Ganci, ever cautious, answered noncommittally while he struggled to figure out who was calling. Benny complained that Ganci no longer passed by Philadelphia. "You've already made your money; now you don't think of anybody anymore," he gibed.

Now Ganci knew. "Oh, but you . . . I had not recognized you, Benny." Benny Zito, Russo was to learn, was a relative from San Giuseppe Iato, a town about an hour's drive southwest of Palermo.

Ganci greeted Zito warmly, inquiring about his father. Ganci recalled that he had been back to San Giuseppe Iato the year before to visit his own father, now in his eighties. Ganci had made regular visits home since leaving San Giuseppe Iato for America in 1966. He was a popular benefactor, sending generous sums back to his Sicilian relatives and friends. No one seemed to know exactly, or care much, where Ganci's money came from.

"Tell me something," Zito asked. "Do you go by Knickerbocker Avenue?"

Ganci paused, suspicious. "No," he said coldly. "Who ever goes there? . . . Why?"

"I'm interested in finding a fellow who is there during this time," Zito said. His name, he said, was Calogero Di Maria.

Calogero Di Maria! Russo knew—and surely Ganci knew—that Di Maria had been killed the previous winter. Two gunmen with hoods had walked into his pizzeria on Avenue U in Brooklyn, set down a bottle of champagne in front of him, and blasted him to pieces. Now Zito wanted to find him? This was bizarre.

Ganci paused again, longer. "But what is he, a pizza man? What?" he asked. Ganci had to know! Russo thought. He must be just playing along. This must be some kind of code. It struck him that Di Maria's pizzeria had been called the Extrabar, the same name as the Palermo restaurant where Ganci and Catalano had been photographed meeting with the Sicilian drug traffickers in 1980.

Yeah, Zito said, Di Maria was a pizza man, from Balestrate. He said he had sold Di Maria a place some time ago, and he had left a sea of debts. "And he's got to pay. . . ."

"We'll find him, Benny," Ganci said.

"Because the time for fooling around is over," Zito said. "I've got to go close the contract because that pizzeria there, I sold it to another guy, no?"

"I understand," Ganci said.

"As soon as we see each other, we'll talk better," Zito said. He expected to be in New York in a couple of days and would call Ganci at his Al Dente pizzeria.

This was promising, Russo thought. Maybe Zito wasn't looking for Di Maria at all. Maybe he was signaling his interest in some kind of deal. Why else would Ganci say he understood? And why would they talk better in person?

Two days later, as he had said, Zito was in New York and reached Ganci at a cousin's barbershop in Queens. Ganci gave him directions to his house. Soon Pat Luzio in the lookout and the surveillance team posted around Ganci's house picked up a light Volkswagen with Pennsylvania plates. Zito had arrived. He disappeared inside the house before anyone could get a good look. Next they saw Ganci raise his brown garage door, open the trunk of his blue Mercedes, remove a brown grocery bag, and disappear into the garage.

That evening Zito called the Roma restaurant and seemed to talk to Gaetano Mazzara about restaurant tables.

"The little dust . . . you pass a rag . . . then the rag dries . . . that little bit of water can be seen, you know," Mazzara said.

Twelve tables, Zito said, "one thousand three . . . but they're good, though, the material, the base."

"Yes, yes, yes," agreed Mazzara. "They're beautiful . . . beautiful tables."

Whatever it signified, the Zito conversation seemed to usher in a flurry of phone calls among Ganci and his compatriots. Within three hours Mazzara called looking for Ganci; he was out, but Mazzara reached him early the next morning. "Don't move from over there because I'm coming," he told Ganci.

Ganci then called Mazzurco, the elfin Lamberti relative. "All right," Ganci told him. "You bring the things in pocket and I will call you . . . understand?"

That evening Giuseppe Lamberti invited the Gancis over. Ganci offered to bring some of his pizza along from Al Dente. For a moment Russo assumed it was another code.

"My daughter wants pizza with extra cheese," Lamberti said.

"What kind, Sicilian?" Ganci asked.

"Ah, bring the American kind."

No, Russo decided, that had to be actual pizza.

Mazzurco later called Ganci. "I've got a couple of plants," he said. "I have a couple of plants to flower. . . . I'm supposed to go out . . . to go to about ten places."

Later Ganci told Mazzurco he was waiting impatiently at home for someone. When Tony Aiello of Caffè Aiello called, Ganci sounded annoyed. "It's been three hours that I'm over here waiting for you. . . . I went to get the things," he said.

"The rolls," Aiello said.

Russo was interested to hear that Aiello was making a pickup from Ganci. Aiello had come up many times before. In addition to the café, he owned Tony's Pizza on 125th Street in Harlem, which informants said was also a drug outlet. Whatever Aiello was picking up from Ganci, Russo doubted it was rolls.

Shortly afterward Ganci summoned Mazzara to a meeting. "Bring those documents," he told Mazzara. The well-coiffed Mazzara soon arrived and handed Ganci a brown package a little smaller than a shoe box.

Russo later listened to Ganci call Benny Zito in Philadelphia. "Tell me something," Zito said, "that young fellow is ready, no?"

"Yeah."

"But not that there's need for any papers for the time being . . ." Zito said.

"Well, taking possession, there's need for the papers . . . that guy won't give you possession without the papers, let's say."

Zito wondered whether he needed an appointment.

"Sure you need an appointment," Ganci said. ". . . You've got to give me an appointment. For example, if you come down tomorrow night or for tomorrow, you've got to tell me at least tonight."

Russo tried to sort this all out. Zito and Ganci were dealing with a young fellow who was ready for something. There had to be some kind of exchange; the young fellow was wary. Zito had to pick up something from Ganci but only after Ganci had made arrangements to have it ready.

DEA undercover agent Stephen Hopson had no reason to think that his investigation in Philadelphia in the spring of 1983 would intersect the FBI's biggest case. The thirty-three-year-old, dark-haired, handsome six-footer had been a DEA agent for nine years, having moved to the drug agency from a job as a county narcotics investigator in Atlantic City. He had already carried out close to a hundred undercover assignments, most of them quick buy-bust operations. Now he was investigating suspected drug-trafficking connections of a Philadelphia pizza magnate, Dominic Mannino, who founded a chain of Mimmo's pizzerias. An arrested drug offender who was willing to become an informant to ease his sentence told Hopson he was working for a Mimmo's franchisee on Roosevelt Boulevard in Philadelphia who might be dealing in drugs. His name, he said, was Benny Zito. Hopson arranged for the informant to introduce him to Zito as a distributor of exercise equipment who might be interested in buying a Mimmo's of his own.

Hopson was building on an earlier undercover breakthrough. For several years a tall, genial DEA agent named Frank Panessa had been working to penetrate a suspected drug ring in Philadelphia. He had targeted a Sicilian, Alberto Ficalora, who operated a pizza parlor and who introduced Panessa to drug-trafficking partners, including Paolo LaPorta, who, it turned out, had been one of contract killer Luigi Ronsisvalle's sidekicks on Knickerbocker Avenue. Ficalora confided that Sicilian associates in New York were major heroin suppliers for the region.

Sicilians were getting pushed around in New York, but that was going to stop, Ficalora told Panessa. "They all lost respect," he said. "But," he vowed ominously, "respect is going to come back from Sicily."

LaPorta confided that there was a bottling company in Marsala, Sicily, that liquefied heroin for easier smuggling into the United States. And he told another tantalizing story: that his group was unhappy with some of the heroin they were getting from Cesare Bonventre and Baldo Amato. The pair, he said, had set up Carmine Galante for the hit in Joe and Mary's restaurant. As a reward, LaPorta said, Cesare had been given control of Sicilian heroin in the United States. But he had been stiffing them, LaPorta said. They had bought $3 million worth of heroin that tested out at a weak 30 percent purity. When they protested, Bonventre insisted it had been 100 percent. "He's stiffing his own people," LaPorta complained to Panessa darkly.

Panessa's infiltration of the pizzeria-based Philadelphia drug establishment helped set the stage for Hopson's sting of Zito. Hopson and a female agent masquerading as his girl friend arranged to meet Zito and his girl friend in June 1983 at Caesar's in Atlantic City. Zito, boyishly handsome with an easy smile and a luxuriant mop of black hair, was flashing a large roll, about $5,000, Hopson noticed. At first they talked pizzerias. Zito told Hopson he had made $200,000 the previous year. Hopson acted interested. He soon met with Mannino, who offered to sell Hopson a less desirable location for $60,000. Hopson said he would think it over. Later Hopson told Zito he had decided against it, but what about going partners in the tavern business? Meanwhile, Hopson confided a problem: He had a deal going with a customer, but he had run short. Hopson was confident Zito would understand the reference to heroin, which he did. He cautioned Hopson that the business was very risky. You had to be careful of police and informants; they were everywhere. Hopson couldn't agree more.

After Hopson left, Zito called Ganci, supposedly looking for the dead Calogero Di Maria but really searching for heroin to supply his new customer: DEA Agent Hopson. "We'll find him, Benny," Ganci promised.

Russo, who was listening to the call in New York, had no idea that a DEA undercover agent had already got his hooks into Zito—just as Hopson in Philadelphia had no idea that Zito's call to his New York supplier was being overheard by an FBI agent.

Zito met Hopson again two weeks later at his pizzeria. Zito said he might be able to help Hopson out with half a kilo for $120,000. Hopson tried to sound casual. Fine, he said, no problem.

But the DEA was cautious about laying out huge sums to drug traffickers. What if the money disappeared? What if the stakes kept going up? Hopson persuaded his superiors to stay in the game.

Russo, meanwhile, was listening to Ganci tell Zito: ". . . that young fellow is ready, no?"

At the end of June Hopson returned to Zito's pizzeria, carrying a green box containing $120,000 in carefully recorded bills. Outside, surveillance agents concealed in a van photographed and videotaped Hopson's arrival. Hopson had decided against wearing a body recorder. Too risky. What if Zito decided to search him?

"This is for the half," Hopson told Zito inside.

"All right."

He tried to draw Zito out. "Be careful driving up with the money."

Zito smiled. "Especially coming back," he said.

Now with Hopson still with him in the pizzeria, Zito called Ganci. Zito needed the "papers"—the drugs—without which Hopson would not give "possession" of the money, as Ganci had so quaintly phrased it. Zito wanted to drive up that night to Ganci's for the pickup.

Ganci repeated he needed a day's notice. Now it was Zito's turn to be annoyed. If he had known that, he would have called the night before, but he had not wanted to disturb Ganci.

Ganci mimicked Zito's whiny tone. " 'Last night I didn't want to call!' What am I, an Arab?" He suggested Zito come by the next night.

"No," Zito said. "Because I have, I have the, how do you say it? . . . I have the young fellow here." He paused. "Did you understand me? If it can be done, you know, ah, I'll take a run late tonight, or else earlier." He paused again. "What do you think?"

"It cannot be," Ganci said.

As soon as Ganci hung up with Zito, Russo listened as Ganci embarked on one of his frenetic bouts of telephoning. First he called the Roma restaurant looking for Mazzara or Castronovo. Neither was around. He tried their homes. Both were out.

Ganci called Zito back. "Ah, I still can't tell you anything," he said.

Zito was disappointed. He did not want the deal with Hopson to fall through: "You know this young fellow . . . is good. He's decided to, to take this thing."

Luzio in the lookout and the trailing surveillance agents then saw Ganci jump in his car and speed to Caffè Aiello. Ganci again came up dry. He called Zito again. "It will have to be tomorrow," he said.

That night Ganci called Bonventre. He was not at his usual Brooklyn haunt, his own Caffè Cesare. Ganci reached him at home. It was already nearly eleven P.M., but they agreed to meet at the café in an hour.

The next day Ganci finally reached Mazzara. They made an appointment at Ganci's for the afternoon. Ganci then called Zito. Zito could come that night. It would be there.

Several hours later the Ganci surveillance squad saw Mazzara's tan Audi pull up outside the orange-brick house. Mazzara reached into the car and extracted a wrinkled paper grocery bag, rolled at the top. He carried it into Ganci's house. Later that night Zito came for the pickup.

Very early the next morning, while Philadelphia slept, one of Zito's associates led Hopson to an apartment and handed him a plastic grocery bag. Inside was a brown paper sack, rolled at the top, and inside the sack was a package of white powder. Hopson took it to the DEA lab. It tested out at one-half kilogram of 83.4 percent pure heroin hydrochloride.

Anthony Petrucci of the DEA's New York office had been following the Ganci investigation closely. A short, rotund former agent of the Bureau of Alcohol, Tobacco, and Firearms, Petrucci had long been convinced, with Russo, Rooney, and Paquette, that the coded calls and large cash transfers were the earmarks of a major narcotics conspiracy. But he was caught off guard, and then astounded, when a DEA agent in the Philadelphia office called him one day in late June 1983 to ask a favor.

They had come across a New York telephone number in an undercover case in Philadelphia, she said. Could Petrucci run it down—894-4739? He didn't have to—he already knew Ganci's number by heart. But what was Philadelphia's interest?

"We're making an undercover buy from a guy here, and he calls that number in New York," the agent told Petrucci.

"Who's the Philadelphia guy?" Petrucci asked.

"Benny Zito."

Petrucci was stunned. "You've got a case on Benny Zito?"

"Since early this year," the Philadelphia agent said.

Petrucci couldn't believe it. "Then we're working different ends of the same case!"

14

NBEKNOWN to the FBI in New York or the Philadelphia DEA, Hopson's undercover drug investigation had tapped into the Cattails case through Benny Zito. The FBI knew that the DEA was investigating pizzerias in Philadelphia. At the same time the DEA knew that the FBI was running a big Mafia drug case out of New York—indeed, both agencies had discussed it at Governors Island in New York Harbor the previous January—but the DEA did not initially know that Zito was calling Ganci. And the FBI did not initially know that Ganci was talking to Zito. Sooner or later, however, considering the deals involved, the two investigations were bound to cross.

Now, the question was: Whose powder was it—Philadelphia's or New York's? The Philadelphia DEA was convinced it had an airtight narcotics case. Hopson had Zito in a half-kilo buy of 83.4 percent pure heroin for $120,000. Philadelphia was ready to take the case down. The New York FBI, on the other hand, was nowhere near a conclusion. There the stakes were clearly greater. Zito's powder had just propelled the investigation into a momentous new dimension. If Philadelphia grabbed Zito now, the arrest would surely spook Ganci and Catalano in New York and expose the wires. Then again, if Philadelphia passed up the opportunity to arrest Zito and the larger case collapsed or evaporated, Zito could skip. What would Philadelphia be left with? Sheer knew how Philadelphia felt; that office was his last posting before New York, and he was still close to many of the agents. For the time being, it was agreed, Philadelphia would hold off.

Meanwhile, across the Hudson, frustration was building among the Newark FBI agents. They had been shouldering a growing burden of the surveillances as the case developed a strong New Jersey dimension. For more than a year they had tailed the Salamones and Sal Greco, who took over Filippo's house when he fled. They had watched Polizzi and his Belleville motel and, of course, Carol, whom Ganci came to visit almost daily. They had spied on Castronovo and Mazzara and the cartons that rolled out of their Menlo Park restaurant. They had even managed to insert a dark-haired, high-cheekboned undercover agent, Hilda Kogut, as a waitress in the Roma restaurant, although she never managed to witness any money transfers. The Newark office had clearly been performing a service role. Every FBI office had to do some grunt work sometimes for another office, but New York was demanding more and more support. Newark had its own investigations to run. And when it came time at the end of the year to report the office's achievements, what would Newark's SAC, the special agent in charge, say, "We helped New York"? How would that impress Washington?

There were other rivalries smoldering behind the scenes. Within New York itself the Justice Department's prestigious Southern District office under Giuliani was at odds with the Brooklyn-based Eastern District, which might have seemed to be the natural home of the case. Ganci and Salvatore Catalano lived and did business in Queens. Filippo Casamento and his deli were in Brooklyn, as was the Pronto Demolition Company. Sal and Giuseppe Lamberti and brother-in-law Sal Mazzurco lived on Long Island. While many of their associates operated out of New Jersey, their dealings, too, were with Ganci. And Frank Rolli, the Alitalia cargo handler who became a government informant and led agents to the forty-kilo seizure in Milan in 1980, had been cultivated and turned by the Eastern District.

But the cash was brought to Manhattan—where Rudolph Giuliani was.

"You could argue this was an Eastern District case," said Assistant U.S. Attorney Charles Rose—who did, to no avail. "Rudy's approach was like the bureau's—bigness," the disgruntled Brooklyn prosecutor said later. "They threw in all the mutts," he said, referring to the lesser defendants. "We would have concentrated more on quality."

The Brooklyn and Manhattan offices had been traditional rivals going back, as the former Eastern District U.S. attorney Raymond Dearie lightheartedly put it, "to the days when our ancestors were breaking stones somewhere in North Africa." Since then there were periods when the two jurisdictions got along better and periods when they got along worse. This was not one of the better times. In 1981 and 1982, before the disparate FBI investigations had coalesced into a discrete case, Dearie watched with skepticism verging on disdain as the bureau launched its "family" strategy, which Dearie suspected was motivated not a little by the prospect of big headlines in the tabloids. He scoffed at Frank Storey's grand vision: "We'll take the family down as a unit." The bureau was playing with mirrors, Dearie decided. It was not going to hypnotize him. Dearie saw the bureau as often manipulative, seeking to play one prosecutor against another as it shopped around for the best deal in the commitment of prosecutorial resources and other support. And the jurisdiction that most often gave the FBI what it wanted, Dearie was convinced, was the Southern District.

The FBI had a different perspective. As Carmine Russo recalled, he had visited the Eastern District three times in late 1982 to get prosecutors there to draw up an affidavit for wiretaps on the phones of Ganci and his associates. Although prosecutor Reena Raggi was eager for the case, Russo said he was turned away each time for lack of sufficient probable cause. The Southern District proved more amenable and aggressive, he said.

"It's certainly true it was harder to get a wire out of the Eastern District than the Southern District," Dearie said. "We took that rather seriously." Not that the Southern District didn't, he hastened to add. But, he said, he held the bureau to a particularly high standard of probable cause on Title III's. In Dearie's view, the bureau's wiretaps were not notably efficient—"not enough return per over-heard hour," as he put it. When the FBI had nothing better to do, he said, it slapped a wire on a mob social club.

In late 1982, after Tom Sheer's arrival in New York, he and Storey invited Dearie and his Manhattan counterpart at the time, John S. Martin, Jr., to review the investigation as it then stood. Sheer hoped to convince the two U.S. attorneys to "cross-designate" prosecutors from each office to work in the other, to counter the rivalries undercutting a cooperative effort. It was to be a futile quest.

Dearie later recalled that he was more than willing to share the investigation with Martin. "I knew the bureau had its way much more in the Southern District than the Eastern District," Dearie said. The Southern District clearly had greater resources: "They could service the bureau better, they had more people. I figured, let's profit from the downside."

"John," Dearie remembered saying, "let's make history. Let's lay aside parti-sanship and backbiting and work together." If the bureau worked more closely with the Southern District, then perhaps the two prosecutors could develop a joint approach. But Martin, Dearie recalled, was determined to pursue it as a Southern District effort.

For his part, Martin recalled a dispute but no particulars. He had taken the job resolving not to be drawn into a fractious relationship with his Brooklyn counterpart, but the traditional rivalries soon surfaced, starting with a tug-of-war over the prosecution of Sonny Black Napolitano—the case in which undercover agent Pistone surfaced—a struggle that Manhattan won.

Martin's departure and Giuliani's arrival in Manhattan in June 1983 quickly exacerbated the hostility. The Eastern District came to see Giuliani as a publicity hound not above big-footing a case away from a neighboring jurisdiction for reasons of political ambition—"grabbing away cases with impunity," as Dearie later put it. Giuliani's office, in turn, dismissed the Eastern District as jealous of Manhattan's preeminent status, and willing to bad-mouth its rival at every opportunity, even lobbying Washington to undercut the investigation. Throughout, according to Giuliani, "Brooklyn sniped at our case," and pressured Washington to get the case brought down quickly. Increasingly Giuliani found himself on the phone to Washington to justify the time the case was taking and to press for the growing commitment of resources that the ever-expanding case required.

"This case couldn't have been done anywhere else," Giuliani insisted later. Given Giuliani's previous number three job at Justice, it was perhaps not surprising that he would enjoy privileged access to former associates in Washington. Generally, what Giuliani wanted Giuliani got. And Giuliani wanted this case. It deserved the best, he and his assistants felt, and Manhattan was the best. Sure, he acknowledged, the investigation could have been divided into five or more separate cases from Manhattan to Brooklyn to New Jersey and elsewhere, "but then," Giuliani said, "they would have been five small cases."

It was politics, countered Dearie. "They weren't going to satisfy Washington with a couple of big cases," he said. "They had to come up with something really big."

Even within the New York office of the FBI there were differences. Tom Vinton, the fierce-eyed narcotics supervisor whom Sheer had brought in to organize the drug case under Frank Storey, thought it was dragging on too long, handicapping other investigations. But Russo thought Vinton was being shortsighted.

To Sheer, the ex-Marine, it sometimes seemed like a battlefield with howitzer shells exploding all around him. "Boom. Boom. Boom. Big fuckin' one-oh-fives." The issues needed an airing. On June 30, 1983, less than a month after Giuliani's arrival in New York, Sheer hosted a meeting at 26 Federal Plaza that drew Giuliani, Brooklyn's Ray Dearie, New Jersey and Philadelphia prosecutors, and representatives from the DEA and the Justice Department. Sheer budgeted an hour and a half for the meeting, which started at 3:30 P.M. He and Luisa had some friends in from out of town. They'd be stopping by to pick him up around five.

In a secure, soundproof conference room, Sheer, according to notes kept of the meeting, outlined the progress of Cattails, urging that the fast-growing investigation of the Bonannos and the drug and money dealings of Catalano and Ganci remain everyone's top priority. He appealed for continued cooperation, recommended that Dearie and Giuliani together appoint the prosecution team, and once again suggested that the two jurisdictions cross-designate lawyers to work in each other's office. Dearie didn't commit himself. A representative from Justice suggested that the Southern District's Louis Freeh be formally designated the prosecutorial coordinator. Dearie demurred, although he agreed to meet with Giuliani to discuss it. Dearie bridled at the Justice official's comments. He was a patsy for Giuliani, Dearie decided. He was also troubled by the fact that Freeh had come from the FBI and hadn't had much experience prosecuting cases. In fact, the two had known each other for four years, since Dearie was a defense lawyer and Freeh the FBI case agent on the Anthony Scotto case. There were more experienced U.S. attorneys in Brooklyn, he felt. But Dearie later denied any obstinacy.

The conference was getting out of hand. Storey took Sheer aside. "Look, Tom," he said, "we can't deal here with twenty years of animosities." Sheer agreed. This was like five-dimensional chess. Luisa and their friends were waiting for him for dinner. At this rate, the meeting would go on all night. They'd all be at each other's throats. Sheer looked at his watch. Then breaking into the bickering he announced to the astonished visitors: "Thank you. The meeting's over" and walked out. But the problems with the Eastern District never could be ironed out, not even after Sheer and Storey took Dearie out afterward for a long lunch. A follow-up conference was held August 25 at the Justice Department in Washington, but again Dearie didn't commit himself. For all practical purposes, Brooklyn was out of the case.

With Philadelphia and New York aware of each other's interest, Hopson continued to meet with Zito, who still thought his new buddy was an exercise equipment salesman. Once Zito asked Hopson if he had a source for mushrooms and tomatoes. Hopson was trying to decipher the request when he realized Zito was talking about real mushrooms and tomatoes; he was just looking to save some money on supplies for the pizzeria. Hopson assured Zito he could get them cheap.

In early July Hopson dropped in on Zito at the pizzeria. Zito was nervous. He rubbed Hopson down to make sure he was not wearing a body transmitter. Hopson acted indignant, but secretly he breathed a prayer of thanks that he had resolved not to wear one throughout this investigation. Zito admitted he was suspicious. "If there's heat," he told Hopson, "I'll be killed."

"Look, if I was the cops," Hopson said, seeking to reassure him, "I'd have arrested you." Besides, Hopson added, "the cops don't pay a hundred and twenty thousand dollars and let the money walk." Zito had to agree. The following week Hopson with an undercover partner met Zito to discuss another buy. Zito complained he wasn't making enough on the deals. They agreed on a higher price of $245,000 a kilo; Zito was looking to make $35,000 for himself.

Hopson asked Zito about his source. "He's an older gentleman, also a pizzeria owner, who sells out of his garage," Zito said. He referred to him as *vossia*, a term of respect, and said he had four or five pizzerias grossing $13,000 or $14,000 a week each.

Two days later Hopson handed over the $245,000 to Zito. Afterward Zito and Ganci spoke to arrange the rest of the transaction. "You're coming down tonight, right?" Ganci asked, his geography off by 180 degrees.

"Yeah," said Zito. "But tell me something. I have around, around, how do you say it? You know, how many are you over there . . . is twenty-one enough of these chocolates or not? . . ."

"Yeah but it should be twenty-one and a half."

"Twenty-one and a half for you guys," Zito said.

"Yeah," said Ganci.

These guys are something else, Russo thought. First they pretended to be talking pennies. Now it was chocolates—or half chocolates. As he figured it, 21½ chocolates were probably $215,000.

That evening the agents were staked out around Ganci's house in anticipation of Zito's scheduled arrival, but by midnight he had still not appeared. Bobby Gilmore was slouched in his Pontiac, half asleep. One A.M. came and went. Two A.M., no action. The agents had all but given up when, shortly after two, a pair of distant headlights drilled wobbly cones of light through the darkness.

Gilmore sat bolt upright. The approaching lights swept the sleeping street. Then a white Volkswagen Rabbit slid to a stop in front of Ganci's house. A man in a windbreaker jumped out and waited at the front door. A streetlight caught the side of his face. The youthful profile and glossy dark hair were unmistakable from the surveillance pictures: Benny Zito. The door opened slightly, and he slipped inside. Three minutes later he returned to the car and removed a shirt box—the money, Gilmore figured. Zito carried it back into the house, reemerging minutes later with a brown paper bag, rolled at the top, tucked under his left arm. He got back into his car and sped back to Philadelphia, followed by a tail of agents.

The next night Hopson picked up his order. It tested out at one kilo of 82.2 percent pure heroin. Hopson was looking for more. He phoned the pizzeria and first reached Zito's brother-in-law, Sal Finazzo, then Zito himself. "He says you've got, ah, some cheese around . . ." Hopson said.

Zito said he had to talk to his supplier: "Well . . . should I tell him to hold it or not?"

Hopson played it cool. He was out of town, he said. "I gotta wait till I come in." Meanwhile, he asked, "Do me a favor? If I can do the one . . . see if, ah, you could lower the thing because I've been coming back now a few times. Maybe they'll give me a break . . . 'cause, you know I'm a good guy."

Zito laughed. "Yeah," he said.

As soon as he hung up, Zito called Ganci—"Uncle Pinuzzo," as he said to Margherita. "Look," Zito told Ganci, "that one of the oven there . . . he is away right now. . . . Maybe he will take one. But he has to give me the answer Thursday."

The next day Zito called Ganci again. Ganci had good news. "Look, ah," he said, ". . . that guy has the two ovens, gas, that you said."

"Huh?" Zito was befuddled.

"That guy has another two ovens," Ganci repeated patiently, "the gas type. . . ."

Now Zito understood.

Russo did not have to wait long to discover who Ganci's guy with the ovens was. It was Salvatore Mazzurco, whom surveillance agents had seen with his relatives the two Lambertis and with Polizzi in the Menlo Park Mall back in March. Mazzurco called Ganci right afterward. Ganci told him to come over the next day and cautioned him to check the purity: "You have to see that the iron is strong."

The beginning of August 1983 brought Hopson back to Philadelphia. He was talking to Zito on the phone when the pizza man was interrupted by another call. It was the police, Zito told Hopson. They were ordering up a batch of pizzas.

Although Hopson couldn't get Zito to lower the price, he was ready for a third buy. Zito sensed his eagerness, so he raised the price again, to $250,000. Hopson had no choice. Zito then called Ganci to say he was coming up the next day.

As before, Hopson painstakingly recorded the serial numbers of the bills, which he then packed in a large box. He gift-wrapped it in white and gold paper patterned with brown bears and black pandas, a design that would show up nicely on the surveillance pictures and videos.

The next afternoon Mazzurco and his brother-in-law Giuseppe Lamberti were seen arriving at the Ganci house. While they were inside, Catalano was observed driving past, looking at the entrance. Shortly afterward Benny Zito drove up in his white Volkswagen Rabbit. He opened the hatch, removed Hopson's gift-wrapped box, and carried it into the Ganci house.

Fifteen minutes later Zito exited with a blue shirt box under his arm. On the sidewalk in front of the Ganci's house Zito ran into Mary Jo, Ganci's young daughter. As the FBI's hidden cameras clicked and whirred, the surveillance agents captured for all time the poignant image of Benny Zito stooping down to kiss Mary Jo with a quarter of a million dollars' worth of heroin under his arm.

The next day Zito met Hopson at a diner in Philadelphia and handed him the box from Ganci. "My associates say, 'Enjoy the shirt,'" Zito said.

Hopson played dumb. "What does that mean?" he said.

"It's the code we use," the unsuspecting Zito confided. He went on to boast that the kilo Hopson had just bought was the best stuff around, with a melting point of 230 to 235 degrees. Tests in the DEA lab confirmed Zito's assurances; the heroin was 78.9 percent pure.

It was later found to have an unexpected dividend: Mazzurco's partial right palmprint on the tissue paper it was wrapped in.

The buys were going so well the DEA decided Zito was ripe for a further sting: Hopson confided he had a new source and offered to supply Zito and his New York associates with heroin from Thailand at $110,000 a kilo, smuggled in by car. With the veteran DEA undercover agent Frank Tarallo posing as the overseas heroin supplier, Tarallo and Hopson presented the offer to Zito at a Hilton hotel outside Philadelphia.

Zito was enticed. He assured them that his associates could purchase between ten and thirty kilos and could probably take all the heroin Tarallo and Hopson could supply. He said some of his associates owned a demolition company where the car with the heroin could be dismantled. Zito said they could also take care of the transport and storage of the heroin.

Zito had only one request: Could they say the price was higher? By telling his associates the heroin would cost $120,000 a kilo rather than $110,000, Zito could make an extra $10,000 a kilo, or $300,000 on thirty kilos. Tarallo had no objection. But he wanted $100,000 up front.

Zito called Ganci for the okay and suggested that Ganci meet Hopson. Ganci curtly dismissed the idea. He didn't get where he was by meeting strangers to negotiate heroin deals. "No, I'm not interested to meet him," Ganci said. "No, there's no need to meet him."

Zito was unsure about proceeding alone. "And who is there? Who can meet him?" he persisted.

"But nobody!" Ganci insisted. "He has to talk with you."

If Zito was unsure, Ganci said, then he should wait. "These are not things that will rot . . . so simply you, ah, you put them in the garage and they stay . . . and when there's the occasion, you use it."

Zito went back to Hopson, insisting that his own okay was sufficient. No, countered Hopson, still trying to surface Ganci; they wanted the guarantees from Zito's suppliers.

Zito argued that he had the guarantees: "If anything happens, they back me up." The others, he admitted, were reluctant to come forward "because . . . they, they're not kids."

Hopson kept trying to draw Zito out. "Do they trust you with that kind of money?" he asked.

Zito should have been insulted but wasn't. "Don't worry about that, yeah," he said.

The following week Zito reported back to Hopson that everything was on hold; there were problems. One of his associates in New York was facing a lung operation. Moreover, Zito told the informant working with Hopson, someone in the Philadelphia Police Department had tipped them off to the fact that Zito's pizzeria was under surveillance and that the DEA had been buying heroin there. The news enraged the agents. Goddamn Philly cops! The agents could try to root out the rat, but it would focus more attention on the leak. They would just have to ignore it and hope it wouldn't matter. The breakdown of the Thai heroin sting, on the other hand, may have been a blessing. After Zito had been enticed, Sheer, the DEA, and the prosecutors decided it might jeopardize the rest of the case, so the proposal was quietly dropped.

In New York Ganci remained under close surveillance. In early July he, his wife, Margherita, and another woman, whom agents took to be Ganci's sister visiting from Sicily, drove to Queens' Booth Memorial Medical Center and went in. An agent quickly followed the trio into the hospital and saw them enter a consultation room and stay for almost an hour.

Several days later, on a sticky Sunday morning, while Rooney was home blacktopping his driveway, Luzio in the lookout and agents posted nearby saw Cesare Bonventre drive up to Ganci's house in a white Mercedes sports car. He was carrying a maroon leather purse, the kind men in Italy, but never America, carry to keep their pockets sleek, free of bulging wallets and keys. Cesare was his usual dapper self, Luzio could see. He wore a striped short-sleeve shirt and a thick gold wristwatch. He stood with his sports jacket thrown casually over his shoulders. He cut a dapper figure, in stark contrast to the two who met him, the pear-shaped Ganci and the stocky Catalano.

They were joined by a fourth man with bushy gray hair and a relaxed smile, Giovanni Ligammari. Back in February the agents had photographed him with Catalano, and the day after the three Bonanno captains were killed in May he had turned up at the Capri Motel in the Bronx. The men exchanged kisses on the cheek and, followed by surveillance agents, walked down the street, talking. Then Catalano took Bonventre's bag and walked to his bakery.

A few minutes later Catalano returned from the bakery with the bag, limper now that it seemed to have been emptied of its contents. He handed it back to Bonventre. Catalano appeared to be conducting the conversation, explaining something to Bonventre. Bonventre then kissed the cheeks of Ganci, Catalano, and Ligammari and drove back to his Caffè Cesare in Brooklyn. Luzio called Rooney at home to fill him in on the episode with the bag. What could it have held? Money, most likely. But it was so small. How much could it have contained? "Why guess?" said Rooney, who soon showed up with a similar bag he had borrowed from one of the women in the office. They went to the FBI evidence safe and pulled out stacks of $100 bills seized in other cases and stuffed the money into the bag. To the agents' astonishment, it held close to $40,000.

Bags of money were still on the agents' minds a few days later, when they followed Ganci to Carol's apartment in New Jersey and watched him emerge with a huge brown plastic bag. Snapping pictures furiously, they saw him stuff the bag into his trunk. Then he got into his car, drove over to a Dumpster, retrieved the bag, and threw it in. Garbage.

On July 21 two men visited Anthony Aiello's pizzeria on 125th Street in Harlem. One of the men, calling himself Frankie, was New York City undercover detective Richard Ford. His companion was "Big Al," a confidential informant, who had agreed to introduce Detective Ford in return for law enforcement consideration in his own case. A woman at the pizzeria told the pair to come back later. When they returned, Ford handed over a bag containing $8,000. She gave him a plastic bag containing, tests later showed, one ounce of 88.7 percent pure heroin. A month later Ford repeated the exercise, purchasing a half ounce of heroin for $4,000. Calculatingly he suggested that the last ounce was bad. "Somebody put starch in the powder," he said.

"Stop playing with yourself," came the answer. "It's not."

Not long after the police buy in Aiello's pizzeria, agents photographed Ganci with Aiello, a large, muscular man with huge arms and often a long cigar in the corner of his mouth. The powder trail, Rooney was pleased to see, was growing clearer.

Ganci was having problems of his own. Carol had smashed up the black Mercedes he had bought her. She was uninjured but took to her bed, sick, as she confided to her diary. Later Ganci drove to the garage where the mangled car sat under a tarpaulin. A few days later, according to her diary, she and Ganci were arguing again.

Ganci had also bought Mary Jo a German shepherd puppy and ended up stuck with the job of walking it, as he lamented to Giuseppe Lamberti: "Because neither Mary Jo or my wife go there and clean up when he does that thing."

"What do you want of Mary Jo?" Lamberti said. She was just a kid.

"Yeah," Ganci said, "but she can do it because . . . not that they do it with their hands . . . and nobody wants to do it. . . ."

Lamberti laughed.

" 'Because it stinks,' she tells me. 'It stinks.' 'It stinks for both of you? It doesn't stink for me?' "

The next day Gaetano Mazzara of the Roma restaurant did not show up for an appointment, nor did he call. Ganci did not understand it. He called home to Mary Jo to leave a message in case Mazzara did call. But Mary Jo wasn't much help either. "I've got to go," she told her father. She was busy playing.

Ganci tried to explain. If the man from yesterday called, he said, tell him Daddy "is waiting for you over there, where . . . where . . ." He realized she had already hung up.

The next evening, highly excited, Catalano called Ganci. Catalano did not get excited often. "But just now a guy came here . . . and he told me that, that guy . . . the TV said his plane blew up in the air!"

Ganci had no idea what he was talking about.

"The crippled one? . . ." Catalano reminded him. "He said he went with the plane!"

Suddenly Ganci caught on. Santo Giordano, the Bonanno family soldier who had been seen at the Brooklyn district attorney's office after the Galante shooting and had been shot and paralyzed the night the three Bonanno captains were murdered, was in a plane crash.

"But what, are you kidding or for real?" Ganci demanded.

"He and someone else."

"But how on television?" Ganci wanted to know.

"Here, we saw it on television," Catalano said. "It fell on the ground . . . while they were flying. . . ."

Ganci was still dumbfounded. "Yes, but I don't understand how it blew up in the air. . . ."

"They had started it . . . he was . . . it was going up in the air."

"Oh, Blessed Mother!" said Ganci.

"And since it was burning," Catalano added, "they were left inside."

For once Russo and Rooney were ahead of Catalano and Ganci. The FBI had known for several years that Giordano owned a small plane fitted with sophisticated radio gear and had suspected the Bonanno soldier of using it to fly contraband in or out of the country. Several days before, a surveillance squad had watched Giordano and a companion examining a single-engine plane at Edwards Airport in Bayport, Long Island. The crippled Giordano could no longer fly a plane unassisted and was using the other man as a copilot.

Rooney was driving past Ferrara's pastry shop in Little Italy at the moment the radio news carried a bulletin about a plane crash in Bayport. He had an intuition. He pulled over to a phone booth and called Russo.

"I think Santo just had a problem," he said.

A few minutes later Russo overheard Catalano's report to Ganci. After so many months in the dark Russo savored the irony of knowing, even before the pair were on the phone, what they would be talking about.

When Catalano and Ganci attended the funeral the next day, Rooney made sure he had agents out copying down the tag numbers of the mourners' cars.

Russo was still trying to sort out all the players on the basis of their voices and the photos snapped by the surveillance agents. Sal Lamberti was an enigma. Smaller than his cousin Giuseppe, he was nonetheless more imposing, with an icy demeanor and eyes that seemed to gleam demoniacally for the camera. He could speak sternly to Ganci. "Someday I've got to bring you a couple kilos of dimes," he told Ganci one day. "This way, once in a while you will call." Russo could see that Sal Lamberti was no underling. The message he had for Ganci involved some "work on the other side" that someone would have to go over to arrange—possibly one of their Italian drug connections, Russo thought.

For every question answered, ten new ones seemed to arise. Russo was spending more and more time glued to the wires, leaving Rooney to arrange surveillances based on what Russo was hearing. As more and more names came up on the phone, more and more people required tailing.

The pressure was getting to Rooney, too. Jane noticed it in his withdrawal from domestic concerns; in the past they had always collaborated closely on all household chores and decisions. When Jane mentioned that they might need a new washing machine, Charlie snapped, "Well go out and buy one. What do you need me for?"

Already close to ninety agents—about one-quarter of the New York office's entire criminal division—were committed to the case. There was a chronic shortage of Sicilian speakers to work the wires. One who was pressed into service was Louis Caprino, a wiry, mop-haired agent who had joined the bureau to work the street but instead found himself imprisoned in the Queens office chained to a tape recorder. He was nearly going mad listening to calls to Ganci's Al Dente pizzeria. Most of all, he came to dread Saturday nights, when hundreds of orders for pizza came pouring into Al Dente and he had to listen to each, deciding whether it might be a coded conversation about drugs. Others, too, had been hurriedly pressed into service. Among them were two young women from the DEA, Nancy Morelli and Gabriele Zacco, who were snatched out of agent school in Glynco, Georgia, and thrown into the New York maelstrom. Nobody meeting them for the first time would have guessed their vocation. Both could easily have passed for college students, office workers, or young career women. Morelli was thin and raven-haired with a long, serious face. Zacco was slightly plump and girlishly pretty. They had just completed twelve weeks' training at the DEA academy when they were rushed to New York to sit on the wires. "Get your ears ready" was all the warning a supervisor gave them. "You're going to do a lot of listening." Sometimes they spent up to ten days in a row in up to twelve-hour shifts listening to calls. They came up to New York so fast and spent so much time on the wires they didn't have time to search for lodgings. Zacco moved in with her parents; Morelli took a room at the Howard Johnson's Motel on the West Side of Manhattan, where her seventy-five-dollar-per-diem allowance barely covered her expenses, not that she had time for fancy dinners or entertainment. She and Zacco found that meals were often a pizza or snack sent in while they sat around waiting for calls to come in; gaining weight for lack of exercise was one of the biggest dangers they faced.

Russo remained the undisputed leader of the listeners. It got to the point where he could sense a change in tone when the people he was listening to shifted their discussion from the mundane to the conspiratorial. He and Rooney, in their own conversations, unintentionally mimicked the code of their adversaries.

"Did those guys go there again?" Russo would ask.

"Yeah," Rooney would say. "But they didn't bring the thing."

"What about the other guy?"

"He didn't show."

They were learning a lot. It was clear that the money Paquette was tracking was generated by drugs, that Ganci was calling the signals, most likely for Catalano, and that their network consisted of Sicilians in pizzerias and restaurants and construction businesses from Long Island to New Jersey. But how extensive was it? Where was the powder coming from, and where was it going, besides to Zito? Where would the case end? Would it end? There seemed to be no natural termination. The longer they worked, the more people came up. Somewhere they would have to cut it off. Where was that point?

In early August, in his former Queens office, Lew Schiliro stroked his long, malevolent mustache and pondered an opening. As supervisor of Rooney's and Russo's squad he had been keeping track of the calls and surveillances and especially all the bags that were changing hands. Watching the bags go back and forth was driving him and the other agents nuts. He had to see what was in at least one of them, to corroborate the phone calls. It was time for a break-through, a bold stroke that would propel the case forward. He had to make something happen. "Sometimes," he said, "the only way to know what's in a bag is to grab it." When he heard from Russo that deli owner Filippo Casamento had made an appointment to meet Ganci on August 7, Schiliro made up his mind: They would grab Casamento and his cargo, see once and for all what was changing hands here. Rooney wasn't around. It was Jane's mother's birthday, and all the family had gone out to Hampton Bays, Long Island, for the celebration. Russo had called him there. "There's something going on," he said.

Rooney made a stab at leaving, but Jane was adamant. She knew he needed some time off. "You're staying for Mother's birthday!" she said, and that was that.

Schiliro ran the plan past the prosecutor Louis Freeh, his 1975 classmate at Quantico. Freeh was dead-set against it. Stopping Casamento, he said, would require an explanation. Worse, the law would require them to disclose within sixty days any occasions on which Casamento was overheard in any wiretaps. That would mean revealing the wires. That would blow the case. Freeh was happy with a "dry" case. He didn't need any powder. He wanted to trace the conspiracy in its entirety—from source to street. He didn't want to jeopardize that with a sudden bust.

Schiliro had an answer. The surveillance agents could arrange with the police to have Casamento stopped on the pretext of a traffic violation. They'd look in the bag, and before they would be forced to disclose any wiretaps, they would simply drop the charges. Freeh remained adamant. They should just tail Casamento, not stop him.

Margherita Ganci had called her husband at Al Dente to say that Casamento was on his way over from Brooklyn. Ganci, nonchalant, seemed more concerned about Mary Jo. "Did she take a bath and everything?" he asked.

It was approaching midnight when Casamento, tailed by surveillance cars, pulled up near Ganci's house. The agents spread out, one parking casually outside a firehouse down the block from Ganci's. Casamento found no spot outside Ganci's, so he parked illegally at a hydrant. He opened and shut his car trunk quickly and disappeared inside Ganci's house. A few minutes later he stepped out again.

Suddenly the midnight peace of the dark street exploded with the deafening clang of the fire bell and the roaring start-up of fire engines. Fire! The hinged doors flew up, and the trucks, sirens wailing, shrieked out. Flustered, the surveillance agent parked there threw his car into gear and tried to get the hell out of the way.

Death in the afternoon: The body of Carmine Galante lies sprawled on the patio of the Joe and Mary Italian-American restaurant on Knickerbocker Avenue in Brooklyn on July 12, 1979, as detectives comb the scene for clues. The Bonanno family boss was gunned down by three intruders, with the suspected complicity of two of his dining companions, Cesare Bonventre and Baldassare Amato. Galante had been moving to dominate the heroin trade, and his killing, prosecutors believe, cleared the way for Sicilian Mafia rivals in America to set up the Pizza Connection. (Photo by William E. Sauro/The New York Times)

All photos, unless otherwise noted, were taken surreptitiously by the FBI during surveillances.

A star is born: Sal Catalano (center, in checkered shirt) meets with fellow Sicilian Cesare Bonventre (in striped shirt), Bonanno hit man Anthony Mirra (right), and Bonanno soldier Joey D'Amico outside the Toyland Social Club of Bonanno underboss Nicky "Glasses" Marangello at 94 Hester Street on September 3, 1977. At the time this series was taken, the FBI had no idea who Catalano was or what an important role he would come to play as leader of a Sicilian faction operating alongside the Bonanno family.

Genesis of the conspiracy: the key surveillance photos taken by Italian Treasury Officer Calogero Scarvaci at Palermo's Piazza Politeama on February 14, 1980, and first given to FBI Agent Carmine Russo in 1982. In the group photo, Giuseppe Ganci is at right. Next to him, in a dark tie, is Giorgio Muratore of Bagheria, Italy, on whose tapped phone in 1980 the Italian police heard about tangerine trees that bore lemons, which police believed was a coded reference to a pending heroin deal. Next to Muratore is Filippo Ragusa, later implicated in a 1983 heroin shipment to a Buffalo tile warehouse. At the extreme left is John Licata, son of slain Bonanno captain Pietro Licata, Sal Catalano's predecessor as street boss of Knickerbocker Avenue. In a separate photo (below) that Scarvaci said he took at the same time, Catalano is pictured alone. Catalano, at his trial, bitterly contested the timing, claiming he was home in Ciminna at the time.

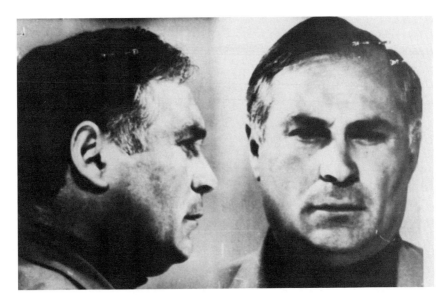

Sicilian Mafia boss Leonardo Greco of Bagheria, a mastermind of the drug pipe-line and money-laundering conspiracy. A heroin shipment seized in Milan in 1980 had been tested near his iron warehouse. (Italian police photo supplied to FBI)

Sicilian Mafia boss Giuseppe Bono, a kingpin of the heroin trade, enjoys a slice outside Ganci's Little Italy pizzeria near Columbus Circle in Manhattan on November 19, 1980, three days after his wedding at St. Patrick's Cathedral and gala reception at the Pierre Hotel. Bono's presence in New York was a big surprise to American and Italian officials.

Guiseppe Ganci (left) and motel owner and builder Frank Polizzi await an incoming call from Sicily at a pay phone near Polizzi's construction office in Belleville, New Jersey, on April 5, 1983.

Baldassare Amato—a miraculous survivor of the Galante massacre in 1979—leaves the Casamento Brothers deli at 2216 Eighty-sixth Street, Brooklyn, on April 20, 1983. At the time he was carrying a large white shopping bag with unidentified contents.

After a key meeting to arrange the heroin shipments, (left to right) Sal Catalano, Giuseppe Lamberti, his cousin Salvatore Lamberti, and Giuseppe Soresi, envoy of the Sicilian Mafia heroin traffickers, leave Ganci's house in Middle Village, Queens, on June 3, 1983.

Pizza man Sal Greco (left), brother of Sicilian Mafia boss Leonardo Greco, and Gaetano Mazzara, co-owner of the Roma restaurant in Menlo Park, New Jersey, meet for a supposedly private discussion in the shopping center parking lot outside the restaurant on June 4, 1983.

Philadelphia pizza man Benny Zito (center) and brother-in-law Sal Finazzo (in black shirt) meet with Giuseppe Ganci at Ganci's house on June 20, 1983, prior to Zito's heroin buys. Below, the Aiello Pickup: Café owner Anthony Aiello (left) visits Ganci on June 23, 1983, after Ganci was overheard on the FBI wiretaps saying he went to get the "rolls." In the garage Ganci—who was Aiello's heroin supplier—opens the truck of his Mercedes for Aiello, who takes out a brown paper bag. (Series continues next page.)

Aiello (above left) leaves Ganci's with the bag and carries it to his Mercedes (below and opposite top).

The Mazzurco Pickup: Salvatore Mazzurco (left) and Ganci meet at Ganci's garage on June 30, 1983. In an effort to bypass wiretapped lines, Mazzurco wears a telephone beeper so cohorts at randomly selected pay phones can signal him to call them back. (Series continues next page.)

Moments later (above), Ganci hefts a thick wad of bills as Mazzurco watches.
Below, Mazzurco leaves Ganci's with a Fiuggi mineral water carton, contents
unknown, and heads for his Mercedes. (This was one of many particularly clear
sequences shot by FBI surveillance agent John Mauzey.)

The Mystery of the Purse: Above left, the dapper Cesare Bonventre—suspected with compare *Baldo Amato in the killing of Carmine Galante—arrives at Ganci's house on July 10, 1983, carrying a man's purse. The contents were unknown to the FBI but Agent Charlie Rooney found that a purse of similar size could hold forty thousand dollars in hundred-dollar bills. Catalano takes the purse to his bakery around the corner, and returns to Ganci's with it (above right). It now appears empty. Below, with the purse between them on the railing, Ganci (left) and Catalano hold a discussion. (Series continues next page.)*

Above, Bonventre joins the group, the purse still on the railing. Below, Catalano gives the purse back to Bonventre, who bids farewell with ritual kisses. Watching at Bonventre's right is New Jersey contractor Giovanni Ligammari, whose later hesitation to front money for a drug deal precipitated its collapse.

Giuseppe Ganci leaves his New Jersey pizzeria, Mr. Bruno's, in Harrison, on July 23, 1983, carrying a plastic bag with unidentified contents.

Castellammare del Golfo. The hometown of Joe Bonanno and his clan, including Carmine Galante and Cesare Bonventre, curves around a lovely harbor and ruined castle fifty miles west of Palermo. (Photo by Ralph Blumenthal)

The Zito Delivery: Benny Zito arrives at Ganci's house on August 2, 1983, carrying a gift-wrapped box containing $250,000 paid to him by DEA undercover agent Stephen Hopson.

Above, Zito steps into Ganci's driveway with the money. Below, seventeen minutes later, Zito exits with a blue shirt box containing one kilo of heroin and stops to greet Ganci's daughter, Mary Jo. (Series continues next page.)

Zito (above), seconds later, stoops to kiss Mary Jo and (below) returns to his car with the drugs. Zito later disappeared and is presumed dead.

At that moment Casamento slipped into his illegally parked car and sped off. The closest agent, Vernon Swint, who had "the eye," was disoriented by the fire trucks. He screeched off in pursuit but lost Casamento. Swint squared the block —and ran into Casamento again on Metropolitan Avenue. *Good,* thought Swint, *I've caught him.* Casamento took off, leading Swint on a high-speed chase into Brooklyn's Sheepshead Bay before stopping at a red light.

The light turned green. But Casamento wasn't moving. Swint, a few cars back, was in a bind. If he didn't move, Casamento would know he was being followed; if Swint swung past Casamento, he would probably lose him.

Suddenly Casamento spun his car around in a half turn and came to a stop. He glared at Swint. Swint tried to think fast. What would any ordinary New York driver do at a time like this? Swint glared back. Then he leaned sassily on his horn. Casamento straightened out his car and sped off in a series of evasive maneuvers. Swint tried to keep up but finally lost him.

Schiliro, back in the FBI office in Queens, was disgusted. He had been sure this would finally net them something they could examine. Russo, with him, was equally crestfallen. He had been on duty now for seventeen hours but he was still so keyed up he jumped in his car and headed over the Brooklyn Bridge. He was determined to track down Casamento himself. Rooney followed in his own car. Both raced to Eagle Cheese in Brooklyn but found it dark and empty. They circled some of the usual Bonanno haunts on Knickerbocker and Thirteenth avenues. No sign of Casamento. Finally, at three A.M., Russo took a swing past Casamento's house. The lights were burning. In the driveway sat Casamento's Cadillac. They might never know now what Casamento had picked up from Ganci and where he might have taken it in the missing two and a half hours. Russo was fuming. He drove home to Staten Island, where his lights, too, were still burning. Carmela was waiting up.

Freeh had no idea how close the agents had come to grabbing Casamento. He would not have been pleased. Even with a police story to cover up the real reason for his seizure, a precipitous bust carried far too great a risk of blowing the investigation. Better wait. There would be many opportunities ahead. If only everyone would be patient.

15

I n late August 1983 Ganci and his mistress, Carol, were followed to the NYU Medical Center in Manhattan, his second visit to a hospital in two months. Russo felt there must be something wrong with his health. Later Ganci called Mazzurco at Pronto Demolition. "I'm just getting home from the hospital," Ganci said. ". . . Hey, fuck! That guy wants me to have an operation. . . . I have a tumor in the lung."

"Oh, Jesus Christ!" said Mazzurco.

"They've still got to do another two tests," Ganci said. "One in the bones. But what the fuck do the bones have to do with . . . with the tumor?"

Ganci was puzzled by something else: Why didn't the doctors ask him for any money?

Don't worry, Mazzurco said, they'll send a bill.

Then it was on to business. "Have you spoken with that guy?" Ganci wanted to know. *Typical,* Russo marveled. *Nothing stops these guys, not even the big C.*

Outside Ganci's house, agents saw an employee of Al Dente unload case after case of boxes marked FIUGGI MINERAL WATER into Ganci's garage. What the hell was it really? Rooney wondered. He hoped to get a chance to find out. Jim Kallstrom was studying ways of getting into Ganci's house to plant a microphone.

180

Rooney was concerned over the risk of exposure, but so far the place was never empty long enough to permit an entry.

Concern that the abortive effort to grab Casamento might have tipped off the deli owner and his cohorts was dispelled by the business-as-usual tone of the subsequent telephone conversations. Within two days Mazzurco was calling Ganci about some people they had met who were "looking for a few documents." Ganci, in turn, called Pronto Demolition, where someone said he was "organizing a few papers, in order, for tomorrow, things."

Rooney had learned a little about Pronto, although he did not know what, if anything, the company actually demolished. He knew what Zito had told Hopson: that his friends had a demolition company where a car carrying heroin could be taken apart. He knew that Ganci and Mazzurco had some connection to the company, whether as owners or partners he hadn't found any records to confirm. He still did not know that the Sicilian Mafia boss Giuseppe Bono was one of Pronto's founders, that Ganci, Mazzurco, and Giuseppe Lamberti each owned a quarter share, and that Giovanni Ligammari shared the remaining 25 percent with another man.

Rooney was especially curious about the petite Mazzurco. He had turned up in the photos Rooney had that were taken at Giuseppe Bono's wedding reception at the Pierre. Two agents had first spotted him coming out of a travel agency with Ganci and another man the year before. The agents followed the two other men when they split off and had to let Mazzurco drive off, unidentified. Rooney had since learned from government records that Mazzurco was born in Borgetto, Sicily, in 1935. He had come to the United States in 1947 and had later been drafted into the Army, serving in postwar Germany with a mortar unit. Surveillance showed he lived on a quiet, treelined street in Baldwin, Long Island, in a modest yellow and lime green house with peeling shingles. He had three daughters and drove a used Mercedes. Mazzurco's wife and Giuseppe Lamberti's wife were sisters.

The DEA had gotten interested in Mazzurco in 1981. One day, to his surprise, Mazzurco received a letter from New York Telephone advising him that the DEA had inquired about his toll records. Usually when a law enforcement agency subpoenas phone records, it accompanies the court order with a formal request not to advise the subscriber. In this case, apparently because of a slipup, the telephone company passed on the information to Mazzurco, who then fired off a letter to the DEA asking why it wanted to know about his phone calls. He followed it up with an application under the Freedom of Information Act for his DEA file. The request for information was turned down by the DEA more than a year later. Mazzurco never did find out what the DEA wanted with him, but in light of his subsequent activities, it did not seem to trouble him much.

In 1978, Mazzurco later claimed, he had been in Palermo when he ran into a lawyer he knew at the stark white marble Mussolini-era federal courthouse. The lawyer was with Sicilian Mafia boss Gaetano Badalamenti. Mazzurco told Badalamenti he had come to buy clothes for a clothing business he had in America. Badalamenti soon introduced Mazzurco to his nephew Vincenzo Randazzo, who, Badalamenti said, was also in the clothing business. Back home in 1978 and working at brother-in-law Giuseppe Lamberti's construction company, Mazzurco said, he was hired to renovate a big house in the Westchester suburb of Pelham. The house (now valued at around $750,000) had recently been bought by Mafia boss Giuseppe Bono, then seeking to escape growing Italian government scrutiny by temporarily relocating in the United States. A dapper gentleman who reminded one real estate agent of the actor Adolphe Menjou, Bono often wore a carnation in his lapel and went around saying he was in the hotel business. Through Bono, Mazzurco met his associate Giuseppe Ganci and then other friends of Ganci's, including Salvatore Catalano. "He told me he came from South America," Mazzurco said later of Bono. He insisted he had never asked and had no idea what Bono did for a living. Nor could Mazzurco remember where he got the $35,000 to $50,000 he said he had invested in Pronto.

On August 9, as Mazzurco and Ganci spoke again, Mazzurco said he could always be reached through Pronto: "They'll call me on the beeper." Surveillance photos had shown the device on Mazzurco's belt, but it suddenly dawned on Russo why, on the basis of what he did overhear, he seemed to miss so many follow-up conversations. Ganci could stop at any pay phone at random, one that the bureau could not possibly have tapped, and leave the number on Mazzurco's beeper. Mazzurco could then also pick out a pay phone at random and call Ganci back. There was simply no way now to monitor such calls. That would explain some of the mysterious gaps in the discussions. He would hear Ganci and Mazzurco discuss something and agree to talk later. By the next call he heard they had already settled the matter and he had missed it. An infernal device, the beeper. Luckily, he thought, these bums were often too lazy to run around beeping each other at pay phones. They supposed it was safe to talk in Sicilian about ovens and chocolates.

A few days later Mazzurco was looking for Ganci again. Margherita explained with pathetic resignation that he was out. "My husband gets lost," she told Mazzurco. "He leaves in the morning, and he gets lost in the American, American way. Even if I were dying, I don't know where he is."

At that moment Ganci was lunching with Carol in New Jersey. Carol and her

friend Ann would soon be opening a new boutique. Ganci was their financier.

Lew Schiliro was still stewing about Casamento's getaway three weeks ago. He
was looking for another chance to make a seizure, something that would give the
bureau a hard look at what was being exchanged, propelling this elephantine case
forward. Another opportunity soon presented itself. On August 30 agents staking
out Mazzurco's house on Long Island were watching him unload several boxes
from his car when a gray Chevrolet pulled up in front. The driver slipped quickly
into the house, and exited a few minutes later, carrying a brown paper bag, and
got back into the car. Agent Denis Collins, watching through a monocular, tried
to radio in the report, but his radio was down. He found a pay phone and called
it in. "Stay on the car," Schiliro ordered. "We think he has drugs. See where he
goes—and pop him."

Grabbing this bozo wouldn't thrill Freeh, but Schiliro would worry about that
later. Schiliro called the prosecutor's office. Freeh was away—as one of Schiliro's
supervisors knew. After months of working late each night, Freeh had finally
yielded to the entreaties of his wife and agreed to take several days off. Like
Rooney's wife, Jane, Marilyn Freeh was a former FBI paralegal. She, too, had
seen little of her husband and had finally persuaded him to take a short vacation
on the beach at Montauk. Rooney, too, was away on Long Island with Jane and
her mother. Meanwhile, Schiliro talked to Richard Martin, Freeh's combative
coprosecutor. Schiliro explained the situation. Martin said he'd try to reach
Freeh. Schiliro also beeped Rooney, who spent the next few hours making calls
in a phone booth, to the point where Jane threatened to deliver Charlie's lunch
plate to the booth. "Boy, are you lucky mother was there!" she fumed.

When Martin told him what was going on, Freeh grew alarmed. Under no
circumstances should anyone be arrested yet, he cautioned. They were overeager,
jumping the gun. Get them to hold off, he urged.

But Schiliro's order to stop the gray Chevy had already gone out.

Collins tailed the unsuspecting driver for half an hour through Long Island
and into Queens, and pulled him over at a parking lot in Howard Beach, near
Kennedy Airport. Schiliro, who had kept in touch with other members of the
surveillance squad, joined Collins there. The driver had several different sets of
identification and car registration papers, but his real name, agents established,
was Giuseppe Baldinucci. They had prepared a story to explain why they had
stopped him, an ostensible traffic infraction, but he never asked the reason.
Collins called the information in, and the name was put through the bureau's
computers.

Collins looked in the paper bag. He was prepared to see white powder. So he was astonished to see money, $40,000 when it was all counted. In Baldinucci's pocket, however, he found a packet of tinfoil. In the tinfoil was powder—550 milligrams, just over half a gram, of 89.2 percent pure light brown heroin—which Baldinucci claimed was cocaine.

He arrested Baldinucci and took him in for questioning. To Collins' surprise, the computer quickly kicked out Baldinucci's name. The thirty-nine-year-old Sicilian was from Borgetto, the same town as the Lambertis and Mazzurco, and had entered the country illegally ten years before. In 1980 he had been arrested in Brooklyn on charges of counterfeiting and mail theft, but he had fled before his trial. He was a fugitive, wanted on an arrest warrant issued by the Secret Service. No wonder he had seemed so resigned; he knew, or thought he knew, why he had been stopped. Not only did the agents not have to explain the reason for stopping Baldinucci, but they never even had to file new case papers requiring disclosure of any wiretaps to the subjects, which would have tipped off Mazzurco and the others that they were under surveillance.

Schiliro was beaming. He couldn't wait to tell Freeh the good news. They had grabbed a bag of money, powerful evidence of some illegal scheme, to be sure, and had done it without having to explain why. Baldinucci insisted that the $40,000 was a mortgage payment that he owed to Mazzurco but that Mazzurco wanted him to bring it to Giuseppe Lamberti instead. As for the heroin he tried to pass off as cocaine—he said it was for personal use. Schiliro and Rooney doubted that Baldinucci had arrived with the money; the surveillance agents had seen no sign of it going in. They came up with a more satisfying theory: Baldinucci had brought the heroin sample to show Mazzurco. Mazzurco liked it and gave Baldinucci $40,000 for a buy. At the going Mafia wholesale rate of about $240,000 a kilo, it would have purchased one-sixth of a kilo. It was more evidence tying the group around Ganci to drug trafficking.

Schiliro was hardly prepared for Freeh's vitriolic reaction. "Are you guys nuts?" Freeh raged. Schiliro had never seen his old classmate so furious, and he had never been chewed out like that. Storey piled on, too. "Yeah, that was a pretty stupid thing to do," he told Schiliro.

But Baldinucci's arrest did not blow the case, just as the telephone company's tip-off to Mazzurco or the police leak to Zito or the bank manager's warning to Filippo Salamone or Swint's burned chase of Casamento or a dozen other giveaways had not blown the case. The news of Baldinucci's arrest would have spread quickly to Mazzurco and Ganci. Undoubtedly they and Baldinucci himself believed he had been seized as a fugitive. In any case, as Dick Martin, Freeh's coprosecutor, later said about the relentless conspiracies, "They couldn't quit. If it had been a part-time thing for them, they might have stopped. But they couldn't. This was their business."

Two days later, on September 1, the irrepressible Ganci, undeterred by his lung cancer, drove to his favorite jeweler on the Lower East Side and then to Clifton, New Jersey. To the surprise of the surveillance agents, instead of meeting Carol, Ganci drove to a nearby Ramada Inn and met Carol's friend and business partner Ann. He and Ann slipped into the motel separately. That evening Ganci had dinner with both Carol and Ann. Did Carol know? the agents wondered.

The next day Ganci picked up Carol and kept another appointment at NYU Hospital. Afterward he bought Carol a pair of shoes at Charles Jourdan and a pretzel from a street vendor. They held hands and window-shopped.

Earlier Ganci and Casamento had spoken on the phone. "I'll give you the check here," the Brooklyn deli owner said. Ganci drove out to Eagle Cheese and left with a large cardboard box that he carried out on his shoulder and put in the trunk of his rust-colored Seville. *A check in a carton?* Rooney wondered. It had to be cash.

A few days later Amato called. "Another day, tomorrow or the next day, we'll make another telephone call, understand?" Ganci said.

Amato understood. "We have to pay that anyway," he said.

Russo was sure he heard *pagare*, "to pay," which seemed to put Amato with them in the drug consortium. Amato's lawyer later challenged that, offering a less incriminating translation. (Later, the jury indicated that it too was unconvinced of the government's version.) Russo shrugged it off. He trusted his golden ears.

Ganci went back to the hospital carrying a suitcase. This time, it appeared, he was planning on staying for a while.

Major events were unfolding outside. On September 9 an Icelandic Air flight from Europe landed in Chicago carrying a passenger listed as Daniel Colombo Monte, a young Brazilian. An air ticket found the following year in an apartment in Madrid indicated that he may have been accompanied by an older man, although that was never clear. Had the flight been staked out, the FBI might have then have seized one of the world's most wanted men, Gaetano Badalamenti, and his son Vito. Instead, the FBI had to wait until April.

Meanwhile other important events were breaking. Lieutenant Joe Polly's NYPD team on the Brooknor investigation and the Buffalo FBI office had simultaneously developed information that a big heroin load was on its way from Naples to a tile dealer, Andrea Aiello, in Buffalo, New York. Aiello, no relation to Tony "Commerciante" Aiello, whom Catalano and Ganci had been dealing with in Queens, was said by informants to have received earlier heroin shipments, including one that had slipped through the federal surveillance net several months before. Working with Mike Fahy of the Customs Service, the FBI narrowed down the possible ships to one scheduled to dock at Port Elizabeth,

New Jersey, on September 13. Agents from Buffalo and New York, including Fahy and Rooney, rushed to the pier where the cargo was being off-loaded.

In the guise of making a routine Customs inspection, the agents feverishly searched the containers until they isolated the shipment of tiles to Buffalo. But nothing suspicious turned up. As a United Van Lines truck arrived to load the tiles with other cargo bound for Buffalo, one of the agents, Thomas Bondanza, grabbed an electric drill and frantically began boring holes into the containers and any other possible hiding places. As he drilled into one of the wooden pallets supporting the boxes of tiles hoisted up on a forklift, it appeared to be hollow. A trickle of white powder streamed down. The agents stared at it, dumbfounded. Rooney turned triumphantly to Fahy. "Would you like a test kit?" Rooney asked. "Or can you guess what it is?" As the agents worked quickly to remove much of the twenty-seven kilos of heroin, worth up to $100 million on the street—and replace it with "sham," a harmless look-alike—Rooney and Fahy conspired to spread the good news as dramatically as possible. As it happened, a big international conference on the Mafia and drugs was taking place on Governors Island in New York Harbor. Judge Falcone and other Italian magistrates and investigators, along with many FBI and DEA officials, were there. Storey was home. Mischievously, Rooney and Fahy called their supervisors' telephone beepers one after the other. Suddenly, remembers Sheer, who was at the conference, everyone's beeper started going off. It was mayhem.

But the extraordinary find unleashed internecine strife in the ranks of the government forces. Sheer assumed it was part of the New York investigation and deployed Kallstrom's surveillance agents to tail the truck to its Buffalo destination. The FBI special agent in charge in Buffalo, Philip Smith, on the other hand, saw the case as the outcome of information his office had developed. He was backed by the U.S. attorney in Buffalo, who was eager to prosecute the case there. Smith insisted his agents would follow the shipment to Buffalo. That was just like New York, Smith figured: "They wanted to believe everything happened in New York." He and Sheer eventually struck a compromise: New York agents would escort the truck as far as Buffalo's territory, where its agents would take over.

But then what? Smith wanted to take the load down—bust the case—in Buffalo, but that sent Sheer up the wall. This was a piece of a gigantic New York investigation, Sheer insisted. Nothing should be done to jeopardize it at this stage.

Smith countered that they had targeted Aiello, a Mafia godfather in Buffalo.

"Bullshit!" Sheer exploded, calling Aiello an insignificant cog in the mob's machine. Maybe, Sheer suggested, he was a big deal in Buffalo but down in New York he was answerable to the major players. Shortsighted action in Buffalo was about to ruin a three-year investigation, Sheer warned. It was, he fumed, "one humongous clusterfuck."

Smith was adamant. He had had Aiello's phones tapped and the wires portrayed him to be directing underlings in New York. This was a special Sicilian operation under the little-known Aiello, Smith tried to persuade Sheer: "He's a 'sleeper,'" Smith argued. "He's not working for the American mob."

Meanwhile, Sheer suggested that Kallstrom's special operations squad assist the surveillance, but Smith didn't think it was necessary. "We can handle it," he assured Sheer. In Buffalo, the shipment on the wooden pallets was unloaded at a United Van Lines terminal and put aboard a smaller truck which carried it to Aiello's warehouse, already staked out by Buffalo surveillance agents. But then, to their dismay, the tiles and pallets were carried into the warehouse out of sight. Hurriedly, Kallstrom's crew was summoned after all to penetrate the warehouse. Overnight, after the warehouse employees had turned out the lights and locked up, the New York agents slipped in and installed a hidden closed-circuit video camera, similar to the one trained on Ganci's house in Queens.

Across Foley Square at the U.S. attorney's office, Rudolph Giuliani had been alerted to the peril by Sheer and Louis Freeh. Giuliani had kept in close touch with his former Justice Department associates in Washington. He had, in fact, personally briefed Attorney General Smith and FBI Director William Webster several times on the investigation. The director kept track of the case in a small notebook he carried with him to record the progress of important investigations. Webster had anticipated just such a crisis. "Are they going to run on us if we're greedy?" he asked Giuliani. Was there, he wanted to know, a danger in holding back too long rather than breaking the case when an opportunity like the Buffalo shipment arose? There was always a danger, Giuliani replied. But the potential rewards of carrying this sweeping case to its end far outstripped the risks. Webster agreed.

Now, from New York, Giuliani called Justice officials in Washington and reminded them of his discussions with the attorney general and FBI director. He urged them to hold Buffalo off.

The next day, the hidden camera videotaped two Sicilians dismantling the pallets and examining the shipment. Despite the switching of the powder, they approved the load, stuffing nearly ten kilos into a suitcase. Telephone taps recorded their plans to drive the load back down to New York—but not before taking two days off for a sightseeing trip to Niagara Falls. Sheer had them tailed back to New York and let them walk around for a few days, meeting with associates, before agents swooped in and arrested seven of them, including Aiello in Buffalo, in what they were led to believe was a routine narcotics bust. The secrecy of the investigation was preserved. One suspect escaped—Filippo Ragusa, who had been one of the original conspirators photographed with Ganci and others in Palermo's Piazza Politeama in 1980. Russo also believed he had been with Cesare Bonventre the year before when ill-fated pizza man Settimo Favia was pressured to settle his gambling debt in the Café del Viale by bringing in heroin from Italy.

Shortly afterward in Philadelphia, Paolo LaPorta told undercover agent Frank Panessa that he feared he, too, was about to be arrested for the Buffalo shipment, although, except for his own statement, investigators had no reason to suspect his involvement.

Two weeks after the Buffalo episode, on a sunny Monday afternoon, surveillance agents followed the pint-size Sal Mazzurco in his brown Mercedes to a restaurant in Long Island City, the Charcoal Grill, where he parked outside and waited. Half an hour later a car drove up with four men who greeted Mazzurco, and all five entered the restaurant. The agents, who snapped pictures furiously, had never seen these men before. One, in his forties, wore a white sports jacket and had sharp, squinty features and black hair combed straight back. Another about the same age had a darker jacket and a balding crown. A third with long hair, much younger and more rakish, had sunglasses tucked into the front of his half-buttoned white shirt. The fourth, in a leather sports jacket, was scrawny and looked like Peter Lorre, Rooney thought later. Shortly before four P.M., after a little more than an hour in the restaurant, the squinty one and the scrawny one got into Mazzurco's car and rode with him to a National Car Rental office, where they rented a car. Rooney himself drove by later with Pat Luzio (who had some free time away from the lookout now that Ganci was in the hospital) to check the renter's name: Emanuele Palazzolo of Milton, Wisconsin. The other two men had gotten into a taxi and were followed to the Roosevelt Hotel in Manhattan, where, agents found, they checked in as Vincenzo Randazzo and Faro Lupo from Switzerland.

In light of the money trail to Switzerland, the meeting of Mazzurco with Randazzo and Lupo was a promising lead, Rooney thought. But a guy from Milton, Wisconsin? Where did he come in? Where the hell was Milton? Where the hell was Wisconsin?

16

AFTER Gaetano Badalamenti left Brazil, having failed to convince Buscetta to take up the war against the Corleonesi, Cristina Buscetta grew increasingly anxious. Her brother's disappearance, followed by that of Buscetta's two sons in Sicily in 1983, had terrified her. Buscetta was spending as much time as possible on his remote ranch in northern Brazil; Cristina had been staying in Rio. Her apartment happened to be two floors down from one owned by another Mafia fugitive, Antonio Bardellino. She and Tommaso decided it would be safer for her to move to São Paulo as soon as she could get the children out of school. In October 1983 Buscetta flew to Rio, where Cristina and the children were waiting to drive with him to São Paulo. There they would split up for safety. Their two oldest children and the youngest would sleep at the home of one friend, and Buscetta, Cristina, and young Tommaso would sleep at the apartment of another friend, Alfredo Mortilli. Buscetta told Mortilli they would arrive in São Paulo on a Thursday. Mortilli said he would leave the key for them with the doorman.

They set off on the long drive to São Paulo. By evening they were tired and decided to spend the night in a motel. They reached São Paulo Friday morning and dropped off the three children at the first house and went on with little

Tommaso to Mortilli's apartment. The next morning Buscetta left with Tommaso to register him for school. It was Saturday, October 22, 1983.

Italian and Brazilian investigators had picked up Buscetta's serpentine trail the previous January, while a federal judge in New York was considering Rooney's affidavit for wiretap interceptions of Ganci and his associates. The Italians had come to Brazil in search of Antonio Bardellino, wanted in connection with a cocaine-smuggling ring operating between South America and Italy. Bardellino had been traced to a Rio apartment in which documents were found that led the police to a phony fish export company called CEICO; the papers detailed shipments of worthless fish to Italy and included lists of phone numbers around the world as well as references to a company called Major Key Sportswear. The police also found, secreted under some furniture, the address of another apartment in Rio that turned out to be listed to Bardellino's wife. The police then checked the toll records of that apartment and came up with calls to the Hotel Regente in Belém, where Tommaso Buscetta had welcomed Gaetano Badalamenti the year before.

The police visited the apartment building and showed the manager a photo spread of wanted fugitives who might have been in contact with Bardellino. The manager, to their surprise, identified a picture of Buscetta, saying he knew the man as Roberto Felice. Until February Felice had lived two floors down from Bardellino, the manager said. Now, in the summer of 1983, he said, a woman named Cristina and her children lived there.

The police then pulled the toll records for that apartment and also found calls to the Hotel Regente, CEICO, and Major Key Sportswear.

The police found that Cristina drove a Chevrolet and contacted every dealership in Brazil until they learned it had been purchased by a partner of her father, Homero Guimarães, and a José Escobar. The Chevrolet dealer who had sold the car identified a picture of Buscetta as Escobar. Police then checked the records at the Hotel Regente in Belém and found that Escobar had stayed there. The noose was tightening.

Next they were able to track down the forger who had been providing false identification papers for the group. From his workshop they confiscated papers showing many of the aliases being used. One document was a driver's license for Homero Guimarães, Jr., Cristina's missing brother, under the name of Otto Levy, who, Cristina's tax records showed, had given Cristina a lot of money. The trail then led to Homero Guimarães, Sr. Records showed that in the spring of 1982, he had transferred a huge ranch in northern Brazil near Belém to Buscetta.

The police found telexes Guimarães had sent to hotels throughout South America at the time of his son's disappearance. One such telex asked: "Have the following individuals: José Escobar, Alfredo Mortilli, Otto Levy, Homero Guimarães, among others, been staying at this hotel recently?" It conclusively linked Buscetta to Guimarães and Mortilli.

By now so many people had been questioned that Guimarães' business partner had learned of the investigation and asked the police what was going on. It was clear that Buscetta had to be seized as soon as he was located.

In September 1983 police who had been staking out Cristina's apartment in Rio saw a new Fiat parked in front. The police tracked down the car's sales papers, which listed José Escobar as the buyer. At least Buscetta still appeared to be in Brazil.

The police developed informants in Cristina's and Mortilli's buildings and at the cleaning company used by Major Key Sportswear. They also checked further into Major Key. It had been formed, they learned, four years before by two investors with $6,000. Within two years the company's listed worth had skyrocketed to more than $1 million. Its business of record was producing promotional jackets for organizations and companies. But the only recorded business transactions were a three-kilo shipment to New York and a five-ton shipment to Paraguay, the latter resulting in a large insurance claim for an alleged loss. The police, noting that Major Key had used its own loaders, suspected insurance fraud.

Through their informant in Mortilli's São Paulo building, the police learned of an October meeting in his apartment attended by many young women, who they suspected were to be used as cocaine couriers.

Early on the morning of October 22, 1983, the Brazilian police informant in Mortilli's building reported Cristina's presence to the police, who set up immediate surveillance. Three hours later they saw Buscetta and a young boy step out of the building, get into a car, and drive off.

Buscetta turned the corner and stopped to buy Tommaso a croissant. Suddenly they were surrounded by plainclothes police. There was no chance to flee. The officers took them back to Mortilli's house—without directions from him, Buscetta realized. That meant the police knew where they had come from. The only ones who knew he was supposed to arrive two days before were Mortilli and the Major Key salesman. Buscetta was certain he had been betrayed.

Moreover, when the police took them back to Mortilli's apartment, there was no immediate search of the premises, another sign that Mortilli had been cooperating. The police took Buscetta into the bedroom while Cristina and Tommaso waited in the living room. One officer, Buscetta said later, then told him that $1 million in U.S. dollars could set him free. Buscetta said $1,000 was all he could come up with, sending the officer into a rage. Buscetta was taken to the police station and the next day to prison. Later Buscetta learned that the same police-man had subsequently approached Cristina one night in a restaurant and, refus-ing to believe they could be as poor as Buscetta claimed, offered to free him for a scaled-down bribe of $50,000.

Meanwhile, others who, unaware of the raid, showed up at Mortilli's house, were also arrested, as were Sicilian associates under surveillance at other locations. Among them: Badalamenti's son Leonardo.

Cristina's father, Homero Guimarães, meanwhile, had grown increasingly alarmed at not having heard from his daughter or Buscetta. Shortly after Bus-cetta's arrest five plainclothes policemen arrived at Guimarães's apartment house for a search. They stopped at the concierge and told him not to warn Guimarães. But the concierge was skeptical that they really were police, and as soon as they left to go upstairs, he alerted Guimarães on the intercom.

When the officers knocked on the door, Guimarães had the maid open it. He saw men in civilian clothes with drawn pistols. Fearing attack, he opened fire first, wounding one of the policemen in the leg. They returned fire, shooting him in the throat, but not fatally.

Records seized in the raids and studied later by the Brazilian police confirmed that relatives of Badalamenti, including Leonardo, had been well entrenched for some time in Brazil. Another of them, Faro Lupo—the rakish, long-haired young man whom Rooney and Russo couldn't identify a few weeks before at the Charcoal Grill meeting in Queens with Mazzurco—was revealed in the records to have recently traveled to New York to open an office of Major Key Sportswear. Airline tickets found in a safe-deposit box of an owner of CEICO, the phony fish exporter, were made out in the name of Badalamenti's nephew Vincenzo Ran-dazzo—who was also Faro Lupo's uncle and another of the participants in the Charcoal Grill meeting. Also uncovered in the raids was a profusion of other records detailing extensive travels by the group throughout Brazil and to Caracas, Rome, Milan, Zurich, and Paris. It would take a long time to make sense of them, but they pointed to a relationship among Buscetta, Badalamenti, and drugs.

Mona Ewell was thrilled by the news of Buscetta's arrest. It had been just one year since she had briefed the assembled Italian and American officials at Quan-tico. For nearly eight years, almost since she had started work as a DEA intelli-gence aide, she had been reading agent reports and informant testimony about the enigmatic and contradictory figure of Buscetta. Now there might be a chance to pin down the myth although she saw no likelihood of gaining Buscetta's cooperation. The Sicilian Mafia didn't work that way.

In Brooklyn, the Eastern District narcotics prosecutor Reena Raggi walked into Charles Rose's office clutching a government cable. "Have you ever heard of Tommaso Buscetta?" she asked.

The brash and usually unflappable Rose nearly fell off his chair. "Everybody's heard of Tommaso Buscetta!" he said. He had been wanted in the Eastern District since 1973, when he was indicted on charges of heroin smuggling with French Connection traffickers Guiseppe Catania, Michel Nicoli, and others. Soon Rose, who had inherited the case, flew down to São Paulo with Ewell and a quiet, soft-spoken DEA agent, John Huber. Ewell had a thousand questions, many of them based on her close following of Frank Panessa's penetration of the LaPortas and Ficalora ring in Philadelphia and their connection to Cesare Bonventre and Baldo Amato.

Since the spring of 1983 Ewell had heard rumors that Buscetta was in Brazil. Before she left for Brazil in October, the FBI gave her some names and phone numbers picked up in surveillances in New York. One was Faro Lupo, who had called a number in São Paulo.

Ewell collected a great deal of information from the Brazilians. According to confidential informants, Buscetta was involved in a consortium of Mafia figures seeking to import heroin from Southeast Asia. The Buscetta group traveled frequently to and from Belém, where Buscetta's ranch near the Amazon River afforded limitless opportunities for smuggling contraband and access to regular flights to Europe.

The police, Ewell wrote in her DEA report, also believed that Buscetta was involved in cocaine smuggling through the phony fish export company CEICO and its shipments to Italy. Major Key Sportswear, they believed, was used primarily to launder money. Recent developments indicated efforts to expand activities to the United States.

According to a Brazilian informant, Gaetano Badalamenti was living in Rio. He went by the name of Francisco Vitale and was in close touch with Buscetta. Moreover, the informant told the police, Buscetta and Badalamenti had aligned their forces to conduct the trafficking. The recent murders in America and Italy of Buscetta's and Badalamenti's relatives were further evidence of the feuds their alignment had provoked. Most recently, Badalamenti's great-nephews Matteo and Salvatore Sollena had been found murdered in New Jersey. Badalamenti was also associated with Major Key; its travel records were found to list his pseudonym Vitale.

Moreover, it turned out, Bardellino, who lived above Cristina in Rio, was the right-hand man of Carlo Zippo, Buscetta's old *compare* from the Brazilian-Italian trading company in New York. Zippo had been arrested earlier in 1983 in Italy on charges of running a cocaine-smuggling operation between South America and

Italy. Another of the group's contacts in Brazil, the police said, was a Neapolitan fugitive from the February 1983 Mafia roundup in Italy that had so infuriated Carmine Russo. His telephone number, it turned out, had been called from Michele Zaza's phone in Los Angeles at the time of Mafia boss Antonio Salamone's visit there. Ewell could barely contain herself at these revelations. There was more. Financial records taken from the Neapolitan showed that he had visited Caracas and had had bank dealings there, evidence that was in line with what DEA Agent Tom Tripodi had told Ewell about Venezuelan money laundering just before the 1982 Quantico conference. These guys were all connected, she kept thinking. It was an intelligence analyst's bonanza.

More connections discovered by the Brazilian police showed that shipments from CEICO were found to have gone to a Naples company called Lo Squalo. A car surveilled in Paris during a meeting of suspected Mafia drug traffickers in July 1983 was owned by Lo Squalo. The meeting coincided with Badalamenti's visit to Paris with his wife and their sons Vito and Leonardo.

The circle seemed complete when Leonardo Badalamenti was found with a telephone number for Carlo Lauricella, an associate of Giuseppe Ganci's in New York.

But the Italians who had rushed over for the Buscetta arrest were not getting along well with the Brazilians. They appeared mutually suspicious and contemptuous. As presumed neutrals, Ewell, Rose, and Huber enjoyed an advantage. They found they could get more from the Brazilians when the Italians were not around, so they made a point of going back to the Brazilians at night to talk to them privately. They were also given access to voluminous police files on Buscetta. Ewell copied reams of files to take back with her to sort out later.

But they had still not seen Buscetta. Aware of the great prize they had captured, the Brazilians had locked him away under ultratight security, out of the Americans' reach. Charlie Rose was determined not to leave without every effort to see Buscetta.

"Someone's got to get in to see him," Rose said of Buscetta. "You," he said, eyeing the lithe blond Ewell, "probably have the best chance."

Ewell went to see the Brazilians. In her most fetching manner she pleaded, "Please, I came all this way. More than anything else in the world I want to see this man. My bosses will kill me if I tell them I couldn't." Besides, she added slyly, how did anybody know for sure they really had arrested the right person?

It worked. The next morning an armored car picked Ewell up at her hotel. She was blindfolded for the ride. When the blindfold was removed, she expected to see a maximum security prison. Instead she found herself in a kind of dormitory, more of a halfway house than a prison, with a communal kitchen and prisoners strolling the halls.

She recognized him immediately; for nearly a decade she had examined every photo DEA had found of him. He had the same high forehead and moplike bushy hair, thick brows, short pug nose, wide, square chin, and bad teeth she had expected. But she was not prepared for the nobility of his bearing; even in custody he seemed regal.

She feigned uninterest.

"Oh, you came to see me," he said knowingly, a half-smile curling his thick expressive lips.

"Oh, no," she lied, flustered. "I'm just, just, looking around."

Among the prisoners Ewell also saw Leonardo Badalamenti, who, as it turned out, was released shortly thereafter on probation, pending possible extradition to Italy—and promptly fled.

As expected, Buscetta was not telling his captors anything. But Rose had an intuition one day when he heard that Cristina had paid a visit to the American Embassy. She was seeing what the Americans were willing to offer her husband, Rose thought. He was getting ready to roll.

But in 1984, when the deal was cut, Buscetta was sent first to Italy. The prospect of returning to the place of his nightmares and being cut off from Cristina and the children filled him with despair. He had a capsule of strychnine that he had kept with him all these years. If he ever fell into his enemies' hands, he had resolved, he would at least deprive them of a final triumph.

17

B y late summer of 1983 Russo and his wires had outgrown the Queens office. At first it had been easy enough to carry on the listening and taping in a portion of the FBI's cluttered sixth-floor quarters in the bronze monolith on Queens Boulevard, but after a sixteen-member Brooklyn North police narcotics squad joined the spreading investigation, the office started to pop its buttons. A separate plant was set up opposite a dentist's office in a nearby building whose owner had helped out the FBI before. Unfortunately the heat went off at night, leaving Russo and Louis Caprino and the other shivering listeners dependent on kerosene heaters and layers of sweaters. The power overload sometimes blew the fuses, plunging the plant into darkness. For laughs, the agents and cops sometimes called up for pizza deliveries from Al Dente, whose employees had no idea that the office to which they were sending pizzas housed their eavesdroppers.

In addition to Ganci's home, his pizzeria was now wiretapped, along with Pronto Demolition, the Roma restaurant in New Jersey, Filippo Salamone's house—since taken over by Salvatore Greco—and Mazzara's and Castronovo's houses. The growing number of wiretaps had sent the bureau beating the bushes for listeners fluent in Sicilian, but it was a difficult quest. The pool was not large to begin with, and prospects had to be carefully screened to avoid taking on anyone who might compromise the investigation, as had been known to happen from time to time. Others were qualified and certified trustworthy but were reluctant to become involved in the exhausting and potentially dangerous work. Rooney had found a Sicilian-speaking clerk in the New York office. Initially she turned the job down as too hazardous, but Rooney prevailed on her to change her mind and join the DEA agents Nancy Morelli and Gabby Zacco.

Across the Hudson, surveillance agents continued to track Ganci's nearly daily visits to Carol, whose private life was taking on a byzantine nature of its own. Carol had a secret, as she confided to her diary on October 4, 1983—she was pregnant. The identity of the father was part of the secret. Carol was dividing her time between Ganci and the someone named Frank, according to her diary. She had been juggling a difficult schedule. She often spent her days visiting Ganci in the hospital, where he was recovering from removal of a cancerous lung, and shopping for the boutique and beauty salon that she and her friend Ann were opening in Belleville with Ganci's money. Nights Carol made love with Frank, although sometimes she had fights with him. She confided to the diary that she was "feeling confuse." Grammar and spelling were never Carol's strong points. She was "upset confusse but felt right. I do feel for Frank," she confessed.

In the beginning of October, a week before the grand opening of Carol and Ann's boutique and beauty salon, Ann complained to Ganci that Carol was not showing up. Ganci by this time was out of the hospital and back at work at Al Dente. By the warmth of their conversation, Russo was reminded of Ganci and Ann's assignation at the motel.

"I should learn to give treatment," Ganci kidded Ann. "I stay in the store with you."

"Oh, I wish you would. I need you. I need you."

Ganci laughed and coughed.

But Ann said coyly she was afraid of tiring Ganci out. She called him honey. He called her sweetie.

"You know you're not here a lot," she complained gently.

"I know, doll. I know. I know."

"And I'm gonna make, I'm gonna make it for you, Joe, so help me God," Ann promised. "With Carol or without Carol, I'm gonna make it. I'm gonna tell you right now I'm gonna make it."

There was nothing wrong with Carol, Ann said. She was just a hypochondriac.

"She is spoiled by me . . ." Ganci agreed. "I spoiled everybody, even the dog."

Then Ganci said suddenly, "We should kill each other."

Ann was shocked. "Huh?" was all she could manage.

"We should kill each other," Ganci repeated.

Ann decided Ganci was joking. "You know what's wrong with Carol?" she said.

"Yeah."

"Nothing!" Ann said. "Nothing!"

". . . I know there's nothing wrong," Ganci agreed. "Nobody likes a worrier. . . . And we're gonna put her to work, don't worry about it."

Ann turned coy again. "Joe?"

"What, darling?"

"When am I going to get mine, mine?"

"Yours yours?" Ganci chuckled.

"Mine."

"Don't worry about it," Ganci reassured her. "Soon."

"All right, sweetheart."

"Okay, my sweetie," Ganci concluded. "Don't worry about it. We're going to fix everything, don't worry."

"All right, honey."

In Philadelphia, agents made a crucial connection in the conspiracy. DEA agent Frank Panessa had been dealing with the LaPortas and Ficalora and their associates for almost a year. Panessa had bought $880,000 worth of heroin, independent of Hopson's buys from Zito that had led directly to Ganci in New York. The discovery of the heroin shipment to the tile factory in Buffalo and the ensuing arrests had panicked LaPorta—a tip-off to Panessa that LaPorta, too, was involved. LaPorta went into hiding. But he confided to Panessa that he owed Bonventre $100,000 for previous heroin buys. LaPorta had two negotiable $50,000 bearer bonds. Would Panessa help him out and accept them for cash? Panessa, with the approval of the DEA, agreed. His partner, William Kean, gave Ficalora the $100,000 for LaPorta in a manila envelope.

What happened next, Rooney and Russo became convinced, tied Bonventre and Amato convincingly into the heroin network. Ficalora gave the envelope with the money to an associate, Francesco Panno, who was then tailed driving up the New Jersey Turnpike and into Queens, where he parked in the lot of a Key Food supermarket. Panno entered the store and walked out with a man whom surveilling agents took to be Baldo Amato. He and Panno were seen talking in the parking lot near two cars with open trunks until they were joined by a third man, later identified as an official of the Pasquale Conte supermarket company. Suddenly, Panno and the third man jumped into the two cars and sped off through red lights, as though fearing pursuit.

Back inside the store, another surveilling agent, John Delmore of the DEA, thought he recognized Amato. As the agent skulked in the produce section pretending to buy bananas, he was certain he saw Amato stare nervously out of the window while pacing back and forth. Then Amato too left hurriedly. The trio had detected the surveillance, Delmore felt sure. They had been burned.

Later Amato's lawyer argued that the man in the supermarket identified as Amato was Pasquale Conte's son, Patsy Conte, Jr., who, at twenty, was nine years younger than Amato and, at five-foot-eight, was several inches shorter. The blurred FBI photos did appear to show Conte. But Delmore, who knew Amato, insisted it was Amato he had seen.

Meanwhile, the diminutive Sal Mazzurco and his brother-in-law Giuseppe Lamberti had another enigmatic conversation about the old man or uncle, a reference Russo had been trying to decode for months.

"Enzo sends you his regards," Mazzurco said.

"Any news from the old man?" Lamberti asked.

Mazzurco said he had not heard anything.

Mazzurco was emerging as a more central figure than Rooney or Russo had first imagined. They knew he was a liaison between Lamberti and Ganci, on one hand, and the so-called old man or uncle and his nephew Enzo—whoever they were—on the other. Mazzurco also was connected to Pronto Demolition and seemed to have a share in a roller rink near Newburgh, New York, where Lamberti had a boutique and a farm. One day the manager of the roller rink called him.

"That friend of mine would like another one today," he told Mazzurco.

Mazzurco was soon followed to the Bronx, where an agent watching through a monocular saw him pull up behind a van registered to the roller rink, called Upskate. He watched Mazzurco retrieve a shoebox-size package from his trunk and hand it to the rink manager, who was followed to another location in the Bronx, where he carried the package into a building.

Several days later Mazzurco told Ganci, "I raised a little bit and . . . but that's about it. The rest . . . are in a separate account." It sounded, Russo thought, as if Mazzurco were trying to round up some money.

Another clue offered itself to Russo toward the end of October. An employee of Giuseppe Lamberti's upstate boutique called Mazzurco to say that "he" called the night before and left a number, 256-4496.

Russo scribbled it down.

"Did he call from down there or from here?" Mazzurco asked.

"From down there," came the answer.

So Russo had a seven-digit phone number for someone in some unidentified place "down there." It was in Rio de Janeiro, but he had no way of knowing that yet. Without the country or area code, tracing it back to the subscriber was virtually impossible. He would have to wait for more information.

Another haunting series of calls unfolded the same day, as Russo heard when he played back the tapes in the Queens plant. Giuseppe Lamberti called Mazzurco in a panic. "I'm supposed to meet the godson of that guy, he's leaving, he's leaving, and I have to meet him, because he's leaving with the ship, with the *Queen Elizabeth.* It should be Fiftieth Street there."

Russo was wondering whom Lamberti was talking about when he supplied the answer. "I need to meet that guy Palazzolo," he said.

Palazzolo? One of the foursome Mazzurco had met at the Charcoal Grill in September had rented a car under the name of Emanuele Palazzolo, Russo remembered. But Paquette reminded him of the Vito Roberto Palazzolo in Europe who had shown up in some of the phone calls by Della Torre and Filippo Salamone. Was this the same Palazzolo? Or two Palazzolos? Were they related like the two Sal Catalanos?

Russo went back to the tape. Lamberti continued: "Because he has to leave . . . he is supposed to leave at five . . . I have to meet him at three."

Russo looked at his watch. He was listening to a conversation that had taken place several hours before. It was already hours past the meeting time. But no one had been assigned to the surveillance. They had missed it.

"It happened again!" Russo raged. He yanked off his earphones and slammed them down on the desk.

Rooney knew immediately what Russo was talking about, but he played dumb. "What happened again, Carmine?" he asked innocently.

"We missed a fucking meeting." Russo explained about Palazzolo and the *QE 2.* "Why didn't we know about it?"

"Take it easy, Carmine," Rooney said. "It's nobody's fault. We're getting short of people." The case, he reminded Russo, was already eating up more agents than had ever been used before in a single criminal investigation. The bureau wasn't going to spare many more. Some surveillances were bound to fall through the cracks.

Russo, muttering, went back to his tape. "And that's why," Lamberti said, ". . . if we meet, I'll give you my car and you'll leave me your car."

"All right," Mazzurco said.

"I don't want to be recognized," continued Lamberti.

Rooney had the ship's manifest checked. It showed Vito Roberto Palazzolo and his wife sailing from Cherbourg, France, to New York and then back to Cherbourg, accompanied by their Mercedes.

Russo found he was not totally bereft of information on the shipboard encounter. Lamberti recounted it on the phone to his cousin Sal Lamberti and said that Palazzolo had spoken of Ganci. It was easy dealing with the round one, Giuseppe Lamberti quoted Palazzolo, "because . . . I know him so long that we have done deals before . . . a lot."

Palazzolo's sign-off was incriminating: "Let's be careful, all of us."

Sal Lamberti said he had spoken to Ganci that morning. "He told me he had tracked down the doctor. . . ."

So now Ganci was in touch with the mysterious doctor, Russo thought. But his confusion deepened a moment later.

"He tracked down everyone," Sal Lamberti continued about Ganci, "and they want, they want the . . . X rays here, these X rays here . . . if he gives them everything, there's no need to conduct tests, he says, there."

It suddenly dawned on Russo that Lamberti was talking about a real doctor and real X rays. What was he supposed to believe?

Ganci was still in pain from his lung operation. As he told Catalano, "Boy, I can't even move." But he shrugged it off philosophically. "Oh, what can I do?" he said. "When I die, I die. I don't care. Ahhh . . ."

Several days later Ganci was at Al Dente when Margherita called to tell him Giuseppe Lamberti and someone else were waiting for him at home.

"Tell them that I'm making a pizza and then I'm coming," Ganci told his wife.

Was this code? Russo wondered.

"Bring it," she suggested.

In the background Lamberti could be heard shouting, "And tell him to bring the calzones!"

"Damn!" muttered Ganci. "And how many things do they want?"

No, Russo decided, that was pizza and calzones.

At the end of October Russo learned through the wires that Mazzurco and an associate were about to leave for Rome. Mazzurco called a number in Sicily that the Italian police were able to trace to Giuseppe Soresi, a hospital orderly from Borgetto. Soresi was a high-level envoy of the Sicilian drug suppliers. He was the black-haired, full-faced man who had visited Ganci at home with Catalano and the Lambertis the previous June, when Ganci had signaled his pleasure over the outcome of the discussions by giving Catalano a nod and a wink that even John Mauzey hidden in the van could see. Mazzurco told Soresi that he was going to see a doctor in Rome and would like Soresi to meet him there.

Soresi asked if Mazzurco could come to him instead. Mazzurco wasn't sure but promised to call when he arrived. Russo pondered this. With the world's best hospitals in New York, Mazzurco is traveling to Rome to consult a hospital orderly from Borgetto.

The man accompanying Mazzurco to Italy, the agents found, was the owner or manager of a Queens foreign car sales agency that Mazzurco also seemed to have some part in. Was Mazzurco suddenly in the car-importing business? Cars were a notorious way of smuggling in drugs. Mazzurco and his companion were followed to the Alitalia terminal at JFK and were watched as they boarded the plane. The next day Mazzurco called home from Rome to say he had arrived safely.

"I'm getting one of those things again," his wife said. Mazzurco didn't understand.

"I'm getting the echo." She coughed, as if for emphasis.

Now Mazzurco understood. They had been suspecting a tap on the phone for a long time, a suspicion given credence by the echo they had begun hearing. So they were not surprised when, in Mazzurco's next call from Luxembourg a few days later, they again heard some interference on the line. Mazzurco's wife suggested it was from the rain. "Yeah, I know that it's raining," Mazzurco said. Once again Russo had the uneasy feeling that his targets knew they were being watched. The FBI was already having some uneasy moments over another of Jim Kallstrom's triumphs—planting a bug in Ganci's car. Upon a court order, bureau technicians had picked the lock of Ganci's blue Mercedes and hidden a small microphone to pick up and transmit conversations in the car. The first test came a few days later when Ganci and Catalano jumped in for a drive, with Catalano behind the wheel.

To the amusement of the agents, some of whom were following in surveillance cars, the bug picked up Catalano poking fun at people who drove without looking back to see whether they were being followed. Like their Al Dente pizzeria employee who never checked for a tail. Catalano said: "The car, he drives . . . near the chair . . . never moves the mirror. He couldn't see anything. Not that he fixes the mirror. Even, while he drives, once in a while, he looks to see if the cars behind him, or cars in the front . . ." he snickered.

"He doesn't look much," Ganci agreed.

Catalano's attention was caught by a woman driver ahead of them who also wasn't looking back. To their glee, the pair made a game of following the unsuspecting woman, tailing her and turning wherever she turned.

"Yeah, see, goes forward that one, what does she know?" Catalano laughed. "Puts the directional on. If she's squeezed, she doesn't look . . ."

But the bug quickly proved disappointing; engine noise and other interference drowned out the conversations. Worse, it sounded as if Ganci might be on the verge of detecting it—and a second one they had planted in the Seville.

"Bring it to the company," one of Ganci's associates could be heard saying in the car. "Tell them, 'I want a new battery. Why do I have to pay for it?' "

Ganci kept trying to get his Mercedes fixed. He took it to several garages, where mechanics hoisted the hood and poked around in the motor and shook their heads. Why was the battery always running down?

The bug, it seemed clear, was draining the power. One of these days, an enterprising mechanic might find the microphone. The bug would have to be deactivated.

Shortly afterward, while Ganci stopped at his pizzeria on Flatbush Avenue in Brooklyn, agents tried to get at the Mercedes to shut off the mike. One agent went to the used-car lot where the car was parked and engaged the salesmen in distracting conversation while another agent moved in close to the car and deactivated the bug by remote control.

But it had been a close call. To be really safe, Rooney decided, the bugs had to go. One night, while Ganci was visiting Carol in Clifton, an agent sneaked up to the parked blue Mercedes, deftly picked the lock, started the car and drove off to remove the microphone in a quiet spot. Unfortunately, Ganci finished with Carol sooner than expected and came out to find—What the fuck?! The car was gone! He looked around dumbfounded. No, that was where he had parked it and now it wasn't there! Ganci ran back to Carol's apartment to call the police.

Surveillance agents who witnessed Ganci's astonishment quickly alerted the agent who had taken the car. Now it was too late for the agent to drive it back. How would it look? Ganci comes out to find his Mercedes gone, calls the police, and suddenly the car drives up? They had to lose the car. But how?

They called Rooney late at home. He had just climbed into bed when the phone rang.

"Now what is it?" said Jane.

They explained the problem to Rooney, who arranged for Ganci's car to be driven to Brooklyn and "found" by the NYPD. The police, treating it as a recovered stolen vehicle, also checked the trunk and discovered boxes of expensive jewelry.

Ironically, Ganci's Seville subsequently disappeared—without the FBI's help. Rooney suspected Ganci had arranged to have it "stolen" to collect the insurance. He soon replaced it with another Mercedes.

On the afternoon of November 7, 1983, the telephone rang in the Castronovo residence in New Jersey. The restaurateur's son picked up.

"Hello," said a voice. "I am Salvatore." He had heard that Castronovo was in the hospital with kidney stones. He wanted to wish him well. He took the number of the hospital and left a message with the son: "Tell him Sal Amendolito called."

Bob Paquette of the FBI and Mike Fahy of Customs had been hunting for Amendolito since 1981, ever since he had been identified as the one who had received cartons of cash from Matassa at World-Wide Business Centres on Madison Avenue. After studying Amendolito's telex and toll records, Paquette was more convinced than ever that the elusive Italian money mover was crucial to tracking the money from its source to its final destination.

Amendolito's name had been put on the watch list that the Immigration and Naturalization Service kept at airports and border crossings to alert government agents to the arrival of foreigners of special interest. But he either had not entered the country or had slipped in under other names.

Then, in July 1983, he was detected coming in from Switzerland. Agents missed him at Boston's Logan Airport, but through the Swissair computer his ticket was traced first to Denver and then Salt Lake City, where, agents later learned, his wife lived. From there he was traced to New Orleans, where he was finally arrested.

Once again the agents faced a dilemma: To confront and question Amendolito risked exposing the investigation; not to take the chance meant possibly forgoing an irreplaceable opportunity. Fahy opted for the risk, putting, he thought, his career on the line. If they could turn Amendolito, it would be a tremendous coup. If he refused and tipped off his partners, it could be a disaster.

They met in the prison in New Orleans. Fahy told Amendolito that if he cooperated fully, the government might consider dropping criminal charges against him.

"No," said Amendolito. "I'll talk about the money, nothing else."

Fahy was astounded. He had never before met such an imperious prisoner who put conditions on his freedom. "I'm offering this guy a walk," he said later, "and he's negotiating with me! What balls!" But then Fahy did not yet know how Amendolito had scammed Leonardo Greco and the Sicilian Mafia.

"Of course, if you're afraid . . ."

"Afraid?"

After Amendolito had agreed to cooperate unconditionally, they flew him up to Paquette's old office in New Rochelle, where he was methodically debriefed. They then learned of his exploits as a money launderer for what appeared more clearly than ever to be a huge narcotics-smuggling operation, although Amendolito insisted he never knew where the millions originated. For the first time they were getting an inside picture of the key financial players and the scope of the enterprise. Amendolito told them of his arrangements with Tognoli and his pickups of boxes of cash from Castronovo at the Roma restaurant, his flights with the money to the Bahamas, the trip to the Chase Manhattan Bank with the yellow bags of money, his disastrous encounter with the Neapolitan furriers and his meetings with Sal—he didn't know his last name was Catalano—and the $1.54 million suitcase. Paquette and Fahy were dumbfounded.

After nearly four months of debriefing Amendolito, Paquette and Fahy had a task for him. They asked him to strap a hidden tape recorder under his clothes and meet an old client, Frank Castronovo.

When Amendolito reached Castronovo, he was home from the hospital, recovering from his operation for kidney stones. He said that he and Gaetano Mazzara had sold their Roma restaurant and that he could no longer work, having suffered cardiac problems as well. Nevertheless, Amendolito persuaded Castronovo to meet him in Manhattan. They agreed on Flanagan's, a dim Irish pub and restaurant on First Avenue in the Sixties; it was all Amendolito could think of at the time. As coached by his government mentors, Amendolito was to draw Castronovo into incriminating recollections of their dealings—namely, the cartons of money Amendolito had picked up from him at the Roma three years before.

"I left Oliviero in a suspended situation where I owed them some money," Amendolito began, recalling, in effect, how he had swindled Tognoli and Leonardo Greco.

Amendolito pulled out a telex he said he had sent Tognoli. Castronovo was cautious, perhaps suspicious. "You don't need to show it to me."

"No, no, it's important that you read the text, that's all."

Castronovo shrugged and read it.

Because the issue was sure to come up, Amendolito broached it first, as if it were of little consequence. He told Castronovo he had been stopped by the FBI and questioned.

"Were you also in prison?" Castronovo asked.

"Yes, they held me, but they didn't—I was not arrested. They . . . held me. I stayed in a hotel here. They picked me up in New Orleans. I was a couple of days in New Orleans. Then they transferred me here in a hotel, and they questioned me here at the hotel, and then I replied that—that I had nothing to do with it."

He then tried to reassure Castronovo: "If they never came to you, it means that everything is all right. Ten days after all this had happened, I was already in Switzerland, trying to contact Oliviero in order to let you know, to avoid to call you directly . . . but there is no danger for me as long as we don't discuss again about money transfers. . . ."

Castronovo narrowed his eyes. "I did not make any transfer," he said.

He must suspect the wire, Amendolito suddenly thought. *But here at Flanagan's he can't pat me down. He doesn't want to make a scene.*

"You didn't make any transfers," Amendolito hurriedly agreed. "I made the transfers."

"But I didn't make any," Castronovo insisted.

"Excuse me," Amendolito interrupted. "I am not talking about you. I'm talking about myself. . . . I am saying that I am in the eye of the hurricane as long as we talk about transfers, okay, because I did make the transfers."

Amendolito tried to draw Castronovo out. "This way in the future there cannot be any implication on the fact that—that physically you consigned money to me. Of this nobody knows."

"I—I consigned you nothing," Castronovo insisted. ". . . I am telling you I didn't, I didn't."

He must *know I'm wired,* thought Amendolito. "Right, right, right, right, right." He rushed to agree.

"Because I didn't," Castronovo continued. "I didn't with you, except . . ."

Amendolito hurtled forward, claiming that he could not do anything further until he had honestly settled his debt with the "real owners of the money," as he put it. He was hoping Castronovo would say something about that on tape. But Castronovo insisted he did not know anything about the source of the funds. ". . . to tell the truth," he said, "if I knew, I would not work in the kitchen . . . like a slob from morning to night."

Amendolito asked for "a helping hand."

"There isn't anybody I can introduce you to because I don't know anybody," Castronovo said. "At that time, when it was done, it was done just like that, give this, okay, find Mike to give to Pasquale. Okay."

Amendolito asked Castronovo when was the last time he had heard from Tognoli.

"For some time, for some time . . . and I have always worked, as you know . . . I did a favor. The favor was done, and that was it. For me everything is done. I do not want to have anything to do with it."

Amendolito wanted Castronovo to let him know whenever Tognoli got in touch again.

"They won't contact me."

"Why?"

"I can't—I am not able to tell you why because I don't know," Castronovo said. "They will not. Maybe it's because something happened there for which they have no reasons to contact me. . . . I am telling you on my part there will not be anything because I don't care about it. These are things that do not interest me. Do you follow me? . . . I agreed to do a favor. I did it, and that's it for me."

"Okay," said Amendolito.

"I—listen, I went too deep already. I went too deep without having eaten or drank anything."

The discussion was over. Amendolito repaid Castronovo a $1,000 loan the restaurateur had given him two Christmases before. He also left Castronovo his phone number, and they parted.

Paquette and Fahy were disappointed. They had hoped Castronovo would say more. But he had said enough to verify the outlines of Amendolito's story. They would have to dig a lot deeper. They would have to be patient.

18

A MENDOLITO'S arrest and willingness to cooperate deluged Paquette with new financial leads. He knew now about the cash pipeline from Castronovo via Amendolito and Franco Della Torre to Switzerland, even though Castronovo had been too cautious to discuss it openly with the wired Amendolito. Paquette knew, too, about Amendolito's link, through his old partner Salvatore Miniati and ironworks manager Oliviero Tognoli, to Leonardo Greco and the Sicilian Mafia. But the more he knew, the more he wanted to know. How did the Swiss connection actually work? What were the laundering channels? Who else was involved? It was time for another trip to Europe. Amendolito would go along. He would reach out for his old contacts and try to revive the cash deliveries, this time as a secret government witness. Getting these transactions on tape and film would make Louis Freeh's job much easier when it came time to prosecute the case. But Paquette, it turned out, didn't accompany Amendolito. In the FBI overseas trips were perks. Paquette had already made two to Switzerland. It was someone else's turn to share the wealth. One of Paquette's delighted fellow agents was tapped to escort Amendolito. Accompanied by undercover agents provided by the Italian and Swiss authorities, Amendolito met with Miniati and Della Torre. But Hutton's tip-off the year before to Della Torre and Vito Roberto

Palazzolo had spooked them. Laundering networks had been dismantled and reconstituted. Amendolito had a good tape-recorded conversation with Della Torre, but all deals were off. Amendolito was unable to reinsert himself into the action.

Back in New York, Paquette was going over an old trail. When Filippo Salamone and his family had driven out to JFK that spring to hand off a gym bag which Paquette was now convinced had been filled with money, the stranger who picked it up had taken a taxi into the city. Agents had missed tailing the cab but had gotten its number and from the driver's trip sheet traced the passenger to First Avenue and Seventy-second Street. Paquette checked his card file. Whom had they come across there? Then he remembered. Salamone's phone bills showed calls to a New York number traced to someone named Enrico Frigerio in a building on East Seventy-second Street. Paquette visited the superintendent. "He's a man from Switzerland," the super told Paquette. "He's often away and lends the apartment out a lot."

This is too good, Paquette thought. He still didn't know who had been there that day with the gym bag, but telephone records from the apartment's phone showed that whoever it was had made some calls to Switzerland. *So Salamone hands off a bag with money that goes to a guy who calls Switzerland.* A telephone trail from the apartment led to a company called Gestinvest in the Seagram Building, which Paquette remembered also housed Finagest, where Amendolito had been first directed to take the cash deliveries from Castronovo. Paquette continued to follow the trail. There were calls from Gestinvest to a resort in Puerto Rico, Palmas del Mar. When Paquette queried the FBI's San Juan office about the resort, the office sent back surveillance photos of Della Torre, Enrico Frigerio, and money-mover Adriano Corti meeting there.

One key figure had quietly slipped back to Italy. Giuseppe Bono, apparently more concerned about the fate of his heroin empire than his own freedom, risked a return home in an effort to salvage his businesses, which were under siege by the authorities. He was soon arrested. The FBI learned of his departure by phone calls to Ganci from a real estate agent advising him of a buyer for Bono's $425,000 house in Pelham.

At the same time, in November 1983, Russo and Rooney were concentrating on trying to fathom the mystery of the new characters who had recently surfaced in the surveillances and wiretaps, like the out-of-towners who had met Mazzurco at the Charcoal Grill two months before. What did it mean when Lamberti told his brother-in-law Mazzurco, "I have spoken about the trip with the guy from the other side, there with . . . where it is hot"?

Mazzurco, who had recently returned from his trip to Italy, was careful not to give away anything on the phone: "Has the guy from where it is hot told you anything?"

"Nothing," Lamberti said. "Vincenzo seems, ah, Vinny seems disoriented. Ehhh, he had me talk to the other guy. And what he wanted was, that . . . the son, though . . . the father wasn't there. . . ."

Vincenzo was sure to call back, Lamberti said. "But as soon as he calls, you've got to tell him, 'Handsome, look, I need those things.' "

". . . Pietro should have them," Mazzurco said.

The son? The father? Is there a Holy Ghost, too? Russo wondered.

The same day Mazzurco, driving his Mercedes, was trailed to Fordham Road in the Bronx, where he met two strangers, one of whom could be seen taking a package from him. A similar transaction was observed several days later.

Afterward the manager of Mazzurco's roller rink called to ask: "Well, did you meet with that guy?"

"Yeah," said Mazzurco. "His brother came. He took, he took the shirt."

The last time someone got a shirt—the package DEA undercover agent Steve Hopson had picked up from Benny Zito, Russo remembered—it had turned out to be nearly 90 percent pure heroin. If this shirt was the same, Russo figured, then Mazzurco looked like a middle link in the dope chain, taking heroin that Ganci had received from Sicily and passing it to dealers in the Bronx.

Meanwhile, agents watching Ganci noticed a seemingly small act that was about to usher in a new phase of the case. It was so minor it might have escaped attention altogether.

Ganci and Mazzurco left Ganci's Al Dente pizzeria and walked a few steps east through the shoppers on Queens Boulevard to the corner of Sixty-eighth Drive. As the agents then watched, Mazzurco copied down the number of the pay telephone there. After he left, an agent, pretending to make a call, stepped up to the booth and memorized the number for himself, 830-9827.

Later that same day Mazzurco at Pronto Demolition called a number in Sicily that the Italian police traced to the sister of Giuseppe Lamberti. She said they had lost the number Mazzurco had given them earlier, so he repeated it, 830-9827. Russo, having been briefed by the surveillance agents, recognized it as the number of the pay phone on the corner outside Al Dente.

"Tomorrow at five o'clock then?" she said.

"Tomorrow at five o'clock in the afternoon," Mazzurco confirmed.

Russo quickly alerted Rooney. The corner pay phone would have to be tapped —fast! They scrambled to draft the Title III order for the FBI director's approval and a judge's signature.

By the next morning the phone was not only tapped but under direct observa-

Hosted by Sal Mazzurco (left), a meeting at the Charcoal Grill restaurant in Long Island City, Queens, on September 26, 1983, gave the FBI its first look at the midwestern group of heroin and cocaine suppliers representing ousted Sicilian Mafia boss Gaetano Badalamenti. Mazzurco is at left. Under the awning (left to right) are Faro Lupo, Emanuele Palazzolo, and Pietro Alfano. The photo `is reversed because it was shot through the mirror of a surveillance car.

Giuseppe Ganci and his commare, *Carol, stroll near her apartment in Clifton, New Jersey, on November 12, 1983.*

Ganci (in dark coat) and Mazzurco wait by the pay phone closest to Ganci's Al Dente pizzeria on Queens Boulevard for an incoming call from Giuseppe Soresi in Sicily on November 19, 1983. In the call, Soresi and Ganci agreed that Soresi's relative Giuseppe Lamberti should travel to Sicily to straighten out a snag in the heroin pipeline.

Italian surveillance: Gaetano Mazzara visits Sicily on December 12, 1983, in another effort to straighten out a snag in the heroin supply line. The photos, displayed in this format by the Italians, show Mazzara, in the light jacket and distinctively swept-back dark hair, with Filippo Nania, the Sicilian Mafia under-boss of Partinico.

Sal Lamberti (on phone) and Mazzurco, outside Al Dente, take an incoming phone call from Gaetano Badalamenti in Brazil on February 8, 1984. The call, in which heroin and cocaine were discussed in coded terms of cotton and acrylic fabric, convinced FBI Agent Carmine Russo that Badalamenti was a key drug supplier to the Catalano/Ganci consortium.

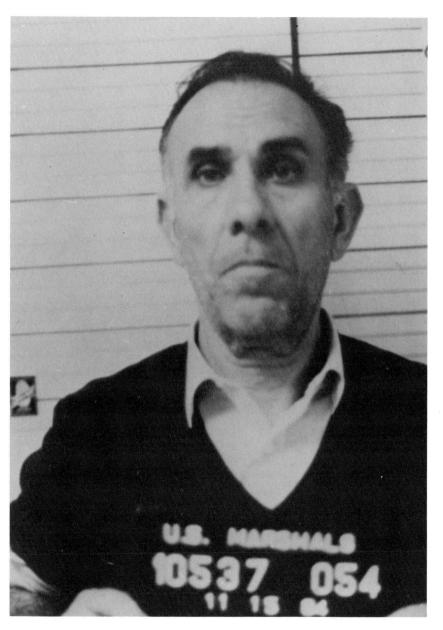

Gaetano Badalamenti in U.S. custody seven months after his arrest in Madrid on April 9, 1984.

Cinisi. The seat of the Badalamenti clan just west of Palermo occupies a strategic location between the mountains ringing the Sicilian capital and the sea. The Cinisi family's sphere of influence took in nearby Punta Raisi Airport, from which billions of dollars of heroin flowed to America in the 1960's and '70's. (Photo by Ralph Blumenthal)

Alfano's home and original pizza restaurant in Oregon, Illinois, photographed by the FBI on January 31, 1984. Behind the house is a new pizzeria that Alfano built on an adjacent lot several years earlier.

Badalamenti's nephew Pietro Alfano (left) and Sal Mazzurco walk out of Ganci's Al Dente pizzeria during Alfano's February 14, 1984, visit to arrange drug deals.

The Pineway liquor mart in Oregon, Illinois, with its outdoor phone booth where Alfano received calls from his uncle Gaetano Badalamenti.

A month before the fall: Six of the Pizza Connection's key conspirators enjoy an outing on Second Avenue in Manhattan on March 6, 1984. From left: Cesare Bonventre, Giuseppe Ganci, Frank Polizzi, Giuseppe Lamberti (hidden), Salvatore Catalano and Baldassare Amato. The group had visited the new Caffé Biffi Amato was building on Eighty-fourth Street.

Tommaso Buscetta, the most important defector from the Sicilian Mafia, arrives at Rome's Fiumicino Airport escorted by Italian security agents on July 15, 1984, nine months after his arrest in Brazil. A blanket conceals a bullet-proof shield. Buscetta's decision to cooperate with investigators became a turning point in the war against the Mafia on both sides of the Atlantic. He later became the lead-off witness in the Pizza Connection trial in New York. (ANSA News Agency, Inc.)

Corleone. Traditional stucco houses line a cobblestone street in the ancient Arab settlement once called Kurliyun, some fifty miles south of Palermo. Corleone is home of the Sicilian Mafia's most fearsome clan and its imprisoned boss, Luciano Liggio. (Photo by Ralph Blumenthal)

Luigi Ronsisvalle, an admitted contract killer from Sicily whose account of a drug meeting and delivery helped convict Sal Catalano, signs an affidavit recanting his testimony in a Sharonville, Ohio, motel room on September 22, 1987. Ronsisvalle subsequently recanted the recantation, claiming he was threatened into disavowing his original testimony. (Photo by Ralph Blumenthal)

Thomas L. Sheer, the FBI's assistant director in New York and the bureau's leading strategist on the Pizza Connection investigation, in his office on December 5, 1986. The following November he announced his retirement after twenty-five years in the FBI. (Photo by Dith Pran/The New York Times)

Rudolph W. Giuliani (left), U.S. attorney for the Southern District of New York, and Louis Freeh, chief prosecutor in the Pizza Connection case, meet the press on October 2, 1987, after mob witness Luigi Ronsisvalle reversed his recantation and reaffirmed his testimony against Sal Catalano. (Photo by Keith Meyers/The New York Times)

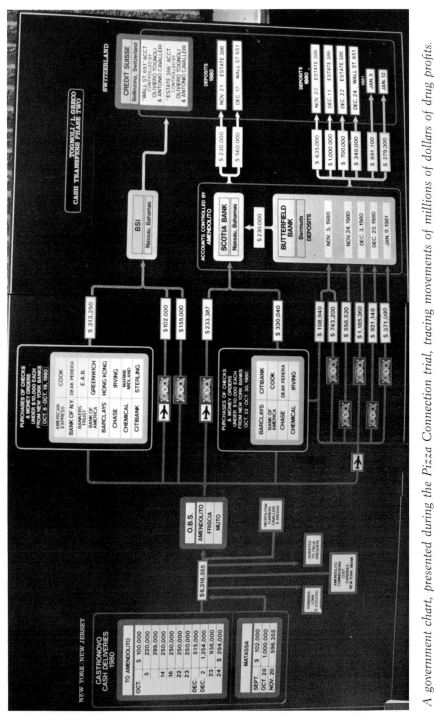

A government chart, presented during the Pizza Connection trial, tracing movements of millions of dollars of drug profits.

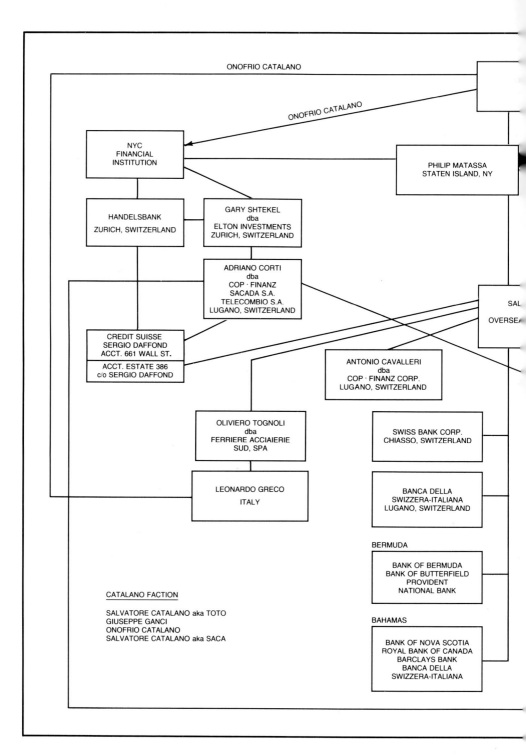

FBI agent Robert L. Paquette's working diagram of financial links uncovered during the Pizza Connection investigation. Many of the bankers and money launderers later testified that they did not know the funds stemmed from heroin sales.

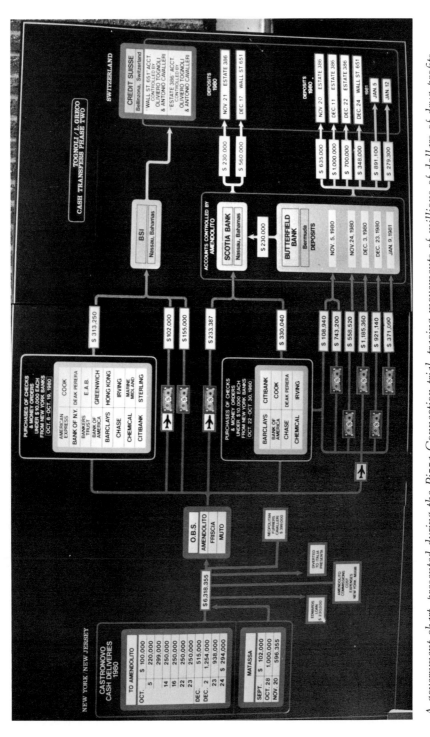

A government chart, presented during the Pizza Connection trial, tracing movements of millions of dollars of drug profits.

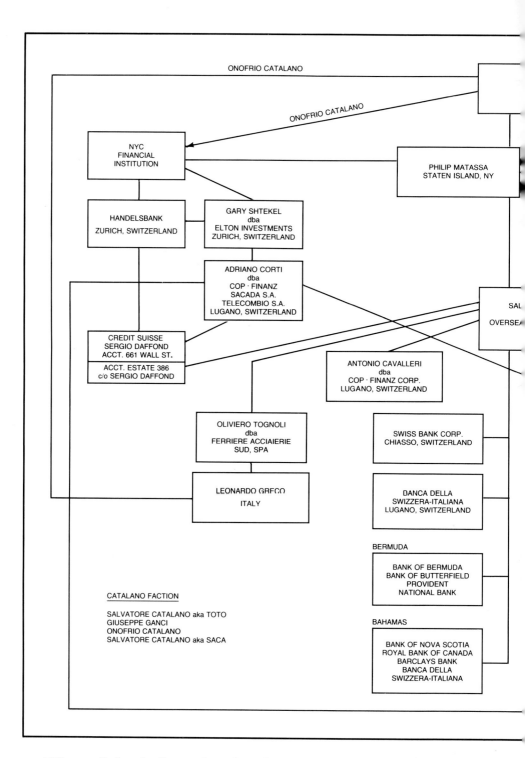

ONOFRIO CATALANO

ONOFRIO CATALANO

NYC
FINANCIAL
INSTITUTION

PHILIP MATASSA
STATEN ISLAND, NY

HANDELSBANK
ZURICH, SWITZERLAND

GARY SHTEKEL
dba
ELTON INVESTMENTS
ZURICH, SWITZERLAND

ADRIANO CORTI
dba
COP · FINANZ
SACADA S.A.
TELECOMBIO S.A.
LUGANO, SWITZERLAND

SAL

OVERSEA

CREDIT SUISSE
SERGIO DAFFOND
ACCT. 661 WALL ST.

ACCT. ESTATE 386
c/o SERGIO DAFFOND

ANTONIO CAVALLERI
dba
COP · FINANZ CORP.
LUGANO, SWITZERLAND

OLIVIERO TOGNOLI
dba
FERRIERE ACCIAIERIE
SUD, SPA

SWISS BANK CORP.
CHIASSO, SWITZERLAND

LEONARDO GRECO
ITALY

BANCA DELLA
SWIZZERA-ITALIANA
LUGANO, SWITZERLAND

BERMUDA

BANK OF BERMUDA
BANK OF BUTTERFIELD
PROVIDENT
NATIONAL BANK

CATALANO FACTION

SALVATORE CATALANO aka TOTO
GIUSEPPE GANCI
ONOFRIO CATALANO
SALVATORE CATALANO aka SACA

BAHAMAS

BANK OF NOVA SCOTIA
ROYAL BANK OF CANADA
BARCLAYS BANK
BANCA DELLA
SWIZZERA-ITALIANA

FBI agent Robert L. Paquette's working diagram of financial links uncovered during the Pizza Connection investigation. Many of the bankers and money launderers later testified that they did not know the funds stemmed from heroin sales.

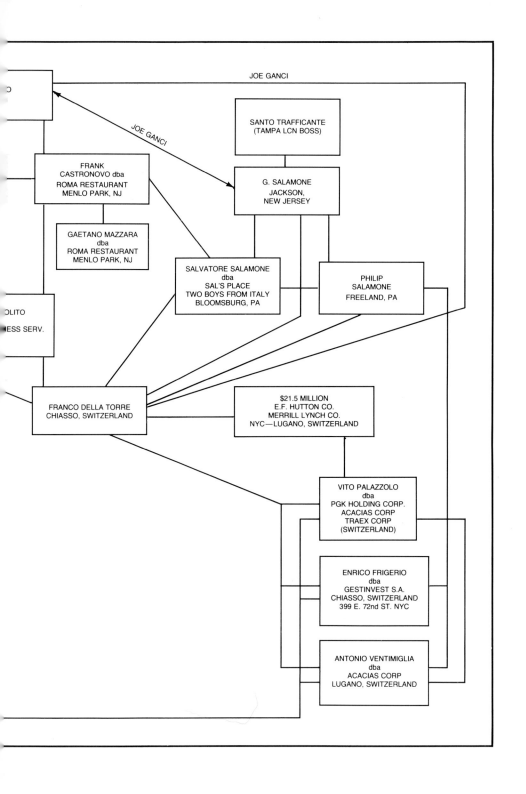

JOE GANCI

JOE GANCI

SANTO TRAFFICANTE
(TAMPA LCN BOSS)

FRANK
CASTRONOVO dba
ROMA RESTAURANT
MENLO PARK, NJ

G. SALAMONE
JACKSON,
NEW JERSEY

GAETANO MAZZARA
dba
ROMA RESTAURANT
MENLO PARK, NJ

SALVATORE SALAMONE
dba
SAL'S PLACE
TWO BOYS FROM ITALY
BLOOMSBURG, PA

PHILIP
SALAMONE
FREELAND, PA

OLITO

ESS SERV.

FRANCO DELLA TORRE
CHIASSO, SWITZERLAND

$21.5 MILLION
E.F. HUTTON CO.
MERRILL LYNCH CO.
NYC—LUGANO, SWITZERLAND

VITO PALAZZOLO
dba
PGK HOLDING CORP.
ACACIAS CORP
TRAEX CORP
(SWITZERLAND)

ENRICO FRIGERIO
dba
GESTINVEST S.A.
CHIASSO, SWITZERLAND
399 E. 72nd ST. NYC

ANTONIO VENTIMIGLIA
dba
ACACIAS CORP
LUGANO, SWITZERLAND

Assistant U.S. Attorney Richard A. Martin (center) questions Mafia turncoat Tommaso Buscetta (left) on the witness stand in the Pizza Connection trial in 1985. Gaetano Badalamenti (foreground) listens. To his right is codefendant and relative Vincenzo Randazzo. Behind Martin and to his right, in the dark suit, is Sal Catalano. Next to Catalano, in the white shirt, is Pietro Alfano. Judge Pierre Leval (top left) presides from the bench. (Drawing by Marilyn Church)

tion by surveillance agents, including Bobby Gilmore, who was parked, as usual, among the gypsies across Queens Boulevard, and John Mauzey, who shivered in his van parked close to the pizzeria. From Mazzurco's conversation it had not been possible to tell whether the call was to come in at five P.M. New York time or Italian time, which would be eleven A.M. in New York. The agents decided to play it safe and be in place before eleven. The six-foot-two-inch Mauzey, with a distinguished thatch of graying hair and a mustache, had arrived at dawn, to be sure of getting a parking space with a good view of the phone booth. Now he had only to sit tight, invisible in the back of the van, with his Canon F-1. The vans were usually plain, without markings; when the bureau used vans marked like utility trucks, the agents had been bothered by customers banging on the vans for phone or electricity service.

As usual when he expected a long surveillance, Mauzey had avoided coffee that morning and drunk orange juice only sparingly. Nature's call would not be appreciated in the van; for emergencies he had a bottle. Once all he'd had to relieve himself in was an empty coffee container, which, at the first opportunity, he covered and put in a nearby garbage pail. To his horror, Mauzey saw a beggar shuffle over to the container. He couldn't bear to watch what followed.

Sixteen-hour stints at a stretch in the van were not unknown; Mauzey's record was twenty-four hours. Just about anything that could happen to a surveillance agent in a van had happened to him at one time or another. He had shivered in subzero weather in winter and, far worse, sweltered in midsummer, when temperatures inside the sealed van could hit 140 degrees and the sweat dripped off his face into his Canon. In winter you could always add extra layers of clothing to keep warm, but in summer, without any air conditioning, you could only strip down to your underwear. Because he did not dare reveal his presence, he and the van had been towed away by traffic control officers; once he'd had to radio the police to shoo away brownies who were trying to hook him up to a city tow truck. He had also watched from the van as a thief swiped headlights from a car down the street. And he had been in the van when some bozo tried, unsuccessfully, to steal it out from under him.

A thirty-five-year-old bachelor, Mauzey boasted an unusually varied background that typed him as an introvert and intellectual: He had been a premed student at the University of Illinois, where he played football and then gave up medicine for a degree in zoology. He enlisted in the Marines and after his tour went to work for a southern Illinois investigative task force. His specialty was surveillance, particularly surveillance photography, but what he really loved doing more than almost anything was climbing mountains. He was thinking about another trip to the rocks of Chamonix when his reverie was interrupted shortly before eleven A.M. by the sight of the portly Ganci in a shapeless coat making his way over to the pay phone with Mazzurco.

Mazzurco slipped his small form into the booth and slyly preempted the phone by picking up the receiver and pretending to talk while surreptitiously holding down the receiver hook to allow the incoming call to get through. At 11:15 the phone rang. Mazzurco jerked his finger off the hook.

"Hey," said a voice that Russo, listening in the plant, later identified with the help of the Italian police as that of Giuseppe Lamberti's relative in Borgetto— hospital orderly Giuseppe Soresi, whom Mazzurco had recently gone to see. Mazzurco handed the phone to Ganci. From the conversation it appeared that Soresi wanted Lamberti to come to Sicily to straighten out some kind of supply problem but that Ganci was not sure the trip was necessary. Ganci chose his words carefully: "The thing that is being manufactured, that guy wants, wants to split it into two things, you understand."

Ganci didn't think it was necessary for Lamberti to rush to Sicily, but he bowed to Soresi's entreaties: "All right, I'll tell him to come over there."

Russo was struck by the authority inherent in the phrase "I'll tell him."

Then Ganci had second thoughts: "He has to come for certain?"

"Yeah, I would say yes," Soresi said.

Perhaps someone could come here instead? ventured Ganci.

"I believe not," said Soresi.

"No, not over here," said Ganci, realizing he might have been misunderstood. "To go up, on top of over there, do you understand?"

What's on top? Russo thought. *Maybe Canada?*

But Soresi was adamant: ". . . if the situation is not completed . . . there is nothing to be done . . . they will not start construction . . . and this is the story."

As Russo decoded it later, unless they resolved this dispute, the heroin manufacturing would not take place.

Ganci sought to convey his urgency; he had waiting customers, too: "Because the guy who has to work over there, he is waiting to work."

Soresi was unmoved: "Because then I won't be able to find the craftsmen anymore."

Accordingly, Lamberti prepared to leave in two days for Sicily. (At the Pizza Connection trial, the jury did not agree that the government had proved the criminal intent of this particular conversation.)

The Italians were quickly alerted and picked up the surveillance as Lamberti, in suit and tie, was met at Punta Raisi Airport on November 26 by Soresi's son. The next day they watched big, black-haired Giuseppe Soresi drive Lamberti to a bar where they met another man, who followed in his car as they continued outside Borgetto toward a hilltop religious shrine, the miraculous grieving Madonna of Romitello. While the Italian agents watched from a distance, the two cars halted at a clearing under the summit, where the men felt they could not be seen, although they were being watched and photographed even then by the Italian police. They got out of their cars, embraced, and talked for about fifteen minutes, at one point walking to the edge of the road out of the view of the police before reentering their cars and departing.

The police had seen enough, coupled with the wiretapped calls in America, to convince them, along with the Americans, that a new heroin pipeline was being readied from Soresi to Ganci and Catalano.

Two days later the ringing telephone startled the Ganci household awake just after five A.M. Ganci picked it up.

Russo, listening to the taped call later, could hear crying in the background. "Come down." Catalano's summons was flat and matter-of-fact.

Ganci, hearing the crying, immediately thought of the Catalanos' baby. Was she sick?

It wasn't the baby, Catalano corrected him. "But maybe they found Alessandro in the car. . . ." Alessandro was the son of Catalano's cousin Saca, but Catalano was really talking about Saca.

"Um" was all Ganci said.

"Pass by here," said Catalano. "I have to go down there quick."

To Russo and other agents who listened to the call and again later to the tape, the strange thing was the deadpan tone of the conversation. Catalano's wife might have been grieving in the background, but it almost seemed as if Catalano and Ganci had been expecting Saca Catalano to be murdered.

Earlier that morning, according to a subsequent police report, the fifty-year-old jeweler from Howard Beach, Queens, was shot to death as he drove through Glendale, Queens, several miles from his cousin's and Ganci's. Saca was hit in the neck and eye by a gunman shooting from an unknown location. The car ran off the road and came to rest in the rear of a house. A man was seen running from the scene but was not apprehended. The investigation later found that Saca had been driving back from the Caffè Aiello when he was shot by someone in the back seat, either a passenger or a hidden assassin.

None of Catalano's associates seemed especially shocked. The next day Frank Polizzi, the Belleville contractor and motel owner, called Ganci. "But who died?" he asked. "Toto's cousin died?"

"Yeah," said Ganci.

"But how?"

"On an accident with the car," Ganci said. He cleared his throat for emphasis.

So, Saca. His jewelry business had long been suspected as a front for money laundering and drug trafficking, even before he had been seen at the very start of the wiretaps in March delivering a package to his cousin Catalano at home and then smoking a cigarette on the balcony. The old Bureau of Narcotics and Dangerous Drugs, as well as the Italian and Canadian authorities, were on to him as early as 1970, as Rooney had read in *The Canadian Connection*.

Rooney and Russo were more stunned than Saca's cousin Toto and their compatriots obviously were. The agents knew from the surveillances that Saca had seemed particularly crazed lately, in one instance all but levitating off the sidewalk, shaking his finger at a seemingly unperturbed Ganci. What the agents didn't yet know was that Saca had become a heroin addict. He had grown nuttier and nuttier and was increasingly jeopardizing their enterprise. Perhaps Ganci had been more upset than he had let on. Now all Rooney could do was arrange to surveil the funeral and see who showed up. Among the mourners he was not surprised to find Cesare Bonventre, who arrived in a black Ferrari he parked ostentatiously outside the chapel—on the sidewalk.

Three days later it was Gaetano Mazzara's turn to rush back to Sicily to resolve an apparently persistent snag in the heroin supply pipeline. Russo heard him frantically calling travel agents to obtain a ticket for the same day. "There is my aunt that does not feel good," he explained. Tommaso Buscetta, still in custody in Brazil, had not yet come to his momentous decision to turn against the Sicilian Mafia, but when he did the following year, among the things he would say was that Gaetano Mazzara had been "made" by the Noce family of central Palermo in the late 1970's for the specific purpose of coming to America to oversee the security of the heroin shipments.

Once again the Italian Treasury Police were waiting at Punta Raisi. Mazzara, in a light sports coat, was recognizable by his full, swept-back coiffure. They followed him to a bar in the Udditore section of Palermo, where an agent played the football lottery as he listened to Mazzara tell friends that he had come to visit his aunt, not mentioning her illness. In the following days he was tailed to the federal court building in Palermo, where he entered and emerged with the Mafia underboss of Partinico, Filippo Nania. Later Mazzara drove to the iron warehouse of Mafia boss Leonardo Greco in Bagheria, the starting point for Contorno's odyssey to the farmhouse three and a half years before. Mazzara left with an unidentified companion, who the officers suspected might be Greco, although at the time he was supposed to be serving a jail sentence. (It was not unheard of in Sicily for prisoners with money and influence to be walking around outside the prison walls when they were supposed to be inside.) Mazzara and his companion were then followed outside Bagheria to a seaside cottage of Frank Castronovo's cousin Carlo. Later Mazzara returned to the warehouse. He subsequently returned to the Castronovo cottage and helped carry a heavy red Samsonite suitcase into the garage.

Back in New York it was clear that some of Ganci's associates were sensing the surveillances, sending a spasm of anxiety through the already hyper Russo.

In early December Giuseppe Lamberti called Mazzurco with a warning about Pronto Demolition: "You got to avoid going over there! . . . Yesterday I had the cops after me!"

"Are you sure?"

"Yeah."

"You're kidding!" Mazzurco said.

"As soon as I left there . . . from the Demolition," Lamberti related, "as soon as I left there, a car in front of there left from there."

"And it came after you?" asked Mazzurco.

"With two of them in there!" continued Lamberti. ". . . As soon as I saw this . . . I went backwards. . . ."

It was not clear that they had detected the agents after all. The FBI surveillance logs for the day showed that after Lamberti and his cousin Sal had entered Pronto, a pizza was delivered by two men in a red car. The deliverymen left just as the Lambertis were departing, and they may have mistaken them for a surveillance car. In fact, surveillance agents rarely worked in pairs, finding that they attracted less attention alone. It was nonetheless disconcerting for Russo to hear that their guys thought they were being watched.

There was an even more disquieting development shortly afterward. Lamberti had chilling news for Mazzurco: "They opened over there!"

"Oh, you heard," Mazzurco said.

It was a serious setback for the bureau. One of Kallstrom's special operations agents had picked the locks at Pronto and planted a microphone inside. But in exiting he was overmeticulous and locked one lock that was never used. The first Pronto employee the next morning couldn't enter, exposing the break-in. The bug was not found. But Pronto was never used by Ganci and Mazzurco and their associates in the same way again.

Mazzurco's manager at the roller rink upstate also thought he was being followed. "Somebody's ass is itching—no?— . . . and . . . we're being watched!" he told Mazzurco.

"But how is this known?" wondered Mazzurco.

"This morning I received a confirmation," the employee said. ". . . I had a green Monte Carlo next to me, with a woman inside."

"That's nice."

". . . next to me."

"Why didn't you speak to her?" Mazzurco asked.

"Why did I have to speak to her for? Fuck her!" He went on: "So, somebody's ass is itching . . . they said they're on top of us twenty-four hours a day . . . it's been known for about a week. I knew about it three days ago. But there was a man who knew it before me."

Who was this well-informed person? Russo wondered. He hoped it wasn't a cop. He was still ticked off over the leak from the Philadelphia police to Benny Zito.

Ironically, when Russo went back to Kallstrom to relay the conversation, Kallstrom insisted they had not used any green Monte Carlos that day. These guys must be starting to see things that weren't there, he told Russo.

A few days later Mazzurco asked his employee if he had seen any more strange cars.

"Sallie, those cops . . . I saw one yesterday. . . ."

Mazzurco was clinging to the hope that he was wrong. "But it's not certain that you saw them," he said, citing an old proverb: "I saw a hundred wolves in a stain."

The employee was not so easily reassured, and his next revelation really shook up Russo. "Sallie, don't you hear that, that guy spoke . . . he spoke with a guy . . . that guy brought another one. . . ."

Oh, my God! thought Russo. *Are they talking about Hopson and Tarallo?* It seemed so, from the next comment.

"And he told him that it's been . . . from the month of July," the employee continued.

July, thought Russo. *That's just when the Benny Zito business started.*

The employee was talking about the FBI now: ". . . he said, he said they're looking at . . . you know . . . and they do a bit of nuisance. But I don't think that they know things." The employee continued, more angrily: "Well, for me they can know all they want. I'll go smack into their balls and all that they are . . . That's all."

"They can see whatever they want," Mazzurco agreed, adding later: "Well, we're always being slandered."

Meanwhile, Pietro surfaced again. Russo had first heard his name from Mazzurco but he still did not know who he was. Pietro asked Mazzurco to get in touch with "that guy who is very full, up to his eyes . . . see what news there is." *That could only be Ganci,* decoded Russo.

Pietro continued: "Tomorrow speak with the guy whom you gave me those suits that time . . . ask him, 'What appetite do you have, what appetite don't you have? What are you going to do?' "

Mazzurco interrupted. "But what interests, what interests us more is the new pants."

New pants? The reference to cocaine went over Russo's head; he made sense of it only later.

Pietro hesitated to commit himself. "I know we are all interested . . . but that guy for the moment, it seems that the factory still hasn't made them. . . ."

Several days later Pietro called Mazzurco again to set up a call from the "old man." Russo could feel a rush of adrenaline again. Perhaps he was getting closer to this phantom—whoever he was. The call was set for two days later at the pay phone near Al Dente.

Mazzurco immediately called dour Sal Lamberti, and his excitement quickly communicated itself to Russo listening in. "Listen," Mazzurco said, "that guy called me . . . that guy . . . the friend from over here . . . and he told me, he says, if we want to talk with the old man . . . I made an appointment to speak with the old man for the day after tomorrow . . . and I don't know if he is here or where the hell he is. . . ."

Two days later, on December 14, two minutes before the appointed time of noon, only Sal Lamberti and an Al Dente worker were at hand. Ganci was home with what he said was an appointment; not even the ubiquitous Mazzurco had arrived. When the pay phone outside rang, the pizzeria employee, not Lamberti, picked it up.

"Hello," said a Sicilian voice.

"Yes," said the employee. "With whom do you wish to speak with?"

"Isn't Joe there?" asked the voice.

"No, Joe isn't here."

"He isn't?" The caller sounded surprised.

"No."

"Not even the brother-in-law?" He seemed astounded that neither Giuseppe Lamberti nor Mazzurco was there.

"No, the brother-in-law left."

"He already left?" Incredulity.

"Yes, he already left . . . why don't you call in the afternoon? One or two hours later?"

"What? One hour or two later?" Disbelief.

"Yes."

"Fine." Resignation.

A few minutes later Mazzurco joined Sal Lamberti at the phone booth. Half an hour later the phone rang again.

This time Mazzurco reached for it. "Hello. Hello. Hello." There was no response. He hung up.

A moment later the phone rang again. Mazzurco snatched it up. "Hello. Hello." He turned to Sal Lamberti with disgust. "You can't hear anything," he said. "Hello!"

Sal Lamberti grabbed the receiver. "Hello. Hello. Hello."

The only response was a mechanical voice intoning maddeningly, "If you'd like to make a call, please hang up and try again. . . ."

Mazzurco walked to another pay phone at the other end of the block and waited. Lamberti joined him. No call. They walked back to the first phone and waited again. Then Lamberti walked back again to the second phone. Still no call. Finally they both walked into Al Dente and called Ganci to tell him what happened.

To surveillance agents staked out around Al Dente and to Russo listening in the plant, it was a puzzling episode. Who was calling? Why wasn't Ganci or Mazzurco there on time to receive the noon call? Why didn't Sal Lamberti, who *was* there, pick it up? Why was he ready to talk the second time?

What Russo and the other agents did not understand was that there were mixed feelings about dealing with the caller, who was under a Mafia anathema. Because of the ban, Mazzurco, who was not a member of the Mafia but an associate, had been designated to deal with him as much as possible, sparing the Lambertis or Ganci, not to speak of Catalano. Russo had not yet figured out that the caller, the old man, was Gaetano Badalamenti, emerging from a foreign exile imposed by the Corleonesi in order to initiate business with his countrymen in New York.

Pietro, whoever he was, seemed to be turning up more and more in the conversations, Russo noticed, although nobody seemed as awful as he was at keeping appointments straight. In mid-December he and Mazzurco were talking on the phone when Pietro suddenly remembered he had forgotten to tell Mazzurco about a crucial call that he had arranged to come in to a certain pay phone. "Goddammit!" he said. "I'm on the road. It slipped my mind completely . . . ah, right now I bet that it's ringing."

Later Mazzurco summed up his feelings when he told his brother-in-law

Giuseppe Lamberti: "That jerk Pietro called me today." Lamberti knew whom he meant—the one from "up there."

But Mazzurco was cautious not to say too much; he was still clearly suspicious of his home phone, as he told Lamberti, "Ah, I'm talking on the phone that's—"

"All right," said Lamberti, quickly grasping the fragmentary warning.

To expand their repertoire of presumably secure pay phones, Mazzurco got the number of the phone booth to the west side of Al Dente, 830-9321, and read it to Pietro. Russo, too, copied it down, and the bureau quickly added it to the growing list of tapped phones. Two days later Pietro reported back to Mazzurco that the person trying to reach them was totally frustrated. He could never get them at the new number and kept reaching some woman.

"It's the number that I gave you!" the exasperated Mazzurco repeated.

Pietro went over it again: "Eight-three-one-nine-three—"

". . . Eight-three-oh," Mazzurco corrected.

Pietro was mortified. "Goddammit, you gave me eight-three-oh . . . Goddammit, then he's right!"

Because of the foul-up, Gaetano Badalamenti, ex-boss of bosses of the Sicilian Mafia, now in hidden exile, had been harassing some hapless woman in Forest Hills, Queens.

Several days later, Ganci and Giuseppe Lamberti were at the newly designated western pay phone outside Al Dente taking a call from Giuseppe Soresi in Sicily. Soresi seemed to Russo to be saying that "the doctor"—Badalamenti—was preparing to set up "residence" in Brescia, near Milan, when the call was interrupted by a deafening racket. Bobby Gilmore and other surveillance agents looked around. There by the pay phone a street crew was beginning to tear up the sidewalk with jackhammers.

Gilmore ran over, formulating a plan as he went. He flashed his FBI badge quickly. "City noise pollution control," he said authoritatively. "This exceeds the maximum decibel standard for ambient noise during the lunch hour." The crew looked up, puzzled. Gilmore added: "Can you guys hold off about ten minutes?"

The surprised workmen shrugged and took a break. Ganci and Soresi finished their call in peace.

The first day of the new year 1984 brought disturbing news to the Lambertis, a bad omen. Giuseppe informed his cousin Sal that one of the group was being followed: "That guy was telling me he was alone . . . he was accompanied!"

"There was a guy there that, who was looking with the binoculars" and taking down license numbers, Giuseppe said.

Russo, hearing this, was discomfited. That had to be the cops—the FBI used monoculars. Put together with the other tip-offs—Ganci's "stolen" car and the Pronto break-in, the suspected wiretaps, the real or suspected tails—it made Russo believe that their targets were catching on to the investigation. How long could the secrecy be maintained?

He listened to the New Year's greetings being phoned back and forth. "I wish you a world of good," a caller told Giuseppe Lamberti. "And let's hope that this year is full of happiness for everyone."

For Lamberti and his associates, 1984 would not be a year of happiness. It would be a terrible year.

In Detroit the federal organized crime strike force had stumbled upon a major discovery. Since the summer of 1983 FBI and IRS agents had been investigating suspected narcotics traffickers in the Midwest when a car with a New York license plate drew the interest of a surveillance team. From the house where the car was parked, calls were traced to the phone of a pizzeria operator in tiny Oregon, Illinois, a small rural county seat on the Rock River some ninety-five miles west of Chicago. An ongoing grand jury investigation had also turned up calls to the pizzeria at the unlikely hour of six A.M., and the telephone trail led to a pay phone in Miami. Quickly the agents became interested in the pizzeria operator, whose name was Pietro Alfano. Alfano turned out to be a forty-seven-year-old Sicilian immigrant with a craggy face, a squinty stare, and glossy black hair combed straight back. He had arrived in 1963 from Cinisi, Sicily, his entry, like that of some of his relatives, facilitated by a private immigration bill sponsored by an apparently well-intentioned member of Congress. When the agents delved deeper into Alfano's phone records, they found a pattern of calls to parties identified as relatives, Emanuele Palazzolo in Milton, Wisconsin, and Samuel Evola in Temperance, Michigan. There were also many calls to numbers in New York City and Long Island. In December 1983 the Detroit strike force asked prosecutor Louis Freeh and Mike Fahy of Customs whether calls from this Pietro Alfano to someone named Salvatore Mazzurco meant anything. Freeh and Fahy, and soon Rooney and Russo, were jubilant. Car rental records had shown that Emanuele Palazzolo was one of the four visitors at the Charcoal Grill meeting with Mazzurco the previous September. The car was later turned in, records showed, in Toledo, Ohio—far from Palazzolo's home in Wisconsin, but close to Evola. Alfano fitted the description of one of Palazzolo's companions. And the name Pietro was heard repeatedly on the wires. The case was branching out across the country. The FBI offices in Chicago and Detroit were alerted to step up surveillances and pull together other evidence for Title III applications. It was time to plant a new crop of wires.

Russo had been harboring a suspicion for some months that Gaetano Badalamenti was the shadowy presence behind the dealings between Mazzurco and the man he had learned was Pietro Alfano, although he did not yet know that Alfano was Badalamenti's nephew. If Russo was right that it was Badalamenti who was trying so hard to overcome Alfano's foul-ups and get through to Mazzurco and the Lambertis, it would be a tremendous revelation, the onetime boss of the Sicilian Mafia penetrating the United States to mastermind a drug pipeline through the Bonanno family. The idea had been jelling in Russo's mind ever since the previous year when he began to hear the tantalizing references to the doctor from far away. For now he and Rooney would keep their speculations to themselves. If they were wrong, no one would know. Because of Russo's hunch, he was seeing the vague coded conversations in a new light. In early January Mazzurco seemed to be waiting for a delivery from Alfano. "Those shirts . . . how are they doing?" he asked Alfano.

Alfano had disappointing news. ". . . I lost the line because the guy who sews is not around." He went on: "Now we are waiting minute by minute . . . because the tailor went up from down there . . . therefore, he will seek to be able to come up here . . . to be able to unravel this thing, more than anything else because it is becoming moldy."

The tailor—could that be Badalamenti himself? Russo wondered. And was he on his way up from down there—wherever "there" was? It sounded as if things had gotten messed up and had to be straightened out.

Mazzurco asked Alfano about the "other shirts."

"Are you talking about the shirts that come from Italy?" Alfano wanted to know. "Or the shirts from over there, where they have come from before?"

"From where they have come from before," Mazzurco said, pointing Russo to two sources of supply.

Russo's suspicions that Badalamenti was behind these calls grew in mid-January with a series of conversations between Mazzurco and Giuseppe Lamberti, who were excited over something they had seen in the Italian-American newspaper Il Progresso.

"Well, you should read it," Mazzurco said. "There's an article."

"Regarding who?"

"The uncle," Mazzurco said. "Well, they make you believe that he was arrested there in Brazil."

Lamberti was dubious; he said he couldn't believe it at all.

The next day, Lamberti said, "that guy" was in the newspaper again, something about a ballerina. But if he were arrested, Lamberti wondered, how could he be making phone calls? He couldn't understand it. All he knew was that somebody with the same name had been arrested and with a ballerina.

Russo was in a frenzy. He had to see *Il Progresso*! He dialed one of its most faithful readers. He knew the number by heart.

"Dad!" he said breathlessly. "You have the *Progresso* from today?"

"Carmine, son! Nice to hear you. How are you?"

"Fine, Dad. You have the paper?"

"And Carmela, how she's doing?"

"Wonderful, Dad, we're all fine. The paper?"

"The boys? How are my boys?"

"Dad!"

"The *Progresso*? I got it right here."

"Dad, you see anything about a guy with a ballerina?"

"A what?"

"A ballerina! A ballerina!"

Russo could hear the paper rustling. It seemed forever until his father got back on the line. "I see it here." He read it aloud in Italian to Russo:

" 'It was revealed that the Argentine police Friday evening arrested Margarita Godoy, a young dancer identified as the mysterious blonde who had been seen last Saturday together with Palermo businessman Antonio Badalamenti, killed in Buenos Aires last week. The lifeless body of Badalamenti was found in his car with a bullet in the back of his head in a street in the suburbs of the capital. According to the declarations of Giovanni Badalamenti, brother of the Italian businessman, who was forty years old, Antonio was the victim of an aborted attempt to kidnap him. The Badalamenti family owns the well-known ice cream parlor Alpino in the center of Buenos Aires and a similar place in Palermo, the city where many of those relatives reside and where they go every year to spend the summer.' "

That was all. Russo thanked his father, sent regards, and hung up. That clinched it. Badalamenti had to be whom Ganci and the Lambertis were dealing with through Mazzurco. Why else would they have gotten so excited about the killing of someone with the same name? But hypothesizing was one thing. Proving it, Russo realized, would be something else. Badalamenti would have to make an appearance or be named directly. And as Buscetta had learned, Badalamenti was very hard to track.

In January Russo and some of the other agents flew to Ottawa for a conference with the Royal Canadian Mounted Police and Italian magistrates who were pursuing related aspects of the investigation. Russo laid out his theory, but to his burning shame, he would always recall, it was patronizingly dismissed by the Italians. That couldn't possibly be Badalamenti, they told Russo; no one had ever heard a boss, or ex-boss, discussing his drug business on the telephone. Russo must be confused.

"It takes a Sicilian to understand a Sicilian," Russo rejoined. He returned home still smarting.

The agents continued to track the movements of Catalano and his circle. On January 4, 1984, Ganci, with Catalano's voice audible in the background, was heard calling Cesare Bonventre to arrange a meeting. Ganci and Catalano were then tailed to Caffè Aiello and then back to Ganci's house, where Bonventre—arriving in a black Ferrari—and bushy-haired Giovanni Ligammari joined them shortly afterward. Ganci soon arranged to meet with Bonventre at a Brooklyn jewelry exchange, and several days later Ganci, Mazzara, and the two Lambertis converged at Frank Polizzi's Casa Polizzi in Belleville for a meeting. The pace was stepping up.

Meanwhile, the cars that Mazzurco and Giuseppe Lamberti had ordered from Europe finally arrived, and the two arranged to drive out to Port Newark to receive them. There were three Mercedeses and a small BMW, with four more coming later.

Ever since he learned of the import plans from Mazzurco's intercepted calls home from Europe, Mike Fahy was convinced that heroin had been concealed in the cars. It was such a classic scheme. He remembered his moment of glory as a young Customs trainee a dozen years before, when he discovered eighty-two kilos of heroin concealed in a Ford Galaxie aboard the SS *Rafaello;* that load, too, had been later attributed to Badalamenti. Now, before Mazzurco and Lamberti could retrieve the cars, Fahy's inspectors were busily dismantling them, searching every conceivable hiding place for what Fahy was sure was the concealed heroin. But no matter how they tore the cars apart, the inspectors came up empty-handed. He couldn't believe it. He had been so sure. Finally Fahy had to admit defeat. Perhaps, he thought later, this had been only a trial run, and the real heroin importation would come later. In any case, these cars were clean. His agents put the cars back together, but they would never run right.

The next day Giuseppe Lamberti drove out in a snowstorm to Port Newark to pick up one of the cars, which promptly broke down on the New Jersey Turnpike. Maybe, Lamberti thought, water had condensed in the gas tank; the motor had not been run for two months while the car was in transport. Fighting frostbite, he tried to flag down passing motorists as they sped past, spraying him with snow and slush. No one would stop. Finally a car pulled over; the driver approached. A long-haired hippie! Lamberti had always hated hippies, but no one else stopped. Lamberti meekly accepted his offer of a lift. The storm had made it impossible to find a tow truck, so Lamberti had to leave the new car in the snow. As a final indignity the police later towed it away.

The next day Pietro Alfano called Mazzurco to set up another pay phone call outside Al Dente, this time at the booth on the western corner of Queens Boulevard—to the right as you come out of the pizzeria of the round one, as Mazzurco described it to Giuseppe Lamberti. Lamberti then called his cousin Sal to be there the following day when the call came in. Whatever compunctions they had had about talking to the person at the other end of the line had been overcome.

On January 20, 1984, shortly before one P.M., the Lambertis were waiting at the booth when the phone rang. Giuseppe picked it up after the first ring. "Hello," he said.

"Hey," came the answer in Sicilian.

At last, Russo thought, he must be listening to the voice of Gaetano Badalamenti.

PART FOUR

GOD WHO IS A COP

... or maybe it's the wind—it can be the wind. ...
—Pietro Alfano speaking on a tapped pay phone

19

"**W**ELL," began Badalamenti, ". . . here we are. . . ."

"The—the, how is the family?" asked Giuseppe Lamberti.

"Well, everything is fine."

"Has there been a problem?" Lamberti ventured.

"No, nothing. What problem?"

So the rumor of his arrest in Brazil was groundless, Lamberti realized with relief.

"So, what can you tell me?" began Lamberti.

"Well, what can I tell you? It seems that the things are not going bad."

"Beautiful," said Lamberti. But then he confessed, "Right now I have . . . once in a while I am being followed."

Russo felt his own pulse quicken. Had they really been that heavy-handed?

"Oh, yes?" Badalamenti didn't sound too concerned, Russo thought with relief. Badalamenti asked about Lamberti's cousin Sal and his operation.

They removed a kidney, Lamberti told him, but he was up and around. In fact, he said, Sal was right there by the phone now.

He loses a kidney and he's standing by the phone in the dead of winter? These guys are indestructible, Russo thought.

Lamberti nudged the discussion to the business at hand. "How are the other things?" he asked.

"Well," said Badalamenti, "in essence, that thing . . . for that thing, I haven't been able to do anything . . . it has not gone anywhere. They should be giving me a response for that thing as of—"

"For the other one?" interjected Lamberti.

"—of four years, five years ago," finished Badalamenti. He did not like to be interrupted.

Russo's mind was racing. A thing of four, five years ago—that must have been an earlier deal. So they were working together back then?

Badalamenti continued. "If it's—if it's that one . . . as the modern one . . . at its disposal. . . . But if that guy wants it sent, I'll send it."

"You can send it," Lamberti said.

The modern one? Russo thought. What's the modern one? Maybe cocaine? Sounded like a new ad campaign: Coke! It's the modern one!

". . . I'm at your disposal," Badalamenti went on. "But however . . . all right. So then I'll have him get in touch. . . . I'm down here. . . . I'm far away."

How far was down? Russo wondered. He needed more clues.

"Anyway," Lamberti said, as if he had just read Russo's mind, "let's be careful. . . ."

He passed the phone to his cousin Sal, who greeted Badalamenti warmly, despite his reservations about taking Badalamenti's original call. Lamberti's Borgetto family was aligned with the Corleonesi. They wouldn't like him to be dealing with one of their enemies. Russo had no way of knowing then how far back they went, how, when Badalamenti had still been on his farm in Cinisi, Sal Lamberti had lived nearby and worked for the Badalamentis for a time. That was long before the murder charge forced Lamberti to flee Sicily. Badalamenti said: "This way, this month of March we can go and collect a bunch of asparagus." It was a reference, Russo guessed, to money; Badalamenti was looking for a nice profit within two months. "For that thing," Badalamenti added, ". . . I've struggled, and am continuing to struggle . . . they have to give me a response for that one of five years, six years ago. . . . Ah, let's hope that it will be positive, because . . . they're having me struggle so much that I don't believe it anymore."

It sounded as if Badalamenti was having a difficult time, thought Russo. He seemed to be taking an unusually direct hand for someone of such exalted position in the Sicilian Mafia. Russo didn't yet know how far out of favor Badalamenti was.

After the call Giuseppe Lamberti filled Ganci in. "I would have liked that you had been there," he said.

Ganci impatiently dismissed the complaint. "Well, what importance is there?" There was no way he was going to get involved with the old man. Ganci did not have to be told what the Corleonesi did to people who lined up with their enemies. And Ganci had thrown in his lot with the Corleonesi.

"Anyway," said Lamberti, "he is still over there, working."

"Is he sick, the poor man?" Ganci asked.

Lamberti understood the reference to Badalamenti's peril. "He is very sick." He couldn't travel here, he went on, "because he is sick." He would call again in a couple of days, Lamberti said.

It was freezing in the Queens plant. It had something to do with the rest of the building heating system; when the building shut down for the night, all the heat went off, and there was no way of keeping part of it on. Here was one problem Jim Kallstrom couldn't solve. The wife of one of the other agents had knitted Russo a blanket, and now he threw it over his shoulders and reached for the thermos that Carmela had filled with hot coffee.

As soon as Russo had heard about the incoming call that he believed would be from Badalamenti, he had alerted Kallstrom, who, Russo hoped, might have a way of tracking the call to its origin. Russo didn't ask how Kallstrom could accomplish this, and even if he had, Kallstrom would surely not have explained; he hadn't got where he was by exposing his technological tricks. When Kallstrom called Russo back after the call and said he might have succeeded in tracing the call, Russo could hardly contain himself. "Where? . . . What? . . . From where?"

Kallstrom enjoyed drawing out the suspense. "It looks," he said, "as if the call . . . came . . . from . . . somewhere in . . . Staten Island!"

"Staten Island!" Russo was dumbfounded. That was where *he* lived! Was it possible? Was Badalamenti hiding somewhere near him in the city's most rural borough at the edge of New York Harbor? No, impossible. In fact, the more he thought about it, the more Russo realized it was the most idiotic thing he had ever heard. Gaetano Badalamenti on Staten Island, going through contortions to call the Lambertis and Mazzurco at pay phones in—Queens! If they were that close, wouldn't they just have arranged to meet?

"Ridiculous," Russo told Kallstrom. Something must have gone wrong with his equipment. He urged Kallstrom to try again.

In Washington DEA analyst Mona Ewell had learned of the strike force investigation that had spotlighted Alfano and flew to Detroit to see what it might mean to her. What she found made her blue eyes widen with astonishment. Here were extensive phone trails from Alfano to New York and to relatives throughout the Midwest. The name of one of them jumped out at her. "Oh, my God," she gasped. "This is Sam Evola. His wife is the niece of Gaetano Badalamenti. It means Badalamenti's people are in the U.S. It means . . . it means . . ." Suddenly a lot of things that had been puzzling her for years were beginning to make sense.

Rooney was also hopeful of unraveling some puzzles of his own, such as what was going on inside Al Dente. Driving past Ganci's pizzeria one day, he had noticed a WAITRESS WANTED sign in the window. Rooney knew just the person to apply for the job and get it—the girlish Gabby Zacco of the DEA. Perhaps now, thought Rooney, they would learn what was cooking there besides the pizza. But like Hilda Kogut in the Roma restaurant, Zacco—who worked in Al Dente for several months, until the risks of exposure began to outweigh the advantages —was not able to add much to what was already known.

Carol and Ganci were on the outs again, or so it seemed from the testy conversation Russo listened to on February 1. Ganci had called Carol at home in the morning, and Carol asked what he was doing.

Ganci was in a sour mood. "I don't know," he said. "Maybe I come down, maybe not. I don't know. I don't really know."

"Well," Carol said coolly, "why don't you let me know so that I'll know what I'm doing?"

"No, it's just, er, go where you gotta go. Why? Why wait for me? If you need to go someplace, go ahead, okay?"

Carol said she didn't have anyplace special to go, but if she knew for sure that Ganci was not coming, she might go somewhere else for a while.

"I don't know what I'm gonna do," said Ganci stubbornly. "Because I gonna call Mr. Lamberti. Let him find me with this money. . . . So when I find him, I'll know what I do. Okay?"

To Russo it was the reference to the money that was the most tantalizing. Ganci had money for Lamberti. He wondered whether it had to do with a puzzling development of several days before. Giuseppe Lamberti had been tailed from his Long Island home to a Brooklyn mob café, where he had stopped to pick up someone. Together they had driven to Lamberti's boutique in New Windsor, where in the parking lot he and two unidentified men were seen looking over a silver Mercedes with Mexican license plates and at one point taking a box out of the trunk. All the agents' antennae had gone up on this one. Mexico had long been a notorious source of heroin to the United States. At an even more dramatic point, the agents later tailed the car to West Point and the home of a visiting Mexican colonel. Had they found a Mexican drug connection to the

United States Military Academy? It took another two and a half months of investigation before the lead fizzled and Rooney established that the visiting Mexican colonel was simply trying to sell his Mercedes to Lamberti, nothing more nefarious than that. That was typical. In any investigation, especially a huge one like this, there were twenty false trails and dead ends for every one that led somewhere. The agents never knew which would pan out, so they had to follow up every one. Often, Rooney reflected, the least likely leads proved most rewarding.

Meanwhile Russo could tell from the calls that Alfano was getting ready for another trip from Oregon, Illinois, to New York. On February 2, unbeknown to Russo, Alfano's relative Emanuele Palazzolo, the skinny pizza maker who had accompanied Alfano to the Charcoal Grill meeting with Mazzurco, rented a car with his relative Alfano in Toledo, Ohio. Alfano's wife and Palazzolo's wife were sisters. And although Russo would be wondering about it for a long time, this Palazzolo had no connection to Vito Roberto Palazzolo, the Mafia money launderer in Switzerland.

Emanuele Palazzolo and Alfano then drove to New York. When they arrived a couple of days later, Alfano called Mazzurco from a phone booth in Astoria, Queens. "I got lost like a monkey," he complained. Mazzurco replied that it would take him awhile to get there "because if the wheels of the car don't work right"—a reference to shaking off a tail, Russo was convinced. They agreed to meet in a nearby Burger King in two hours.

Why would these guys drive from Ohio to New York when they could fly? wondered Russo. He could guess. They drove because they had something they didn't want to carry through the security checks at an airport. But if they dropped something off in New York, something like narcotics, they could fly back, couldn't they? Records later showed that Palazzolo dropped off his rental car on February 4 at La Guardia Airport.

That night the new midwestern wiretaps revealed that Alfano had hardly reached home from his whirlwind trip to New York when his relative Sam Evola called. Evola, a robust, mournful-eyed drywall contractor from Temperance, Michigan, was married to Badalamenti's niece Cristina, who as a youngster in the late 1940's had been the fugitive Badalamenti's beloved little companion. "Yeah, I left him everything," Alfano told Evola. "This way on Monday, they'll give me everything back. You know, mine and theirs."

Earlier in New York Giuseppe Lamberti asked Mazzurco about the visit: ". . . documents, did he bring you everything?"

"Yeah," said Mazzurco.

Lamberti soon passed by Mazzurco's house and picked up a package.

A ledger recovered two months later from a secret compartment in Mazzurco's closet recorded the transaction: At the Burger King, Alfano had delivered two kilos of cocaine to Mazzurco.

But Rooney had bad news for Russo. The surveillance squad, stretched thin that day, had followed Lamberti in his rounds instead of splitting off to follow Mazzurco to the Burger King meeting with Alfano. It was a major loss, Russo realized, especially since Alfano had brought "documents." The delivery, the long car trip to New York, the plane trip home, the "modern one," the "thing of four, five years ago," the "asparagus"—everything pointed to a drug handoff at the Burger King. And they had missed it.

Russo was livid. "Why does this crap keep happening?" he demanded. "What kind of idiotic . . . moronic . . . assholes—"

"Carmine, let's not exaggerate. It doesn't keep happening," Rooney said. "It happens. It has happened. It'll probably happen again. But we've got a great record. I mean, come on."

Rooney managed to keep his cool. It was his makeup. Things just didn't get to him the way they got to Russo. Good thing, too. One Russo was terrific. Two Russos would have been disastrous. But Rooney was also feeling the strain. One morning Jane happened to mention the cars she had been seeing parked every morning by the school across from the house.

"What cars?" Rooney asked.

"Cars, by the school." Jane was surprised Charlie hadn't seen them. "They've been there for several days."

"Was anybody in them?" Rooney asked.

"Some men."

"Some men!" Rooney was incredulous. "There are cars with men across from the house for days and you don't say anything?" What was going on with Jane? He didn't tell her everything that was going on in the investigation, but she knew enough about what he was working on, or should, to be concerned when strange cars started showing up across from the house.

"Well, it's your job to notice things," Jane said. "Maybe the only things you don't notice are what's happening with your family."

The disclosure alarmed Rooney. What if his house or Jane—or the kids!—were being watched? He called the bureau. He wanted the cars checked out. As it turned out, no one was after him; a child at the school was in the middle of a custody battle, and investigators hired by the disputing parents were watching the kid.

Russo looked for a way to recoup the damage done by the missed Burger King surveillance. To his relief, and Rooney's, Alfano was no sooner back home in

Illinois than he called Mazzurco to remind him of an important incoming call the next day at noon, important enough for Alfano to fly back to New York to be there when it came in. This time the surveillance squad made sure to stick with Mazzurco as he drove to La Guardia, picked up Alfano, and took him to Al Dente, where they met with Giuseppe Lamberti at the pay phone, the one to the right as you came out of the pizzeria.

Lamberti appeared jumpy, the agents noted. He kept looking around furtively and copied down license numbers of nearby vehicles, including a customized van, not the bureau's, on Queens Boulevard and an unmarked police car that just happened to drive up to the pay phones. Once he even put his face up to a window of one of the FBI surveillance vans and peered inside. Lamberti was about to try to yank the door open when—to the relief of the agent inside—he was called away by one of his associates. Kallstrom knew his vans could withstand scrutiny. They had been registered to seemingly legitimate companies with elaborate pedigrees. Besides, anyone who called Albany to check the registration of a bureau vehicle automatically triggered a counterinquiry in return; the registrations of bureau-owned vehicles were specially coded to reveal any efforts to expose them.

No call came into the outside Al Dente pay phone on February 6. Alfano, cursing, danced around the booth for an hour and a half as his feet numbed with cold. What had gone wrong? He called home. Perhaps there was a message explaining the problem. There was not. Maybe the phone was out of order. Lamberti went across the street and called the booth. No, it was working fine. Alfano, still baffled, headed back to the airport for the flight home, to Oregon, Illinois, but first he placed another collect call home. He and his wife had devised a little code to frustrate eavesdroppers: He would call collect using the name Dean.

When his wife picked up the pizzeria phone, Alfano said, "Hello, Dean?"

He immediately realized his error—but then compounded it. "Oh," he said, "Me Dean. You Don." But there were still no messages, his wife told him. Alfano couldn't understand it. Hadn't it been all arranged?

The mystery was dispelled the next day when Badalamenti reached Alfano at Emanuele Palazzolo's pizzeria in Milton, Wisconsin.

"Anyway, I called over there and nobody answered me," Badalamenti complained.

Today? But it was supposed to have been yesterday! That's why Alfano had traveled all the way to New York, to receive Badalamenti's call, in the presence of Lamberti and Mazzurco. Badalamenti thought it was today? Somebody had screwed up the arrangements. Alfano had a sinking feeling he was the one.

He imagined Badalamenti dialing the Al Dente pay phone over and over as it rang and rang and rang. . . . Alfano shook his head to banish the sickening image. Perhaps the call could now be rescheduled for the next day without him.

"Anyway," said Badalamenti, turning the conversation to the two Lambertis, "I'm in a hurry to talk to them . . . because over here I have two factories that are ready."

Badalamenti then passed on a message for Mazzurco and his associates: "If you want to deal personally, come over here. . . ." In other words, Badalamenti added, "forget about the messengers."

"I know," said Alfano, "because we'll hit."

To Russo it sounded as if Alfano were admitting he and Badalamenti were likely to hit or trigger border watch lists. Badalamenti obviously found it too incriminating an admission for the phone. But then he, too, compounded the error. "Because we'll hit! Why don't you be quiet?" His dumb nephew was always blurting out stupid things. What if the phone were tapped? They had to assume that it was. One day Alfano would push him too far!

They rescheduled the call to the Al Dente pay phone for the next afternoon. ". . . tell them that you desire fish," Badalamenti reminded Alfano.

". . . don't hesitate to call me," Alfano signed off grandly.

Badalamenti could almost be heard to bristle.

"What?" he said.

"Don't hesitate to call me."

"What's there to hesitate?" Badalamenti asked dryly.

Alfano was caught in a bind. Badalamenti was pressing him to collect the "fish" owed by the New Yorkers for the two kilos of cocaine that Alfano had delivered. Russo had been right to erupt over the missed surveillance; the bureau had lost a precious opportunity.

Alfano was not a forceful negotiator. Although he led his uncle to believe that he had made the arrangements for payment, in fact, Mazzurco had told Alfano that they did not have the money—and would not until their customers in turn had paid them, a response Alfano was afraid to report back to Badalamenti. Trapped between his fearsome uncle and the unbudging Mazzurco, Alfano was trying to finesse a way out. In advance of Badalamenti's phone call, Alfano pleaded with Mazzurco that in case Badalamenti asked for the money for "those things that I brought . . . tell him that they're ready."

"Don't even say tomorrow or we're still negotiating," Alfano cautioned.

But if the money really was not ready, Mazzurco protested, how could he say it was? "Because," he added, "I don't want to be embarrassed."

Alfano begged him to go along and tell Badalamenti, "It won't be more than a day."

The next day, February 8, 1984, brought the call Russo had been hoping for, dreaming of, virtually since the case began.

Sal Lamberti and Mazzurco were walking out of Al Dente just before the appointed time of one P.M. when the pay phone on the western corner began to ring. Mazzurco ran to pick it up. After a few minutes of preliminaries Badalamenti said: "Fort Lauderdale, you know where it is?"

"Sure I know," Mazzurco said.

"From there they will go over there . . . will that be fine with you guys?"

"Well, I think so," Mazzurco said.

". . . I think that by the beginning of next week . . . or they will come with twenty-two parcels or with eleven parcels, whatever you guys prefer . . . it's his opinion to come with all twenty-two parcels . . . or containers, no? . . . That would be all right for you guys, no?"

"I don't know about the twenty-two," Mazzurco said. It sounded like a lot.

"Now there's another thing," Badalamenti went on. "I met the guy with the shirts of four years ago . . . but there's a little problem. . . . There's another guy here that has, there's ten percent acrylic. I understand little about this."

"But ten percent is not bad," Mazzurco said.

The cost "over here," Badalamenti said, "is about forty-five cents. And over there it will cost about sixty cents . . . and the price is good. . . ."

One of them could come to see him, Badalamenti said. Or he could send two containers to start—"What could we lose?" But he needed an answer. "It would be good that as soon as we talk again, you can tell me . . ." he said. ". . . This is one thing. Closed."

Russo was exultant. It was so transparent! Badalamenti was offering to deliver either eleven or twenty-two "containers," undoubtedly kilos, of some drug. There was a second offer from the guy with the shirts of four years ago, and a third whose product was 10 percent "acrylic"—that is, 90 percent pure—for $60,000 each, delivered. The way Badalamenti had skipped over the containers, without mentioning a price, made Russo suspect they were not as important as the other stuff. Perhaps they were kilos of cocaine. The other two deals must involve heroin.

Russo suddenly realized that the sound level in the plant had risen to a roar and that he could hardly hear the conversation. He looked around. There were more than a dozen cops and agents milling around, swilling coffee, jabbering, laughing. It infuriated him. Here he was trying to listen to this—this most important conversation in the case—he was sure of that—and there was this social hour going on around him. A fucking party!

"Shut the fuck up!"

The laughter died suddenly, cut off, as if a plug had been pulled. There was dead silence. Russo realized everyone in the plant was staring at him. So what? What did he care? Let them look. It was on his shoulders now. He had the key to the case right here. A Sicilian Mafia boss *on the phone to Forest Hills, Queens,* masterminding a series of drug deals. *Himself!* This was historic.

Badalamenti was still talking. "Now," he said, "let's return to that thing of four years, five years ago . . . you guys already know the stuff. You know every-thing. However"—he cleared his throat—"the worst little problem . . . first is that the price is . . . high. It will go to about ninety cents . . . to get over there. . . . But anyway, it would be acceptable."

Mazzurco agreed.

"If there were not another thing," Badalamenti added, ". . . since they don't have an importing license . . . he wants half imported for himself. That then over there . . . he would divide it in his stores . . . but this thing, I don't digest it very well."

Russo's mind was racing to keep up with the words and their hidden meaning. He could go back over all this later. For now it sounded as if the price of this better heroin was $90,000 delivered. But there was a hitch. The manufacturer had no means of getting his own shipments into the United States and insisted that as a condition of sale Badalamenti smuggle in the manufacturer's shipments as well. Badalamenti didn't sound happy about that.

"Well," reasoned Mazzurco pragmatically, "if it is an essential thing that in order that . . . er, for those containers of ours to arrive—"

"No," said Badalamenti, "ours do not enter into this. It is he, it is he who needs us. . . . He would make the furniture for us. . . . He does not have an importer's license . . . we have the license." In return for making the "furniture" for them, Badalamenti went on, this source was asking for 50 percent because he did not have his own "license." Badalamenti's tone turned grim. "This is difficult," he said.

So, Russo thought, half of what Badalamenti smuggled in would belong to the source. Badalamenti was right; those were tough terms.

Mazzurco was conciliatory. "Well, it's up to you to do as you want to do the thing."

The next day a follow-up call clarified dealings. This time Giuseppe Lamberti picked up the pay phone outside Al Dente when Badalamenti called to say that in two days he was sending someone to Fort Lauderdale—"the thing where it is hot"—with the twenty-two containers.

Lamberti asked about the suit that cost sixty dollars.

". . . They are—they are shirts. . . ." Badalamenti corrected him. That was the cheaper heroin with the 10 percent impurity, for $60,000 a kilo. The suits were the purer stuff, for $90,000. Lamberti was getting them mixed up.

Badalamenti asked what suits were selling for in America these days. "Well," Lamberti explained, "the good suits . . . you're talking . . . a hundred eighty dollars . . . a hundred seventy-five . . . a hundred eighty-five . . . it depends . . . a hundred ninety, it has also gone to. It depends on the situation." Right on target for mob-imported heroin, Russo realized. Hopson, he remembered, had paid Zito as much as $245,000 a kilo.

Badalamenti said he would send two shirts "to try"—the "cheaper shirts." The other shirts, he said, "are the ones that . . . you've always worked."

"However, the trouble is this," Badalamenti added. "The nuisance is that he wants half of it because since they don't have the importer's license . . . They want that, that we import them, with our license. . . . And we will deliver them over there. And I don't like this."

"Do we need them?" Lamberti asked.

"Heh, certainly," said Badalamenti, "because . . . they have the shirts and they will keep the shirts. . . . What do you say? Do you like it?"

Lamberti responded with a proverb: " 'A person in good sense does not know in another's house.' You are over there, and you know how things are over there. . . ."

As for the eleven or twenty-two containers, Badalamenti said, "I have them ready." He added: "This worker—this worker says he is ready to do six days a week. He doesn't want to work on Sundays."

Badalamenti had something particular in mind. "You should not get upset," he went on. ". . . Instead of having him do three days by you and three by me . . . let's do four by me because . . . don't get upset—"

Lamberti finished the thought for him. "I understand. Right now you have more of a need."

Badalamenti was not satisfied with a fifty-fifty deal. He wanted a two-thirds, one-third split. He needed it right now. It was not an auspicious way to start a partnership.

20

SQUAD supervisor Lew Schiliro and narcotics coordinator Tom Vinton were not convinced that the wires had turned up Badalamenti, and they told Russo as much in one of their frequent huddles in the squad area at 26 Federal Plaza. Along with the skeptical Italians, they thought it improbable that the notorious Sicilian Mafia boss would be dialing for dollars in America, periodically calling from some foreign hideout to rouse befuddled housewives at wrong numbers in Forest Hills, Queens. What proof did Russo have that he was listening to *the* Badalamenti?

Russo reminded them how excited Mazzurco and Lamberti had been over the *Il Progresso* article about a Badalamenti relative, mixed up with a ballerina, who was shot dead in Buenos Aires in January. There had been a second conversation about a later *Il Progresso* article mentioning yet another Badalamenti who had been killed. *"Il Progresso?"* Schiliro rolled his eyes. So, he said, they talked about someone named Badalamenti in an Italian newspaper. How did that show this was Badalamenti on the line? Well, Russo recalled, didn't the DEA's Mona Ewell say that Alfano was Badalamenti's nephew and that Sam Evola was married to Badalamenti's niece and that many of the phone conversations referred to the "uncle"? Badalamenti could be their uncle, the supervisors countered, but Alfano didn't have to be talking to him; the "uncle" could be anybody. All these guys did was use code words; Russo would be the first to admit to that. Maybe, they said, Russo was getting overly caught up. Russo tried to tell them what he was hearing; the authority in the old man's voice; the deference in Alfano's. But what it boiled down to, Russo had to admit, was a hunch. He had a hunch it was Badalamenti. Screw them. He'd show them.

In the four years since Russo and Rooney picked the files out of their mailboxes, the case had ballooned to unrecognizable proportions. What had begun in the aftermath of the Galante murder as a look at a group of unknown Sicilians on the Bonanno turf of Knickerbocker Avenue now engulfed a vast international money-laundering network, where cash-stuffed cartons and suitcases changed hands in hotel rooms and darkened doorways to be spirited overseas by some of the nation's largest financial institutions; a Turk's morphine-base supply operation that launched its own armada of vessels and counted its profits in the hundreds of millions of dollars; and a heroin distribution pipeline fed by Mafia traffickers in Sicily and an exiled Sicilian boss, and operating through pizzerias and boutiques and construction companies stretching from the eastern seaboard to tiny hamlets throughout the American heartland.

By February 1984, eleven months after the wires had begun transforming the case into the FBI's largest single criminal investigation, more than a hundred agents and police officers were detailed daily on both sides of the Hudson to keep track of Catalano, Ganci, and their expanding circle of underlings and associates. Several dozen more FBI and DEA agents in Illinois, Wisconsin, and Michigan were assigned to watch and listen to Alfano and his midwestern relatives.

Tom Sheer and Rudy Giuliani and the supervisors and prosecutors on their staffs believed that they had hooked into a gigantic Mafia heroin empire. So far they had traced intricate paths of money and mob connections on both sides of the Atlantic. But aside from transactions with the hapless Benny Zito that led back to Ganci, Mazzara, and Mazzurco, little of the drug flow had surfaced. Now the phone calls between Alfano, Mazzurco, and Badalamenti—or whoever else was on that other end—were providing a glimpse into this mysterious landscape as well. The irony was, now that the case had broadened beyond all imaginings, its focus was quickly narrowing to a circle of crucial telephone calls. It was as if the blazing sun of the case were being concentrated through a powerful lens onto one searing point.

On a crisp Saturday in February, shortly after the phone calls of the suits and shirts and acrylic, the telephone rang in Alfano's pizzeria on South Fourth Street in Oregon, Illinois. As soon as he heard his master's voice on the line, Alfano snapped to. "Roll call!" he quipped.

"Did it become daylight?" Badalamenti asked dryly. It was actually a few minutes past noon, but Badalamenti knew his nephew's penchant for staying in bed late into the day.

"It became daylight just now," Alfano answered smartly.

Badalamenti got quickly to the point. "For that matter about the salted sardines," he said, ". . . what are you doing? Monday will you be there to play cards?"

Alfano had no more of an idea than Russo what in the world Badalamenti was talking about.

Still, Alfano answered automatically, "Yes."

"There at the salted sardines," Badalamenti said.

"At the side?" Alfano asked uncertainly.

"At the salted sardines!" repeated Badalamenti.

Alfano sighed. Not another trip to the "big city," he lamented.

"At the salted sardines, yes!" Badalamenti repeated impatiently. What time would Alfano be there? he wanted to know.

Alfano was still not sure what his uncle meant. "But at the side, though," he said.

"About what time?" repeated Badalamenti.

"At noon," Alfano said. He repeated the name uncertainly: "Salted sardines." He was still not sure. "Or the 'big one'?"

"Yes," Badalamenti said, unhelpfully.

They agreed on Monday at one o'clock.

Alfano still had no clear idea of where he was supposed to go. "Where you wanted me the day before yesterday?" he asked.

Badalamenti put it to music, singing out in frustration, "At the salted sardines." And he added: "Hardhead!"

". . . At the side . . ." Alfano was still mumbling to himself. He took one last stab at it. "At Filippo's?" he asked.

Badalamenti's tone turned icy. Unlike other men, he rarely burst into a rage or otherwise lost his temper. But to those who knew what he was capable of, his absence of visible fury was somehow more fearsome. After all that, his numbskull nephew had just blurted out a name. "Well, since you have to do this," he said acidly, "what's there to do? . . . Then, then we have to find another one. . . ." Badalamenti would have to think of someplace else.

Alfano, oblivious to his uncle's exasperation, was still grappling with it. "Then you want me to go down there? . . . At the salted sardines?"

"My regards to you," said Badalamenti. The conversation was over.

To make matters worse—but better for Russo—Alfano proceeded to rehash the episode in a conversation the next day with his equally obtuse brother-in-law Emanuele Palazzolo, a slight, befuddled-looking figure who ran a pizzeria across the state line in Milton, Wisconsin, and whose picture at the Charcoal Grill the previous September had reminded Rooney of Peter Lorre. To Palazzolo, Alfano confided that he had been half asleep when Badalamenti had called just past noon. " 'What do you mean, at the salted sardines?' " Alfano recounted the conversation. " 'At the side?' He says no, and he wouldn't give me an answer. 'At the big city?' and he wouldn't give me an answer. . . . At a good moment," Alfano continued, "I mentioned a name . . . Filippo. Boy, he didn't want this name mentioned."

"No?" asked Palazzolo.

"Because you know," Alfano explained, "he's always afraid."

The phone call Badalamenti was to have made to Alfano at the "salted sardines" was rescheduled for the pay phone to the right outside Al Dente. Once again Alfano was commanded to fly from Illinois to New York to be at the phone with Mazzurco when Badalamenti called. It was an ill-fated flight. The departure out of Chicago's O'Hare was delayed by fog, and Alfano had to take a train to another airport after fighting with three taxi drivers who refused to make the trip. Meanwhile, he kept calling his wife in Illinois, instructing her to tell Badalamenti to reschedule his call for later in the day. The flight departed but nearly made an emergency stop in Buffalo before finally landing at La Guardia. Mazzurco picked up the shell-shocked Alfano at the airport for the ride to Al Dente and Badalamenti's phone call. The phone rang on schedule, and Alfano snatched it up.

"We are here," he said crisply.

". . . Listen," said Badalamenti, "they told you the town over there, no?"

"No," said Alfano, "they still haven't told me."

They seemed to be talking, Russo realized, about arrangements to transfer the eleven or twenty-two containers in Florida.

Badalamenti told Alfano to get the name from the others there; he preferred to say as little as possible over the phone. Over the amount he had already collected, Alfano was to bring an extra "hundred," Badalamenti said.

Alfano, he went on, should arrive Friday night, at a hotel whose name he would provide, Badalamenti went on. "Saturday morning they will call you." Alfano's code name, Badalamenti said, was to be Mr. Rossi.

Alfano should rent a car in a nearby town, Badalamenti went on, because "ten things . . . now will arrive."

At the "town of the sun," as they were calling Fort Lauderdale, Alfano would turn over the $100,000 when the delivery was completed. There was someone else Alfano should see "that would not be further than thirty . . . that is, from the town of the sun."

"You mean Naples then," Alfano blurted out proudly.

"Yes," said Badalamenti, exasperated.

The phone was passed to Sal Lamberti and then to Mazzurco. Badalamenti could not understand why Giuseppe Lamberti was making himself so scarce. "But why doesn't this boss ever want to come?" he asked. "What is it? What? What does he have? Does he always have things to do?" Badalamenti was exaggerating. Giuseppe Lamberti had talked to him on January 20. But his sense was right— Lamberti found dealing with the disgraced boss distasteful.

". . . Eh, he has a tail going after him," Mazzurco explained. He did not tell him the other reason: that Badalamenti was anathema to other Mafia members, and Lamberti was reluctant to be caught dealing with him.

About those "shirt" samples they had talked about, Badalamenti said that it might not work out, that his supplier had expressed himself badly: Instead of talking about lire, he had been talking about dollars. Badalamenti said he had scolded him: "We're not in America; we are here in Italy." Consequently Badalamenti said the figure would be twenty more than he had previously told Mazzurco.

Was he trying to pull a fast one here? Mazzurco wondered. Russo had no better idea than he did. But the conversation contained one vital tidbit: Hadn't Badalamenti said he was in Italy?

Meanwhile, Badalamenti went on, he was still trying to duplicate that earlier deal, "the supplier that we had five years ago." The samples were coming next week, Badalamenti said.

He saved the worst for last, and he tried to pass it off casually. "Give . . . some money to my nephew, now," he said, "because he has to leave it over there. Because I don't have any more . . ."

Mazzurco paused. They, too, were waiting to get paid; they didn't have the money either, he said.

Badalamenti did not want to hear that. "You have to give it to him," he said of the money for Alfano, "because he has to leave it for them" in Fort Lauderdale.

Mazzurco tried to explain it again; clearly Badalamenti did not understand. The "samples" Alfano had brought them had been sold, but the money had not yet come in; therefore, Mazzurco could not yet pay Alfano.

Badalamenti was insistent. "Listen, he has to leave it there. Therefore, there is nothing to be done."

Mazzurco was adamant. "I tell you . . . at this exact moment, today . . . it's the same as—as . . . squeezing a rock."

"You guys have to prepare it," Badalamenti said, his tone hardening.

At the first mention of Fort Lauderdale, Jim Kallstrom and his special ops people had swung into action, drafting plans to ensure that Alfano and Mazzurco and whoever else showed up for the eleven or twenty-two containers would do so under bureau surveillance. There was no time to lose. Kallstrom borrowed a Coast Guard transport plane and crammed it full of his special ops wizardry: eighteen squad members, six surveillance cars, and enough other equipment, Rooney thought admiringly, for another Grenada invasion. By coincidence, Sheer happened then to be attending a major case seminar in Tampa and talked frequently with Kallstrom and Storey in New York about the arrangements to send the team down. Sheer then briefed the FBI's special agent in charge in Miami, where he assumed Kallstrom would land. But Kallstrom and his contingent arrived in the territory of the Tampa office—surprising the hell out of the FBI's Tampa SAC, who asked Sheer with bemusement: "I don't mean to be impertinent, but what are you doing down here with your own army?" The embarrassed Sheer then advised him of the operation.

Kallstrom's first project was to infiltrate the staff of the Howard Johnson Motel in Fort Lauderdale. As Storey and Vinton saw it, the turning over of the drugs would be a perfect occasion to take down this case. And they wanted agents in place to do so. Indeed, they felt if they saw drugs changing hands, they would have no choice. Vinton in particular was looking forward to closing out this case and moving on. He had a lot of big narcotics cases languishing because all the agents were on this case. "What is this, Vietnam?" he grumbled.

Louis Freeh was for holding out. As Giuliani's assistant U.S. attorney masterminding the prosecution of the case, he felt it was a long way from being wrapped up. He believed Russo's hunch that they were on to Badalamenti was right. If they took the case down prematurely, Badalamenti would surely escape, and Freeh wanted to catch him. The sources of the drugs were also still unclear. Badalamenti was not Catalano's and Ganci's only supplier. What about Soresi and the people he represented? The trail had already wound halfway around the globe. Where else might it lead? Freeh confided his dismay to his boss. Giuliani agreed. He hadn't shepherded this crucial prosecution past envious rivals only to have it undercut now by precipitous arrests. He called his former colleagues in the Justice Department, who were sympathetic. And he called Tom Sheer.

Giuliani often began his calls with a long rhetorical question. This time was no exception. "Tom, I know the pressure your agents have all been under, but considering the opportunity to surface more of this case, it would be a shame now after all your efforts to blow the chance for a tremendous breakthrough that could take down the infrastructure the way we always said the bureau could—wouldn't it?"

"Shit, yeah!" Sheer agreed. He wanted this case pushed to the utmost as much as Giuliani did. Rudy was preaching to the converted. But a vast FBI apparatus had been set in place in Florida. Who knew which way events could turn? A surveillance could be burned. Someone could find a microphone. There could be a shoot-out. They would probably have to make some split-second decisions. He hoped they'd be the right ones.

"Louis and Carmine are convinced, Tom," Giuliani continued, "that if we can just hold off, Alfano will lead us to Badalamenti."

"I'm going to try to hold it together, Rudy. You're looking at it from a prosecutorial point of view. But this sucker's taking on a life of its own." God knows what Kallstrom already had going down there. Probably the whole staff of the Howard Johnson was made up of agents by now.

Alfano wanted Mazzurco to come down to Florida with him for the pickup, but as Mazzurco told his brother-in-law Giuseppe Lamberti, Alfano "has some sick head." Nothing would get Mazzurco to go to Florida. He was still spooked by a little-noticed arrest the previous June in Miami; it had sent a shudder through their enterprise, but not surprisingly in a country of thousands of overlapping law enforcement jurisdictions, it had not attracted the attention of Russo or Rooney in New York. Guido Cocilovo, a customs broker who several years before helped heroin traffickers slip their loads in through Alitalia at JFK, had been arrested as he was about to board an Amtrak train to New York with six kilos of cocaine in his baggage. Officers staking out the station had seen him acting strangely and asked to see his driver's license. When it turned out not to match the name on his ticket, they questioned him further. "Cocilovo had begun to sweat around the upper lip area," the police report said. His hand was shaking, and as one of the officers later reported, "he is just becoming a nervous wreck at this point." With his permission the officers searched his bags and found the cocaine. Cocilovo tried to act surprised, as if he had no idea how it had got there, and offered no explanation. "I am like a newborn baby," he insisted in the police car on the way to the station house.

Mazzurco was particularly nervous because Cocilovo had been working for them and had been in on the "deal of four, five years ago" that Badalamenti had transacted with Ganci. Cocilovo had not talked; Mazzurco and Ganci and their associates were safe. But Mazzurco had no desire to retest the perceptiveness of the Miami police.

Relations between Alfano and his uncle, meanwhile, were going from bad to worse. Each day it seemed that Badalamenti was yelling at him for something new. How did he get involved in all this? It was getting too complicated. Alfano was stuck in the middle. Badalamenti called him again at the Illinois pizzeria to find out if he had collected the $80,000 owed by Mazzurco and delivered the money to a currency broker at the World Trade Center to be wired to Badalamenti. "That thing, did you do it?" Badalamenti asked.

"Which one?" asked Alfano, confused.

"Those little shirts . . . the eight little shirts . . . did you leave them?"

"No."

"But, damned cuckold!" Badalamenti growled. "What am I going to do with you?"

Alfano thought Badalamenti's instructions had been to wait. He'd gone to New York, but he didn't remember having to drop off any money.

Then why did Alfano bother to go at all? Badalamenti demanded.

"But what do I know?" said Alfano.

Badalamenti ground his teeth. "Ah, you're making me go crazy . . . to, to ask you, so then, when you go someplace, why do you go? . . . Why did you go there for then? . . . To go and see . . . the library there?"

Alfano was reduced to silence.

"Let's go," said Badalamenti, fed up. "Give me that number in code."

Alfano didn't understand.

"The one you wanted to give me," Badalamenti prompted.

Now Alfano understood. "*S-T-E*," he began to dictate.

"*S-T-E*," repeated Badalamenti.

"*U.*"

"*U.*"

"*R.*"

"*R.*"

"*E.*"

"*E.*"

"*R.*"

"*R.*"

"*M.*"

"*M.*"

"*E.*"

"*E.*"

"S."

"That's all," said Alfano.

Russo stared at the word he, too, had just copied down. STEURERMES. What the hell did that mean? It sounded German. What had Badalamenti said? "Give me that number in code." But how to decipher it?

As if by way of an answer, a few minutes after hanging up on his uncle, Alfano was seen leaving the pizzeria and rushing the fifty yards over to a phone booth outside a liquor store in a small shopping center. Alfano had used this phone to take calls from Badalamenti before, and the bureau had added it to the growing list of intercepted phones. The code must correspond to the number somehow —but how?

Now the phone rang, and Alfano picked it up.

Badalamenti started right in. "Bitch of a cuckold, with you one has to . . . as soon as I get ahold of you . . ."

Alfano was contrite. "You're right." he agreed.

Badalamenti was not mollified. "I'll cut your head off!" he said.

"You're right," Alfano repeated.

"Anyway," Badalamenti said, "tomorrow you've got to have them make this deposit."

Alfano was typically confused. "Eight or eighty little shirts," he was saying.

"Eighty!" said Badalamenti.

In addition to the $80,000 to be deposited for him with the currency broker, Badalamenti told Alfano, more was needed: "And you bring a hundred."

Alfano panicked. "And where am I going to get all of these?" he asked.

"What do you mean, where are you going to get them? Didn't you have them give it to you?" Badalamenti reminded Alfano he was supposed to collect the money from Mazzurco.

Alfano had to admit he had not been able to collect it. "But they don't even . . . have salt for their salt shaker," Alfano said.

"They have to find it!" said Badalamenti. "Tomorrow they have to deposit it, and you'll have to bring those."

"But—but don't you see they're crying?" Alfano said. He was being squeezed in the middle again.

His feebleminded nephew was siding with the New Yorkers—that was typical. Badalamenti could care less about their problems. "They're crying . . ." he said. "It's not that I have a bank."

Someone with Badalamenti got on the line to give Alfano the name of the hotel in Fort Lauderdale: "Then it's called Howard Johnson. Are you familiar with this . . . ?"

"Yeah," said Alfano. "I'm familiar with this person, Howard Johnson."

As soon as he finished with Badalamenti, Alfano instructed Mazzurco to use a pay phone in New York to call him at the pay phone outside the liquor store in Oregon, Illinois, which the FBI had already tapped. But even using two pay phones they had every reason to think were secure, and speaking in Sicilian, the two were circumspect, Russo noted.

Alfano again asked for "eight things"—the $80,000.

Mazzurco protested that he had already explained the situation to Badalamenti. At best, he said, he could bring forty.

Alfano dismissed $40,000 as inadequate. "The water won't boil in the pot," he said. He said he had been told by Badalamenti in no uncertain terms: "Tell them to find it, wherever."

Later Mazzurco complained to his brother-in-law Lamberti: "I spoke with that engineer from far away . . . before he does the—the engineering that he has to do . . . he is looking for money."

Alfano had his own problems. That night he was home with vomiting and the runs. "Now I'm waiting for another phone call . . . to go where we went the first time," he told his relative Sam Evola, who found it all amusing.

Alfano did not appreciate Evola's chuckles. "Please, I'm going crazy," Alfano said. He mimicked Badalamenti's orders to deliver the money to the currency broker: " 'Take it to them. No, don't take it to them.' Then I get there. 'Didn't you take it to them? Didn't you tell me no? Bring it to them!' God what a pig! . . . But what am I, made of steel? Oh, St. Joseph!"

Evola sympathized with Alfano. "He directs someone, 'Attention!' And they run."

Alfano suddenly had an idea. "How are you situated?" he asked Evola.

"Well," said Evola. "About fifteen . . . maybe a little less I don't know. I haven't counted them."

They spoke cautiously about a prospective customer at a car wash who might help them raise money with a substantial drug order. But he was already in debt to them.

Alfano went back to fulminating against Badalamenti and the difficulty of following his confusing orders: " 'Go and pick these pears.' Then he gives you another one. During the last thing, you've forgotten the first thing."

"You have to run with it," advised Evola. "Or else . . ."

". . . You can't go backwards," agreed Alfano. "You cover your eyes and go forward. . . . But let me laugh at where the fuck I am."

Once again that night Alfano and Mazzurco discussed their predicament. Mazzurco explained once more that they had distributed what Alfano had brought them and were waiting for payment themselves.

"Then we're all on hold," said Alfano sadly.

"We're on hold," Mazzurco agreed. "What do you want from me?" He told Alfano, ". . . I had already told him . . . that I'm . . . the rock. The rock is dry . . . and it can't be squeezed any more. What the fuck does he think that I was saying to him?"

Alfano said he had no choice then but to tell his uncle of the delay. He knew Badalamenti wouldn't like it.

"And now I'm jammed up," Alfano sadly told his relative Emanuele Palazzolo that night. ". . . I have to bring those things. They don't have those things." The people in Florida, it was clear, were expecting Alfano to arrive with the money. "What am I going to bring them?" he said. "Testicles?"

The next day, when Badalamenti called the pizzeria, Alfano had an easy solution. He wasn't going to Florida. He had nothing to bring, so he wasn't going.

Badalamenti could not believe it. Alfano was just going to stand up the people waiting down there to meet him. "But who told you not to go?" Badalamenti demanded. "Then you're going to leave that guy walking around like this?"

He told Alfano to get down there—fast.

Alfano had just called Northwest Airlines to book his flight to Fort Lauderdale under an alias when Badalamenti called back. He told Alfano to hold off. Meanwhile, he said, "Make an appointment for me with that big guy for tomorrow."

"For tomorrow?" Alfano repeated. He was trying to think who the big guy was. "The one with the glasses," said Alfano.

"Heh," said Badalamenti.

"Yeah . . . the big guy," said Alfano.

"The big guy," said Badalamenti.

"Yeah," said Alfano. He still was not sure who Badalamenti meant.

"I understand . . . the . . . one . . . fine!"

As Badalamenti hung up and the line went dead, Alfano could be heard mumbling questioningly, "the medium one . . ."

Badalamenti wanted to talk to Giuseppe Lamberti—the "big guy" was a reference to his size more than to his standing in the Sicilian Mafia, where his cousin Sal was more important than he—but Lamberti didn't want to talk to Badalamenti, as he informed Mazzurco when the little guy called to arrange the call for the next day. Lamberti said he had another appointment. Badalamenti could just as easily talk to his more important cousin Sal.

The next day Badalamenti called Alfano to confirm the phone appointment. It was set for one P.M., said Alfano, finally glad to have something definitive and positive to report. And he added proudly, "The big guy." Nobody had told him Lamberti planned to be far away when Badalamenti called.

Badalamenti wanted to know where Alfano would be the next day. "Here," said Alfano, at the pizzeria in Oregon.

Badalamenti hesitated. Alfano panicked. "There?" he asked.

"Yeah," said Badalamenti.

Alfano was befuddled again. "Where?" he asked. "At Naples . . . or at the big guy."

Suddenly the line went dead. Alfano was sure that his uncle, furious, had hung up on him.

Two minutes later the phone rang again. "The line fell," said Badalamenti.

"Ah, the line fell." Alfano sighed with relief. So Badalamenti had not hung up on him after all.

"So then," continued Badalamenti, "you will be there, at the prickly pears?"

Alfano cleared his throat to gain another second to think. What the devil was the prickly pears?

Badalamenti sensed his confusion. "Don't you remember when we went to get the prickly pears?" he asked.

"*When we went . . .*" *So Badalamenti* had *been here with Alfano,* Russo thought. *Badalamenti in America. Perhaps in Florida.* But Russo had the same question as Alfano: *Where or what the hell were the prickly pears?*

"Yeah," said Alfano, still not sure.

What time would he be there? Badalamenti wanted to know.

"Whenever you say . . . now?" answered Alfano helpfully, desperate to please.

The line went dead again.

"Hello?" said Alfano. "Hello. God is a pig!"

Nine minutes later the phone rang again. "Tomorrow what time will you be there?" asked the same voice.

At noon, Alfano said. And the appointment with the "big guy" was set for—

Suddenly the line went dead again.

"Yeah, but then . . ." Alfano realized he was disconnected. "Ah . . . fine," he said to himself.

At precisely one P.M., right on schedule, the pay phone rang outside Al Dente. Sal Lamberti began with a mild apology for his cousin's absence. "For him it is, it is difficult to be here," he said.

Badalamenti was also conciliatory. He had not realized that they had already paid Alfano "three things directly." Still, he thought he had been "embarrassed," he said. "You guys have to do me this favor," Badalamenti went on, alternately beseeching and commanding. "Tomorrow you guys have to do it. You—you have to see how you guys can do it."

Sal Lamberti was not encouraging. "If you squeeze a rock"—he reminded Badalamenti once again—"no juice comes out." They had already squeezed all they could.

"Don't embarrass me," Badalamenti repeated.

"It's got nothing to do with embarrassment," Lamberti said. They just did not have it.

". . . Well, go get them . . . with interest, whatever way you can," said Badalamenti, more urgently now. "Do me this favor, because then between the other things I will do . . . for you guys. . . ." The line went dead.

Lamberti couldn't believe Badalamenti's nerve. They should borrow from the bank to pay Badalamenti!

Within minutes Badalamenti had restored the connection. "Hey," he began again, "you guys have to do me this favor."

It was too late to stop the guy from going to Florida, he said; he was already on his way with the goods.

Lamberti saw the problem. But to Badalamenti's dismay, Lamberti then turned him over once again to Mazzurco. All Badalamenti could do was to lay out his plight once again: "That guy is on the street with twenty-two," he said, ". . . because he didn't get to know that the payment had not been made. . . . Please let me know that this payment was made by you guys."

Mazzurco could make no promises. And Alfano, for the time being, stayed home. There was no point in traveling down to Florida with nothing.

Typically, Alfano and Mazzurco could not even agree on the amount owed. Mazzurco figured $40,000; Alfano calculated it at $140,000.

Mazzurco blew up. "What hundred and forty!" They had owed eighty and paid forty. They left only forty.

Listen, Alfano said, ". . . I brought you those two things . . . so that they could become the Madonna!" Alfano seemed to be saying that he had brought Mazzurco the two kilos to be turned into money.

Mazzurco interjected, "If they haven't even become God yet! What do you want from me?" If Mazzurco's customers had not yet paid him, how could he pay Alfano?

When Badalamenti called back later, Alfano had good news. "Well," Alfano began proudly, "those guys have gotten four little shirts together . . . and that makes a total of fourteen." He had $100,000 and had gotten $40,000 from Mazzurco; that made 140.

Badalamenti sounded relieved. Alfano should take "ten"—$100,000—with him to Florida and wire the remaining $40,000 plus another $40,000 to Badalamenti.

"Okay," said Alfano, embellishing, "I'll take ten with me, little shirts, because the little kids, the kids are nude. But the eight shirts, do I have to take it to that family that the older guy told me to?" The same currency exchange office in the World Trade Center that Badalamenti's elder son Leonardo had mentioned?

"Yes," said Badalamenti.

"The thing is," Alfano said, "I can do this thing tomorrow. Today is Tuesday." Then, he reckoned, comes Wednesday, Thursday. . . .

"Today is Thursday," Badalamenti said dryly.

"Today is Thursday? Today is Thursday?" Alfano appeared stunned. Then it would be done on Friday, Alfano said.

No sooner was everything in place in Florida than Badalamenti changed signals again, reaching Alfano in the pizzeria on February 23, just before his departure for Fort Lauderdale. "Tomorrow cancel everything, and then I'll call you," Badalamenti said.

The deal was falling apart. The evening before, surveillance agents had watched Catalano, Ganci, the two Lambertis, and Giovanni Ligammari slip through a side door of a boarded-up deli in Glendale, Queens. They came out two hours later. The next day Ligammari called Mazzurco. Ligammari said he he was going to "Big Head's because that talk of last night. . . . I thought about it, and I'm not too happy about it. Did you understand? . . . I haven't been able to sleep . . . the thing is all mixed up."

Ligammari, one of the investors in the heroin consortium, had told them he had doubts about the deal. They had been counting on his money to pay Alfano.

21

L IGAMMARI's second thoughts threw the consortium made up of Catalano, Ganci, the Lambertis, and Mazzurco into confusion. During an urgent meeting in Ganci's house, Mazzurco called Giuseppe Lamberti at home to fill him in on the crisis. Catalano was there, too, along with Ligammari, who also spoke to Lamberti on the phone. "I'm fighting with everybody here," Ligammari said.

As soon as he returned from Ganci's house, Mazzurco called Alfano at his pizzeria. To Alfano's dismay, Mazzurco could not say when the money might be available.

Alfano was reaching the breaking point. "I know I'm not blaming you," he told Mazzurco. "But . . . it's not right that these people are doing this thing. Or should I come back over there and take everything back? Bloody Christ! With no shame!"

Mazzurco tried to calm him down. "If they're taking their time," he said, referring to the drug customers who owed them money, "what can I tell you?"

"But God is a pig! Give them a little push," insisted Alfano.

"And you also shouldn't have done what you did," countered Mazzurco. "You made promises!" Because Alfano had promised his uncle, was it Mazzurco's problem?

252

Alfano tried to soothe Mazzurco. There was no reason for the two of them to be fighting. "It's this damned need that we have . . ." Alfano was losing control. "Nerve, nerve, nerve, nerve, nerve, nerve, nerve, nerve, nerve! For a nothing thing . . . they're taking all this time! But God is a pig!"

Mazzurco tried to round up what he could, calling Ligammari's son with the message that "those people want ten and need an answer."

Then, as if Alfano didn't have enough to worry about, in the wee hours of Saturday morning, February 25, Emanuele Palazzolo's sleep was interrupted by a collect call from his aunt Lia in Sicily, calling from a pay phone in Palermo.

Palazzolo immediately assumed it was an emergency with his mother; she had not been feeling good lately. No, Lia reassured him, his mother was fine. "It's only that we are under control . . . for all the places. Don't talk to me about anything," she warned. " 'How are you? How is it going? Exclamation point,' and that is it. Be careful even over there by you guys."

Palazzolo, no genius, immediately ignored her advice and blurted, "But who told you?" Aunt Lia had the presence of mind not to answer.

Palazzolo immediately called Alfano, who answered the phone groggily.

"Sleeping?" Palazzolo asked.

"No, we're playing cards, Emanuele."

The sarcasm was lost on the simpleminded Palazzolo. "With who?" he asked.

Then he started to relate the story, how he had been sleeping "and the bell rang." So, he told Alfano, "try to keep it short."

Alfano didn't have a clue to what his brother-in-law was talking about.

Palazzolo explained that they had called from the "big country. . . . And we have to tell the others . . . also . . . because over there and here and everywhere. . . . The guy with the stripes went to tell them."

What, again! Russo was furious. Again some crooked cop had spilled the beans. They had been lucky until now. But one of these days a leak would blow the investigation. If he could get his hands on the bastard who tipped them off in Sicily!

After Palazzolo hung up, it dawned on Alfano that he still didn't understand. He tossed and turned for a while, and although it was now after four A.M. he called Palazzolo back.

". . . but was it the big, big country or here?" he asked.

Palazzolo gave up on the code. "From over there, Palermo."

Alfano was relieved. "I thought it was over here. Pig of God! . . . Instead I understood here. Emanuele, you made me so scared! Pig of God!" But the warning had little effect. That evening Alfano and Evola were on the phone rehashing the situation. (In the end the jury did not find that the government had proved the criminal intent of these two calls.)

Evola was home stewing over the money owed them by the customer from the car wash. They had sold him some coke and had been counting on his payment toward the money Alfano was to take to Florida, but he, too, had been stiffing them.

"God has been on our side," Alfano said. "Because that guy from the big country—nothing yet." Badalamenti was giving them a breather, but any day now he could call again and order them down to Florida to deliver money they didn't have.

"God has helped us, Turi . . . God has helped us," Alfano concluded, addressing his relative by his traditional diminutive.

Evola was skeptical. "I don't know if He has helped us." For one thing, Evola said, the customer who owed them money had suddenly become impossible to find. "This guy will put us in the bag," Evola warned. "He is pulling our leg, can't you see it or not? . . . I don't like being taken for a fool."

The next day, February 26, a relative, Filippo Galbo, called with grim news for Alfano. "Do you know who they took out?" he said. "The brother, the son of Uncle Nino." He was a young relative of theirs, a Badalamenti who had gone to work in West Germany. He was petite like Palazzolo, Galbo recalled, and "to get a word out of him . . . you needed pliers."

"Who?" Alfano had trouble recalling him.

"Agostino . . . in Germany."

Now Alfano remembered.

"Yeah, they went and cleaned him up there . . . they took him out," Galbo went on.

The terrifying news spread quickly through the Badalamenti clan, who immediately recognized it as the latest manifestation of the ferocious vendetta of the Corleonesi. Alfano called his wife's brother, Giuseppe Trupiano, at his pizzeria in Paris, Illinois. "They did it as a vengeance against his brothers, maybe," Alfano said. He was getting excited. Perhaps he was thinking of himself. "And he gets killed right there! They wanted to get his brother. I don't know who . . . and they got him involved. They got Agostino involved. They're always dishonorable. They get wicked with people who are not involved in anything. He did nothing."

Alfano recalled that Galbo had been alarmed, saying, "Let's hope they don't cross the ocean."

"What can we do?" Alfano said he told him. "We're here."

As for Badalamenti, who knew what he thought? He didn't discuss such things, Alfano and Trupiano agreed. "The doctor doesn't call to carry on a conversation," Trupiano said.

Later Alfano's wife supplied more details in a conversation with her brother Trupiano. Quoting from an account in an Italian paper, she said, they went at little Agostino "with the knife—maybe they wanted to know something."

"Did they cut him up . . . piece by piece?" Trupiano sought the grisly details.

"In the head . . . the teeth," she said. ". . . then they shot him . . . but first with the knife."

The macabre discussion reinforced Russo's conviction that this was indeed the clan of Gaetano Badalamenti and that Badalamenti was the voice at the other end of the phone line. Schiliro and Vinton were no longer so skeptical.

Mazzurco was looking for Alfano. He misdialed twice, finally reaching him at the phone outside the liquor store in Oregon, Illinois, where Alfano was dancing around to keep warm. Mazzurco had collected $80,000 for Alfano. "Tomorrow," Alfano said, "bring those eight little shirts over there." He was freezing in the phone booth. "Dammit, it's cold! I'm dying. God is a pig!" Mazzurco said he had forgotten where to deliver it.

Anna Alvarado, Alfano reminded him; "do you remember that lady?" Mazzurco recalled they had been to her office before, at the World Trade Center. The account was called Duke, Alfano said.

Russo quickly alerted Paquette. It sounded like another channel to move funds.

That afternoon Badalamenti called Alfano at home. "The two letters of . . . the package you sent to me . . . the two first ones I recall," Badalamenti said. "But the others, I don't remember the other five. Can you spell them?"

"S-T-E," Alfano began.

"U-R-E."

"R."

"M."

"E."

"S."

"O."

The O seemed to throw Badalamenti. "This O seems too much."

Alfano insisted it was right. Then he changed his mind. "No. No. No. No. No, without the O. You're right."

"Very good," said Badalamenti. Once again he had caught his nephew in a mistake.

"In twenty minutes," said Alfano, "I will be there."

The last time Alfano had dictated the word to Badalamenti Russo learned that it was the code for the pay phone number outside the liquor store in Oregon. But what was the key to the code? Maybe the Detroit office could crack it. A query was sent by teletype. Agent Jerome Cox, who was one of the Detroit strike force members responsible for the crucial pinpointing of Alfano through phone records the year before, decided to try his hand at the puzzle. His mother-in-law, a crossword buff, was eager to help. Cox knew from the surveillances and wiretaps that the number in the phone booth was 732-3428. Seven numbers. How did that come out to STEURERMES, a ten-letter word? He and his mother-in-law turned the word around again and again. It made no sense. Then Cox had an idea. What if the first three letters were the area code—815? Then the rest of the phone number would correspond to the URERMES part. His mother-in-law wrote out the phone number and beneath it aligned the letters:

732-3428

URE-RMES

Then Cox rearranged the numbers in numerical order. There was no number 1, so he left a dash, 2 was E, 3 was R, 4 was M, 5 was blank, 6 was blank, 7 was U, 8 was S, 9 was blank. Now he rescrambled the letters rearranged in numerical order: - ERM - - US -. But what about the area code, 815? He knew 8 was S; it fitted for the first letter of STEURERMES. Then 1 was T. And 5 came out to E. But E already corresponded to 2. Something was screwy. The best Cox and his mother-in-law could come up with for the key to the code was TERM - - US -. But what the hell was that?

Exactly twenty minutes later the phone rang at the liquor store. "Listen!" Badalamenti commanded when Alfano picked up. The Florida deal was set again. Alfano would bring the $135,000 he had assembled, plus whatever he was supposed to pick up the next day.

"Certainly." said Alfano. *This time,* he thought, *I really do understand it.*

He rushed back to the pizzeria and called Evola. The winter wind was blowing hard, but there was no snow. At Evola's the weather was worse—a near blizzard. Now Evola's customer from the car wash would never show up with the money, which they needed more than ever. It seemed that the customer was having trouble collecting from his customer, and as so often happened in the world of drug trafficking, one collapsed deal was setting off a long line of tumbling dominos.

"Bitch of the Madonna," Alfano cursed. "He will mess us up on this trip." Without that money, how could Alfano do what he had promised Badalamenti?

It was now Monday. He had until Friday. Friday he had to be in Florida with the money.

Keep calling the deadbeat every hour and a half through the night, Alfano told Evola, even if it drove his wife crazy.

That afternoon Badalamenti called Alfano to check on whether Mazzurco had delivered the money for him at the World Trade Center. Alfano said he was waiting to hear.

"I hope we won't be embarrassed again?" It was more of a statement than a question.

"Well, I don't think so." Alfano didn't want to sound too confident.

Alfano put in another angry call to Evola's customer. Again the man's wife answered that he was still out. "God is a pig! What am I going to do with your husband?" he shouted.

Evola called back. "Okay, Turi," Alfano said. "Time is running out."

"I know it is running out," Evola agreed. They had to collect that money soon.

"You should put yourself at the back of his door," Alfano said. "Go inside and sit inside. As soon as he comes, you kill him with a hammer."

Evola laughed.

Alfano didn't know anymore whether or not he was serious. "You've got to make chopped meat of him and sell it," he went on. Anything to get the message across to the deadbeat: "Get ten cents and bring it, son of a bitch!"

Evola said he would drive over there and wait for him.

". . . Go there, why?" said Alfano, really worked up now. "Smack him in the brains. There's one thing, like you said before, a shot to the head. That's all, because if he had it, he would come.

"Let me, let me finish this thing," Alfano prayed out loud. "If I get to finish, God, pig Jesus Christ!"

Evola tried to sound casual. "Whatever happens happens, that's all," he said.

His guy *had* to come across, Evola said a moment later. "If not, I'll truly break his horns."

Alfano recalled how they had been repeatedly stood up. "Oh, wicked God, nobody tells me the truth, honest and precise!" He sighed.

If nothing happened tonight, Alfano said, he would drive to the man himself. "I'll give him a punch in the face and come home."

"And that's all you can do," Evola soothed. "You haven't had this satisfaction, that's all."

"Jesus Christ! Nailed to the cross!" Alfano was reaching the breaking point.

Evola, too. "There is a snowdrift," he said. "Ten feet of snow. I should put myself in it and never come out."

As if Alfano didn't have enough grief, Mazzurco called in a froth. "But where the hell do you send me?" he began.

Earlier the surveillance agents had trailed Mazzurco to 1 World Trade Center, where they saw him remove a brown briefcase from his trunk and take the high-speed elevator to the thirty-third-floor offices of a currency brokerage, Manfra, Tordella & Brookes, Inc., a foreign exchange house licensed to operate as a bank. They could not immediately determine what took place inside, but Russo got a good idea from overhearing Mazzurco's later angry recriminations with Alfano.

"Do you know what they were looking for?" he raged. ". . . passports, documents, they have to report it. . . ." Mazzurco told Alfano that the woman there, Anna Alvarado, had been expecting checks for $120,000, not $80,000—and not cash, as Mazzurco had brought. "Dammit!" Mazzurco fumed. "But always doing these mix-ups! I don't believe it!" Was there ever anything Alfano didn't screw up? Mazzurco was a nervous wreck now. "What Christ! Just figure what shape I'm in over here." (At the trial, Alvarado testified that she had no recollection of these events.)

Alfano had too many other problems to be sympathetic. Mazzurco just had to see to it; that was all there was to it. But Mazzurco was reaching the breaking point. "Why do I've got to see to it? You've got to see to it."

Alfano was oblivious. One way or another, Mazzurco had to be responsible for coming up with the money, even if he had to carry it down to Florida himself.

"No, dear," corrected Mazzurco tartly. "I'm not going anywhere from here."

"But without them," wailed Alfano, "where am I going to go? Jesus Christ is a pig!"

"Don't ask me," said Mazzurco. "I did my part."

Then Alfano received an unexpected boost. Evola's drug customer, the guy from the car wash who owed them the money, called. Alfano was exhilarated. But it wasn't welcome news. He needed more time, the man said. His customer was away.

"I can't stand it anymore," Alfano blurted. ". . . I swear . . . because you all tell me three days and then months go by. I get really embarrassed like a dog. Vulgar God!"

The desperation of his plight haunted Alfano. ". . . Listen to me," he said. "I have gotten four telephone calls tonight and this morning, and I told them I was ready. I can't tell them—God is a pig!—what's happening. . . . I told him, 'Go ahead with it, that everything is ready.' . . . We are already with our heads under the gun."

". . . Right now my head hurts," the man said.

"My head can't hurt right now," Alfano said, almost boastfully. "Because if my head hurts, then a thousand people's heads will ache. . . ."

Badalamenti called back. Alfano reluctantly shared the news of the latest problem. Badalamenti, stunned, said he would call back.

The next day Evola heard from his drug customer, who said he was finally going to meet, in turn, with his customer. The money would be available Friday. But Friday was too late, Evola protested. Alfano was supposed to be in Florida Friday.

They were all trapped, Evola added. "Yeah . . . because now, it's going to finish smelling," he said, ". . . it's going to end up stinking. . . . You have to believe me like a brother. It's going to end up stinking."

"I believe you," the other man said. "I believe you."

"You've got to believe me," Evola repeated. "It's time to run. We have one more day," he added, "to see if we can, ah, ah, save face."

Alfano had now reached his customer's customer who was holding everything up. The man started to explain, but Alfano soon cut him off. "Wait, don't say another word," he began. "Hold on a minute. These things, all these madonnas, will they be ready tomorrow?"

"No, no!" said the man. The money was not ready. "We decided for Friday night."

"Goddammit," said Alfano. Friday night would be too late. Couldn't it be done tomorrow?

No, said the other.

Then why hadn't Evola's customer told him that in the first place?

He was a kid, the other explained. ". . . As soon as something goes wrong, he becomes ashamed," he went on. ". . . It's, you know, the way we Italians are . . . he gets so ashamed that he becomes almost paralyzed."

Alfano was unmoved. "He's paralyzed, and he also paralyzed fifty thousand people, and that's bad," he said.

Nevertheless, Alfano prepared for his trip to Florida, hoping somehow to make up the missing funds. He called his simpleminded brother-in-law Emanuele Palazzolo, who in his own car with Alfano's son could follow Alfano to Florida. Palazzolo was out, but his wife was getting spooked. She had been hearing strange noises on the telephone, as she explained to Alfano: "Because when they hang up, three things hang up."

Meanwhile, half a world away, in the monstrously overcrowded Brazilian business capital of São Paulo, a Brazilian woman was in the process of renting an apartment for six months for herself and two men who went by the names of Antonio Ferraro and Riccardo Vitale. Their real names were Vito and Leonardo Badalamenti, and they were sons of the fugitive Sicilian Mafia boss.

22

Tom Vinton couldn't understand it. "How big is this group if they're arguing over a few thousand bucks?" he asked Frank Storey.

"That's how they are, Tom," Storey said. "They could have a million dollars in the bank, and they'll argue over a traffic ticket. That's the way they are."

Vinton was unconvinced. He also had lingering doubts about whether it was Badalamenti on the line after all. "Carmine, if this is Badalamenti—"

"What do you mean, 'if'?" Russo bristled at the doubt implied in Vinton's conditional phrase. "What the hell you think I've been doing here for a year?"

Vinton's black eyes widened with anger, accentuating the natural fierceness of his features. He clenched his powerful jaw and controlled himself. He knew that weeks of sleepless nights in the frigid plant had taken their toll on Russo. He was a goddamn volcano.

Rooney and his family were on edge, too. Late one night the phone rang and Jane heard a gruff Sicilian voice asking for Charlie. "Who . . . who wants him?" she asked tremulously. She couldn't make out the name. "Who?" Her heart was pounding fast. Then she recognized the caller's voice. It was Carmine's father. He wanted to know how the family was doing.

Russo was listening carefully for any sign of sudden alarm by Catalano, Ganci,

260

and their compatriots, tip-offs that they had detected the saturation surveillance. But their conversations seemed reassuringly mundane. Catalano said his brother was getting tickets for a Diana Ross concert at the New Jersey Meadowlands. Did the Gancis want to come? Ganci was delighted. He, too, liked Diana Ross. Meanwhile, Catalano said, he had been expecting to hear from the "horseman" —Sal Ferrugia—but he had not yet called. Eleven months before, in April 1983, agents had photographed Catalano and Ganci meeting at the Villa Maria in Queens with Ferrugia, acting boss of the Bonanno family in the absence of the jailed Rastelli. Catalano's reference showed they were still well plugged into the Bonanno leadership. Everything was normal.

On March 5, 1984, Giuseppe Lamberti told his cousin Sal that the next day they were having lunch with the "tall one." Russo was always interested in the doings of Cesare Bonventre. He was especially intrigued when the group that turned up the following day in Manhattan included not only Lamberti, Bonventre, and his constant companion Amato but also Polizzi, Ganci, and Catalano, all spiffily clad in suits or jackets and ties. Bonventre was dapper as ever in a camel's hair chesterfield coat. Catalano sported a three-piece suit. Ganci's girth was swathed in a sports coat and argyle V-neck sweater, beneath which he, too, wore a tie. Something was being celebrated. Surveillance cameras caught the extraordinary sextet examining an apartment project at the site of the Amato family deli on Second Avenue at Eighty-fourth Street. The deli had burned down not long before, and in its place an apartment building was going up over a sleek new Italian café and restaurant called Biffi, opened by the Amato family. Agents watched the group marching to lunch at Lusardi's restaurant and strolling down Second Avenue—an exuberant crew in perhaps their last happy moment.

Evola's drug customer finally called; he could come by Saturday morning. But when he arrived, he did not bring everything Evola and Alfano had been expecting. As Evola informed Alfano, he brought "a little of those things"; the rest would take longer.

Alfano was crushed anew. "God is a pig there where he is put! This cuckold wretched guy! . . ." He called the man's customer, who had apologized for him before. "Are you guys kidding over there?" Alfano demanded. ". . . What kind of a stunt is this?" Alfano was at the end of his rope. "I can't do anything else anymore. I tried to straighten things out, but I can't do it anymore. Here it's an embarrassment nice and clear, nice and clear and specified. . . . I could grab this guy and crush him like grapes and the other guy, too. . . ."

Evola was piecing the money together, collecting some thousands here, some thousands there. But putting together the eventual $400,000 was a grueling task.

"It's the truth," commiserated Alfano, swearing, ". . . God who is a cop!"

Badalamenti called him again at the liquor store; it was early March and still bitterly cold in northern Illinois. Alfano had to dance around to keep his toes from freezing. He scarcely knew where to begin anymore with his uncle: ". . . I'd like the pleasure, if it's possible for you, two hours to talk to you, to clarify and straighten out and fix, do certain things. And to analyze certain things."

Badalamenti was not impressed. "Yeah, but for now," he said, "what's the news?"

Alfano frantically attempted to explain the situation: "No, I'm short six little shirts. For these six little shirts, I, at that time, took two little suits, and I brought them to them. I told them, 'In two days, please, make them become little shirts.' It's been a month, and they said they still haven't been able to make them become little shirts. Is it possible, this life? I told them, 'Why are you trying to embarrass us?' Therefore, I won't be able to put together twenty-three little shirts . . . with mine, I'll get to fourteen little shirts."

"What do you mean, fourteen?" Badalamenti asked. Only $140,000?

"Of my own I'll get to fourteen. If they had also given me mine, the little shirts that I brought out there, awhile ago, to have them become better shirts, I . . . we would have been in good shape."

"And what of theirs?" Badalamenti wanted to know.

"Only six little shirts have come forward," Alfano admitted.

What Alfano seemed to be saying, as best Russo could decode it, was that Alfano had given Mazzurco some coke to sell—the two little suits—and had been expecting to be paid back $60,000—the six little shirts. But Mazzurco had not come across with the money, apparently because his group had not been paid by its customers. Now Alfano was short of money to take to Florida; instead of the $230,000 he had been expecting to get toward the $400,000 he needed, he had assembled only $140,000.

He began the story again. "I brought them two little shirts—"

Badalamenti cut him off. "I've already heard it once. You've told me three times. Don't tell me again!" Go somewhere to get the money, he commanded. Go to a bank if necessary. "I won't be able to earn enough to pay for the phone calls," he grumbled.

When Mazzurco called back, Alfano's message was desperate. "You guys have to see to it. . . ."

"Nothing, absolutely not," said Mazzurco.

"This is it," said Alfano.

"Forget about it!" said Mazzurco.

As the drug deal was collapsing in early 1984, Russo frantically tried to pinpoint Badalamenti's location. Some calls seemed to indicate that the fugitive boss was someplace warm, perhaps in South America. But recently Badalamenti sounded as though he might be in Italy. Then there had been the reference to the "prickly pears," possibly in Florida, where Badalamenti hinted he had met Alfano once before. Is that where he was? If so, there was a chance they could seize him there with Alfano. Russo also knew that if the bust were to go down in Florida and Badalamenti were not there, he would escape their net, perhaps for good. Russo had worked on this too long to let that happen.

Mike Fahy believed, with Russo, that they were on to Badalamenti, and he also favored holding off until they could seize him, as Fahy encouraged Freeh. "Anyone can get dope, Louis," he said. "We have a chance to get *the man.*"

Freeh didn't need convincing. He had run this prosecution from the beginning as a largely "dry" case, without dope. He was going for conspiracy. This was the biggest damn conspiracy he had ever seen, and somewhere near the middle of it, he, too, was convinced, was Badalamenti. Giuliani agreed. So did Tom Sheer, and so did FBI headquarters, as Randy Prillaman, who supervised the case for the bureau in Washington, told Frank Storey. "We can let the twenty keys go if we have to," he told Storey. The object was to stick with Alfano to get to Badalamenti. The contingency had been approved by FBI director Webster, the only official, along with the DEA administrator, who could make such a judgment.

Storey was indignant. *Let twenty kilos of cocaine into the country?* No way. A conference call was hurriedly set up to link Storey and Prillaman, along with the agents in charge of the FBI offices in Miami, Philadelphia, Buffalo, Chicago, and Milwaukee, all of whom had pieces of the case. With Schiliro and Vinton at his side at 26 Federal Plaza, Storey argued that nothing justified letting this deal go through. "We can't let the twenty keys walk," he insisted. It would be illegal. "Look," he went on, "we accomplished what we could. Badalamenti, he's one person. If we take down the network, what does he have left anyway?"

Headquarters hung tough. Giuliani, with Sheer's support, had convinced Justice that taking down the case now would be premature. Badalamenti was a prize. No one had ever captured a top Sicilian Mafia boss like him before— certainly not in the United States, if that was where he was. Since 1978, Prillaman said, Badalamenti and his allies had been responsible for 80 percent of the heroin reaching the United States. Considering how much had already come in, twenty-two more kilos of anything would be minuscule. It was worth the risk. "If we don't get a choke hold on the organization now," Prillaman argued, "we'll never bring it down."

Storey was outgunned. He was convinced that Washington regarded the case now as a political issue; so much had been invested in time and effort that the bureau had to come in with something spectacular. But was that the right rationale to miss a chance to bust a big coke load? What haunted him was that if he let the load through to catch Badalamenti and they missed Badalamenti and the load, it could be his ass, not anyone else's. When the conference call ended, the issue was still not resolved.

Suddenly a key clue turned up. On March 4 Alfano got a call from Vincenzo Randazzo, another Badalamenti nephew. Russo and Rooney had since identified him from earlier phone conversations as one of the other men photographed with Alfano and Emanuele Palazzolo at the Charcoal Grill meeting with Mazzurco the previous September. Randazzo said he had to talk fast; he had only seven francs, and they were going fast.

Russo immediately thought of France. But then Randazzo said: "Listen! Listen! I can return to Brazil; it's useless that I remain in Switzerland. Now, like a fool, I have to return to Brazil. . . ."

Russo quickly got in touch with Kallstrom. Badalamenti's calls were probably coming from Brazil. But where?

Back in Illinois, Alfano was trying to scrape together the money he needed to take to Florida. But he suffered another setback when Evola's drug customer called with more bad news: "Look . . . they're only half of those—of those pizzas from the other day."

"Oh, they're only half?" Evola gave a bitter laugh but said he'd take them anyway.

Mazzurco, calling from a candy store near his home, told Alfano he had collected "a little . . . I already have another twenty in my hands."

But he warned Alfano, "It's not to happen, it's not to happen again."

That evening Badalamenti called Alfano at the pizzeria. "Listen to me!" he began.

"Tell me," Alfano answered eagerly. Just as long as the old man didn't blow up.

"If you can get ready—"

"Uh," said Alfano.

"—that tomorrow . . . you call there now."

"Ah."

". . . at the big city—"

"Uh."

"—for tomorrow to give that thing . . . those things there. . . ."

So he had to go to New York again—to the World Trade Center? Alfano thought with distaste. All right, if it kept Badalamenti from blowing up again. He waited for the details in a call to the liquor store pay phone.

At home in Michigan, Evola was standing by with a packed suitcase, waiting to accompany Alfano. It hardly mattered anymore that the customer who was supposed to deliver the reduced payment had stood him up.

Alfano, in turn, waited at the pay phone for Badalamenti's instructions. When the phone rang, Russo heard the operator say "I am calling from Brazil, sir. . . . Wait a moment, please. . . ."

Badalamenti *was* in Brazil. Russo dialed Kallstrom again. A special operations team was already mobilizing for the trip to Brazil, Kallstrom said, while other specialists worked frantically to trace the phone signal to its source.

Alfano, insecure as ever, started babbling excuses, until Badalamenti cut him off with an authoritative "Listen to me!"

"Tell me," Alfano succumbed.

"Bring them a hundred," Badalamenti ordered, referring to the people Alfano was to meet in Florida after picking up the money from Mazzurco in New York.

But there was a new twist. To get the money to him now, Badalamenti said, Mazzurco would have to bring the money, not to the World Trade Center but to someone named Louis Reich, whose phone number he gave Alfano. Whoever brought the money to Reich, Badalamenti said, should explain it was for "Eddie from São Paulo."

Rooney immediately had the number traced. It came back to the law offices of Louis S. Reich, in the Empire State Building.

What Russo did not know, and would not know for some months, was that Badalamenti had come up with a new method of transferring funds, agreed upon after the disastrous experience with Manfra, Tordella & Brookes, which had required too much embarrassing documentation. "Eddie from São Paulo" referred to an Argentine national in the leather business in São Paulo. The previous year Reich had set up a company in New York to accept commissions for the leather dealer. In this case Badalamenti had arranged with the dealer to receive payments from New York through his channel. Accordingly, Reich had been informed that someone was going to come in and give him $120,000 for transmittal to Brazil.

Alfano described the process to Mazzurco: "Tell him this gift is from Eddie from São Paulo. . . ." And he urged: "Don't waste any time because tomorrow I have to be there, see?"

Alfano prepared to fly to Florida, as the surveillance agents already in place in Fort Lauderdale and Naples went into a high state of alert. The argument over whether to take down the case then and there had not been resolved, but the agents had to be ready to swoop in at a moment's notice. Alfano made reservations to fly first from Chicago to New York. The ticket agent quoted him a fare of $496, sending Alfano into a fit, before she suddenly corrected herself: "Oh, that's round-trip."

"I'll kill you, ma'am," Alfano joked. He settled on an earlier flight that was cheaper. He was dealing in millions of dollars of dope, but Alfano, like his partners, was a tightwad.

Alfano was still trying to cajole money out of the recalcitrant drug buyer who had stood them up so many times before when suddenly they halted their conversation. They could hear the eerie sound of a distant phone being dialed.

"Someone is dialing," Alfano whispered.

"Someone who is dialing," the other agreed.

". . . or maybe it's the wind," said Alfano quickly. "It can be the wind."

"I don't know," said the other man, equally spooked. What were these phantom phones? Was someone else on the line?

Nothing was working smoothly. They were jinxed. When Mazzurco called Louis Reich to arrange the money drop-off, he was told Reich was on vacation until the following week.

Badalamenti ordered Alfano to hold up his trip to New York. "Therefore, we're stopped, in midair," Alfano told Evola sadly. That was just as well, Evola said; the guy with the money hadn't shown up either. If they ever got their hands on their lying customer from the car wash, they agreed, they'd know how to take care of him. Then Alfano had a disconcerting thought: What if someone was planning the same fate for them?

"They could make us like . . . they could . . ."

"A pizza." Evola finished the thought.

"A pizza!" Alfano agreed.

"Inside a pizza," Evola said. "Ping, ping, ping, ping . . . piece by piece . . ."

". . . they would make chopped meat of us, precisely," Alfano said.

In New York, meanwhile, Ganci had been on the phone looking for Cesare Bonventre. "He didn't keep an appointment, and I was worried," Ganci said.

Odd, thought Russo. Why would Ganci be worried about Cesare? For any reason? Or was Ganci just getting tense? Ganci told Giuseppe Lamberti that his blood pressure had hit 190, and the doctor thought he was nervous.

On March 13, unbeknown to the FBI, three Italian nationals with false passports checked into the Copacabana Hotel Residence in Rio. Records seized later identified two of them as Gaetano Badalamenti and his son Vito.

Within days, Jim Kallstrom scored a spectacular technical breakthrough. Working with the Brazilian authorities, he succeeded in tracing one of the calls from Badalamenti to a cluster of pay phones in a shopping center outside Rio. The Brazilian police and a boyish-faced FBI agent, Denis Collins, who was among five agents flown to Rio March 19, rushed to the location, but more than half an hour later there was no sign of Badalamenti.

Surveillance was also noticeably stepped up in Italy, disrupting the plans of their Italian suppliers, Giuseppe Lamberti reported to Ganci: ". . . they had everything prepared . . . but then the weather got bad and . . . you know it started to rain hard; everyone went to take cover. . . ."

Meanwhile, Lamberti advised Mazzurco, a relative was coming over from Italy to help settle things. He was called Ugly, the son of Peppino the Ugly. Shortly afterward, surveillance agents followed Mazzurco and Sal Lamberti to JFK, where they picked up a short, roundish man with a benign face. He looked more morose than ugly. The visitor was later identified as Giovanni Cangialosi, a relative of Giuseppe Soresi and a trucker from Borgetto.

Agents following Cangialosi saw him, together with Mazzurco, Ganci, and Giuseppe Lamberti, pull over at a rest stop on the Southern State Parkway near Valley Stream, Long Island, where they used the pay phone. It was an incoming call, the agents realized. They were now using this phone to receive calls. The agents had been caught unprepared. Quickly Rooney and Freeh drafted a Title III intercept application for the highway phone. The request was telefaxed to Washington for the FBI director's approval. Randy Prillaman carried it to Judge Webster on a Saturday night. As more pay phones needed tapping, Prillaman repeated the performance the next two Saturday nights, until it seemed that every Saturday night found him at Judge Webster's home.

In record time, Kallstrom's agents were ready when the phone on the parkway rang; it was Soresi calling. Soresi had come to New York in June 1983 to arrange heroin shipments from Sicily, and Giuseppe Lamberti had visited him to straighten out a snag in the supply operation. Now he was calling from Borgetto, struggling to evade the mounting Italian police surveillance.

"Is it still raining?" asked Sal Lamberti, who took the call.

"It is sleeting," Soresi said.

"Sleeting right now?" Lamberti was surprised. "Well," he said, "anyway, it has to stop."

Several days later Soresi called at the highway phone again.

"How is the weather there?" asked Giuseppe Lamberti.

"Well, it's still doing. . . ."

"Damned weather," said Lamberti. "It never ends!"

In the Midwest, meanwhile, after the furious calls of recent weeks an eerie telephone silence descended.

"What the goddamn is happening?" a nervous Alfano asked Evola. ". . . I am waiting minute by minute for the blood of God. We are trapped!"

Even as they spoke, hundreds of agents were reconnoitering the homes and pizzerias of the Sicilians they had been tailing for so long. Depending on what happened in Florida or Brazil, they might have to move in quickly.

In Rooney's home, the telephone also fell silent. Rooney couldn't understand it. Then he found that the kids, in conspiracy with Jane, had taken the phone off the hook to guarantee them some time with their father. The respite was short-lived.

Badalamenti, meanwhile, called Alfano at the pizzeria.

"Hey . . . dirty misery," was Alfano's greeting. "How are you?"

"Fine," said Badalamenti. "How are you?"

"Fine," mimicked Alfano, emboldened by his despair. "You're making me die. . . ."

Now Badalamenti grew furious. "But when are you going to stop . . . always with these words . . . ?" He set up a call for the next day at the liquor store pay phone.

Within seconds after the call came in Kallstrom's specialists had locked in on it and traced it to a phone booth near the center of Rio. Collins and his Brazilian counterpart, communicating in sign language—neither spoke the other's language—rushed to the scene. An operator at the phone complex remembered Badalamenti—but he had slipped away again.

In New York Mazzurco and Ganci agreed they had had it with Alfano; they were sick and tired of his whining. If he called again begging for money, they agreed, they would brush him off. "Look," Mazzurco said, "I'm going to shrug my shoulders when he tells me something." He would just play dumb, he said, insisting he had to ask the others.

"Let's do like that guy in the film about Giuliano," Mazzurco added, remembering a movie of the legendary Sicilian bandit king. "He says, 'If they were there, I was sleeping . . . if I was sleeping, I didn't hear anything.' "

The next day, as agreed, Badalamenti called Alfano at the liquor store. Again

Kallstrom's specialists immediately homed in on the call. Badalamenti began by chiding his nephew. "Be careful when you talk on the . . . certain words. . . . I understand but that they slip out but . . ."

"I know . . . I understand."

The call was emanating from another phone booth in Rio. Collins and his Brazilian partner were on their way.

Badalamenti was still talking. "You have to be careful," Badalamenti reminded his nephew. The time had finally come, he said, for Alfano to travel to New York to deliver the money he had collected.

In Rio, Collins and the Brazilian ran to reach the phone booth before Badalamenti finished the call. But it was empty.

In New York Mazzurco and Soresi's visiting emissary Giovanni Cangialosi picked up Alfano at the American Airlines terminal at La Guardia and drove him to Pronto Demolition. The agents tried not to inhale deeply the Greenpoint neighborhood's noxious vapors as they watched the three, followed shortly by the two Lambertis and several unidentified men, disappear into the brick warehouse building. Several nauseating hours later the agents watched them exit, Mazzurco driving Alfano back to La Guardia for the flight home.

It was April Fools' Day 1984. Badalamenti called Alfano again at the pizzeria. "Listen to me!" said Badalamenti. "How are you all? Are you all fine?"

Once again Kallstrom's agents locked in on the call, tracing it to yet another public phone booth in downtown Rio.

"All fine," said Alfano expectantly.

"Eh," said Badalamenti. "Ready for—"

The line went dead.

Alfano was dumbfounded. He went over the abrupt conversation to himself: " 'Eh, listen to me . . . all fine. . . . Say hi to everybody'—and he hung up?"

Within minutes Badalamenti had called back. He had gotten cut off, he explained. Alfano was relieved. At least it was not something he had said. "Look, I went," Alfano said.

"Yes?" Badalamenti said, waiting to hear more.

"No . . . they aren't," said Alfano mysteriously, clearing his throat. Russo guessed that Alfano was saying that Mazzurco and his associates had refused to go with him to Florida. "Anyway," Alfano added, "everything is there, let's say."

In Rio, Collins and the other agents and their police partners converged on the phone booth. Badalamenti was gone again. Armed with Taurus revolvers issued by their Brazilian hosts—the Americans were not permitted to bring their own pistols to Brazil—the agents decided to stake out the previous booths in case Badalamenti returned. But he never did. Collins felt sorry for his Brazilian counterparts. They were part of the elite unit that had arrested Buscetta the year before, but they had no walkie-talkies or other advanced equipment.

In New York tension was rising. Ganci picked up Catalano and drove him to Al Dente. Ganci called home twice to get numbers for Amato and Ligammari, whose change of mind had precipitated the financial crisis in which they now found themselves. Catalano could be seen pacing nervously in and out of the pizzeria, sometimes peering out of the window.

The next morning Catalano rushed with Ganci to make a morning appointment at Pronto, where Sal Lamberti had also come. That evening Ganci called Catalano at home. "You're saying the rosary?" Ganci asked.

"What can I do?" replied Catalano.

"I called the guy from today . . . the guy you saw," Catalano went on. ". . . he is wanted to be seen . . . by the horseman . . . the guy from down here."

Sal Ferrugia again. Catalano was obviously keeping in touch with the Bonanno acting boss.

The next evening Mazzurco's visiting Sicilian houseguest, Cangialosi, got a call at Mazzurco's house. "Have you cultivated the tomatoes?" asked the caller.

Cangialosi laughed.

"Have you prepared the soil for the tomatoes?"

"Well, almost," said Cangialosi.

"Have you heard anything? Will this thing be organized?"

"Yes, yes!" said Cangialosi.

A few days later the tap on Carol's phone in Clifton, New Jersey, picked up a strange conversation between Carol and her mother. Carol had been talking about Ganci: ". . . 'cause remember last time I told you they shot one of his friends while he was driving. . . ."

Carol's mother remembered the story of Saca.

"Well, now one was missing for a month! . . . And his wife is going to have . . . er . . . her first baby . . . the same day I'm having mine she's having hers . . . and now he was missing for a month. . . . So I says, 'Oh,' I says, 'she wanted the cops or the detectives to look for him.' He goes, 'Oh, no, we're looking for him.'

"Ain't that terrible?" Carol continued. "Well, he must have did something. Even Mike said he's probably dead."

The mother questioned whether he would ever be found.

"Well, they'll find him somewhere," Carol said.

Who was missing? Russo wondered.

23

O N the mild, sunny morning of April 5, 1984, Pietro Alfano was at the register of his pizza restaurant in Oregon, Illinois. His wife, Maria Cristina, was sprinkling flour on the marble slab and rolling out the thick circles of dough. Alfano gazed through the sun-diamonded window to the trees along South Fourth Street. Tiny green buds were beginning to sprout at the tips of the branches. Maybe the harsh prairie winter, and his nightmare, were finally over. The ringing phone, like an instrument of torture, seemed to mock his hopes.

More than four years of FBI investigation, hundreds of thousands of hours of surveillance, 1,000 rolls of surveillance photographs, and 100,000 monitored telephone conversations across the country and around the world were boiling down to this moment.

In Florida Kallstrom's agents were still staked out in Naples and at the Howard Johnson Motel in Fort Lauderdale, although it seemed less and less likely that Alfano, Mazzurco, and their partners would resolve their financial impasse. But the way the calls had seesawed, the deal could be revived at any moment. The FBI had resolved to take down the case at the first opportunity. The time had come. In preparation hundreds of federal agents around the country had spent the last two weeks split into arrest and search teams shadowing Catalano and

Ganci and the other targets of the investigation going back to 1980. At a command they would come streaming forth.

"But what is it, didn't we understand each other?" Badalamenti's voice on the other end of Alfano's pizzeria phone was dangerously muted.

Kallstrom tried to zero in on the call once again in Brazil.

"But . . . no, perhaps no," sputtered Alfano, confused.

"But didn't we have an appointment there?"

Alfano remembered the appointment well. "At four o'clock," he said.

"At three o'clock," corrected Badalamenti, his voice controlled, but steelier.

How much time, he wanted to know, would it take Alfano to get where he was supposed to be?

Five minutes, Alfano promised. He tore off his apron and ran out of the pizzeria. Ten minutes later the liquor store pay phone rang.

"All right. Listen to me," said Badalamenti. "Next week you have to be there. . . . Listen to me . . . make it . . . for Madrid."

Madrid! So Badalamenti was no longer in Brazil! The agent listening to the call in Illinois motioned frantically for someone to call Russo in New York.

And, Badalamenti added, "put some money in your pocket . . . about ten."

As soon as Badalamenti hung up, Alfano called the travel agent. "Tomorrow for Madrid," he said, adding: "Let's see if we can do it low fare."

In the plant in Queens, Russo was ecstatic. No one doubted any longer that they were closing in on Badalamenti.

That evening Alfano told his brother-in-law Emanuele Palazzolo that he would be taking a trip.

"But where is it, below or above us?" asked Palazzolo.

"Above and to the right, who knows?" said Alfano. Where the hell was Madrid anyway?

Then Alfano remembered something. "In fact, fuck! I have to call that one from the farm because tomorrow he's bringing us the corn. But let me tell him, let me tell him not to bring it." It was too late now for the people who owed them money to try to come across. The time for that was past; they had been stiffed too often. ". . . He can stick it up his ass!"

The next day, April 6, Pietro Alfano did not open the pizzeria. Often on mornings when he did not have to be in the restaurant, Alfano remained in bed until the ringing telephone woke him at noon, but today Alfano was up early. As he climbed into his car, a man in a dark sedan on the next block watched Alfano through his side-view mirrow. He plucked a small radio mike off the seat and spoke into it.

Two hours later Alfano, followed by a procession of agents, pulled into Chi-

cago's O'Hare International Airport. He parked, unloaded two suitcases, and checked in at the KLM counter for a flight to Amsterdam and connection to Madrid. He paid no attention to two fellow passengers—Charlie Mandigo of the FBI and Anthony Greco, Jr., of the DEA—who boarded behind him and positioned themselves in separate seats with a good view of the traveling pizza maker.

That afternoon Badalamenti called Alfano's pizzeria. Maria Cristina said her husband would be arriving the next day on KLM.

"That's fine," said Badalamenti.

The morning of April 7, after the jet had landed at Barajas Airport in the Spanish capital, Agent James Kibble of the DEA, waiting in the terminal, watched Alfano file through immigration and customs control. With an imperceptible nod, Kibble signaled to Deputy Chief José María Rodríguez Merino of the Antidrug Brigade of the National Police. They watched as Alfano was greeted by a handsome, black-haired young man. The two chatted for a moment at the taxi stand, then stepped into a cab and sped off, too engaged in conversation to notice the cars that began falling into place behind them. After a fifteen-minute drive the cab pulled to a stop outside a high-rise apartment building in the outlying Santa María residential quarter of Madrid, where Alfano and his companion unloaded their luggage and disappeared inside apartment 1C.

The cars that had followed the cab quickly emptied out, and Chief Merino and his men in plain clothes took up positions around the building. The men sat and waited. They waited all afternoon. That evening, the dark-haired young man who had met Alfano at the airport and a companion, possibly his brother, left the apartment to go to a nearby bar, where they made some calls before returning to the building. The police waited through the night and into the next morning.

Shortly before noon Alfano emerged from the building, accompanied by an older man with dark-rimmed eyes below a furrowed brow. Agents followed the pair as they strolled down the street toward a bakery. Almost immediately Alfano's companion sensed they they were being watched. He also knew there was no escape.

Just as they reached the front of a municipal police station, one of the policemen decided he had them. He stepped out of the shadows with a drawn pistol. Alfano and his companion were hustled into the station house.

Inside, the questioning began.

"Are you Gaetano Badalamenti?" Chief Merino asked Alfano's companion.

"No," said the man evenly in accented Spanish. "I am Paulo Alves Barbosa."

"Where do you live?" asked Merino.

"I don't know, in a hotel," the man said.

"Do you know Alfano?" Merino persisted.

"I don't know. I don't know," he said.

Then it was Alfano's turn. "Do you know that man?" Merino asked, pointing to his companion.

"No. No," said Alfano.

"Where do you live?" he asked Alfano.

"A hotel."

"Which hotel?"

"I don't know," said Alfano.

Leaving the two locked up, Merino and his men returned to the building and banged on the door of apartment 1C. A woman's voice answered.

"Madam, open the door," Merino shouted. "It's the police. If not, I will come in." The door swung open.

The table was set for breakfast. By the table stood a plain-featured woman in her fifties with thick brown hair. Theresa Vitale Badalamenti was accompanied by the young man who had met Alfano at the airport—her son Vito. He was wearing a bathrobe and had obviously just come out of the shower.

"Your husband, Gaetano Badalamenti, has been arrested," Merino said.

"That is not my husband," said the woman. The young man said he was renting the room and was not related to the woman or the arrested man. Both were taken in for questioning. The woman was later allowed to leave and quickly fled.

A search of the apartment was put off; the $10,000 in $100 bills that Alfano had brought would not be found inside a white espadrille in the bedroom closet until two weeks later, by which time the breakfast meal had turned foul and moldy. But before leaving the apartment with the woman and young man, Chief Merino spotted a pair of bifocals that he thought Badalamenti might need in jail and took them back to the police station. As he was about to hand them to their owner, he gave the case a quick shake. A tiny wadded-up ball of paper rolled out.

Curious, the officer smoothed it out.

ERMES PEP SROARET, it said.

Within hours Rooney and Russo had received the news from the American Embassy in Madrid: Gaetano Badalamenti, onetime boss of the Sicilian Mafia's ruling commission and one of Italy's most hunted fugitives, had been arrested by the Spanish police. Also seized were his son Vito—Leonardo had spied the arrest and narrowly escaped—and Pietro Alfano, who had long since run out of Sicilian curses. It was a Sunday, but Rooney and Russo had gone on full alert from the moment that Alfano, leading his invisible retinue of federal agents, had left Chicago for Madrid.

Meanwhile, in the departure lounge of Alitalia Airlines at New York's JFK Airport, Mazzurco waited with a stumpy, mild-faced traveler about to board his flight to Rome. After three weeks in New York, Giovanni Cangialosi was return-ing to Sicily, carrying, among other things, a precious cargo of telephone numbers from pay booths on the Southern State Parkway. As Mazzurco waved a last good-bye and turned away, NYPD's Lieutenant Joe Polly and Agent Louis Caprino, who had been closely watching the farewell, moved in. Caprino had been finally taken off wiretap duty in the claustrophobic plant, where he had listened to all the Saturday night pizza orders he hoped he would ever have to listen to in his life. He followed the passenger into the jetway leading to the aircraft.

Just outside the plane, Caprino called his name: "Giovanni Cangialosi!" Cangialosi turned, surprised.

Caprino told Cangialosi to turn away with his hands behind him. He relieved Cangialosi of his packages, which contained a batch of I LOVE NY shopping bags, $6,060 in dollars and lire, and a piece of Marriott Hotel notepaper listing seven area code 516 telephone numbers. The agent slipped cuffs around Cangialosi's wrists while reciting the litany of Miranda warnings that law enforcement officers can now reel off in their sleep ("You have the right to remain silent . . . anything you say can be used against you . . . you have the right to an attorney . . ."), and the agent added a warning of his own. "Stay calm," he cautioned. "Don't give me any problem."

Caprino and Polly bundled Cangialosi into a car and drove him to the FBI Queens office. Russo rushed in to meet them there.

"I want to make a call," Cangialosi said.

"Oh, sure," Russo said. There was no way Cangialosi would get within miles of a telephone tonight, Russo would see to that. Tomorrow he could make all the calls he wanted.

Rooney had spent the afternoon and evening of April 8 with prosecutor Louis Freeh and Mike Fahy of Customs, preparing arrest and search warrants for a judge's signature. They had gone through this exercise several times before, drawing up arrest papers just in case they suddenly had to bring down the case sooner than expected. Each time the warrants had been allowed to expire, unused. But this was the real thing.

At nine P.M. Rooney forced himself to break off, retrieved his brown Pontiac, and drove home for a late dinner with Jane. The children were already asleep. Two hours later he was back at New York FBI headquarters in Foley Square, in a heavily curtained room behind a locked door with a red sign, AUTHORIZED PERSONNEL ONLY—CP ID REQUIRED. In the early hours of April 9, 1984, the FBI's command post, its version of the Pentagon's war room, was filling up with supervisors and officials from the FBI, DEA, Customs Service, police, and U.S. attorney's office. Tom Sheer arrived at four A.M. from his home in Connecticut. He was glad to see coffee already perking and piles of doughnuts that had been brought in by agents anticipating a long night and day.

Rooney, in a suit and tie, stood at the center in front of the first tier of curved desks bearing phone consoles and computers. Russo was to show up later. Not there was Bobby Paquette, whose long-sought transfer back to Connecticut had come through the month before; he was already off and running on another undercover investigation. Next to Rooney loomed Sheer, in a blue suit and tie and plain white shirt. Flanking Sheer were officials of the DEA and police. Facing Sheer on the right side of the room sat Louis Freeh, there to insure that the raids would stand up later across the street in the United States district court when he tried the longest federal criminal case in modern history. His boss, Rudolph Giuliani, was not present, for he realized this was not his show. His presence in the command post that morning might seem gratuitous. His time, he knew, would come.

Next to Freeh sat the DEA's Frank Tarallo, who had long since shed his undercover identity as Benny Zito's would-be Thai heroin supplier. On Tarallo's other side was Frank Storey, the organized crime supervisor who whipped the case together under Sheer. Standing next to Storey, near his special operations desk in the corner, was Jim Kallstrom, happily reaping the rewards of his "people and widgets." And next to Kallstrom was Mike Fahy, hoping that this typical bureau extravaganza would not steal the show entirely from his dedicated Customs agents. Behind an outer tier of desks sat Tony Petrucci, the rotund DEA agent who had first realized that Philadelphia's Zito case and New York's Cattails case were parts of the same investigation; Tom Vinton, who had pushed so insistently—too impatiently, in Russo's view—for this day; and squad supervisor Lew Schiliro, twisting his sinister-looking mustache with insouciance.

In the front of the room an agent stood poised with a marker ready to toll the morning's results on large erasable panels. A wall of clocks ticked off the minutes in time zones across the nation and around the globe. Clerks and supervisors hunched over telephone and computer consoles. For a moment no phones rang, no commands crackled.

Just before six A.M. on April 9, 1984, Tom Sheer gave the order. "Let's go," he said.

In Oregon, Illinois, and other sleepy midwestern towns, in Brooklyn, Queens, Long Island, New Jersey, and Philadelphia, more than four hundred federal agents, police officers, and sniffer dog teams moved into position for a sweeping series of raids orchestrated by Rooney and others in the electronics-jammed command post. The teams carried sledgehammers, crowbars, flashlights, cameras, plastic bags, gloves, and guns. Throughout the night team members had gathered at preselected meeting points near their targets, flicking their headlights in rituals of recognition practiced for the past several weeks in accordance with the "seven P's": "Proper Prior Planning Prevents Piss-Poor Performance." Many team members sported blue windbreakers splashed with the big yellow letters FBI. Nobody wanted to be mistaken for an intruder.

A thousand miles from the command post, forty-eight hours after Alfano—unbeknown to his family—was arrested in Madrid, agents knocked on the door of the Alfanos' two-story white wood-frame house in Oregon, Illinois.

Maria Cristina admitted them to the back entrance. "Where is your husband?" an agent asked innocently.

"He is in Arizona," she said, "looking for new business." With her were the Alfanos' twenty-two-year-old daughter, Suzy, and three younger sons. Visiting at the time was Alfano's brother-in-law Emanuele Palazzolo and his wife, Fannita.

"What's going on?" asked the petite, rumpled Palazzolo.

"You are under arrest for narcotics conspiracy," said Agent Joseph Cincotta. Palazzolo put his head in his hands and began to weep.

As the agents searched the house, Suzy Alfano slipped on a bulky overcoat and headed out.

"Where are you going?" asked Agent Paula Brand.

"I'm just driving my aunt Fannita home to Milton," she said. Brand let the women go—but not before frisking Suzy and retrieving from her coat pocket a Smith & Wesson five-shot .38 special. Suzy said it was an old coat the family kept handy for anyone to put on who had to run outside for a moment. She said the family had found the gun in the house when they had moved in seventeen years earlier. After checking, the bureau found the pistol had been reported stolen from the glove compartment of a Wisconsin car parked in a Chicago garage in 1979. In Aunt Fannita's purse, agents found a $1,000 bill and two $500s. None of the agents had ever seen such large bills before.

In Alfano's house the agents found hollow-point bullets for the gun and two bulletproof vests. They found a gas-powered dart gun that shot hypodermic needles filled with a sodium chloride solution and Xylazine, a sedative used to knock out horses, although the puzzled agents looked in vain for any horses around the pizzeria. In the converted barn next door they discovered another bulletproof vest, a six-shot Taurus Brazilian revolver, a Smith & Wesson 9-mm automatic, an AR-180 Armalite semiautomatic rifle with a scope that was the particular envy of the searching agents, and an Ingram MAC-10 submachine gun with a silencer and shoulder brace.

They also turned up some scraps of paper. One was marked STEURERMES; another, TERMINUSA.

Simultaneously seven FBI agents, two IRS agents, and two local police officers were converging on Sam Evola's house in Temperance, Michigan, just over the state line from Toledo, Ohio.

"It's all over, Sam!" his wife, Cristina, heard one of the raiders shout as they clamored for entrance in the predawn chill. In the Evola house the agents collected a bag of white powder from a file cabinet.

"Is this heroin?" one of the agents asked.

"No," said Evola. "It's cocaine."

As an agent placed Evola under arrest, the stocky contractor insisted—or so the agent later testified—"You can't prove nothing on me."

The line was almost too good. Later Evola's lawyer told the jury, "Do you believe in this day and age that that man back there came out with that Jimmy Cagney statement?"

In the house Agent Thomas J. Love found a passport showing travel to Brazil in 1982. The agents also went through Evola's wallet. In it they found a sheet of notebook paper with some strange words, one of them TERMINUSA.

They asked him later what it meant.

"It's the name of my uncle's cow," said Evola. "In the old country," he insisted, "it was common to name your pet animals."

Across the Hudson from the FBI command post, fourteen federal agents in Oakhurst, New Jersey, entered the house of pizza man Salvatore Greco, brother of Sicilian Mafia boss Leonardo Greco in Bagheria.

Several of the agents drew their guns as Greco restrained his large Doberman pinscher.

"My hands are clean," Greco said. "I no touch dope."

In Greco's yellow Mercedes station wagon Agent William McComb found $13,000, including $10,000 in $100 bills. Greco claimed it was from the pizzeria. In the adjoining pizzeria Agent Gregory Forry stood on the counter and began removing panels of the ceiling. He thrust his head and arms deep into the dusty opening and spied a blue duffel bag. Something about the bag was odd, he thought. Then it dawned on him: The opening was strewn with plaster dust, but the bag was clean. It must have been put there recently. He opened the bag. Inside was a plastic sack, and inside it was a Styrofoam case containing a loaded Israeli Uzi machine gun. In a Foodtown shopping bag Forry found a Mach II .380 caliber machine gun, with loaded magazine. He also found a 1939 German Luger with twenty-eight rounds in the magazine. And a silencer for the Uzi. The

Uzi and a pistol turned out to be among eighteen automatic rifles, machine pistols, and other weapons purchased by Sal Salamone, Filippo's brother, under false names, in 1982. According to a deed agents found in the house, Greco had bought Filippo's house for one dollar the previous year, when Filippo and his family fled in a rush after learning of the FBI's financial investigation.

In nearby Sayreville-Parlin, New Jersey, Gaetano Mazzara, former coowner of the Roma restaurant in Menlo Park, was just getting up for the day, along with his wife, grown son, and two grown daughters. Austere, even in pajamas, Mazzara let the eight agents in and asked, "Can I just wash up and shave?" Agent Richard Kaier assented but took the precaution of accompanying Mazzara to a bathroom just off the master bedroom.

He was giving the bathroom a search when Mazzara nervously directed Kaier's attention to an area in back of the bidet—a European fixture the agent was puzzled to encounter. He checked behind the bowl and found a hollowed-out area at the base. Inside he saw the dull glint of a gun. Mazzara started to reach for it helpfully. "Hold it," Kaier commanded, extracting a Colt .38. In Mazzara's shaving kit he found bullets. Elsewhere in the house, searchers found several types of ammunition, a balance scale of the kind used to weigh narcotics, plastic freezer bags used to package drugs, and $60,157 in cash in a safe.

In Sayreville, Roma partner Frank Castronovo's house yielded $37,200 in $100 bills sealed up in the wall behind a telephone.

In Belleville and Nutley, New Jersey, other teams were searching the office, house, and car of motel owner and restaurateur Frank Polizzi. In the motel office Agent Charles Urso found a loaded .38 in a sock.

"Do you have any guns?" Agent Richard H. Brandes asked Polizzi before searching his Mercedes.

"No," Polizzi said.

"What about this?" asked Brandes, extracting a .38 from the glove compartment. From Polizzi's pockets, he took papers with the telephone numbers of Bonventre, Mazzara, and Catalano.

In upstate Stone Ridge, New York, near Kingston, agents drove cautiously up the long driveway to the country farm of contractor and boutique owner Giuseppe Lamberti. Suspicious, Lamberti came out of the house with a shotgun.

The agents froze.

"FBI!" one shouted. "Drop it!"

Lamberti didn't move.

"I said, 'drop it!'" the agent shouted. "DROP IT!"

Lamberti dropped it. Inside the house agents found another shotgun, this one with a sawed-off barrel for easier concealment and transport, a rifle, and two pistols. In Lamberti's Long Island home they found a showcase of rifles and shotguns, ammunition, and literature describing the Uzi machine gun. There were phone listings for Ganci, Casamento, Giuseppe Baldinucci—and Giuseppe Bono in Pelham. There was also a passport showing travel to Brazil and a list of guests who attended a daughter's wedding and their cash gifts. Under a notation "Did not come—sent money" was "Badalamenti 1000."

Agents who searched Bonventre's home on Eighty-third Street in Brooklyn found a loaded .22 caliber rifle and bullets for four different pistols, but no sign of Bonventre. In Bonventre's Caffè Cesare on Thirteenth Avenue Agent William Jenkins found court papers from the Philadelphia prosecution of Paolo and Giovanni LaPorta, the case worked by the DEA undercover agent Frank Panessa that contained evidence of a $100,000 drug payment destined for Bonventre in New York.

Baldo Amato was also nowhere to be found. Searching his house in Brooklyn, Agent John Farmer found another set of court papers, this one from a heroin case in the Eastern District.

On a quiet treelined street in affluent Baldwin, Long Island, agents with a sniffer dog searched the split-level ranch house of Salvatore Mazzurco. They retrieved two pistols and parts of a third, a cigarette pack filled with bullets, a money-counting machine, two cigar boxes with white powder, $1,406 in U.S. bills, and $31,000 in Canadian bills. They also found $19,900 in cash between the towels in a bathroom cabinet, $9,500 in a suitcase in the closet in the master bedroom, $500 in a china cabinet, $1,600 in a foyer closet, $2,980 on top of a breakfront, and a certified check for $100,000 made out by Mazzurco to someone else.

Pat Luzio shook his head incredulously as the money seemed to tumble from every nook and cranny of the house. In his own wallet he had just twenty dollars.

Under a trapdoor of a closet in the master bedroom the agents found a red-covered spiral notebook full of numbers. They also found copies of court papers Mazzurco was translating into Italian. The 1981 case dealt with Frank Rappa, an accused heroin trafficker, who was to have picked up the heroin-laden Ford Galaxie that trainee Fahy had discovered aboard the SS *Rafaello* in 1971. There were also ten shares of stock in the Pronto Demolition Company issued in 1980 in the name of Giuseppe Bono.

In the trunk of Mazzurco's Mercedes, under the spare tire, searchers found a balance scale and, by the rear seat, in a storage compartment, a first-aid kit. Inside the first-aid kit nestled a loaded .38.

At a neat brick garden apartment house at 67-20 Seventy-eighth Street in Middle Village, Queens, a location that surveillance agents had come to know better perhaps than any other, Agent Robert Liberatore arrested the fat silver-haired man who answered the door. In Giuseppe Ganci's house, they found a loaded Beretta automatic pistol with the serial number obliterated, a silencer, a loaded .32 and extra bullets, and a bullet magazine wrapped in an Italian newspaper. There were accountings of household expenses for Giuseppe Bono, a business card for Mimmo's pizza in Philadelphia with the name Benny on it, and a beige notepad with numbers and the names of Bonventre, Onofrio, Filippo and Claudio Esposito, the Swissair clerk who couriered money to Switzerland for Ganci beginning in 1980. In the breakfront the agents found $60,000; and in a metal sentry box in the den closet, another $56,000. Mary Jo's Barbie doll, the agents noted with consternation, had a real fur coat.

Agents also raided Carol's apartment in Clifton, New Jersey. Scattered around the small garden unit were sixty-two pieces of jewelry—diamond necklaces, bracelets, brooches, rings, and earrings—later valued at $260,000. There were five fur coats, later valued together at $65,000. There were also two AR-15 automatic rifles, a MAC-11 machine pistol, bullet magazines, and a thousand rounds of ammunition.

Russo was assigned to the squad sent to arrest Catalano, the key target after Badalamenti. How would Catalano take it? Russo wondered. Russo rang the doorbell outside the simple white-balconied garden apartment near the Lutheran cemetery in Glendale, Queens.

Caterina Catalano came to the window.

Russo explained their mission in English and Italian. "Wait a minute," she said. Nothing happened. The agents rang again. Nothing.

They battered down the door with a sledgehammer.

Catalano was in his pajamas, gazing at the agents in disbelief. Russo read him his rights, cuffed his hands behind him, and led him to a waiting car while Caterina berated the agents who stayed behind to continue the search, which, virtually alone of the locations raided, yielded virtually nothing of interest.

Another team, meanwhile, was going through Catalano's bakery, fragrant with loaves of fresh bread and pastries. In a file cabinet in the back office, Agent Ronald Eichorn found .25 caliber bullets and, in a closet, .22 caliber bullets. In the back room agents removed the sunken ceiling and discovered a white paper bag with six .38 caliber rounds.

In the FBI command post an agent in front of the tiers of desks kept scribbling and erasing names on the board as the toll of arrests mounted. Two names were still missing. Where the hell were Cesare Bonventre and Baldassare Amato? Once again, just like the day Lilo Galante got whacked, they seemed to have disappeared.

After bringing in Catalano, Russo joined Rooney in the command post. They looked at each other, Rooney rolled his eyes, but neither said a word.

24

B Y SIX P.M. on April 9, 1984, twelve hours after Tom Sheer had kicked off the raids with a quiet "Let's go," Rooney and Russo and the rest of the triumphant squad assembled at the bar of Dino's, a popular Italian-Greek restaurant on Third Avenue in the Twenties that Joe Polly had discovered. Dino's had become a favorite after-work place; it was on the way home for many agents and far enough away from Foley Square to afford them some anonymity. As they hoisted their beers, all eyes were fixed on the evening news broadcast that blared from the TV over the bar. Like everyone else who had grown up in the blue glow of the electronic hearth, they wanted confirmation of the day's events by seeing them broadcast on the evening news.

At home in Staten Island, Carmela Russo had known for several days that something was up, although she still didn't know what. Carmine seemed more serene on the few occasions when she saw him; he still didn't say anything about the case, but she sensed it was going better.

"Ma, lookit this!" Vincent, their seven-year-old, was watching TV when the story of the arrests filled the screen. He heard "FBI" and somehow knew it was about his father. Carmela came running in from the kitchen, drying her hands on her apron. "Daddy did all this!" Vincent said proudly. Carmela nodded. Her eyes were filling so fast with tears she could hardly see the screen. She didn't know whether she was thrilled or angry. All she could think of were those terrible months when Carmine would tiptoe into the house after midnight, heat up the food she had left on the stove, and explode if she said the wrong thing.

The apartment door clicked open. This time he didn't tiptoe in. Carmine Russo, a smile at last lighting up his thin, harried features, stood in the doorway as the boys flung themselves into his arms. Carmela, dabbing at her eyes, joined the whooping throng. What he had put her through, Russo realized. He vowed to make it up to her, his eyes, too, filming with tears. He turned away to swipe them with a grimy hand.

The phone rang. "Carmine, son!" His father's voice was bursting with pride. He had just come from a walk on Eighteenth Avenue, he related, and the arrests were the talk of the Italian neighborhood. What they were saying, the elder Russo told his son, was: "When the FBI gets you, they get you good!" Russo hoped they were right.

Rooney reached his home on Long Island at about the same time. Jane and the children, too, had excitedly watched the news on TV. "It's over?" Jane asked hopefully. "Are you home now to stay?"

Rooney shook his head. "It's just starting," he said.

Rooney was right. Now that the arrests had been made, the case entered a critical new phase. For more than four years, since early 1980, when Russo and Rooney had inherited the Galante/Bonanno case that had ballooned spectacularly into the Sicilian Mafia money-laundering and drug investigation, the FBI, DEA, Customs Service, and NYPD had been trying to make sense of all the cryptic dealings and communications. At first it was just a surreptitious passing of cartons and paper bags by people the agents had never come across before. Slowly they were identified, along with the nature of their packages of cash and drugs. Finally their clandestine conversations were exposed. Only now, after the astonishing finds of the arsenals, money, jewels, financial ledgers, and other incriminating records and booty, could the government begin to make sense of the labyrinth of trails that continued to perplex Rooney and Russo and all the other investigators. What was in the twenty-two containers Badalamenti never had a chance to transfer to Alfano in Florida? Heroin? Or cocaine? How did the supply operation work? What were the links binding Catalano and Ganci and their partners to Badalamenti and his relatives? Where did the money go? What did the seized ledgers signify? What was TERMINUSA? How quickly could the government prepare for trial? If the agents or prosecutors had fouled up anywhere or couldn't pull the evidence together fast enough, everyone they grabbed could go free. The thought sent Russo's stomach churning.

There was one other major puzzle: Where was all the dope? For all the bags that were transferred and all the millions of dollars generated, no real cache of heroin or cocaine had been unearthed at the homes or offices of any of those arrested. Evola's ounce of coke and the traces of heroin powder in Mazzurco's house hardly counted. The Benny Zito sales were never traced back to the heroin's source. The forty kilos assembled by the Adamitas in Milan in 1980 were seized, thanks to turncoat Frank Rolli, before they ever reached America. The heroin concealed in the wooden pallets bound for Buffalo was intercepted and substituted before it ever reached its buyers. Mike Fahy had been sure he would find heroin in the imported cars, but the cars were clean. It wasn't in Greco's tomato cans or in Ganci's garage. It wasn't even in Ganci's huge stock of Fiuggi water—the bottles turned out to contain only water. Yet the heroin had been there—that was clear from the millions of dollars that had changed hands. Rooney and Russo reasoned that it had been cleverly hidden where Mazzara, Mazzurco, Ganci, and others could put their hands on it when they needed it but where neither surveillance agents would spot it nor searches would turn it up. Possibly their supply had just run out at the time of the raids. "We weren't on the right people," Frank Storey reflected later. "Somewhere there was a missing link." Seizing drugs, anyway, had not been a prime goal of the case; rather, it was exposing the Sicilian Mafia faction and, later, finding Badalamenti. The whereabouts of the actual drug caches was one mystery the investigation never solved.

There were other puzzles. Benny Zito had vanished without a trace. Perhaps he had fled before the raids. A more likely scenario was that he had accurately predicted his own demise when he told Hopson, "If there's heat, I'll be killed."

The missing Bonventre and Amato, unlike Zito, eventually turned up. Bonventre was found a week after the arrests, his body hacked in half and stuffed in two glue drums in a warehouse in Garfield, New Jersey. The agents might never have found Bonventre's remains if it had not been for a tip from someone who knew exactly where the drums had been stored—and that they would soon be on their way to Wisconsin. The informant named one of the underworld killers as Cosmo Aiello (who turned up dead himself five weeks later). It took three weeks for the NYPD's Jack Clark and other experts to positively identify the glue-corroded and badly decomposed remains from dental charts and the indestructible gold chain Bonventre had worn.

The grisly discovery did not surprise Russo. He knew how the swaggering Bonventre had intimidated and infuriated associates, and he remembered DEA

Agent Frank Panessa's account of how the Philadelphians were incensed at Bonventre for gypping them with diluted heroin. There was no end to the number of people who were ready to do Bonventre in, Russo reflected. No, he was not shocked, nor had he been nearly five years before, when Carmine Galante got his—thanks to Cesare, Russo remained convinced. Now it was Bonventre's turn.

Amato turned himself in the day his *compare's* body was reported found. At a court hearing Russo made a point of showing Amato the gruesome photos. Amato looked for a moment as if he might faint.

"Baldo," Russo said, "you saw what happened to your cousin. You could be next. Do yourself a favor, and talk to us. We can protect you."

Russo thought he saw a flash of hesitation in Amato's obsidian eyes. Then they turned impenetrable again.

"I appreciate that, Mr. Russo," Amato said. "But I have no enemies. Talk to my lawyer."

In Detroit Agent Jerry Cox had continued to ponder the mystery of STEU-RERMES. The searches provided an answer. He had gotten close, as close as TERM - - US - . Now Cox could see that the key he was after was TERMINUSA, the word scrawled on a piece of paper found in Evola's wallet. The key word was also on a paper in Alfano's house. Using TERMINUSA to denote numbers 1 through 9— zero was the unused letter O—Badalamenti and his relatives were able to convey telephone numbers back and forth in code. URERMES of STEURERMES, Cox had already figured out, was 732-3428, the pay phone at the liquor store in Oregon. IMRSURR, found in Evola's wallet, came out to 543-9733, the number of Badala-menti's São Paulo apartment. And ERMES PEP SROARET, also found on the wad of paper in Badalamenti's glasses case, was 830-9321, the number of one of the pay phones outside Al Dente. (ERMES was 23428, the key digits of the liquor store phone. PEP was not immediately decipherable.)

And just what was TERMINUSA besides a word with no repeating letters? The explanation had to await Badalamenti's extraordinary testimony.

Tommaso Buscetta had been a prisoner in Brazil since October 22, 1983, when he was arrested on a tip while driving his son to school. After Mona Ewell of the DEA and prosecutor Charlie Rose of the Eastern District had rushed to São Paulo, along with the Italians, in hopes of interrogating the long-wanted fugitive mafioso, Buscetta languished in well-guarded custody while the Brazilians figured out what to do with him. Badalamenti's arrest in Madrid nearly six months later provided a solution. The Americans and the Italians both wanted Buscetta. Both nations also wanted Badalamenti. A deal glimmered.

Not all the Americans were convinced that Buscetta was as significant a catch as Ewell thought. Some in the FBI called Buscetta a "dirtbag," with little value as a witness. Others saw him as slippery and untrustworthy. The DEA and FBI, too, had their frictions over Buscetta. It tickled the DEA's John Huber to say that Buscetta never quite trusted the FBI and preferred dealing with DEA agents.

Charlie Rose had an inkling that Buscetta was considering turning against the Mafia when he learned that Cristina had made several visits to the U.S. Embassy. He guessed that she was trying to make a deal for her husband. A deal was in fact at hand, but not the one Buscetta had intended. The United States agreed to drop its claim on Buscetta, allowing the Italians to proceed with their extradition request to the Brazilians. The Italians, in turn, would give the Americans first claim on Badalamenti in Spain.

To Buscetta the prospect of returning to the place of his nightmares, home of the vengeful Corleonesi and graveyard of two of his sons and numerous other relatives, consumed him with despair. He still had his capsule of strychnine, which he had been saving for a last way out. Now he swallowed the poison.

Buscetta survived his attempted suicide to be returned to Italy and become the most important Mafia turncoat in history. In extensive interrogations by Investigating Magistrate Giovanni Falcone, in debriefings by DEA analyst Ewell and other U.S. representatives, and in exhaustive courtroom testimony, Buscetta created a voluminous testament that stands as the most authoritative description ever provided of the inner workings of the Sicilian Mafia and its American ties.

As recorded by the Italians and translated by the American authorities, Buscetta's "confessions" began: "I wish to preface my statement by saying that I am not an informer, in the sense that what I am going to say is dictated by the fact that I intend to win favors from the courts. Nor am I an informer in the sense that my disclosures are not motivated by mean calculations of self-interest. I have been a mafioso, and I have made mistakes for which I am prepared to pay in full my debt to justice, without asking for any discounts or gifts of any kind. Instead, in the interests of society, of my children and all young people, I intend to reveal everything that I had knowledge of regarding this thing which is the Mafia, so that the new generations can live in a more dignified and more human manner. . . ."

Buscetta then lifted a trapdoor over an immense and horrible catacomb. He revealed more of the workings of the Sicilian Mafia than anyone before or since, but he did not tell all. He refused to discuss his political connections or knowledge of the so-called third, or governmental, level of the Mafia, the first being the members or soldiers and the second, the bosses. Hinting at revelations he would never make, he told Judge Falcone that these stories would be disbelieved as the ravings of a madman. "I am not willing to go beyond this topic," he said. "I would be considered crazy. I would end in the loony bin. . . ." Or, he might have added, the morgue.

Two months after he had begun with Judge Falcone, he finished, concluding his testimony with these words: "I have made these statements of my own volition, and I am in full possession of my mental faculties. In so doing, I have been guided solely by my own conscience and not by a desire for revenge or vendetta. Revenge, you know, has never brought back what was lost forever. My decision, therefore, matured over the course of time, is not based on personal rancor and still less on the hope of availing myself of any rules for easier treatment of those who turn state's evidence, as they say. The truth is that I have realized for some time that the times in which we live are incompatible with the traditional principles of Cosa Nostra and that the latter, correspondingly, has been transformed into a band of ferocious assassins inspired solely by the thought of personal gain.

"I do not fear death, nor do I live in terror of being murdered by my enemies; when my turn comes, I will face death serenely and without fear. I have chosen to follow this road, and there is no turning back. I will fight with all my strength to see Cosa Nostra destroyed.

"I am well aware of the humiliation and suspicion I will have to bear and of how many people who are poorly informed or acting in bad faith will vilify the choice of road that I have taken, but even if I am subject to derision or, worse yet, called a liar, I will not retreat one inch and will seek to convince all those who are still undecided to follow my example in order to put an end once and for all to a criminal organization that has brought nothing but struggle and desperation to so many families and has contributed nothing to the development of society."

Later he added a postscript to his biographer Enzo Biagi: "The things that made a mafioso out of me don't exist anymore," he said. "All I see is a desperate search for money, many betrayals, and absurd murders. Children should never be touched."

In November 1984 it was Badalamenti's turn at extradition. Louis Caprino, who had arrested Cangialosi at JFK in April, and Pat Luzio, who had long manned the Queens lookout, were sent to Madrid along with heavily armed U.S. marshals to escort Badalamenti and Pietro Alfano to the United States for trial.

To the agents' surprise, when an armored Spanish van delivered Badalamenti to the airport, they were directed aboard a C-141 military cargo jet, with only webbing for seats. Security was so tight that not even the crew had been informed of its mission. After they were airborne, the young Air Force pilot leafed through the Army newspaper, *Stars and Stripes*, which carried a big story about the departure from Spain of notorious Sicilian Mafia boss Gaetano Badalamenti. Luzio watched the pilot's eyes widen as he gulped and slowly turned around to gaze at the grim-faced man with the deep-hollowed eyes who sat strapped into a webbed seat behind him.

"Is—is . . . that *him?*" he asked, pointing at the newspaper and glancing quickly at Badalamenti, who glared back. Luzio nodded.

Security requirements had even precluded telling the crew they would be flying passengers back to the United States. As a result, no extra food had been loaded aboard for the nine-and-a-half-hour flight. The crew shared its rations with its passengers, but Badalamenti refused to eat or to use the toilet.

Caprino tried to engage Badalamenti in conversation, suggesting that he might help himself by cooperating with investigators. Badalamenti seemed willing to listen until Caprino raised the accusations of drug trafficking. Badalamenti turned to ice. "You can accuse me of anything," he said, "but never call me a drug dealer." The discussion was over.

Within days of Badalamenti's retrieval, agents conducted a raid carried over from the spring sweeps. Tony Aiello—Commerciante as Luigi Ronsisvalle knew him, who ran the Caffè Aiello and once had gone all the way to Ganci's house to pick up "rolls"—had not been arrested with the other defendants on April 9. Louis Freeh had wanted to gather additional evidence against the husky, black-haired Aiello. He would assume he had not been implicated, Freeh figured. He might also flee. On November 14, 1984, agents raided Aiello's house in Queens. They seized nine pistols and rifles, five of them loaded, considerable amounts of jewelry, and $91,000 in cash. But not Aiello. As might be expected, considering that he had had seven months' warning since the initial raids, Aiello was a fugitive. The same day agents also raided the Queens home of Aiello's father, Vito, where they found a pistol and a wrapped package containing the $30,000 paid by an undercover detective, Richard Ford, for heroin the month before at Tony's Pizza on 125th Street. They found another package concealed in the dropped ceiling containing $898,127.

Three months later, in February 1985, Detective Kenneth McCabe of the NYPD was startled to get a call from a long-forgotten figure of his past. Calling from his prison in Sandstone, Minnesota, where he was doing five to fifteen years for one of his thirteen murders, was Luigi Ronsisvalle. He was calling, he said, to offer some new information against Salvatore Catalano. Ronsisvalle, who was due for release shortly, having served more than the conventional one-third of his sentence, was first called to testify before the President's Commission on Organized Crime, in Florida. Freeh read about the testimony in the *Daily News* and invited Ronsisvalle to New York for further debriefing. Ronsisvalle said he had two new pieces of information to offer. He now remembered having seen Catalano and Ganci huddling in a Knickerbocker Avenue café in 1977, after which he was told that the heroin "pipeline" had been reopened. Ronsisvalle also remembered that in late 1977 or early 1978 he and Felice Puma drove a hundred-kilo load of heroin up from Florida in Puma's red Porsche and delivered it on Knickerbocker Avenue to an associate of Salvatore Catalano while Catalano stood nearby. Why Ronsisvalle never reported the episodes in 1979, when he was first debriefed about his other contacts on Knickerbocker Avenue and his dealings with Michele Sindona, was never explained satisfactorily, but his new accounts electrified prosecutors preparing the case against Catalano. This was powerful new testimony tying the elusive Catalano directly into the heroin conspiracy.

Rooney had another job for Ronsisvalle. He took out his photos from Giuseppe Bono's wedding. Rooney had copied the pictures, cut away the tuxedos and the background, and pasted just the heads on plain sheets. The photo display had provoked great hilarity in the FBI; agents called it Rooney's "pumpkin heads." Now Rooney took out his pumpkin heads and files of surveillance pictures and showed them to Ronsisvalle, who recognized, but couldn't always name, some of the figures Rooney and Russo had been trying to identify for nearly five years, people like Key Food's Pasquale Conte, with whom Ronsisvalle had his bitter run-in on Knickerbocker Avenue. Rooney and Pat Luzio also took Ronsisvalle on a car tour of his old haunts on and around Knickerbocker Avenue to seek his recollection of people and places he hadn't seen since 1979.

In the summer of 1985 Freeh and the other prosecutors flew to Europe to take testimony from many of the arrested money launderers, among them Franco Della Torre, the dapper Italian who brought the suitcases of cash to Merrill Lynch; Paul Waridel, the refrigerator-size confidant of Yasar Musullulu; and Enrico Rossini, who had worked with the still-fugitive Vito Roberto Palazzolo in financing the Sicilian Mafia's drug deals through E. F. Hutton. The government depositions were taken during June 1985 in the cantonal courthouse in Bellinzona, Switzerland, amid the breathtakingly beautiful Italian lakes. A Swiss magistrate presided according to Swiss law while former federal judge Edmund L. Palmieri represented the federal judge in charge of the American case, Pierre N. Leval. After decades of stonewalling foreign efforts to penetrate the secrecy that shielded so many illegal financial dealings in Switzerland's banking community, the Swiss authorities began a historic cooperative effort with American investigators. The billions of dollars in dirty money they had been sheltering were no longer worth the negative publicity and accelerating resentments of worldwide law enforcement agencies, to say nothing of the legal and social implications of harboring the criminally generated fortunes. The testimony of the cooperating witnesses filled in many of the gaps in the story of how the drug millions found their way back to Switzerland and Italy. Rooney and Freeh and another prosecutor, Robert Bucknam, then moved on to another urgent task: interrogating the Turks who supplied morphine base to the Sicilian Mafia.

The trip began in an upbeat mood. On the flight to Ankara Rooney traded his FBI cap to a Lufthansa stewardess for two bottles of champagne. One later exploded in Rooney's shoulder bag, which he then lugged, dripping wet, past distracted Turkish customs officers.

The Turkish government had promised to cooperate and make available some arrested associates of Musullulu for questioning although Musullulu himself was a fugitive. The Americans had great expectations. Here were figures who not only could tie the delivery of billions of dollars worth of morphine base to the Sicilian Mafia but could also shed light on the role of the Bulgarians in the drug and arms markets. Some intelligence reports had the Bulgarians selling narcotics that their border agents had seized and using the proceeds for arms purchases to aid terrorist groups.

"How do we know they will talk to us?" wondered Rooney.

"Of course they will talk," a Turkish official assured them. "Otherwise we will cut off their heads."

That not-so-subtle coercion, Freeh realized, would taint their testimony in an American court of law. In the end the Americans didn't even bother questioning the Turkish prisoners. Meanwhile, Rooney, who liked to boast of his cast-iron stomach, was felled by something he ate. He later blamed it on a bad hamburger at an American envoy's cookout. But en route home he recovered sufficiently to down a platter of Wiener schnitzel and sauerkraut and several beers at the Frankfurt airport.

September 30, 1985. Autumn had officially begun, but warm Indian summer breezes blew through lower Manhattan as legions of blue-suited lawyers and a crowd of news reporters converged on the columned United States Courthouse at 9:30 A.M. They set their briefcases on the X-ray scanner, walked through the metal detector, and made their way to a paneled hearing room jammed with tables and plastic chairs for the opening day of SS 84 Cr. 236, the 236th criminal indictment of 1984—*United States of America* v. *Gaetano Badalamenti et al.*

So this was Badalamenti. A newsman laying eyes on him for the first time— standing, in fact, fewer than ten feet away in the crowded hearing room—was struck by his plainness. A Sicilian elder in a bluish gray suit and white socks, Badalamenti stood, taciturn beneath his thinning woolly hair, bushy brows, lined forehead, and dark-rimmed eyes that seemed more baleful than intimidating. He hardly looked like a notorious Mafia boss who had lost a murderous struggle with the Corleonesi and sought to mastermind a drug empire from exile. Yet intimations of his authority flashed through. When other defendants behind him were chattering away too carelessly, Badalamenti turned around and silenced them by merely lifting an eyebrow. In their drab suits and open shirts and Leatherette and cotton jackets they resembled a gathering of building superintendents. The exception was Salvatore Catalano, whose narrow-eyed expression emitted a palpable aura of command. But there were few people for Catalano to talk to. His closest sidekick, Giuseppe Ganci, had been cut from the case. Ganci was dying of lung cancer and would be tried separately if he lived.

Although the bail set was among the highest ever levied—$4 million for Badalamenti, $3 million for Catalano, and more than $1 million each for many of the others—all but Badalamenti, his son Vito, his nephew Vincenzo Randazzo, and Sal Salamone, the hapless Pennsylvania pizza man and gun buyer, made bail and were out of jail. In Catalano's case the huge sum was pledged by dozens of relatives and associates who put up their houses and businesses as collateral.

The defendants had settled into plastic chairs and donned the black wireless headsets carrying simultaneous translations of the proceedings in Sicilian when a stentorian command cut through the babble: "Places, everybody! All rise!" A black-robed figure with an aesthete's narrow face topped by a tangle of reddish brown locks came striding into the chamber. United States District Court Judge Pierre N. Leval had only recently finished presiding over the gargantuan *Westmoreland* v. *CBS* libel case; now he was beginning a case that would in the next seventeen months dwarf all the others. The longest federal jury criminal trial on record had begun.

25

T HE grand jury indictment returned shortly after the April 9 raids had named thirty-eight defendants, later pared down to thirty-five, twenty-two of whom were present in court for the beginning of jury selection on September 30, 1985. Ganci was absent. Bonventre had been murdered, possibly Zito, too. The rest were being sought in Italy or Switzerland. Among those were Filippo Salamone, Vito Roberto Palazzolo, Faro Lupo, Guiseppe Soresi, Franco Della Torre, Leonardo Greco, Oliviero Tognoli, and Salvatore Miniati. As it was, the number of defendants in court made the trial monumentally complex. By the time it was over, many lawyers wondered whether they would ever again see a spectacle like this. Most hoped not.

Almost everything about the trial was extraordinary. To begin with, Judge Leval agreed with the government that the case was triable as a single conspiracy rather than a series of smaller criminal prosecutions. He admitted to having had substantial doubts early on because of the way different pieces of evidence applied to different defendants. But he had concluded that the case was a single conspiracy and that all accused participants could be tried together, cumbersome as that might be. "It seems to me," he ruled, "that there is strong and convincing evidence that there is a kind of central New York/New Jersey Sicilian axis functioning over a long period of time on a consistent and concerted long-range purpose to import and distribute narcotics."

It was a momentous decision for several reasons. As a matter of law, in a single-conspiracy case all defendants are chargeable with all acts committed in the course of the conspiracy, regardless of how remote they may be from any of the particular acts charged. Thus prosecutors would not have to prove that the Pietro Alfano who spoke to his uncle Gaetano Badalamenti in 1984 received or even knew of Frank Castronovo's cash deliveries to Amendolito in 1980. It would be enough, for a guilty verdict, to show that they knowingly participated in a common conspiracy to import heroin. But to do this, the government had to establish the conspiracy from its beginnings and tell its story in compelling detail that, pieced together, made the epic that became known as the Pizza Connection. Had the cases been tried separately as a series of a dozen smaller prosecutions, the same broad tale would never have emerged. Moreover, the magnitude of the single proceeding guaranteed the case immense public attention and a place in legal history.

The ruling that sustained the prosecution saddled the defense with a crushing burden. The voluminous evidence compiled by the government in nearly five years of investigation seemed virtually impossible to combat, leaving one of the defense lawyers to complain, in an extraordinary admission out of the presence of the jury, that the government was "proving the case to death." And the more the start of the trial was delayed by legal motions on both sides, the more time the FBI and Freeh had to continue their investigations and nail down the government's case. Assuming that the accused were, in fact, guilty, it would have been to their advantage to press for an immediate trial, so as not to give the government further time to gather evidence. If, on the other hand, they were innocent, they could afford to spend more time preparing their defense case. But the defendants protested their innocence, and contested each stage of the prosecution, giving the government the time it needed to perfect its case and, as it emerged, to seal the defendants' fate nearly three years later before the jury. No one would deny that the four years of investigation by Rooney and Russo and the hundreds of other FBI, DEA, Customs, and IRS agents and the police on four continents had presented the defense with all but insurmountable obstacles.

The trial began in a jammed hearing room but soon graduated to a chandeliered fifth-floor courtroom. Picking the jury and twelve alternates took a month and would have taken far longer had those in the pool suspected that they would be sitting not the six months estimated by the judge but nearly eighteen. The names of the jurors were kept secret for their protection, although Judge Leval never put it to them so bluntly; Buscetta had alerted the government to a possible effort to corrupt or intimidate the jury, not an unknown hazard in Mafia trials on either side of the Atlantic.

The case presented huge logistical problems. A soundproof booth had to be constructed for the three simultaneous interpreters who spelled each other in roughly hourly segments at $250 a day each and translated the proceedings for the Sicilian-speaking defendants, who sometimes dozed off with the headphones on or took them off and followed the proceedings in English. In all, the unflappable interpreters processed some ten million words, the equivalent of reading aloud fifty fat novels. An entire "war room" at the U.S. attorney's office was set aside for the prosecution's evidence: hundreds of cassettes containing the estimated hundred thousand telephone conversations recorded on the forty-seven court-authorized wiretaps, representing at least one year's worth of uninterrupted talk; hundreds of videocassettes and thousands of photographs from the thousand rolls of thirty-six-exposure film shot by the surveillance agents; and untold thousands of pages of witness depositions and financial records collected from Turkey, Switzerland, Italy, and Brazil. Domenico "Mimmo" Buda, a bantamweight computer student from Calabria whose sister was married to an FBI agent, was deputized as a marshal specifically to keep track of the growing mountain of material.

Rooney was in the courtroom every day, monitoring the statements of both sides for accuracy and making sure, among other things, that the weapons seized in the raids, along with the heroin Benny Zito had sold DEA agent Steve Hopson, were available for prominent display to the jury. Somehow, nothing seemed to drive home the prosecution's case so dramatically as the sight of the arsenal of deadly weapons on the government table. Russo was not to be seen; he had already taken up his new assignment as the FBI's assistant legal attaché at the American Embassy in Rome and returned only to testify about the accuracy of the wiretap translations. When he took the stand, Russo was a slick, even arrogant witness, deftly parrying the questions of the cross-examining defense lawyers while he bobbed his head and body in the manner of a prizefighter. Sometimes he answered the question before it was fully asked. Carmela had been very worried about Carmine's appearance in court. Everyone now knew that he bore a large share of the credit—or blame—for making the case. Would the Mafia try to retaliate against him? Without her husband's knowledge, but in collusion with Carmine's father, Carmela arranged for bureau protection for him. When Russo learned about it later, he didn't know whether to be annoyed or touched.

The government's opening argument on October 24, 1984, was ringingly set forth by an austere member of the prosecution team, Robert Stewart, the head of the government strike force in Newark, who had been brought into the case to ensure the widest possible cooperative effort by the key jurisdictions involved. Stewart had studied the courtroom seating plan and knew where each defendant would be located. He whirled around on cue and pointed his finger directly at a defendant as he named him or, more impressively, consulted his notes on a yellow pad while reaching behind him and picking out the defendant in question. The jury would have to grapple with many names and events, Stewart predicted. "Yet," he went on, "the basic story of what occurred in this case is not very complicated. It is, stated in its simplest terms, the buying and selling of a commodity year in and year out, over and over again." The commodity in question, he said, "was massive amounts of contraband narcotic drugs, heroin and cocaine." What also made the case significant, he continued, was that all those involved in the buying and selling were members or associates of the Sicilian or American Mafia who during just a part of 1982 and 1983 had earmarked for distribution in the United States over a ton and a half of pure heroin worth more than a third of $1 billion, of which more than $60 million was smuggled out to Switzerland to pay the suppliers. In all, the government estimated, the shipments of drugs imported by the Mafia during the life of the conspiracy, 1979 to 1984, were valued at $1.6 billion.

There it was, the Mafia in a courtroom. Before Giuliani's tenure the word "Mafia" had rarely been uttered in the halls of justice. Now not only was the criminal brotherhood a centerpiece of the Pizza Connection, as the case was already being widely called, but it also stood at the core of other major prosecutions unfolding contemporaneously in nearby courtrooms: the trial of Gambino family figures, including boss Paul Castellano, the most powerful Mafia leader in America, who in December 1986 became another victim of the Mafia retirement program when he was gunned down outside Sparks steakhouse in Manhattan, and the trial of the Mafia ruling commission itself, featuring such longtime mob untouchables as Anthony "Fat Tony" Salerno of the Genovese family, Anthony "Tony Ducks" Corallo of the Lucchese family, Carmine "Junior" Persico of the Colombo family, Philip "Rusty" Rastelli, acting boss of the Bonanno family, and Anthony "Bruno" Indelicato, whose fingerprints had been found in the Galante murder getaway car.

Stewart, with his closely cropped gray hair and sober demeanor, retold the story of the Galante killing and spotlighted the suspicious escape of Bonventre and Amato. Amato's lawyer, Paul Bergman, strongly objected, challenging the murder's connection to the case. Nearly four months later Judge Leval agreed, ruling that the government had not provided sufficient evidence to support its contention that Galante was killed because he stood as an obstacle to Catalano, Ganci, and Bonventre. Although Lefty Ruggiero had told undercover agent Joe Pistone that Galante had been killed for refusing to share, the judge ruled that the government's scenario was largely speculative and could prejudice other defendants while lengthening the already massive case. Accordingly he barred further evidence of the Galante killing. The story of the murder later found a home in the Mafia Commission case, where the government successfully presented the same evidence against Bruno Indelicato, who was later convicted. But defense counsel contended that the trial had already been tainted and that it had an appealable issue in Stewart's opening narration of the shootings in Joe and Mary's restaurant.

After the defense lawyers had given their opening statements, prosecutor Dick Martin announced: "Your Honor, the government's first witness is Tommaso Buscetta."

Those in the courtroom who expected a thug, a Mafia renegade tempered by two decades of life on the run, were astonished by the courtly, soft-spoken fifty-seven-year-old Sicilian in a conservative blue suit who took the witness stand and matter-of-factly parted the curtain shrouding the innermost sanctum of the Sicilian Mafia. A crack in his controlled demeanor was seen only once, when he put a trembling right hand to his face. Buscetta had reportedly refused $5 million offered him by jailed Corleonesi boss Luciano Liggio if he would not testify; rebuffed, Liggio was said to have offered $1 million to anyone who could slip him a gun in the Palermo courtroom when Buscetta was on the stand.

Buscetta's testimony had been awaited with great public anticipation, fueled by frenzied media coverage and the genuine drama of the appearance of a Mafia intimate who had betrayed the world's most viciously powerful criminal cartel. Few who had seen it could forget the haunting news photograph of Buscetta being returned to Italy from Brazil: Below the huge bull-nose prow of an Alitalia 747, dozens of Italian security officers are scattered on the tarmac beside their cars; everyone is looking up at the plane's front doorway. Descending the stairs with a striped blanket thrown over his wrists to hide a bullet-proof shield is the dwarfed figure of Tommaso Buscetta.

By making Buscetta the leadoff witness, the government succeeded in seizing media attention and spotlighting the Sicilian and American Mafias as never before in a courtroom. Apart from Badalamenti, however, Buscetta had little to say about the defendants; indeed, of the twenty-two, Badalamenti was the only one he knew well. He knew Filippo Casamento slightly from his time in New York and had heard that Gaetano Mazzara had been made a member of Palermo's Noce family to look after its drug-trafficking interests in America. He knew of Sal Lamberti. But Buscetta's true value to the prosecution lay in his ability to describe the ritualistic and terrifying world of the Mafia. As for his own involvement in the drug trade, Buscetta contended that his only role was to put bosses Antonio Salamone and Salvatore Inzerillo in touch with each other for a onetime drug deal. As arguable and self-serving a position as this was, in view of all the incriminating testimony against Buscetta by the convicted French Connection traffickers, neither side had much interest in portraying Buscetta to the jury as a drug kingpin. The government did not care to taint its chief witness, and the defense was reluctant to associate such a key Mafia figure with drug trafficking. As some of the defense lawyers noted cynically, although Buscetta was under oath, having sworn to tell the full truth about his criminal past, the perjury statutes were enforced by the government.

Buscetta threw the government one major curve. Questioned on the stand about his knowledge of Badalamenti's involvement with drugs, Buscetta responded to prosecutor Martin: "I never saw, nor did he speak to me personally, nor did I see him dealing with others in drugs. I was certain he was not working in drugs."

The answer clearly stunned Martin and the rest of the government team, while buoying Badalamenti and his lawyer, Michael Kennedy. Was Buscetta protecting Badalamenti? Did the two have a secret understanding? Or was Buscetta merely saying he had no personal knowledge of Badalamenti's involvement?

Martin tried to recoup his position with follow-up questions, but Buscetta became more obtuse: "He was not against, and he did not deal in drugs."

Later Buscetta clarified his responses by saying, "In order to work in drugs, he would have had to have support in the U.S. in Mafia circles, and for him this was impossible." In other words, Buscetta assumed that Badalamenti, as an ousted boss, would have been rebuffed in any efforts to traffic in drugs. However, Buscetta conceded, he had never heard Badalamenti express any opposition to drugs.

It helped the government gain back some ground, but the damage had been done. Reasons for Buscetta's unexpectedly literal testimony on Badalamenti could only be guessed at and went to the heart of the mysterious interplay between the two Mafia outlaws now facing each other across a federal courtroom.

After the trial Buscetta returned to the anonymity of a protected federal witness. Like his fellow Mafia turncoat Salvatore Contorno, he was living somewhere in America under another name and guarded by U.S. marshals while he sought to mastermind one more deal, a lucrative book contract that would provide for Cristina and their children. Buscetta had talked to prosecutors and judges on two continents; if he was going to talk any more, he was determined to get paid for it.

From the beginning of the trial a wave of illness engulfed the defendants. Baldo Amato was out with a toothache. Randazzo had a toothache. Greco had a bronchial infection. Casamento had rectal bleeding. Evola had an eye emergency. Greco had dental surgery. Casamento had a toothache. Castronovo had a heart attack. Palazzolo had neck surgery. Evola fell off a scaffold and broke his ankle. Polizzi had swollen eyes and a sore throat. Ligammari had back pain. Mazzara had a fever. Vito Badalamenti needed blood. While some of the ailments were undoubtedly real, "Sicilian flu" at trial, too, was in keeping with Mafia tradition. As an Italian jurist noted several years before in a conference paper,

> No prominent Mafia boss is without his sheaf of impressive-looking medical documents, confirming that he suffers from serious illnesses—illnesses that prevent him from travelling to the place where he is supposed to be held in detention, or coping with the rigors of preventive imprisonment, or attending a court hearing. In most cases, the illnesses in question are either non-existent or they are common ailments (such as arthritis, diabetes, or liver disorders) which suddenly become severe should they chance to afflict a representative of the Mafia. Several Mafia bosses have been suffering for years from incurable diseases, according to their medical certificates; we must expect their imminent demise. . . .

Not all the stricken were feigning. In February 1986, after the trial had been under way for just over four months, Ganci died of lung cancer, never having recovered sufficiently to stand trial. His codefendants won permission to attend the funeral.

In fairness, jurors and lawyers, too, were periodically felled by illness. Nine months into the trial Sal Salamone's lawyer Robert Fogelnest suffered a massive heart attack. But the trial lasted long enough for him to undergo surgery, convalesce, and return to finish arguing his client's ultimately doomed case. Meanwhile, Salamone, in desperation, asked prosecutor Martin to represent him.

"I have another client, Mr. Salamone," the government lawyer replied.

One woman juror cracked under the pressure of the case, smashing the window of the marshals' van that carried the jury to and from court.

The introduction of the wiretap evidence presented special problems. In one of the many unusual arrangements of the precedent-setting trial, actors were hired to read the parts of Badalamenti, Alfano, Ganci, and others in the phone conversations. At first, to the indignation of the defense, the readers—inevitably dubbed the Pizza Players—embellished their roles with pseudo-Mafia accents until the judge directed them to stop. One day one of the readers appeared in court in a dark suit, black shirt, and red tie. "If he continued to dress like that," warned Amato's lawyer, Paul Bergman, "he could get indicted."

The trial was well under way when FBI Agent Michael Slattery and Thomas Loreto, a thin, curly-haired Customs Service agent, sent to the FBI lab for testing the slip of paper that money launderer Sal Amendolito said Catalano had given him with his phone number some six years before, as Catalano prepared to hand over a suitcase with $1.54 million. Within several days the results were ready. "I've got a surprise for you," one of the technicians reported back. There, on the paper, was a clear Catalano thumbprint, a devastating piece of evidence that left Catalano's shrewd and aggressive lawyer, the six-foot-five-inch Ivan Fisher, uncharacteristically shaken. All he could do was cast doubt on the unlikely sequence: Did Amendolito really stick the slip of paper from Catalano in his Rolodex and keep it for three years, as he claimed, until the FBI suddenly decided to have it tested three years later? "What could Fisher do?" Fahy of Customs quipped later. "Cut off Catalano's hands?" The evidence got to Catalano, as judged by interpreters in their soundproof booth. Catalano's seat in the courtroom was just to the side and rear of the booth, and the tension beneath his seemingly unperturbable exterior was often betrayed by nervous foot tapping. When he became very agitated, the interpreters inside could hear his foot rapping a tattoo on the booth.

Inspired by the discovery of the Catalano print, Slattery tried another long shot. He sent to the FBI lab the paper bag in which Benny Zito had delivered heroin to the DEA undercover agent Steve Hopson three years before. To everyone's amazement, the paper bore a handprint of Gaetano Mazzara's. A third test found Mazzurco's handprint on tissue paper of yet another Zito heroin package.

The skeptical defense asked why the government had waited so long to conduct the tests, to which prosecutors replied that until suspects were identified, there was no one to whom any prints could be matched.

"I call Gaetano Badalamenti to the stand!"

The trial was two weeks into its second year—Judge Leval had made a point of wishing everyone a happy new year as the mammoth proceeding marked its first birthday on September 30, 1986—when Michael Kennedy answered the suspenseful question: Would his client Badalamenti testify in his own defense?

Kennedy had kept everyone guessing; probably he did not even know the answer himself until his client told him. Defending an accused Sicilian Mafia drug trafficker was not Kennedy's usual métier. Ruddy-faced and alternately soft-spoken and hot-tempered, Kennedy had made his reputation representing radicals, including defendants accused of running guns for the Irish Republican Army. Kennedy said in fact that Badalamenti had engaged him because he didn't want a known mob or drug lawyer as his counsel. Kennedy insisted that he would not have taken the case had he believed that the "old man"—as he called Badalamenti with a respect that seemed to border on affection—was involved with drugs. To Freeh and Russo and others who had studied the intercepted telephone calls between Badalamenti and Alfano, Mazzurco and the Lambertis, it was a laughable contention, but Kennedy stuck to it all the same. When he agreed to take the case, he said, he had not yet seen the wiretap transcripts. But after the verdict he still said he was perhaps the only person in the world besides Badalamenti himself who continued to believe that the Sicilian was not a heroin trafficker. As Kennedy initially told the jury, Badalamenti was a "proud, dignified, simple, yet remarkable man" who "refused to have anything to do with narcotics or trafficking or money."

On this morning the mournful-eyed Badalamenti arrived from his cell in a dark suit and red tie. Led by marshals into the courtroom, he turned around and waved to his wife, Theresa. Perhaps he seemed a little more cheerful than usual. Then Kennedy ended the suspense: Badalamenti would testify. Freeh would get his chance to cross-examine the former boss of the Sicilian Mafia Commission.

Badalamenti took the oath in a deep, throaty voice. "Did you ever have anything to do with drugs or drug trafficking?" Kennedy asked him.

"Never!" said Badalamenti.

Later Kennedy asked him whether he was "personally" opposed to drugs.

"My answer is yes," Badalamenti said. "I believe the people who use it don't know what they are doing."

Kennedy sought to take the edge off some of the questions sure to be raised by the government about Badalamenti's aliases. Badalamenti alluded to his persecution by the Corleonesi. Asked again by Kennedy why he had adopted aliases, Badalamenti turned sullen: "I have already stated why. However, if my reply is not clear, I can repeat it." Then Kennedy led him onto more hospitable terrain, discussing his relatives and upbringing in Cinisi. There was a brief but fruitless attempt to call Badalamenti's nephew Vincenzo Randazzo as a defense witness; the government had agreed to allow Randazzo to plead guilty to an immigration charge, and he had been dropped from the ranks of the defendants. But he made clear he would invoke his Fifth Amendment privilege against self-incrimination if called to the stand. Later, when Randazzo was ordered by the government to present himself at the airport for deportation to Italy, he disappeared.

Kennedy had trouble finding areas on which to question his client without exposing him to legal jeopardy in Italy, where he was also facing major charges. "There is no question I could ask Mr. Badalamenti," Kennedy acknowledged to the court, out of the jury's presence, "that in my opinion as a professional is not fraught with peril."

He led Badalamenti through his business experience as a contractor for Punta Raisi Airport and a trucking entrepreneur. "I paid all my taxes," Badalamenti declared. "I made money. I spent money." And where were those business records? The government wanted to see them. Kennedy said neither he nor his client had them.

What, Kennedy wanted to know, was "Terminusa"?

"I have used it since I was a partisan," replied Badalamenti, confirming use of the nonsense word as a code for the numbers 1 to 9.

Kennedy plunged ahead. "What did the conversations have to do with?"

"Mr. Kennedy, I will not explain for two reasons," Badalamenti said. "I have never betrayed and I will never betray my secrets. The other is that it would cause me harm in Italy."

If the conversations were not about drugs, Kennedy gently prodded, how could the disclosure hurt him?

In Italy, Badalamenti responded, he was being charged not just with drug trafficking but with other crimes. "It is a dreadful matter."

Pressed further, Badalamenti threw the trial into an uproar by invoking his Fifth Amendment privilege. Judge Leval held an off-the-record conference with both sides and pronounced himself mystified. He had never heard of a case, he said, in which a defendant testified to his innocence and then claimed the Fifth when it came to the central evidence against him. He would have to study the law on it, the judge said. He soon ruled that once a defendant takes the stand to address major issues in the case, he abrogates his Fifth Amendment privilege.

Now it was Freeh's turn. Under government cross-examination, Badalamenti, contradicting Buscetta, denied that he had been present with Joe Bonanno and Tommaso Buscetta at a meeting in Palermo in 1957.

"Are you a member of Cosa Nostra?" Freeh asked.

"I have never said it, and if I were, I would not say it," Badalamenti replied. "I would respect my oath."

"Are you now or have you ever been a member of La Cosa Nostra?" repeated Freeh.

"You know, if I were to say yes, I would have big problems in Italy," Badalamenti said.

"Is the Mafia oath important to you?"

"Yes, if I took it," Badalamenti said.

Freeh, citing Italian military records, challenged Badalamenti's contention that he had served with the partisans against the Fascists in World War II, especially since Badalamenti admitted he had never heard of British Field Marshal Bernard Montgomery or U.S. General George Patton. The records, Freeh said, showed that Badalamenti was attached to his Italian army unit after he claimed to have deserted to join the partisans. Kennedy challenged those records, setting off a shouting match—out of the presence of the jury—between him and the judge, who threatened to hold the lawyer in contempt.

Kennedy bristled. "The way you are handling this courtroom is an embarrassment to any of us who are members of the bar," he told Judge Leval.

"I could care less what your opinion of me is," the judge retorted.

Freeh bored in on Badalamenti, but the Mafia boss remained imperturbable, telling Freeh at one point, "Please don't raise your voice because you don't frighten me."

Later he added: "If I am the depository of a secret, there is no one who can get it out of me. So many have tried, all different ways, torture included."

Freeh tried to get Badalamenti to explain his extensive use of pay phones, but all Badalamenti would say was: "I have never wanted other people to know my business."

Wasn't drug dealing the real subject of those calls? Freeh persisted.

"It is not drugs," said Badalamenti. "I cannot explain what it is."

For his refusal to answer the questions put to him on cross-examination, Badalamenti was later convicted of criminal contempt before another Southern District judge.

Catalano's defense consisted largely of alibi witnesses who testified that Catalano was home with his family in Ciminna at the time of the meeting at the Piazza Politeama in February 1980 and that therefore, the photograph of him taken by the Italian Treasury Police must have been taken at another time. But one of Catalano's witnesses, a factory worker from Ciminna, undermined his own credibility when he was asked about the Mafia.

"What's that?" he said. "I don't know what it is. Is it something that one eats?"

Mazzurco, when he took the stand in his own defense, offered similarly incredible testimony. Asked about the balance beam scale, widely used by drug dealers and found in his car trunk, Mazzurco claimed: "I was going to take that scale to Roma Imports to weigh some macaroni packages."

He also made some key admissions, which may have sealed the fate of one of his codefendants. Asked on cross-examination whether he had really been talking over pay phones about shirts or whether that was a code, Mazzurco said: "Well, you can call it code. I call it speaking in a cryptic way. . . ." He also acknowledged that he "suspected" Ganci, Badalamenti, and Sal Lamberti of belonging to the Mafia and that he "believed" that the Mafia did exist.

How did he explain his palmprint on tissue paper in the box of heroin Ganci gave Zito for DEA Agent Hopson? Mazzurco claimed he had delivered a shirt to Ganci, who had then used the same paper and box for the heroin.

As for a ledger found in Mazzurco's house listing what clearly appeared to be transactions of kilo quantities of heroin, Mazzurco said it actually referred to gems, although it was the first time anyone had heard of precious stones being bought and sold by the kilo. "What if you give him emeralds and he brings back coal?" Freeh asked.

Mazzurco said being cheated had never occurred to him.

"What kind of gold, what kind of rock is ninety percent acrylic?" Freeh asked.

"We were talking of imperfections," said Mazzurco blandly. "Perhaps you are not familiar with the Sicilian people and their way of talking," said Mazzurco. "Sicilian people, we have been abused going back maybe thirty-two hundred years, always by different nationalities, specifically the Greeks, the Arabs, the Spanish, the French, the English, all the way down the line, and we have learned that in order not to—when we are speaking, if there are other people listening to us, to always speak in a manner that those people would not understand us. It is our nature, our inborn nature to the Sicilian people."

Freeh let Mazzurco's speech sink in. Then he asked: "Were the Greeks persecuting you when you said, 'I'm supposed to bring them ninety-five cents' and you meant ninety-five thousand dollars?"

None of the defendants mounted a persuasive defense. Amato's witnesses, for example, claimed that the product he and Ganci were importing was Italian coffee for his sleek new Caffè Biffi on Second Avenue and Eighty-fourth Street. Castronovo's lawyer contended that the $37,200 found sealed up in a wall in his client's house was the proceeds of a bank account he had closed because the bank wasn't giving enough interest.

How much interest, asked Freeh, did the wall give?

For sheer implausibility, nothing matched the testimony of Salvatore Greco's main alibi witness, his accountant Justin Pisano. Pisano offered his diary in evidence in an effort to prove that on the day in 1980 that the government claimed Greco was at the farmhouse near his brother Leonardo's iron factory testing a heroin shipment, Sal Greco was really with Pisano in New Jersey looking over a pizzeria for sale. What about the diary entries indicating that Pisano had been at the opera then? prosecutor Robert Stewart wanted to know. What about *La Troviatta*, as Pisano had spelled it in his diary? Pisano denied he was an opera fan. The listing really referred to a client named Troviatta, he insisted.

Then what about *Carmen* listed for another night? Stewart asked.

Pisano said that, too, was a client named Carmen.

And, said Stewart, seizing on another entry, was *Barber of Seville* an appointment for a haircut? Pisano acknowledged that was an opera.

It was a stellar prosecutorial performance, backed by Pat Luzio's strong supporting role. Earlier that morning, after he had got his first look at the suspicious diary, Freeh dispatched Luzio to the *New York Times* morgue to check the newspaper's opera listings for the specified days six years before. Luzio had less than two hours before Stewart was to go before the jury, but he found the information and got it to court just in time for the prosecutor's devastating cross-examination.

Freeh had noticed that while virtually all diary entries were in ink, certain ones relating to Greco were in pencil and chronologically out of order, as if Pisano had scribbled them in later. Stewart noted that Pisano was claiming that his diary entry recording his visit with Greco to the Neptune City pizzeria took place on a date two years before Greco had bought the place. How, the prosecutor demanded, could Pisano have known in 1980 that Greco would acquire the pizzeria two years later and call it Neptune City?

Pisano stared at the diary for a long time. There was dead silence in the courtroom. "I don't understand how I wrote Neptune City," he finally replied weakly. Freeh later denounced it as one of the most blatant fabrications he had ever encountered.

Another gaffe may have been committed by Emanuele Palazzolo's lawyer, who, in submitting her version of wiretap transcripts, provided a name that Russo and other government experts had been unable to decipher. The name was Guido Cocilovo. He was the former Alitalia customs broker who had been arrested in June 1983 at the Amtrak station in Miami with six kilos of cocaine. It was that arrest that had so spooked Mazzurco and his associates that they later refused to travel to Florida with Alfano to pick up the twenty-two "containers" sent by Badalamenti. Cocilovo had not talked, and the police had not been able to find out for whom he was working. Thanks to Palazzolo's lawyer, the government learned that Cocilovo's name had come up in a telephone conversation between Alfano and Palazzolo in 1984. Cocilovo, it then became clear, was among those who had been moving Badalamenti's drugs to Mazzurco in New York and had been doing so for years. He had, in fact, been a courier of a previous shipment, referred to by Badalamenti on one of the taped calls as "the thing of four, five years ago."

Gaetano Mazzara's defense was set to follow Mazzurco's, but as his embarrassed lawyers informed Judge Leval, he had disappeared a few days before, on Thanksgiving eve, as Mazzurco's testimony was concluding. One of Mazzara's lawyers, Harriet Rosen, had been with him in New Jersey on the Wednesday before Thanksgiving, going over his defense case. In the afternoon she had to return to the city, and he drove her to the bus stop. The holiday traffic was so bad, she later said, they agreed he would not attempt to drive her into Manhattan. The next night, after Mazzara had missed Thanksgiving dinner, his family reported him missing.

Freeh was angry but not surprised. He had figured that some of the defendants, despite their astronomical bail, might try to flee, especially now that the defense cases were proving so flimsy. Vincenzo Randazzo, Badalamenti's nephew, who was to have been deported to Italy to face charges there after pleading guilty to immigration violations, had failed to report to the airport as scheduled and had also disappeared, although his lawyer claimed he was under no legal obligation to surrender himself as the government insisted. But Mazzara's dire position was clear. He had been deeply implicated when his palmprint was found on the paper bag containing one of the kilos of heroin Benny Zito sold to Agent Hopson. No wonder he had skipped. At the government's demand, the remaining defendants who were out on bail were quickly rearrested and remanded, over the bitter protests of their lawyers.

The following day Mazzara's lawyer, white-faced and trembling, returned to the afternoon session of the trial. "Your Honor," said Harriet Rosen, "during the lunch recess I learned some overwhelming and sad news that my client, Gaetano Mazzara, has been reported to have been found dead." That morning Mazzara's shot and beaten body had been found partially wrapped in a plastic garbage bag in a warehouse section of Brooklyn. He appeared to have been tortured. His legs were twisted and broken, and an X-shaped mark had been cut into his scalp. Most significant, perhaps, the medical examiner later found marks indicating that a pliers had been applied to his tongue, perhaps in an effort to tear it out. That, Charlie Rooney and Louis Caprino speculated, could indicate that he was killed on the orders of a codefendant who was fearful, after Mazzurco's damaging testimony, that Mazzara, too, might take the stand and crack under cross-examination.

There was another school of thought. Government intelligence reports indicated that Mazzara had continued to deal in drugs during the trial, and some of his codefendants may have felt that his actions so jeopardized their cases that they wanted him out of the way. No one knew for sure. Naturally none of these facts or speculations into possible motives were shared with the jurors; all they were told was that Mazzara had died. Later Judge Leval questioned them privately to see whether they might have heard anything of the murder that could overshadow the testimony and prejudice them against the remaining defendants, although the jurors were under orders from the beginning of the trial to shun TV reports, newspaper accounts, or conversations touching on the case in any way.

While agents investigated the Mazzara murder, making scant progress, Mike Slattery, the agent who, with Tommy Loreto of Customs, had requested the delayed fingerprint check on Amendolito's slip of paper with Catalano's print on it, had been trying to find the missing Vincenzo Randazzo. Randazzo had been sought ever since he failed to appear at JFK for his deportation after his guilty plea to immigration violations. Figuring that Alfano might lead them to his fugitive relative, Slattery drove to Newark International Airport to follow Alfano and Palazzolo as they returned from a weekend trip home to Illinois during the trial. As he tailed the pair in a cab, Slattery noticed he had company—three men in a blue rental Oldsmobile also seemed to be tailing Alfano. *They must be marshals,* Slattery thought. *But they don't look like marshals.* He and the three strangers in the other car followed Alfano up the New Jersey Turnpike, through the Lincoln Tunnel, and to the Greenwich Village hotel Alfano and Palazzolo were staying in during the trial. The two got out of the cab and entered the hotel to register. The blue car with the three men also stopped. Slattery was getting the creeps. *These guys are not marshals. Who the fuck are they?* Slattery got out of his car and crossed the street to a pay phone, where he could pretend to make a call while watching what happened next. Out of the corner of his eye, he saw one man get out of the car and walk toward him. He was coming up from Slattery's back. Slattery was reluctant to turn around for fear of establishing eye contact and attracting the man's attention. On the other hand, Slattery was afraid not to keep an eye on him. A cop had just been shot dead at a diner in Queens. Who knew what was going on? The man came closer. Slattery broke into a sweat. His free hand inched toward his gun belt. The man was at the phone booth. Slattery forced himself to look away and talk into the dead phone. The man was right at his back now. Slattery couldn't see what he was doing. Then Slattery heard his footsteps echo away. Moments later the man passed again, this time on his way back. He crossed the street and walked up to the the hotel, peering into the lobby where Alfano and Palazzolo stood at the reception desk. Then he got back into the car with the other two men and drove off. Slattery tried to keep pace with them and he got as far as Brooklyn before losing them. But he had gotten the rental plate number—and it would soon lead to a surprising breakthrough.

Now that the agents and marshals knew where Alfano was staying, they checked the phone records from his room and found calls to a Greenwich Village apartment. They put the apartment under watch—and found Randazzo, who was arrested as a fugitive. He was later acquitted of all charges in Italy.

The defense had rested, the summations were on, and the trial was four months into its second year when some of the lawyers came in with T-shirts reading PIZZA CONNECTION DEFENSE TEAM. Below was the picture of a pizza with a slice cut out and the dates 1985–19? It was almost over. But not quite.

On the evening of February 11, 1987, as Pietro Alfano and his wife were leaving Balducci's delicatessen in Greenwich Village, two men stepped out of a red car and shot Alfano three times in the back before escaping in a waiting blue van with New Jersey plates. The next day, as a comatose Alfano clung to life in the hospital, the trial was in an uproar. Badalamenti's lawyer, Michael Kennedy, soon joined by all but one of his defense colleagues, moved for a mistrial, saying it was "impossible to proceed in an atmosphere of fear, intimidation and chill that pervades this courtroom." Tensions ran high, symptoms of a split between the Badalamenti and Catalano factions that reached the point where Catalano's lawyer, Ivan Fisher, felt compelled to say, "There is nothing to suggest that Mr. Catalano had anything to do with what happened to Mr. Alfano." Some of the defendants asked to be placed in protective custody. And many spoke darkly of the Sicilian Mafia war that, as Alfano once feared, seemed to have jumped the ocean and begun to rage on the streets of New York. This time it was impossible to keep it from the jury. One juror admitted to the judge that he had overheard the remark "They killed another one." Another juror, who lived in Greenwich Village near the scene of the shooting, had practically stumbled across it—he had actually heard the shots—and could not avoid learning what had happened.

The suspected attackers were tracked down with astonishing speed. Rooney immediately remembered the rental car that Slattery had seen tailing Alfano from Newark International two months before. The customer was traced and turned out to be a convicted New Jersey bank robber, Frank Bavosa, who owned a blue van. A search of his house yielded records indicating he had a gun and had recently traveled to the Midwest with another man; the FBI learned that an acquaintance of Bavosa had said the two plus a third man had been in the van the night of Alfano's shooting. And, she said, they had recently been hired for $40,000 to do something involving guns. Bavosa was arrested and then told the FBI and NYPD that they had participated in the shooting and had been paid $40,000 to kill Alfano, allegedly because of his continuing drug-trafficking activities. Investigators then said they located an informant who said that the contract had been arranged by Pasquale Conte, Sr., the Key Foods official listed in FBI records as a captain in the Gambino family, and Vincenzo Pullara, thirty-two, of Bensonhurst. Conte was arrested shortly afterward at Kennedy Airport. He was carrying a one-way ticket to San Juan, $7,000 cash, and a passport with a visa for Argentina. At his Long Island home ten guns were found. He was released after posting $3.4 million bail. But within a few weeks the case against Conte and Pullara suddenly collapsed. The informant, by then identified as Salvatore Spatola, a convicted heroin and cocaine trafficker, clammed up, and the government was forced to drop its charges against Conte, although it said it was continuing the investigation. Alfano survived, paralyzed below the waist for life. The motive for the attack remained a mystery. Was it Badalamenti's revenge? Catalano's? Or an attempt to create a mistrial?

The verdicts came surprisingly quickly on March 2, 1987, after only six days of deliberation. Some of the defense lawyers later calculated that the deliberations for some defendants could have lasted only a few minutes. Obviously, that was all the jurors needed, especially after consulting a 394-page digest of the key wiretaps and other evidence, prepared by the prosecution, that Judge Leval allowed the jurors to take into the jury room. Eighteen of the nineteen remaining defendants were found guilty; Badalamenti's son Vito was the only one acquitted. Baldo Amato's black-haired brother Vito rushed to the courtroom. "All?" he kept asking Guiseppi Lamberti's lawyer, Anthony Lombardino, in a stricken tone. "All?"

Perhaps the happiest of the defendants, after Vito Badalamenti, was the elfin Mazzurco, who, the jurors decided, had not supervised five others and so did not get convicted of the more serious counts of helping mastermind the conspiracy. "It was the only time," said grinning defense lawyer Joseph Benfante, "where I got hugged and kissed by a convicted client facing thirty years." Mazzurco could be eligible for parole, Benfante calculated, in a mere ten years.

The paralyzed Alfano had also been found guilty. But Judge Leval, ruling that the shooting had deprived Alfano of a complete trial—although his defense case had concluded—later overturned the conviction.

On the eighth floor of the U.S. attorney's offices, preparations for a party were under way. Marshals carrying bottles of champagne strode toward Giuliani's large office with its panoramic view over lower Manhattan. Giuliani's law library was thronged with TV cameramen and reporters. Giuliani took his customary place behind the microphones, along with prosecutors Freeh and Martin, all three in red ties, and fellow prosecutors Bucknam, Stewart, and Andrew McCarthy. They were flanked by the mustachioed, ruddy-faced Robert Stutman, special agent in charge of the DEA in New York, and Mike Fahy of the Customs Service. The verdicts had come so quickly there hadn't been time to reach the FBI's Tom

Sheer, who was out of town, or, apparently, anyone from the New York Police Department. Rooney was there, but as a mere agent he had been instructed not to stand at the microphones with the luminaries.

"This is a great victory for law enforcement," began Giuliani. "It's an outstanding result. I couldn't have hoped for anything better." If the efforts continued, "there is not going to be a Mafia in five to ten years."

The sentencing came three months later, in June. Asked if he wished to address the court, Badalamenti did not even bother to stand up. "I have nothing to say," he said in Sicilian.

Ivan Fisher said a few words for Catalano, who also disdained to address the court. "This fellow is forty-six years old," he told the judge. "Does it make any sense for the U.S. government to lock him up beyond fifty-eight, fifty-nine or his sixtieth birthday?"

At the prosecution table Rooney, in a gray suit, sat impassive. Giuliani, also in gray with a maroon striped tie, entered the courtroom with his deputy Dennison Young. They took seats near the front. Giuliani's face was unreadable.

Judge Leval sentenced the sixty-four-year-old Badalamenti to forty-five years in prison, noting, however, that according to the extradition agreement with Spain, he would have to be released after serving thirty years, when he would be ninety-four. He also fined him $125,000.

Catalano, forty-six, also got forty-five years and was fined $1.15 million. And in a novel application of a restitution statute, Judge Leval directed Catalano to contribute another $1 million to a fund for the rehabilitation of drug addicts. The others also got between fifteen to thirty years, with fines and restitution payments in most cases totaling several hundred thousand dollars.

Polizzi, unlike the others, did speak on his own behalf, embarking on a rambling and emotional monologue beginning with his illegal entry into the country in 1958 and going on so long the judge had to interrupt him so he could continue sentencing the others. Then he let Polizzi resume. In an effort to prove that he couldn't have been involved in drugs—"I never believe in drugs because I hate drugs"—Polizzi said that his wife's brother had been taking drugs but "we straightened him out. . . ." Polizzi also invoked his right to a hearing on the information about his mob ties that the government had provided the court prior to sentencing. It was a big miscalculation. Prosecutor Robert Bucknam tried to warn Polizzi's lawyers that it would not be a smart move. But the big florid-faced contractor with the pompadour would not be swayed. As a result, the government got to air far more of its damaging intelligence on Polizzi: his membership in the DeCavalcante family and his trips to Florida to visit the aging New Jersey Mafia boss Sam "the Plumber" DeCavalcante; his business partnership with his uncle, mobster Anthony Riela; his meetings with other mobsters; even a county prostitution and sexual assault charge for endangering the welfare of a child. It was an interesting historical juxtaposition. A quarter century before, Polizzi's boss DeCavalcante was secretly tape-recorded in extensive discussions of Mafia conspiracies —perhaps the only real parallel to the Pizza Connection tapes.

Sam Evola, who had been arrested with the cocaine sample, entered a surprise last-minute guilty plea, hoping to mitigate his sentence. But standing in a windbreaker beside his lawyer, he declined to provide information on the crimes of the conspiracy, as prosecutors usually require of those admitting guilt. Freeh, contemptuous of the last-minute plea, brought to court a tape recording made by an undercover officer showing that Evola's brother continued to sell drugs after the Pizza Connection had surfaced.

"Is this public?" a startled reporter asked Freeh.

"It is now," the prosecutor said.

Judge Leval, unimpressed by Evola's deathbed conversion, sentenced him to fifteen years, drawing a venomous outburst from Evola's wife, Cristina, Badalamenti's niece.

"Christ on the cross!" she swore at the prosecutors who she felt had double-crossed her husband. "I hope they get what they deserve!"

In August 1987 Alfano pleaded guilty by telephone from his hospital bed rather than risk having the conviction reinstated on appeal or having to go through a retrial. The plea, during which Alfano admitted his role in the drug conspiracy, carried a mandatory minimum sentence of ten years and a maximum of thirty.

One convicted defendant remained unsentenced—Baldo Amato. His lawyer, Paul Bergman, had argued to Judge Leval that the government's recitation of the Galante killing, before it was ruled out of the case, had fatally prejudiced the case against Amato. That, coupled with what Bergman called an erroneous FBI identification of Amato in the Key Food parking lot when the $100,000 was brought up from Philadelphia, warranted a directed acquittal or at least a mistrial, Bergman contended. The judge took it under consideration. More than a year later, after extensive talks between Bergman and Freeh, they agreed that Amato would drop his appeal on the Galante issue in exchange for a limited sentence, set by Judge Leval at five years, of which Amato had already served twenty-two months. He later agreed to drop all right of appeal in exchange for a three-month furlough before returning to prison.

Carmine Russo should have been happy. The case turned out to be everything he had thought it would be. He had said the voice on the phone was Badalamenti, and it was. (Palermo's assistant chief prosecutor, Giusto Sciacchitano, was the only one of the Italians who had initially ridiculed Russo's suspicions who was gentleman enough to congratulate the Sicilian-American FBI agent for his perspicacity.) But Russo was glum. There had passed out of his life something he knew he would never experience again. He felt the loss most poignantly at night, when he tucked his youngest son into bed under the hand-knitted blanket he had used to wrap around himself while he listened to the tapes on those freezing nights in the unheated plant.

Charlie Rooney felt it, too. He would have the time now to work on the steam locomotive in Riverhead, but somehow it was no longer so alluring. The case of a lifetime was over. He suspected he would never see another one like it again. It was a letdown for Freeh and Martin and Schiliro and all the other prosecutors and agents whose lives had been shaped by *the* case for so long. Soon Martin was to join Russo at the American Embassy in Rome, Schiliro and Rooney were to be off to Washington, Sheer was to retire, and Freeh to take over the strike force in the Southern District. The Pizza Connection was not the only gang broken up by the verdicts in Foley Square. New teams of agents were already grappling with new conspiracies, and no fewer than twenty-four FBI offices around the country were deeply engaged in major investigations of Sicilian Mafia groups. In Washington Frank Storey was readying a massive series of raids for the spring of 1988. "We'll never start from zero again," said a proud Tom Sheer.

In September 1987, half a year after the convictions of Badalamenti, Catalano, and the others, a stranger called the town house office of Catalano's lawyer, Ivan Fisher, on Manhattan's East Side. The message was intriguing: Call Luigi Ronsisvalle at a number in Cincinnati. Ronsisvalle was the happy hit man who along with Salvatore Contorno and Salvatore Amendolito had built the government's successful witness case against Catalano. As such, Ronsisvalle would presumably be a prime target of Catalano's fearsome ire. Why would he step out of the shadows of the federal witness protection program to reveal himself to Catalano's lawyer? Why indeed? Fisher wondered. But he quickly returned the call.

Ronsisvalle told a startled Fisher that he might be amenable to recanting his testimony against Catalano. He invited Fisher to fly out to a Cincinnati motel and see him. Fisher thought there was a good chance he was being set up. As a prominent criminal lawyer who defended notorious drug kingpins and crime bosses—although he always maintained he was not a "mob lawyer" with its connotations of partnership with the Mafia—the flamboyant long-haired Fisher had been targeted before, without success, by federal agents eager to tie him into the conspiracies of his clients. The government had also tried to seize his legal fees as the fruits of criminal undertakings, but the effort was overturned on appeal. Now, Fisher suspected, it was trying to nail him for tampering with a witness. Fisher had good reason to believe Ronsisvalle was going to ask for money in connection with recanting his testimony against Catalano. After discussing the matter with Catalano in prison and with Catalano's other chief lawyer, Mario Malerba, Fisher decided he had no objection to paying Ronsisvalle with Catalano's money. Didn't the government also pay witnesses? But he wanted no suspicion that he had attempted to suborn a witness. Most of all, he wanted it to be done in the open. He wanted a witness. He asked me to come along and tape the entire conversation, and I did. I, too, had qualms. Was I being drawn into a case of possible witness tampering? Was I being used? The answers were clearly yes. But the story, my editors agreed, was too good to pass up.

Ronsisvalle met us in the bar of a Holiday Inn in suburban Sharonville, Ohio, outside Cincinnati. He was squat with a belly, thinning hair, and squinty eyes in a pleasant, porcine face. He spoke in the throaty Italian accent I remembered from his testimony, but off the witness stand he conveyed charm and good humor. He insisted he had framed Catalano on the drug charges to help himself with the authorities. He was particularly bitter over what he recounted as callous treatment at the hands of marshals of the witness protection program. But he was also afraid of Catalano and was clearly hoping to get money from him. Fisher avoided the money issue, exasperating Ronsisvalle. "You still not talking about them goddamn things," he complained to the lawyer, rubbing his thumb and forefinger together.

"Mr. Ronsisvalle . . ." Fisher boomed in the bar.

"Shhhhhh," hissed Ronsisvalle, looking around. "Please, Mr. Fish, no say that name around here." The lawyer apologized profusely.

Ronsisvalle's stated change of heart was persuasive. At one point he blurted, "I got three daughters. God is my witness. If I lie to you now, may my daughters drop dead with the worst things God can give to human beings. I'm swearing to you on my three daughters." He also said: "Mr. Fish, I want you please, from the bottom of my heart, I want you to accept my apology for what I done to Toto Catalano. I swear to God I feel so bad. I feel like crying." He killed thirteen people without compunction. Now a lie was making him cry. This was some story.

Why was he doing this? I kept wondering. I asked Ronsisvalle if he was afraid of Catalano. His answer was telling. "Not anymore," he replied. I realized what he was saying: With his change of testimony he had bought himself life insurance; Catalano wouldn't want him to die before he could recant in court.

In our two visits Fisher paid Ronsisvalle $2,620 to cover, the lawyer said, Ronsisvalle's unpaid hotel bill and other expenses and pay for a trip to his daughters. Fisher also collected Ronsisvalle's signature on an affidavit recanting his testimony against Catalano.

In Ronsisvalle's motel room, crowded with the pathetic belongings of a life lived on the run—portable radio/cassette player with dozens of tapes, paperbacks, extensive bar, and scattered toiletries—the ex–hit man asked us to wait a moment while he made a call. He dialed a number and said, "Hi, babe, what time I gonna see you tonight?"

Fisher's heart lurched. *This is it! It* is *a setup!* Fisher had seen this happen to clients countless times before: the transaction in the motel room; the phone call; a coded tip-off. He waited for the agents to rush in for the arrest. But he hadn't done anything wrong, he told himself. And *The New York Times* was his witness.

Ronsisvalle hung up. No agents burst in. He had been talking to a girl friend, one of the many bored Cincinnati housewives and shopgirls he had been bedding as the only diversion of his sordid life. But Fisher was spooked. The $2,620 he had paid Ronsisvalle for expenses on behalf of Catalano was apparently the only money Ronsisvalle would see, although I couldn't be sure that he hadn't gotten more out of my presence. But that would have undercut the whole point of Fisher's public exercise. For the recantation to work, it would have to withstand scrutiny.

"That's all I gonna get?" Ronsisvalle said disappointedly. "Well, my understanding was maybe something else as soon as Mr. Catalano be home. But it sounds to me, Mr. Fish no talk about."

"You bet your bippy Mr. Fisher no talk about," the lawyer agreed.

"That's the total?" Ronsisvalle persisted.

"That's Toto and total," said Mr. Fisher, never one to pass up a good pun.

We flew back to New York, Fisher to file Ronsisvalle's affidavit with Judge Leval and seek a new trial for Catalano, I to write a forty-five-hundred-word story on Ronsisvalle's recantation for *The New York Times*. The page one article was illustrated by a photograph I took of Ronsisvalle in the motel room signing the recantation.

The consternation was predictable. A key trial witness, one who also testified before the President's Commission on Organized Crime, recants his testimony and is given cash—on film and on tape. From then on the confusion mounted. Giuliano and Freeh were furious. What were Fisher and Ronsisvalle trying to pull? Why had Ronsisvalle changed his story? How did *The Times* get in the middle of this? The prosecutors began a grand jury investigation. Fisher's cocounsel, Mario Malerba, embarrassed, I suspect, by disclosure of the dealings with Ronsisvalle, denounced Fisher in court for filing for a new trial for Catalano prematurely. Malerba sought to withdraw the application. Fisher thereupon withdrew as cocounsel for Catalano altogether. Giuliani, paradoxically, defended the new-trial application as submitted, arguing that Catalano's lawyers should not be allowed simply to withdraw the application for resubmission later; they should be burdened with defending this one or be barred from easily submitting another. Judge Leval ruled there was no harm in allowing the application to be withdrawn.

I called Ronsisvalle at the motel and found him hung over and incoherent from a monster binge. He had spent all of Fisher's money on a succession of sodden parties. Now he was at the very bottom. His lawyer said later that Ronsisvalle had bought a gun and put the barrel in his mouth, ready to kill himself. But he couldn't pull the trigger. When I called Ronsisvalle at the motel the next day, he had checked out.

Where was Ronsisvalle? I got my answer several days later, when Giuliani produced him at the federal courthouse in Foley Square. Now Ronsisvalle had a totally different story. He swore that the only reason he gave Fisher the recantation was that two Sicilian-speaking men had approached him on the street in Ohio, said they knew where his wife and daughters were living, and threatened to kill them unless Ronsisvalle called Fisher to change his testimony. Fisher pronounced himself dumbfounded—and I believed him. Ronsisvalle's latest account raised many unanswered questions. How had the Sicilians found him in the witness protection program? Once he had been threatened, if he had been, why hadn't he immediately called the marshals and relocated himself and his family? In court, Ronsisvalle pleaded guilty to obstruction of justice for, he now said, falsely swearing that his testimony against Catalano was fabricated when in fact, it had been true all along.

How was the health of Ronsisvalle's daughters? I wondered.

It was a bizarre finale to a strange episode in a monumental case. In our two meetings, including some time that I spent alone with Ronsisvalle and in our telephone call, he never hinted he was acting under duress, although he expressed general fear of Catalano. In fact, as far as I could make out, he seemed mainly interested in getting a substantial sum of money for his recantation. I was skeptical that Ronsisvalle had ever been threatened as he claimed. I was never called before the grand jury, and Fisher was called only to produce the tapes I had made and given him copies of. No further development in the investigation was announced, although a grand jury investigation was still open in May 1988. On January 14, 1988, Ronsisvalle appeared once more in federal court in Foley Square, this time to receive a suspended five-year sentence for his admitted obstruction of justice for falsely recanting his sworn testimony in the Pizza Connection case. Ronsisvalle was free again and melted once more into the shadows of the witness protection program.

Like Ronsisvalle's strange exit, the severing of the Pizza Connection left haunting questions that the government's case, exhaustive as it was, never managed to resolve. What happened to all the money? The Italians were later able to trace and seize some $250 million in property and other assets but another billion dollars or more had disappeared. Where were all the drugs, apart from the buys and seizures that had turned up in the case? They had undoubtedly been sold and distributed, but how had they entered the country and where had the caches been secreted? How many other financiers and drug suppliers and middlemen and receivers had conspired, undetected, with Badalamenti, Catalano, Ganci, and their cohorts? Who had periodically tipped off the conspirators here and in Italy, threatening to blow the case? And perhaps most important, what did it all mean? Did the gargantuan effort and expense justify the results? What would be the case's ultimate impact?

Sheer and Giuliani, Freeh and Fahy, and Rooney and Russo and Paquette and the other lawmen here and abroad who had worked on the investigation since it began with the slaughter in Joe and Mary's restaurant in 1979 were not naïve enough to believe that they had struck a conclusive blow against the Mafia, whose demise had been so foolishly predicted too many times before. Nor dared they hope that the heroin supply would be diminished. As the DEA's Tom Cash often observed, interdicting drugs was like squeezing a water balloon—it always bulged out someplace. But at the same time the mountain of intelligence data from the immense commitment of investigative forces, the growing cooperation of the American and Italian authorities and other governments worldwide, and the historic defections of Buscetta, Contorno, and lesser Mafia renegades signaled a turning point in a long struggle. Who would have thought, exulted Giuliani after the verdicts, "that we could convict the head of the Sicilian Mafia." Or, for that matter, the ruling commission of the American Mafia's five New York families. Or much of the leadership of the five families themselves as well as many other mob bosses around the country. Tom Sheer's confidence that the FBI would "never start from zero again" was well founded. The bureau was not likely ever to return to its former state of innocence and ignorance.

Some of the fugitives were also being run down. In November 1986, a tip led FBI agents and detectives to a pizzeria in Patchogue, Long Island, where, after a wild car chase, they seized Anthony "Commerciante" Aiello. He had lost weight, dyed his hair, grown a beard, changed his name to Frank Manno, and moved with his wife to the suburban Long Island community of Hauppauge. He had been sought for two years, ever since the bureau—which had deliberately passed over Aiello in the Pizza Connection raids of April 1984—just missed grabbing him in a second phase of arrests the following November, when agents found $900,000 in his father's house. Aiello then had been playing cards at a friend's and had slipped out the back door as agents converged at the front. Convicted in March 1988, Aiello was sentenced to life in prison plus 140 years and fined $375,000.

A few weeks earlier, Vito Roberto Palazzolo, the fugitive Italian-born Swiss money launderer who had helped arrange the millions of dollars of cash deliveries to the Turkish morphine supplier Yasar Musullulu, and who had sailed in on the *Queen Elizabeth II* to meet with Giuseppe Lamberti in 1983, was arrested in South Africa in possession of a false passport and several million dollars. Palazzolo, who was no relation to Alfano's relative, Emanuele, had been sought since 1986 when he never returned from a holiday furlough from prison in Lugano, Switzerland. While hiding in the land of apartheid he had cemented relations with some members of Parliament and had been photographed at a reception for Prime Minister Botha. Television videos of the reception were, in fact, what tipped off Italian investigators to Palazzolo's presence in South Africa in the first place. He was quickly returned to prison in Switzerland.

A watershed had been reached in Italy, too. On December 16, 1987, after nearly two years of trial—longer even than the Pizza Connection case—a Palermo jury convicted 338 of 452 Mafia defendants charged with operating their underground empire largely on drug profits. Among the 19 top bosses sentenced to life in prison in the so-called maxi-trial was Michele Greco, the nominal head of the Sicilian Mafia Commission, who had been flushed out of hiding and captured shortly after the trial began in February 1986. Also sentenced to life in absentia were two notorious fugitives: Pino Greco, the ferocious killer implicated in General Dalla Chiesa's assassination and the attempted murder of turncoat Salvatore Contorno; and Salvatore Riina, who remained Italy's most elusive and mysterious Mafia boss. Pippo Calò, the arriviste boss of Tommaso Buscetta's Porta Nuova family, was given twenty-three years, and virtually all of the other leaders and soldiers Buscetta exposed also received long prison terms and heavy fines. Buscetta and his fellow *pentito*, or penitent, Contorno, received three and a half and six years, respectively, although both remained free and hidden under heavy government protection in the United States.

The verdicts were greeted with silence. For once, the courtroom of cagelike cells in a Ucciardone Prison annex that had cost the Italian government $18 million to build did not echo with the catcalls and jeers of the prisoners. They had fallen silent, as if acknowledging that a new era had dawned. In the Mafia's Sicilian homeland, the brotherhood's aura of invincibility was crumbling.

Here in the United States, the prosecutions and changing demographics were also taking a toll on the Mafia. Internally, its recruitment was lagging, thinning the ranks. The grandsons and nephews of the old bosses were drifting out of the mob's orbit, away from perilous lives as "men of honor" and into less dubious enterprises and professions. Over the last twenty years, the bureau figured, the number of "made," or inducted, members in the twenty-four American Mafia families nationwide had been halved to some seventeen hundred soldiers and leaders plus some thousands of associates. (New York City's five families traditionally accounted for half the nationwide total.) If the government siege continued, Giuliani liked to say, the American Mafia could be reduced within the next five or six years to little more than a street gang.

Many of the successes were attributable to RICO, whose promise was only beginning to be fullfilled a decade and a half after its enactment. Initially, recalled G. Robert Blakey, the Notre Dame University law professor who was one of the act's progenitors, the concept of attacking organized crime through the enterprise itself rather than one or another of its usually lowly functionaries was widely disdained. As the FBI saw it, if the strategy wasn't invented by the bureau, it could hardly be any good. But Blakey's lectures and the successes of pioneers like Giuliani were persuasive. The Sherman Anti-Trust Act was enacted in 1890, but it was not successfully applied against Standard Oil until 1911, Blakey liked to recall. The real implications of RICO, too, might only emerge after two decades. The civil provisions were particularly overlooked, Blakey felt, although prosecutors Giuliani in Manhattan, Andrew Maloney in Brooklyn, and Robert Stewart in Newark had broken new ground by initiating civil RICO lawsuits—triable under easier standards of proof than criminal cases—barring mobsters from control of union locals long in the thrall of the underworld.

But RICO was no magic bullet. Exaggerated hopes for its success, Blakey noted, were based on three widespread assumptions of the 1970's, all of which had turned out to be untrue. One was that the organized crime–connected drug epidemic was a finite problem largely restricted to the underprivileged. It turned out to reach into the highest economic and social spheres. The second was that it was largely a domestic law enforcement problem. But it was clearly international. The third was that it was amenable to strong law enforcement pressure and criminal sanctions. But the murders of judges and police chiefs in Italy and the anarchistic violence of the drug cartels in Colombia laid that myth to rest as well. "There are plenty of people RICO was not designed for," acknowledged Blakey. "It's already obsolete."

Many experts shared Blakey's sober view. The NYPD's Jack Clark particularly saw no reason for complacency, as befitted a tough cop who after twenty-six years of breakthroughs still found himself tailing bad guys day after day. In his lectures to eager young police recruits, Clark likened the Mafia to a wheel, with the bosses and underbosses and *consiglieri* at the hub, and spokes of capos radiating out to the soldiers on the rim. Soldiers were forever getting busted or killed. They were expendable. In recent years, the government had been taking out the spokes as well. They too were replaceable. Now the government was trying to rip out the hub. But deep inside the hub, Clark liked to say, were the bearings.

Even government successes contained the seeds of new problems. The prosecution of traditional organized crime created a vacuum into which powerful new ethnic criminal cartels were surging. Most menacing was the ascendency of a Chinese organized crime network rooted in ancient triads or criminal societies, an underworld empire, if anything even more disciplined and ferocious than the Sicilian Mafia. Its fast-rising influence was trackable in the soaring quantities of Southeast Asian heroin reaching the streets of New York. In 1982, Southeast Asian heroin accounted for only 3 percent of the supply in New York, according to the DEA. Within five years it had reached at least 40 percent. It was probably even higher, some experts theorized, because some devious Chinese traffickers had learned to disguise their heroin as a Southwest Asian product traditionally imported by the Mafia. The Chinese gangs had long had headquarters in Hong Kong. But with China's pending takeover of the former British crown colony set for 1997, many experts had reason to fear that the triads would shift their operations to the United States in years to come. With less of an ethnic diaspora to draw on than the Italians, some experts believed, Chinese mobsters in the United States might stand out more and thus prove easier to thwart. But their secretive clans promised to be even harder to penetrate than the Mafia, if only because the FBI and other investigative agencies were woefully short of Chinese agents.

Beleaguered on both sides of the Atlantic, the Mafia was losing its grip over narcotics and with it, some of its vast wealth, power, and invincibility. Traditional organized crime—that is, the Sicilian Mafia—had long controlled the Southwest Asian heroin that accounted for half or more of the six tons or so of heroin flowing into the United States each year. In recent years, as Chinese-smuggled Southeast Asian heroin cut sharply into the Mafia's near monopoly, the percentage of Southwest Asian heroin in the United States dropped to 30 percent—and the Mafia had lost some of that to other organized crime groups. Clearly, the Mafia's grip on the racket was weakening.

But the new heirs to the drug empire of the underworld threatened to be every bit as difficult to dislodge. "I don't know who has a solution—*I* don't," said Blakey of Notre Dame. "Some kid twenty-five years old somewhere may be thinking about it. There may be a military solution. Or no solution."

The war raged on.

In the predawn hours of March 31, 1988, more than 200 federal agents from

14 field offices converged on the homes, apartments, pizzerias, boutiques, and other businesses of 64 suspected drug traffickers spread from Long Island and New York City to Pennsylvania, North Carolina, and Texas. At the same time, across the Atlantic, the Italian authorities sought another 169. Within a few hours, some 150 of the 233 targets of a new assault on the Sicilian Mafia's drug empire were in custody and the rest were being rounded up or hunted in what officials called the largest international drug case ever developed by the Justice Department and the biggest joint antidrug operation ever mounted by the two nations. This scheme, according to the government, had a new twist: exporting sought-after South American cocaine to Italy in exchange for plentiful heroin. Once again government tape recorders whirred with hundreds of intercepted telephone conversations. The Sicilian voices spoke of "suits" and "shirts," "the guy from the shoes," "red wine" and "white wine"—references, the government once again contended, to cocaine and heroin (beige and white). And although one of the callers was heard to warn, "Enzo, we are on the phone; I don't like too much bullshit on the phone," still they talked. They talked because they had business to do and there was no other way to do it.

Several of the targets bore familiar names. There was a Catalano—Domenico —who appeared to be no close relation of Salvatore "Toto" but who lived on the same road near an airstrip in Marlboro, New York, north of Newburgh, as Toto's late cousin Saca had. There was Claudio Calderone, a former employee of Salvatore Mazzurco and Giuseppe Lamberti's Pino Europa boutique in New Windsor, south of Newburgh, where some of the Pizza Connection's illicit business was transacted under the cover of clothing deals. The government charged in its new complaint that Calderone was an unindicted coconspirator in the Pizza Connection case, and that he had acquired ownership of the boutique from Mazzurco and Lamberti after their arrests and in a venerable tradition had been selling heroin out of the business. Most significant, the new case turned up Emanuele Adamita, the former New York pizza man who with the turncoat Frank Rolli had unwittingly led DEA agents to Milan in 1980 for the forty-kilo seizure that became a prelude to the Pizza Connection case. Adamita had been seized then in Milan after bringing the heroin, concealed under phonograph records in tin canisters, to a freight forwarding office for shipment to Brooklyn. In March 1987, after seven years behind bars in Italy, Adamita was foolishly granted a furlough from which, like Vito Roberto Palazzolo in Switzerland, he never returned. A month after his escape, according to the complaint, Adamita was back in New York, telling a customer he could provide heroin and cocaine. Unfortunately for Adamita, that customer was a confidential informant working undercover with the FBI. A new pizza case was under investigation.

Eleven months later, the dark-haired Adamita was in a suite of the Parker Meridien hotel in Manhattan meeting with one of his good customers. The fugitive trafficker put his arm around his companion and said he considered him family. You couldn't be too careful today, Adamita cautioned, the cops were everywhere.

There were rats all around, his customer agreed. Whereupon he paid Adamita for a pound of heroin and accepted delivery, kissed Adamita on the cheek—not on the lips as some reports later had it—revealed himself to be a DEA undercover agent, and told Adamita he was under arrest. The stunned Adamita began to weep.

We're getting good at this, Frank Storey, at FBI headquarters, thought later. "It was a great effort, much broader than anything we did before," he told reporters. "The Pizza case taught us how to do it."

NOTES

Throughout four years of following the saga of the Pizza Connection, I had one powerful advantage over the FBI: I knew how the story ended. In writing this book, I knew which characters were important and what would happen to them in the end. That was vital for shaping the story into an intelligible narrative. But it also created a dilemma: how to make the story unfold for the reader in a fair reflection of the fitful and dramatic way it did for Charlie Rooney and Carmine Russo and all the other federal, local, and foreign law enforcement agents who worked on the case. I would like to think I succeeded in conveying the reality, although in truth the case proceeded in a more disjointed way than any reader would have the patience to follow. I chose to tell the story chronologically, as the investigators experienced it, and without encumbering the text with excessive sourcing or disruptive footnotes. Yet some explanation of sources is in order. The bulk of the material comes from testimony in the mammoth court case and the 41,910 pages of trial transcript it produced. That did not include the tens of thousands of pages of evidence, including wiretap transcripts, Buscetta's "confessions," depositions of Swiss money launderers, and FBI, DEA, and police reports. To flesh out the often skeletal court record, I conducted interviews with more than two hundred FBI and DEA agents and criminal justice officials, supervisors, prosecutors, and defense lawyers here and in Italy. The dialogue given in these pages comes largely verbatim from the wiretaps or court testimony and depositions. Where there was no sworn or electronic record, as in conversations between law enforcement agents, the dialogue is based on the best recollections of participants. A more detailed description of sources, in the order in which the material appears in each chapter, follows.

CHAPTER 1

In the government's view, the murder of Carmine Galante decisively set the stage for the heroin consortium of Sal Catalano and Giuseppe Ganci and their compatriots. Considering everything else that emerged during the investigation and trial, I find this view persuasive, and therefore, I use it to open the story. In the trial the defense argued that the account of the killing had no place in this case, and the court, for reasons I cite in Chapter 25, agreed. Yet what may have have been a prudent legal ruling does not necessarily represent the preponderance of the historical record and since a writer's rules are looser than a lawyer's, I chose to include, indeed to showcase, the slaying. Moreover, the same evidence of the circumstances of the murder was recounted in witness testimony and other evidence presented in March 1987 in the Mafia Commission trial in the Southern District. It is from this record that I extracted the witness accounts of the killing. I also consulted news reports of the murder in *The New York Times*. On June 16, 1987, among other occasions, I also visited Knickerbocker Avenue and the various sites, including the former Joe and Mary's restaurant, that figure in this story. The restaurant is now a Chinese takeout place.

CHAPTER 2

On February 20, 1977, *The New York Times* ran a long and excellent profile of Carmine Galante by Lucinda Franks that furnished many details of his routine as recorded by NYPD and federal surveillance agents. The NYPD lieutenant whose assessment of Galante is quoted in the article is Remo Franceschini.

For the accounts of Russo's role in the case, I interviewed him at length at the FBI offices in New York on April 13, 1987, and on June 9 and 10, 1987, in Rome, where he was then posted as a legal attaché. I interviewed Rooney—who had remained based in New York through the end of 1987—on some two dozen occasions beginning in 1985, with most of the interviews taking place at the Manhattan U.S. attorney's office and the FBI's Queens office, after the trial ended in March 1987. I also interviewed Rooney on several occasions in 1988, after he had been reassigned to FBI headquarters in Washington. Material on how both agents, as well as others, fitted into the case and on how the case was viewed and handled by the bureau was furnished from 1985 through 1987 in more than two dozen interviews with Tom Sheer, as criminal director and assistant director in New York. I also interviewed Sheer on several occasions in 1988, after he retired to become a private security consultant.

Jack Clark of NYPD organized crime intelligence, in interviews in February 1988, verified details furnished to the FBI.

Results of the forensic investigation of the Galante murder scene and the surveillance at the Ravenite Club were provided in the Mafia Commission case and by Jack Clark, as cited above.

I was present as a *Times* reporter at the Brooklyn DA's office on July 31, 1979, when Cesare Bonventre and Baldassare Amato surrendered for questioning.

The Nassau County arrest of Bonventre and Amato is detailed in police reports and grand jury testimony of Officers Michael Ricco and George Kuhlkin in 1979. The evidence was presented as an exhibit in the Pizza Connection case.

Luigi Ronsisvalle testified at length at the trial in January 1986. FBI and DEA reports of his debriefings as an informant were exhibits in the case.

Calculating the value of heroin is a tricky business. I use a figure of approximately $200,000 a kilo when it was sold by Mafia importers like Catalano-Ganci to suppliers like Benny Zito in 1983, and between $2 million and $4 million a kilo, depending on how much it is cut, or diluted, by the time it is sold on the street. Of course, not all shipments reach the street.

CHAPTER 3

The Russo and Rooney accounts are from interviews as cited above.

The data on the FBI's belated recognition of the Mafia are from Richard Gid Powers' *Secrecy and Power* and Peter Maas' *The Valachi Papers.* (For these and other books cited below, see the full references in the bibliography.)

Most of the Catalano biography emerged during his bail hearing in the Southern District in June 1984. Some material was also provided during the trial. On June 4, 1987, I visited Ciminna to see the church and other sites in Catalano's hometown.

The history of Palermo is recounted in M. I. Finley et al.'s *A History of Sicily.* Some of the Mafia history was provided by Daniele Billitteri of *Il Giornale di Sicilia* and by other residents.

Palermo seventieth among Italian cities in per capita income and seventh in consumption: statistic cited in Mary Taylor Simeti, *On Persephone's Island.*

The Piazza Politeama episode is recounted in officially translated trial testimony of Treasury Officer Calogero Scarvaci in November 1985. I visited the central Palermo piazza many times during my trip to Sicily in May and June 1987.

The account of Salvatore Contorno is from trial testimony in January 1986. DEA and FBI and Italian reports on Contorno, including his Italian interrogations, were exhibits at the trial. The account of Emanuele Adamita's trip to Italy and the seizure of the forty kilos was given in trial testimony in December 1985. In later 1984 and several occasions in 1985 and 1986 I interviewed Assistant U.S. Attorneys Charles Rose and Mark Summers of the Eastern District about the roles of Adamita and Frank Rolli, among other issues. I had two brief telephone interviews with Rolli, who is in hiding, but was unable to arrange a meeting.

CHAPTER 4

For Carmela Russo's reactions to the case, I interviewed her together with her husband in Rome on June 10, 1987.

The data on the Giuseppe Bono wedding is from a June 30, 1986, interview with Tony Petrucci of the DEA.

For a history of FBI undercover operations, I interviewed former undercover agent Gail Tyrus "Ty" Cobb in New York on December 18, 1986, and under-cover supervisor Robert Lill at bureau HQ in Washington on December 22, 1986. On December 4, 1986, I spoke briefly with former undercover agent Joe Pistone, who was then working on his own book and was hesitant to provide any substantial information. He subsequently corroborated my account, based on his testimony in the Pizza Connection case in January and February 1986, and his testimony in the Napolitano and Balistrieri prosecutions in 1982 and 1984. Pistone's autobiography, *Donnie Brasco: My Undercover Life in the Mafia*, pub-lished in early 1988, helped fill in some gaps.

CHAPTER 5

Tommaso Buscetta's story is based on his trial testimony in October and November 1985 and his voluminous so-called confessions to Judge Falcone in Palermo in 1984. The confessions became a Pizza Connection case exhibit, along with many once-confidential reports of the FBI, DEA, and NYPD. Beginning in 1985, through Buscetta's counsel, Philip Douglas, I sought repeatedly to interview Buscetta, who is in hiding, to no avail. He would talk only for pay of unspecified thousands of dollars or a partnership in any writing project, demands precluded by my professional constraints. Two works in which Buscetta did collaborate do provide information unavailable in the public record, Enzo Biagi's anecdotal biography *Il Boss è Solo* and Tim Shawcross and Martin Young's *Men of Honor: The Confessions of Tommaso Buscetta*.

For Mafia history and sociology, I relied heavily on multiple interviews with Pino Arlacchi, former consultant to the Italian Anti-Mafia Commission, in Rome and New York in 1986 and 1987. Arlacchi's book *Mafia Business* is an invaluable treatise on underworld economics. Other useful data are from Jane and Paul Schneider's *Culture and Political Economy in Western Sicily*, Finley et al.'s *A History of Sicily*, Norman Lewis' *The Honored Society*, and Frederick

Sondern's *Brotherhood of Evil.* Joseph Bonanno's autobiography, *A Man of Honor,* obviously self-serving, is nevertheless often surprisingly candid and, in view of the use later made of it by Rudolph Giuliani, historically note-worthy.

The material on Gaetano Badalamenti is largely from his trial testimony in October 1986.

CHAPTER 6

The material on Rooney and Russo is from interviews, as cited above.

The account of Robert L. Paquette's entry into the case is from multiple interviews with him from 1985 to 1988.

The material on Jim Kallstrom is from interviews with him from 1986 to 1988, FBI surveillance logs, and interviews with other agents and supervisors, as cited above.

The Citam conversations are from Italian wiretap reports offered as trial exhibits.

The Esposito testimony is from the trial in March 1986.

The Amendolito narrative is taken from his lengthy trial testimony in February and March 1986. Amendolito's account was seriously challenged chiefly by Catalano's lawyer, Ivan Fisher, but not even the astute Fisher could belittle the discovery of Catalano's thumbprint on the slip with his name and number from Amendolito's Rolodex. Other material is from interviews with Paquette and with Mike Fahy of Customs on February 26, 1987.

CHAPTER 7

The account of the evolution of the Sicilian Connection out of the French Connection and the complicity of French intelligence in narcotics trafficking is chiefly based on multiple interviews with Thomas C. Tripodi from 1984 to 1987 and on a February 1987 research report by Tripodi, for which I paid him $800. It was the only occasion in which I paid any source, and the context was as follows: I had already interviewed Tripodi on some half dozen occasions starting shortly before his retirement from the DEA in 1985. He had freely provided his information without pay. He subsequently began his own security consulting business and offered to prepare a digest of key material on foreign intelligence involvement in narcotics trafficking to which he said he had research access. Because it was questionable whether I could easily locate the same material myself, I gratefully engaged Tripodi for the assignment. I contrast this instance with Buscetta's insistence that he be paid to speak about his criminal career (one he said he had repudiated out of moral conviction). Tripodi was not seeking to sell his information—which, in any event, he had always provided gratis—but sought only to be compensated for his consulting time on a well-defined and legitimate research project, a request I did not find unreasonable or professionally compromising. Tripodi's material complemented other excellent data on the same subject in Alfred W. McCoy et al.'s *The Politics of Heroin in Southeast Asia.* Other corroborative data appear in DEA reports on Operation Caesar, including MTF 320, December 1978, File No. GFXA-79-8001.

Buscetta's account is from his confessions and intelligence reports, as cited above. The allegations of Buscetta's involvement in the French Connection are based on testimony of Michel Nicoli, Claude Pastou, and Giuseppe Catania in the Southern and Eastern Districts in 1973 and 1974.

CHAPTER 8

The Russo, Rooney, Paquette, and Fahy accounts are from interviews, as cited above.

The Bono wedding account was provided by Petrucci, as cited above.

Francis J. Storey's account is from an interview on January 20, 1988.

The money-laundering data is from an excellent paper, "Hot Money, Flight Capital and the Global Crisis of Debt," delivered in November 1986 by R. Thomas Naylor of the Economics Department of McGill University in Montreal. A fuller account is available in Naylor's *Hot Money and the Politics of Debt.* Additional data are taken from the money-laundering report of the President's Commission on Organized Crime, October 1984.

The Paul Waridel and Yasar Musullulu narrative is from Waridel's deposition in Switzerland in June 1985, presented as a trial exhibit.

The testimony of Louis E. Brown was offered at the trial in March 1986. The Merrill Lynch documents were an exhibit in the trial. The Franco Della Torre deposition was taken in Switzerland in June 1985 and offered in evidence at the trial.

CHAPTER 9

The Buscetta narrative is drawn from his trial testimony and confessions, as cited above. Badalamenti denied parts of Buscetta's account, as noted in Chapter 25, but Badalamenti's credibility was eroded by his refusal to answer questions under cross-examination.

CHAPTER 10

The accounts of Sheer, Storey, and Russo are based on the interviews cited above.

Reena Raggi's account was related in an interview on January 15, 1986.

Mona Ewell's data are from interviews with her at DEA HQ in Washington on March 27, 1986, and June 11, 1986.

CHAPTER 11

The wiretap conversations starting here and continuing throughout the rest of the book are from 1,144 translated transcripts compiled for the trial and contained in chronological order in eight thick loose-leaf volumes. Throughout the course of the trial the government's translations of some words and phrases were challenged by the defense, but the vast bulk of the electronic record stood as offered by the prosecution. I have, by necessity, boiled down the conversations, while, I am confident, preserving their essence.

The Ganci surveillance was re-created from an interview with Bob Gilmore on September 16, 1986, and my visit with Gilmore, on the same date, to cited locations in New York and New Jersey.

CHAPTER 12

The account of the lookout is from multiple interviews with Pat Luzio, along with Rooney, in 1987 and 1988.

The surveillance of Filippo Salamone is from the trial testimony of Agent Richard Kaier in April 1986, surveillance logs, and Gilmore, as cited above.

The data on Quantico is drawn from a visit there on November 10, 1985.

Carol's diary was a trial exhibit. After some reflection, I decided there was little point to identifying her here beyond her first name. Although close to Ganci and a beneficiary of his dealings, she was not accused as a participant in the conspiracy. She and her friend Ann are the only characters not identified in full. Without exception, there are no pseudonyms and no composite characters in this book.

CHAPTER 13

The account of Rudolph W. Giuliani is gathered from multiple interviews I conducted with him from 1984 to 1987.

The account of Stephen Hopson is from his trial testimony in May 1986.

Frank Panessa's account is from an interview at DEA HQ in Washington on March 27, 1986 and from his testimony to the President's Commission, meeting in Miami, February 20–21, 1985.

The joining of the Philadelphia and New York cases was related by Petrucci during multiple interviews in 1986 and 1987.

CHAPTER 14

The account of the tensions and rivalries in the case is based on interviews, as cited above, with Giuliani, Sheer, Rooney, and Rose (of the Eastern District). In reconstructing the meeting of June 30, 1983, Sheer read from contemporaneous notes.

The account of Louis Caprino is from an interview on November 9, 1987.

The controversy over seizing Casamento, and later Baldinucci, was related by Lew Schiliro and Louis Freeh in multiple interviews in 1987.

The account of Vernon Swint is from the trial testimony in May 1986.

CHAPTER 15

The Mazzurco material is from his trial testimony in November 1986.

I interviewed Dick Martin on March 13, 1987.

The account of Baldinucci's arrest is from the trial testimony of Denis Collins in June 1986. Additional material is from my interview of Collins on February 2, 1988.

The account of the heroin substitution at Port Elizabeth, its seizure in Buffalo, and the rivalry over the operation is from interviews of Sheer, Giuliani, and Fahy, as cited above, and Philip Smith on March 11, 1988.

CHAPTER 16

Buscetta's account is from his trial testimony and confessions, as cited above, as well as DEA reports provided as trial exhibits.

Ewell's account is from interviews with her, as earlier cited.

CHAPTER 17

I interviewed Nancy Morelli and Gabby Zacco of the DEA on December 20, 1985, and January 23, 1986.

The account of Amendolito's arrest is from the interviews with Paquette and Fahy.

CHAPTER 18

The account of Amendolito's continuing role in the investigation is from Paquette.

I interviewed Agent John Mauzey on April 1, 1987.

The account of how the investigation came up with Alfano is from a telephone interview with Agent Jerome Cox of the FBI's Detroit office on January 26, 1988.

Russo provided the account of his use of *Il Progresso.*

The story of the Customs Service's search of the cars is from Fahy.

CHAPTER 19

The account of the bureau's efforts to pinpoint Badalamenti is from Russo.

Ewell described her surprise over finding the link to Badalamenti in Detroit.

The account of the strange cars outside the Rooney house is from Rooney and his wife, Jane.

The noise pollution episode was related by Gilmore.

CHAPTER 20

The account of the disagreement over the identification of Badalamenti is from Schiliro, as cited above, and Tom Vinton, interviewed on March 2, 1987.

The Florida surveillance was described by Storey, Sheer, Freeh, and Giuliani.

The Cocilovo episode is from reports of the Metro-Dade Public Safety Department in June 1983 and circuit court testimony in August 1983, presented as trial exhibits.

CHAPTER 21

The "STEURERMES" story is from Cox, as cited above.

The records of Badalamenti's apartment rental in Brazil were later recovered from his Madrid apartment after the raid of April 9, 1984.

CHAPTER 22

The account of the tensions between the agents is from Russo and Storey.

Storey and Fahy provided the account of the debate over taking down the case in Florida. I also interviewed Randolph Prillaman by phone on February 17, 1988.

The account of the effort to trace Badalamenti to a phone booth in Brazil and to seize him there is from Russo, Rooney, and Collins.

CHAPTER 23

The scene at the Alfano pizzeria is based on material from Oregon residents, news accounts in the Oregon *Republican Reporter,* and weather data for April 1984.

The arrest of Badalamenti and Alfano was recounted in trial testimony by Merino in September 1986.

The arrest of Cangialosi was recounted in the trial by Caprino in September 1986.

The events preceding the raids and the scene in the command post were recounted by Fahy, Rooney, and Sheer. I visited the command post on several occasions from 1985 to 1987.

The search of the Alfano house was recounted in trial testimony by Brand in September 1986. Accounts of the other searches are also from the trial testimony of agents.

The Lamberti gun episode is from an interview with Sheer; the Catalano arrest from an interview with Russo.

CHAPTER 24

The account of the celebration at Dino's is from Rooney; the homecomings from Russo and Rooney.

The "STEURERMES" episode is from Cox.

I interviewed John Huber of DEA on January 14, 1986.

Buscetta's statement is from his confessions to Judge Falcone.

The account of Badalamenti's extradition to the United States is from an interview with Caprino on January 7, 1988 and an interview with Pat Luzio on January 14, 1988.

Ronsisvalle told me of his call to McCabe in an interview in Cincinnati on September 18, 1987. Ronsisvalle's new information was the subject of FBI reports offered as exhibits in the trial.

The Swiss depositions were trial exhibits.

The account of the trip to Turkey is from Freeh and Rooney.

I was present for the start of the trial on September 30, 1985.

CHAPTER 25

Most of the material in this chapter comes from the trial transcript or my notes in court.

The quote on Mafia sickness is from a 1982 Italian paper by V. Macri, cited in Arlacchi's *Mafia Business,* p. 146.

The episode of the Catalano fingerprint is from an interview with Tom Loreto of the Customs Service on February 26, 1987.

The theories of the Mazzara murder are from interviews with Caprino, Rooney, and Schiliro on November 9, 1987.

The account of how Alfano's surveillance helped break the case of his attempted murder is from interviews with Mike Slattery on April 1, 1987 and February 10, 1988.

The story of the Alfano shooting investigation is from a deposition of Agent Robert J. Liberatore on February 18, 1987.

The Ronsisvalle recantation episode is from interviews with Fisher and Ronsisvalle on September 18 and 22, 1987.

BIBLIOGRAPHY

Arlacchi, Pino. *Mafia Business.* London: Verso, 1986.

Biagi, Enzo. *Il Boss è Solo.* Milan: Arnoldo Mondadori, 1986.

Bonanno, Joseph, with Sergio Lalli. *A Man of Honor: The Autobiography of Joseph Bonanno.* New York: Simon and Schuster, 1983.

Charbonneau, Jean-Pierre. *The Canadian Connection.* Ottawa: Optimum, 1976.

Finley, M. I., Dennis Mack Smith, and Christopher Duggan. *A History of Sicily.* New York: Elisabeth Sifton Books, Viking, 1987.

Freemantle, Brian. *The Fix: Inside the World Drug Trade.* New York: Tor, 1985.

Lewis, Norman. *The Honored Society.* New York: G. P. Putnam's Sons, 1964.

Maas, Peter. *The Valachi Papers.* New York: Bantam, 1968.

McCoy, Alfred W., with Cathleen B. Read and Leonard P. Adams II. *The Politics of Heroin in Southeast Asia.* New York: Harper & Row, 1972.

Mustain, Gene, and Jerry Capeci. *Mob Star: The Story of John Gotti.* New York: Franklin Watts, 1988.

Naylor, R. Thomas. *Hot Money and the Politics of Debt.* New York: Linden Press/Simon and Schuster, 1987.

Newsday staff and editors. *The Heroin Trail.* New York: Holt, Rinehart & Winston, 1974.

Pileggi, Nicholas. *Wiseguy: Life in a Mafia Family.* New York: Simon and Schuster, 1985.

Pistone, Joseph D., with Richard Woodley. *Donnie Brasco: My Undercover Life in the Mafia.* New York: New American Library, 1987.

Powers, Richard Gid. *Secrecy and Power: The Life of J. Edgar Hoover.* New York: Free Press, 1987.

President's Commission on Organized Crime. *The Cash Connection: Organized Crime, Financial Institutions and Money Laundering.* Washington: October 1984.

President's Commission on Organized Crime. *Organized Crime: Federal Law Enforcement Perspective.* Washington: November 1983.

Schneider, Jane, and Peter Schneider. *Culture and Political Economy in Western Sicily.* New York: Academic Press, 1976.

Shawcross, Tim, and Martin Young. *Men of Honor: The Confessions of Tommaso Buscetta: The Man Who Destroyed the Mafia.* London: Collins, 1987.

Simeti, Mary Taylor. *On Persephone's Island: A Sicilian Journal.* San Francisco: North Point Press, 1987.

Sondern, Frederick, Jr. *Brotherhood of Evil.* New York: Farrar, Straus & Cudahy, 1959.

Sullivan, William C., *The Bureau: My 30 Years in Hoover's F.B.I.* New York: W. W. Norton, 1979.

Talese, Gay. *Honor Thy Father.* New York: Dell, 1971.

Tosches, Nick. *Power on Earth.* New York: Arbor House, 1976.

INDEX